BETWEEN A ROCK
AND A HARD PLACE

D1570122

BETWEEN A ROCK
AND A HARD PLACE

African NGOs, Donors and the State

Edited by

Jim Igoe

ANTHROPOLOGY, UNIVERSITY OF COLORADO AT DENVER

and

Tim Kelsall

POLITICS, UNIVERSITY OF NEWCASTLE UPON TYNE

CAROLINA ACADEMIC PRESS
Durham, North Carolina

Library of Congress Cataloging-in-Publication Data

Between a rock and a hard place : African NGOs, Donors and the State / edited by Jim Igoe and Tim Kelsall.
    p. cm.
    Includes bibliographical references.
    ISBN 1-59460-017-1
1. Non-governmental organizations—Africa—Case studies. 2. Civil society—Africa—Case studies. I. Igoe, Jim, 1964– II. Kelsall, Tim, 1970– III. Title

HC800.Z9E4434 2004
300'.96—dc22

                                                              2004006334

CAROLINA ACADEMIC PRESS
700 Kent Street
Durham, NC 27701
Telephone (919) 489-7486
Fax (919) 493-5668
www.cap-press.com

Printed in the United States of America

CONTENTS

Figures and Tables

PREFACE

Jim Igoe

The 1990s were the decade when African NGOs reached their zenith as the preferred institutional vehicle for development, governance, and emergency relief on the continent. During this decade, much was written about African NGOs. Theory on NGOs and civil society in Africa proliferated in the fields of political science, anthropology, and geography. Scholars working in development and conservation bureaucracies also generated NGO theory. As many observers have opined, however, much of what is known about NGOs is based more on what is believed about them than on empirical observations of what NGOs actually do in practice.

Fortunately, this situation is gradually changing as scholars who went to study African NGOs for their dissertation research in the 1990s are beginning to publish their findings. For the first time "thick description" of African NGOs is becoming available, often to the chagrin of western donors and African NGO leaders.

As far as we know, this volume represents the first survey of ethnographic NGO case studies from around the continent. All of the authors in this volume lived and worked with African NGOs for extended periods of at least a year. They shared the aspirations and frustrations of African NGO leaders. They also experienced the swings between exuberance and despair (and sometimes back again) which frequently occurred at the community level during the heady years of the NGO revolution.

Bringing these studies together was no easy task. The seeds for this volume were planted in 1999 by Tim Kelsall and Sara Rich Dorman, when they began organizing a special issue of the *Oxford Journal of Development Studies*, which unfortunately never materialized. In 2001 I suggested to Tim that we put some of the articles submitted to the special issue together in an edited collection, and we set about trying to find a suitable publisher. In 2002 Carolina Academic Press agreed to publish this volume.

Through H-Net Africa and word of mouth, we received over thirty submissions in one form or another. In addition to NGO case studies, we received technical reports and even a play about NGOs in Zimbabwe. We also received a couple of pieces that were theoretically compelling, but not ethnographic enough for this collection. Four submissions that were accepted for the volume unfortunately never materialized.

The nine case studies that ultimately appear in this volume tell a compelling story about the state of African NGOs, a story which has profound implications for governance and development on the continent in the new millennium. Ron Kassimir, our discussant for a conference panel launching this collection, noted that all of the case studies in this book betray a sense of disappointment at the shortcoming of African NGOs. This is undeniably true, but this disappointment is tempered by an equally palpable respect for African NGO leaders who struggle to foster positive changes under what are frequently near impossible circumstances. I personally have wondered how well I would do if I found myself trying to operate under the kinds of circumstances that the case studies in this volume so vividly describe.

This double perspective of admiration and disappointment parallels what Dorman (this volume) describes as the current tendency to either "romanticize" or "pathologize" African NGOs. We seek to avoid either of these myopic perspectives to the extent that we can. Rather we seek to illuminate the structural difficulties of African NGOs caught between the "rock" of western donors and the "hard place" of the African state. Tired as I am of working on this project, it has been a real pleasure to read these case studies over and over, as each new read reveals astounding parallels for African NGOs operating from Cape Verde to Zimbabwe. I believe that these studies taken together will have important implications both for academic theory and NGO practice.

Acknowledgments

It is a decade since we began working on NGOs in Africa; in that time numerous people, in the field and in the academy, have shaped our views of the dilemmas that NGOs face. Some of them deserve special mention.

Tim Kelsall

I would like to thank Erwin Kinsey of Heifer Project International and Dirk Booy and Sarone ole Sena of World Vision Tanzania, all of whom welcomed a PhD student poking his nose around when few others were willing to be so open. I would also like to thank everyone in World Vision's capacity building division in Arusha and the staff and members of the Area Development Project in Moshono, for assisting in field research. Much of what I know I owe to my research assistant, Jehovah Roy Kaaya. Samantha Goodwin and Bobby McKenna were loyal friends in the field; Claire Mercer both friend and intellectual companion. Tom Young, my PhD supervisor, was a constant source of ideas and encouragement. The research would not have been possible without the support of Leandra and Jean Box. And lastly I thank Jim Igoe, for providing me a roof over my head in Arusha, many memorable moments, and for pushing me to work on this book.

Jim Igoe

I would like to thank first and foremost my research assistants Edward Oloure Parmello, Lengai Mbarnoti, and Lobulu Sakita. I also thank the citizens of Simanjiro District, Tanzania, who graciously tolerated my presence in their midst for nearly three years. I am grateful to the following people within Tanzania's Pastoralist NGO movement: Saruni Ndelelya, Martin Saning'o, Makko Sinadai, Lekei Milikan, Moringe Ole Parkipuny, Maanda Ngoitiko, Peter Toima, Daniel Murumbi, Duncan Getognond, Augustino Maragu, and Christopher Duguay. I would also like to acknowledge the works of Tundu Antiphas Lissu and Issa Shivji, whose integrity and clarity of analysis have been a constant source of inspiration for me as both a scholar and an activist.

Thanks to Hamisi Nguli at COSTECH for his assistance, coffee, and engaging conversation. From my graduate school years, I owe thanks to Tom Barfield, Sutti Ortiz, James Pritchett, Alan Hoben, Bob Hefner, Jane Guyer, and Frederick Barth, all of whom have fundamentally influenced my thinking. From my adjunct years I am eternally grateful to Michael Stone, Mike Woost, David Anthony, Bill Bissell, Glenn Stone, Steve Ferzacca, Hillary Rodrigues, and Laurie Hart. From my tenure track years I must thank Steve Koester, John Brett, Kathy Pickering, Annie Ross, and Terry McCabe. Special thanks to Eugene Mendonza for helping to find a home for this volume. Special thanks also goes to Erica Bornstein for all of her theoretical input on the article that I wrote for this volume. Of course, I must also thank Tim Kelsall for getting this project started and the best Italian meal I've ever eaten. Finally, I wish to express my undying gratitude to my wife, Glady, whose support for my work never wavers, as well as to my boys, Erick and Vincent, who are a constant source of inspiration.

Both of us would like to thank our contributors—Sara Rich Dorman, Ben Rawlence, Marie-Emmanuelle Pommerolle, Erica Bornstein, Marina Padrão Temudo, Elizabeth Challinor, Tim Docking, and Stephen Jackson for their fantastic input and commitment to this project, as well as for their remarkable patience. Finally, no acknowledgement would be complete without thanking the following cast of characters: Beth Pratt, Simon Heck, Claire Mercer, Dan Brockington, and Peter Rogers.

Editors and Contributors

Editors

Tim Kelsall is Lecturer in African Politics at the University of Newcastle upon Tyne and joint editor of the journal *African Affairs*. He received his doctorate from the School of Oriental and African Studies, University of London in 2000 and is currently working on issues of accountability in Africa.

Jim Igoe is an assistant professor in the Department of Anthropology at the University of Colorado at Denver. He received his doctorate from Boston University in 2000. His dissertation research examined the impacts of economic and political liberalization on pastoralist communities in Tanzania, especially the emergence of indigenous NGOs of the Maasai and Barabaig ethnic groups. His current research deals with natural resource conflict and community-based conservation for indigenous communities living in and around national parks. He is author of the book *Conservation and Globalization: A Study of National Parks and Indigenous Communities from East Africa to South Dakota*. He is executive director of the NGO BRIDGE (Bridge for Indigenous Development and Grassroots Empowerment).

Contributors

Erica Bornstein is an anthropologist who is currently a Fellow at The Society for the Humanities at Cornell University. Her recent book, *The Spirit of Development: Protestant NGOs, Morality, and Economics in Zimbabwe* (Routledge 2003), is based on ethnographic research with Christian NGOs in Zimbabwe. Her published articles include: "Child Sponsorship, Evangelism, and Belonging in the Work of World Vision Zimbabwe" (*American Ethnologist*), "Developing Faith: Theologies of Development in Zimbabwe" (*The Journal of Religion in Africa*), and "The Verge of Good and Evil: Christian NGOs and Economic Development in Zimbabwe" (*Political and Legal Anthropology Review*).

Elizabeth Challinor is affiliated to the Center for the Study of Social Anthropology in Lisbon with a research grant from the Foundation for Science

and Technology, Portugal. She was the first representative of the Portuguese
NGO Oikos in Angola from 1990–92. She is currently working on a book on
the anthropology of development in Cape Verde where she has carried out
ethnographic fieldwork. She teaches on a post-graduate course in Humanitarian Assistance at the University of Fernando Pessoa, Porto and has set up
evening courses on issues related to development and globalization in collaboration with the School for Higher Education of Viana do Castelo.

Timothy W. Docking is a 2003–04 White House Fellow working at the U.S.
Department of Agriculture. Most recently he directed research on African affairs at the U.S. Institute of Peace. Tim's recent research has focused on political development, the nexus between AIDS and violent conflict, American foreign policy towards the continent, the West Africa regional war and terrorist
threats in the Horn of Africa. He has held several research fellowships including a Fulbright (University of Mali) and has served as a Peace Corps Volunteer and an election monitor. He has published numerous articles on democratic transitions, peacekeeping and conflict in sub-Saharan Africa. Tim
holds a Ph.D. in political science from Boston University.

Sara Rich Dorman is a Lecturer in African and International Politics at the
University of Edinburgh. Her DPhil thesis (Oxford, 2001) examined the politics of Zimbabwe's NGOs, with particular reference to their relationship with
the state. Current research projects include a monograph on Zimbabwean
politics (*Nationalist Politics in Zimbabwe, 1980-2002: State, Society and Elections)*, a project examining state-society relations in Eritrea and comparative
studies of post-liberation states.

Stephen Jackson is Associate Director of the Conflict Prevention and Peace
Forum, a program of the Social Science Research Council in New York. A relief worker in Somalia, Rwanda and Angola during the 1990s, he holds a
Ph.D. in Cultural Anthropology from Princeton. His dissertation research
examines the interplay between local and international dynamics of violence
in the D.R. Congo throughout the recent war. Previously a director of the International Famine Center at the National University of Ireland, Cork, his
research interests include the political economy of war, global/local conflict
linkages, principles and practice in humanitarian affairs, the political manipulation of ethnic identity, politico-ethnic violence, the postcolonial state,
and regional conflict formations.

Marie-Emmanuelle Pommerolle is reading for a Ph.D. in politics from the
Centre d'études de l'Afrique Noire (Bordeaux, France). Her dissertation is a
political sociology of local human rights NGOs in Kenya and Cameroon. Her
research interests are militancy, collective action and democratization, and law

and politics. She currently teaches politics to undergraduates at the Institut d'études politiques de Bordeaux.

Ben Rawlence lived and worked in Zanzibar from 1995 to 1997. With a BA from the University of London (SOAS) and MA from the University of Chicago, he has worked for the Global Security and Cooperation program of the Social Science Research Council, the International Peace Academy and as a consultant to Human Rights Watch on Zanzibar. He now works as Foreign Affairs adviser to the Liberal Democrats in the UK Parliament.

Marina Padrão Temudo is a senior research fellow at the Instituto de In-vestigaçao Cientifica Tropical (Tropical Research Institute), in Lisbon. She has conducted ethnographic field research mainly in Guinea-Bissau, but also in Cape Verde, Mozambique, Saint Thomas and Principe and Guinea-Conakry. She is interested in the study of "development landscapes." Other key issues of her research are: changes in gender relations, social capital and seed manage-ment in times of war, and local land tenure systems in Africa.

Between a Rock and a Hard Place

CHAPTER 1

INTRODUCTION: BETWEEN
A ROCK AND A HARD PLACE[1]

Jim Igoe

Department of Anthropology, University of Colorado at Denver
james.igoe@cudenver.edu

Tim Kelsall

Department of Politics, University of Newcastle upon Tyne
tim.kelsall@ncl.ac.uk

The Wake of Africa's NGO Revolution?

The Danish Ornithological Association (DOF) has received a grant of
1.3 million Euros from aid funding body DANIDA to promote the pro-
tection of rare birds and to support democracy in the provincial town of
Morogoro, Tanzania.[2]

In the mid-1990s few observers would have guessed that the popularity of
African NGOs could possibly wane in less than a decade. Indeed, the rhetoric of western donors portrayed these organizations as a panacea for Africa's
development and governance problems—a "magic bullet" that would find its
target no matter how poorly fired (Vivian 1994). During this period, NGOs
became a growth industry, on a continent where most economic sectors were

---

1. We are grateful to Ben Rawlence for his careful reading of an earlier draft of this introduction, and the numerous insightful comments that he made in response. All of Ben's
comments have been incorporated into this current iteration.
2. Tanzanian birds to get protection cash, *The Copenhagen Post*, 1–7 November 2002,
p. 3.

in decline (Fowler 1988). Not surprisingly, NGO research became a growth industry as well.

As the unrealistic expectations of western donors failed to materialize, however, support for African NGOs began to decline. This process was accelerated by the events of September 11th 2001, which prompted donors to redirect aid money toward African states in an effort to reduce the terrorist threat. In East Africa several bilateral and multilateral donors have quit NGO based aid, redirecting almost 100% of their funding budget to ministerial support.[3] Many African NGOs have found their funding significantly reduced and are now experiencing a freeze in the freeze/thaw cycle of a fickle development industry (see Jackson this volume).

This decline of support for African NGOs will doubtless prove as tragic as the abundant and uncritical support they enjoyed in the 1990s. During the heady days of the global NGO revolution, William Fisher (1997) warned against this eventuality, pointing out that grassroots NGOs were bound to fail to live up to the unrealistic expectations of western donors and academics. It would be unfortunate, he opined, if donors and academics abandoned grassroots NGOs without understanding the processes that caused them to fail. It would be even more unfortunate if they overlooked the strengths of grassroots NGOs—what they might have achieved if given the right kinds of opportunity and support.

The studies in this volume were researched during the zenith of Africa's NGO revolution, when Fisher was warning of the decline of grassroots NGOs. Due to the inevitable delays of academic publishing, they are appearing in the context of the decline he foresaw. It is too early to say, however, whether they represent an autopsy of Africa's NGO revolution. The decline in NGO funding had varied from region to region and from organization to organization. It is important to note, however, that the conditions these studies describe have continued to change since they were written. In this respect, this volume supplies the type of analytic record that Fisher called for in 1997: what went wrong with African NGOs, what went right, and what could have gone better under more optimal circumstances.

We hope that these studies will be useful for ongoing NGO interventions in Africa and elsewhere. Even more importantly, we hope that they will not be overlooked when African NGOs re-emerge as the favored institutional ve-

---

3. Special thanks to Simon Heck and Beth Pratt for reading a recent draft of this introduction and offering this information.

hicle for development and governance interventions, as they almost inevitably will in the freeze/thaw cycles of development assistance. Some NGOs have already become the "darling of the donors," fallen out of favor, repackaged themselves, and re-emerged as the "darling of the donors" once again—all within the space of a few years. Individual NGO leaders have done the same (Igoe 2003). More importantly, these studies have value not just for future interventions, but also in understanding how politics work in Africa, especially the politics of aid.

On the theoretical side, these studies are a caveat against perspectives that fail to account for the ever shifting nature of the global system in which development and governance interventions are formulated and implemented. They are also a celebration of the critical and ethnographic approach to theory and to understanding political processes, which positivist models cannot capture. While positivist models of development and governance come and go in response to geopolitical change, the ethnographic approach remains viable in any context. The studies in this volume apply ethnographic approaches to Africa's NGO revolution of the 1990s. While this revolution may have passed, the importance of locally understood political contexts should never be lost. The ethnographic perspective not only illuminates these contexts, but more importantly the ways in which they articulate with ever shifting global networks of institutions, ideas, and money. Illuminating the articulations between "the local" and "the global" is essential to understanding Africa's NGO revolution.

At the end of the 1980s, the Soviet collapse led some enthusiastic observers to proclaim that we had reached "the end of mankind's ideological evolution and the universalization of western liberal democracy as the final form of human government" (Fukuyuma 1989: 4). In the context of our current geopolitical crisis these proclamations, which were made less than twenty-years ago, now appear ridiculous. Such proclamations are especially important to theories of civil society as a catalyst for the globalization of liberal democracy and free market capitalism. As will be demonstrated below, such theories informed donor ideals that African NGOs equalled civil society, and were therefore essential to the economic and political liberalization of African countries.

The ethnographic studies presented in this volume take place in the putative space of African civil society. They reveal that it is a murkier and less stable space than most civil society theories would suggest. They illuminate the ways in which African NGO leaders negotiate it. This perspective reveals that NGO leaders—along with other cultural entrepreneurs—are painfully aware of the shifting nature of the global system upon which they depend for their livelihoods—and which holds important opportunities for improving conditions in their communities. In order to successfully negotiate this space they must be flexible—able to abandon one approach for another as conditions demand. These conditions present difficult challenges to development and governance interventions that are premised on conditions of stability and predictability. They also challenge prevailing theoretical models of governance and development. In order to reveal these conditions, our studies must penetrate current myths about civil society and NGOs in Africa. We conclude, however, by suggesting possible ways forward in light of the conditions that we reveal.

Before introducing the perspective of the assembled studies, however, it is necessary to address their historical and theoretical context. The following section outlines the historical processes that contributed to Africa's NGO revolution. We then address the various theoretical perspectives that sought to explain this revolution during the 1990s. We conclude with a discussion of the importance of the ethnographic perspective for understanding African NGOs and the common themes that emerge from the studies in this volume.

The Global Associational Revolution and the Rise and Fall of African NGOs

Ten years ago Lester Salamon, director of the Center for Civil Society Studies at Johns Hopkins University, proclaimed (1993:1):

> A veritable associational revolution now seems underway at the global level that may constitute as significant a social and political development of the latter twentieth as the rise of the nation state was in the latter 19th century.

This proclamation now seems almost as short sighted as the idea that we had reached "the end of history" in 1989. It also ignores the fact that states and NGOs are both means to an end, but the ends of development and governance are constantly changing according to western priorities. Most recently, for instance, concerns about civil society and democratization have taken a back seat to security imperatives. As the studies in this volume reveal, Africans rarely have a voice in determining policy imperatives. As George W. Bush's recent trip to the continent dramatically illustrated, policy is set from outside every time. It is important to note, therefore, that African NGOs did not deliver in the manner expected not merely for technical reasons or inaccurate understandings. Africa's NGO dream failed for two primary reasons: 1) it was launched on the wrong assumptions; and 2) it failed to address the fundamental power imbalance between givers and receivers of aid, as well as between African elites and their constituent communities.[4]

Furthermore, if the current conflict in Iraq is any indication, the line between the state and the NGO sector is becoming increasingly irrelevant—as is the line between the state and the private sector. In June of this year (2003), President George W. Bush informed American NGO leaders that they were in fact "an arm" of the U.S. Government—and that they had an important job to promote U.S. interests in Afghanistan and Iraq. Furthermore, NGOs receiving funding from the U.S. Government were not to speak to reporters or publicly express critical opinions of U.S. foreign policy.[5] Meanwhile corporations like Halliburton and the Carlisle Group are given non-bid government contracts for the reconstruction of Iraq. In this context the efficacy of particular types of institutions becomes less important than the question of whose interests they serve.

In the early 1990s, however, it was widely believed that NGOs would become the foundation for a global civil society. This was reflected in a global proliferation of NGOs. The reasons for this proliferation, and the beliefs that accompanied it, are numerous and complex. Generally speaking, however, it is closely associated with two global political transformations: 1) The Reagan/Thatcher revolution, with its emphasis on free markets and the downsizing of government; and 2) The collapse of the Soviet Union and the rise of civil society in Eastern and Central Europe.

These global transformations coincided with a growing perception that NGOs "were more efficient conduits for development than often-discredited official agencies" (Masoni 1985:8). So widespread were these perceptions that Judith Tendler (1982), an insider to development for over thirty years, labelled them "NGO Articles of Faith": assumptions that NGOs are by their very nature altruistic, autonomous, cooperative, efficient, empowering, participatory, and transparent. While these assumptions are frequently contradicted by NGO performance, they have remained a powerful justification for the funding of NGOs in Africa and elsewhere.

The influence of these transformations became visible by the end of the 1980s. At the beginning of this decade NGOs were an obscure vehicle for development interventions. By the end of it observers were suggesting, "the

---

4. This paragraph is almost completely constructed from the insights of Ben Rawlence.

5. Klein, Naomi (1993) "Bush to NGOs: Watch Your Mouths." *Globe and Mail (Canada)*, June 20, 2003.

1980s may turn out to be the NGO decade for rural development in Africa" (Bratton 1989; see also Sandberg 1994; Charlton and May 1995; and Edwards and Hulme 1996). Alan Hoben, formerly senior anthropologist at U.S.A.I.D. and the World Bank, described how NGO officers rose from total obscurity to being among the most sought after people within these agencies during this period.[6]

NGOs proliferated even more rapidly in the 1990s. While multi-lateral and bi-lateral aid still dominated development and governance interventions, NGOs "displaced governments as the primary recipients of a number of categories of Official Development Assistance," especially those related to emergency relief assistance (Charlton and May 1995). Across the board, NGOs received a far larger slice of the development money pie and have become significant players in the impoverished economies of Sub Saharan Africa. A study of NGO sectors in 42 countries, headed by Salamon, indicates that if all the funding for NGOs worldwide were amalgamated into a single country, it would be the eighth largest economy in the world, a total of $90 billion annually. In nine of the countries in the study, the NGO sector is growing at four times the rate of the economy, 23% versus 6%.[7]

In Canada, NGOs received 22% of the total aid funds, both public and private (Brodhead 1987). In France, where charitable organizations were previously illegal, 60,000 new NGOs were being registered every year. From 1992 to 1997, 100,000 NGOs were registered in the former Soviet Union. In the Netherlands and Israel, which are two of the countries included in Salamon's study, one in eight workers is employed in the non-profit sector. In developing countries, the proliferation of NGOs is equally dramatic. India leads the way with over a million registered NGOs. Brazil has 300,000.[8]

Africa's NGO revolution was not nearly so dramatic. Relatively speaking, however, the growth of NGOs on the continent was significant. In 1988 the Environmental Liaison Center in Nairobi estimated that there were between

---

6. From personal comments to Jim Igoe, who was Hoben's advisee at Boston University.

7. Salamon cited these numbers in a speech to an annual meeting of National Voluntary Organizations in Montreal in September of 1999. The speech was covered by the Montreal Globe and Mail in an article entitled "Citizens' Groups New Agents of Change: Researcher studies rapid worldwide growth of $90-billion non-profit sector" by Andre Picard (09/20/99).

8. *Ibid.*

8,000 and 9,000 NGOs in the whole of Africa (Ng'ethe 1991). Current figures from South Africa indicate that there are 98,920 registered NGOs in that country alone. These organizations contribute 1.2% to the country's Gross Domestic Product and employ 645,317 full time staff, which represents 10.2% of the formal non-agricultural workforce.[9] In Tanzania, where there were only 25 registered NGOs in 1986, by 1994 there were 813 (GOT 1994). This number is closer to 1,800 if non-registered organizations are included (Mercer 1999). Ghana had 80 registered NGOs in 1980. By 2001 it had 1300.[10]

In terms of funding, NGOs in Africa began receiving an increasing share of bilateral aid. By 1989, the European Economic Community was contributing $600 million annually to African NGOs (but now has shifted back to ministerial funding).[11] During this same year the Canadian International Development Agency was giving 12% of its total aid to Africa to NGOs. Multilateral agencies like the United National Development Programme (UNDP) and the World Bank began seeking NGO partners and encouraging joint ventures between African governments and local NGOs (Bratton 1989). In fact, it was rare to find a development, conservation, or governance intervention for sub Saharan Africa that did not involve local NGOs in some capacity.

In the wake of this initial enthusiasm, western donors and NGO researchers have grown disappointed as African NGOs have failed to live up to their original expectations. A major reason for this disappointment, however, is that these expectations were unrealistic. These nascent organizations were so poorly understood that there was still no consensus on how to classify the various types (Vakil 1997). Nevertheless, donors expected them to do everything from promoting good hygiene to promoting women's rights, from introducing micro-credit to introducing rural Africans to the value of resource conservation, from planting mandarin orange groves to planting the seeds of democracy across the continent.

Considering these expectations, the relative paucity of funding compared to the monumental tasks at hand, and the lack of trained NGO personnel, it

---

9. These numbers were compiled by the Graduate School of Public and Development Management at Wits University and coordinated by the Centre for Civil Society Studies at Johns Hopkins (www.globalpolicy.org/ngos/role/globdem/funding/2002/0731fund.htm).

10. These numbers will compiled by Paul Opuku-Mensah from the files of the Ministry of Employment and Social Welfare, Government of Ghana.

11. Personal communication from Simon Heck, based on his experience as a development consultant in Kenya.

is surprising that African NGOs have been as successful as they have over the past twenty years. Rather than assume that NGOs have universally intrinsic qualities, it is more fruitful to assume that they will reflect the socio-historical conditions of the locale in which they operate. On a continent where most governments are highly dependent on foreign aid for their continued survival, this shift of donor money from African states to the NGO sector was significant indeed. Its significance is even greater when one considers that per capita incomes in sub Saharan Africa dropped by 21% in real terms from 1981 to 1989, while income inequalities have continued to grow in the wake of structural adjustment reforms (UNDP 1996 and UNDP 2000). Africa's NGO revolution occurred at a time when unprecedented numbers of civil servants were made redundant by the downsizing of African states that accompanied these reforms, which coincidently presented new opportunities by creating a liberal environment for the registration of local NGOs.

Donors walked into these conditions in the early-1990s with large sums of NGO funding. Most were beholden to inflexible funding cycles that required them to disburse this money within a relatively short period of time. Unfortunately for them, local NGOs were scarce on the ground. This situation resulted in an over abundance of donor money channeled to a select few NGOs (cf. Tendler 1975). In Tanzania this created a situation where "any NGO that was able to present a veneer of respectability was virtually assured a surfeit of money" (Kelsall 1998). NGO registration was happening so rapidly during this period that the Tanzanian Government suspended NGO registration in 1996 as it was unable to process all the articles of incorporation that it was receiving. Similar processes in other parts of the continent led to the popularization of the briefcase NGO: organizations that existed only on paper, registered for the express purpose of parting donors with their money.

By the late 1990s, there was a growing perception among both donors and the African public that African NGOs were dominated by sophisticated con artists. An op-ed piece in the *East African* from 1999 described the situation in Kenya as follows:

> Against the backdrop of worsening poverty in Kenya, the NGO sector has recorded a dramatic increase in numbers, especially since the advent of political pluralism. By the mid-nineties, the formation of NGOs had become something of a fad among the professional upper-middle classes. The perception among ordinary folk was that this was

a get-rich-quick gimmick dreamed up by resourceful individuals to exploit gullible foreign donors.[12]

The briefcase NGO stood as a stark antithesis to the original promise of NGOs as institutions of grassroots democracy. It is likely, therefore, that donors and researchers became overly focused on them, thereby overlooking innovative and dynamic grassroots initiatives. Maren (1997: 166) describes this situation in the context of famine relief in war-ravaged Somalia. One of his Somali informants, Osman Raghe, sought to establish a local NGO to assist in the reconstruction of his country:

> Then he learned that it wasn't that simple. The UN invited Somali NGOs to register and apply for grant money. Suddenly more than 1,000 Somali NGOs appeared from the rubble of the city. Local businessmen began calling themselves NGOs, competing for contracts or sub-grants from foreign NGOs. Driving along Mogadishu's bullet-scarred streets one saw the signs: The Somali Society for the Protection of Children, Somali Children's Aid, and Action for Children. It was endless. Some were cynical attempts to make money. Others were a practical result of the fact that in Somalia, as in much of Africa, relief and development are the most dynamic growth industries. While (foreign) NGOs and the UN helped create this atmosphere, they held in contempt many of the Somalis who tried to cash in on the relief and development explosion. No matter what Raghe did, he was seen by foreigners as another Somali profiteer jumping on the aid bandwagon to make a buck.

While individuals like Raghe are seemingly less common than NGO leaders of a more opportunistic stripe, they have undeniably been part of Africa's NGO revolution. Most NGO researchers working in Africa have encountered selfless individuals who struggle to bring about positive change in the face of seemingly impossible odds. Their situation is the inspiration for the title of this volume, as they are truly caught "between a rock and a hard place." On one side they must deal with western donors, on whom they depend for support, and whose agendas frequently do not match their own. On the other they must deal with government officials who feel threatened by their activities and who may be competing with them for legitimacy and/or funding. It also includes other NGO leaders, some legitimate and

---

12. Ohayo, J. (1999) "They Drive Pajeros; They Alleviate Poverty; Yet No One Loves NGOs." *The East African,* March 29th–April 4th.

some not, who are competing with them for the same limited pot of money. Finally it includes NGO opportunists who cast suspicion on everyone in the NGO sector.

The unfortunate mistake made by many NGO analysts is to mistake the institution for the process. As Fisher (1997: 458) points out, "the transformative potential of the NGO sector may emerge less from ordered and controlled participation than from relatively chaotic sets of multiple opportunities." NGOs in Africa opened up new types of socio-political space, simultaneously presenting new opportunities. Some took advantage of these opportunities to enrich themselves; others used them to promote grassroots democracy. Some even successfully accomplished both. As Fisher also points out, the space created by these activities may present future opportunities for new types of activism and progressive initiatives. It is the fluidity of these spaces, and their associated opportunities, that should be of interest to NGO researchers, rather than the success of failure of a particular NGO (op. cite). The nature of these spaces is a central theme of all the studies in this volume. Before turning to these studies, however, it is first necessary to examine the theoretical perspectives that emerged around Africa's NGO revolution in the mid-1990s.

Theoretical Perspectives

The Liberal Project and African NGOs

As the previous section has pointed out, Africa's NGO revolution coincided with an ideological assault on the state that originated not in Africa, but in the New Right politics of the west. Freeing the economy from the shackles of state intervention was presented as the way to restore global economic growth. The Bretton Woods institutions—previous champions of the state—fell into line. The World Bank's 1981 *Accelerated Development in Sub-Saharan Africa* reflected this transformation, arguing that African economic failure was caused by excessive state interference in the market. After almost a decade spent trying—unsuccessfully in most cases—to dismantle the state, the multilaterals came round to the idea that some kind of state was necessary to development. The point was to get an appropriate state, accountable to the interests of its population. With the publication of *Sub-Saharan Africa—from crisis to sustainable growth* in 1989, politics and democracy moved to center stage in development debates (World Bank 1989). The valorization of NGOs can be dated from this moment.

To appreciate the logic of this position it is important to recall that performance of African states in the 1970s was hardly beyond reproach. In the eyes of liberal scholars, and not a few Marxists, African governments were developmentally inept for a number of reasons. To begin with, they lacked sophisticated managerial capacity and were consequently ill-suited to ambitious central planning. The states that arguably went furthest in this direction—Ghana, Guinea, Tanzania, Ethiopia and Mozambique—tended to take small leaps backward. Secondly, African states tended to have shallow historical roots—they were superimposed upon highly diverse populations, few of whom even imagined themselves as part of a national community. This made them difficult to govern, with an ever-present danger of disaffected politicians whipping up ethnic or religious storms. Where political legitimacy was weak, and where managerial capacity was low, African leaders sought to buy political consent in rough and ready ways—dispensing patronage in the form of state employment, contracts and funds through ethnic networks. Particularistic practices such as these frequently compounded problems of inefficiency and waste, as state officials viewed their offices as prebends, created for the sole purpose of facilitating self-enrichment. (*See* Bates 1981; Callaghy 1988; Diamond 1987, 1988; Hyden 1981, 1983; Olukoshi 1998; Sandbrook 1985).

This fact was related to another one: African societies tended to lack a powerful and self-confident capitalist class constituted outside of the state, which saw its political role as one of ensuring that the government created conditions conducive to capitalist investment. Instead, individuals with capitalist aspirations were acutely dependent on the award of state contracts, credit and licenses, such that the ability to make money also became inseparably linked to the personal favor of those in political power. More often than not, those with the ability to make money quite simply *were* those in power, so closely were politics and business intertwined. Naturally, this situation placed a high premium on the ability to win and maintain political office, to the extent that in some states, electoral contests became ferocious life or death competitions and politics a literally cut-throat affair (*Ibid.*).

Aside from aid, the key source of funds to feed the swelling stomach of this insatiable beast was peasant export crops. Frequently these were heavily taxed to the point at which peasants started selling them outside of state channels, or simply stopped producing them altogether. Instead of raising prices, it was more usual for states to try to compel peasants to grow cash crops, sometimes on expensive and poorly conceived development schemes. With funds from agriculture drying up, states were less able to buy political consent by redistributing patronage. Coercion became more common, and in cases this spiralled out of control provoking bloody civil wars, often with an ethnic dimension. This type of instability acted as a further deterrent to rational capitalist investment and an increased incentive to predation.

Or so the liberal story goes. Certainly the state, crippled by its own internal contradictions, was in retreat in many African countries by the end of the 1970s. This condition was often compounded under Structural Adjustment in the 1980s. It was in these circumstances that the actual and potential role of NGOs became more visible. Beyond the crumbling state structures, researchers discovered that Africans were getting on with their lives, devising new ways of making an income and organizing community associations. The first became known as "informal economic activity," and the second as "associational life," or "civil society." Gradually these phenomena came to be seen as the keys to Africa's regeneration. The informal economy was represented as a seedbed of dynamic indigenous capitalism, and associational life as a site of empowerment and bulwark against authoritarian rule (Chazan 1988; Diamond 1988; Bangura & Gibbon 1993).

With the fall of the Berlin Wall democracy was thrown into the mix. Entities ranging from rural women's credit societies to football clubs to urban legal advocacy groups were classified as civil society. In only the latest in a long line of examples of the development industry's incurably faddish optimism, these organizations were presented as a virtual developmental panacea, with enormous expectations attached to their role (Clark 1991).

NGOs were perceived as "close to the people" and therefore capable of "putting people first." The idea was that development as previously conceived had been too hubristic, centralized, and top-down. It had exploited the poor peasants to create expensive, unsustainable white elephants and idle over-privileged bureaucracies. NGOs would ensure that development was equitable and not exploitative, that it was sustainable and not environmentally destructive, and that it respected indigenous knowledge and employed culturally appropriate technology (Poulton and Harris 1988). According to Farrington et al (1993: 100): "The social transformation that many NGOs are seeking to effect is deemed in NGO-lore to derive directly from an empowered rural poor who will identify the roots of their poverty and then change them."

Linked to their "people-centeredness," the entire modus operandi of NGOs was thought to be democratic. In the eyes of liberals, they came to be viewed through a neo-Tocquevillian lens. They were pictured as little schools of civilized politics, veritable vessels of democratic pedagogy. In their classrooms, Africans would learn how to be good, civil citizens who would know how to critique their leaders, would be tolerant of opposing political viewpoints, and would respect electoral processes and the rule of law (Diamond 1994). The very experience of associating and cooperating together in NGOs contributed another crucial ingredient to development and democracy—social capital (Diamond 1994 and Hyden 1997). NGOs would help build up a stock of knowledge about how to cooperate, together with vast reserves of goodwill toward neighbors and even strangers, which would mean that working together for development, as well as acting as citizens to hold government to account, would be easier to achieve.

Next, NGOs were constituent units of civil society. They were there to convey society's voice to the state, to admonish it when it made inappropriate policy or discharged its duties poorly, to protest against it if it took an authoritarian turn, and generally to champion causes that all reasonable people would regard as desirable, such as gender equality, protection of the rights of the child, sustainable development, AIDS awareness, and anti-female genital mutilation, not to mention the protection of rare species of bird.

The tone of some of the liberal literature is unmistakably celebratory. Indigenous grassroots organizations are presented as democratic crusaders in a Manichean struggle against an illiberal, authoritarian, often patriarchal state. They are presented as authentic, self-propelled vehicles of emancipation. NGOs are intimately linked in this discourse to democracy, development and autonomy, an almost irresistible combination, constituting the three points of a discursive arrowhead designed to penetrate, effortlessly, freedom loving liberal hearts.

Anti-NGOs

But not everyone was so smitten. The pro-NGO literature provoked a vigorous riposte, which can be divided into two main strands: communitarian and socialist. These unlikely bedfellows are united in their antipathy to liberalism and the liberal project; NGOs as key vectors of the latter, have unwittingly earned their ire. But why are they so steely-hearted?

The interesting thing about the communitarian critique is not that it doubts the ability of NGOs to fulfill the liberal mission with which they have been charged. In fact, communitarians are completely convinced by liberal claims for NGOs; they just don't like what they are trying to do (Williams 1993 and 2000 and Williams and Young 1994). Liberals want to use NGOs to foster horizontal, contractual forms of association. Old ways of life, old communities, old institutions, and old selves are earmarked for destruction, when communitarians prefer that they be conserved (*ibid*).

The idea that NGOs are really about transforming people and eradicating their traditional ways of life will doubtless strike some westerners who work in the sector as surprising, since they tend to think of themselves as people who want to help others. But the idea that NGOs are the advance guard of a "liberal project" paints them in the pose of neo-colonial missionaries - agents of a form of cultural imperialism.[13] Funding for NGOs begins to look less like support for indigenous democracy and people's rights, and more like the foisting of a foreign culture on the vulnerable peoples of the South.

Williams and Young (1994) drive home their case by drawing an analogy between the Governance Agenda and the historical process by which pre-industrial European populations were transformed into citizens of modern states. They cite Foucault, who describes an apparatus of modern disciplinary power, composed of institutions such as the workhouse, the factory, the school, the army and the prison, which created a population at once politically docile and congenial to exploitation. These practices were underwritten by a desire to create a citizen governed by a circumscribed, self-regulating, self-disciplined autonomy (Foucault 1977, 1982, and 1991; Barry et al 1996). At the same time they point to the way in which the liberal state often consolidated itself through violence, smashing forms of corporate community—such as Scottish clans—that stood in its way (see Young 1995).

Liberal philosophy valorizes choice. But, communitarians argue, it only values choices of the correct, liberal kind. Inscribed in the work of canonical liberal thinkers such as Rousseau, Locke, Smith and Mill, is, they argue, a deep intolerance of the choices that non-propertied, uneducated, or non-western peoples make (Williams 1993; Williams and Young 1994; and Young 1995). In traditional liberal credo, it is illegitimate to abolish private property, circumcise your female children, or vote for a political party that supports *sharia* law. If people are to be given the right to choose, it must be certain that they make the right choices. In some cases, this means that they will need to be transformed (see Abrahamsen 2000). Sometimes this is accomplished by force, at others more insidious methods are used: a micro-physics of capillary power that infuses the body of the citizen and the state. In Africa's case, the capillaries come in the shape of NGOs (Williams 1993 and Williams and Young 1994). Communitarians re-

---

13. Some literally *are* missionaries, so this jibe is unlikely to unsettle them, but others who have a secular outlook will probably be more upset.

sent the ways in which NGOs work to reconstruct Africans on a western template. NGOs, in this optic, become the unwitting agents of a silent ethnocide.

Elements of the communitarian critique are also held by Marxists. Hearn (1998 and 2000), for instance, demonstrates that USAID has used its funding practices in Kenya and Ghana to create indigenous NGOs in a liberal mould, with the anticipated effect of promoting a liberal economic and political agenda. It is not the erasure of "traditional" communities that Marxists are unhappy about, it is that the liberal agenda pre-empts the possibility of socialist emancipation. The critique comes in a variety of forms. In the first place, it doubts the developmental capabilities of NGOs, seeing them as plagued by lack of coordination, amateurism, infighting, and narcotic religious zeal. Hanlon's book on Mozambique (1995) is a classic example of this kind of literature. He pillories NGOs, not just because of the above problems, but because they inherit, by default, the blame for the collapse of FRELIMO's noble socialist dream.

Because they divert donor funds from governments, other Marxists regard NGOs as complicit in an international project to undermine the state, the only institution capable of protecting Africans from the "gales of global capitalism." Marxists are skeptical of the liberal interpretation of the African crisis. While all states shared some of the features of the liberal narrative (the downward spiral of state illegitimacy, corruption, economic decline, violence, less legitimacy, more corruption, and so on), only a minority shared them all. They question the process by which the worst aspects of a variety of distinct historical trajectories have been woven into a single cautionary tale about the pitfalls of state intervention in development. The ideological effect of this kind of horror story is to facilitate the imposition of neo-liberal blueprint solutions, rather than to create fair international economic arrangements, or to tailor development policies to the specific conditions of a diversity of states (see Leys 1994).

NGOs, in the view of Marxists, either wittingly or unwittingly, underwrite this process. They tend to be concerned with welfare provision, and therefore serve merely to pick up the pieces left by the onslaught of Structural Adjustment. The very presence of charitable organizations provides a veneer of respectability and serves to legitimize the entire neo-liberal project.

As for the idea that NGOs can foster democracy, this too is deemed suspect since they are associated with liberal definitions of democracy. Liberal democracy is democracy for the middle classes. Marxists would much rather support genuine social movements made up of peasants, workers and the unemployed. The ability of donors to steer radical social movements into unthreatening forms of bourgeois politics, by turning them into NGOs, is deemed by them a retrograde step. They prefer "popular" groups that offer a more boisterous challenge to world capitalism and to African leaders, imperialism's crony compradors (Saul 1997).

Added to this is a set of concerns oriented to the perspective of African social activists or NGO leaders. The dependence of African NGOs on their Western counterparts merely replicates the patterns of dependency that tie African governments to the former colonial powers. In addition, donors are sometimes criticized for being culturally arrogant and condescending, failing to appreciate the value of their African staff. Often they fail to grant sufficient funds to their African counterparts, and require excessive reporting and auditing procedures. In addition, the process of gaining funds is sometimes so time-consuming that organizations are diverted from their original objectives. In sum, many would like to see African NGOs being granted more money and more autonomy (see Manji and O'Coill 2002).

The NGO Industry's Auto-Critique

Elements of the Marxist critique echo an internal critical discourse conducted by NGO staff themselves, aided by researchers closely linked to the NGO industry.[14] At the turn of the 1990s, NGO ideologues ruminated on the opportunities presented by an enlargement in scale. Clark (1991) argued that NGOs were often, "idealistic, bottom-up, democratic, flexible, responsive and anti-elite," even "anti-management." Putative strengths, these characteristics could also be construed as weaknesses. Sheldon Annis argued that "small scale" could mean "insignificant," "politically independent" could imply that NGOs were "powerless" or "disconnected" and "low cost," could mean that they were "underfinanced or poor quality"(cited in Farrington *et al* 1993: 23).

In spite of their emphasis on "scaling-up," NGO supporters were also wary of closer engagement with state and donors. In a major contribution published in 1997, Hulme and Edwards (1997: 3) asked, "Are NGOs losing the special relationship with the poor, with radical ideas, and with alternatives to the orthodoxies of the rich and powerful, that they have claimed in the past?" NGOs,

---

14. This is hardly surprising, since many of these individuals were originally fired by the ideas of Paulo Freire and other leftists, even though the sector has lately been decidedly embourgeoisified.

by now receiving a very significant proportion of their funding from bilateral or multilateral donors, were said to be abandoning the ideals and advantages that previously distinguished them. NGOs had become over-bureaucratized, over-professionalized, too focused on moving money and the balance sheet. According to Hashemi, "NGOs have to make a choice: between the four-wheel drive vehicle that comes with government licensing and donor funding, and the much harder conditions involved in living alongside poor people" (cited in *ibid*: 15). Part of this shift in NGO outlook has taken place, as Pearce implies, via the marginalization of the more radically minded elements *within* NGOs (Pearce 2000: 20).

The shift was accompanied by a set of anxieties about accountability. There were worries that Northern NGOs (NNGOs) were becoming too "upwardly accountable" to official aid agencies; that Southern NGOs (SNGOs) were more accountable to NNGOs than vice versa; and that neither were very accountable to the poor, their supposed constituencies (Bebbington and Riddell 1997: 124–25). In addition, there was a realization that injecting resources into organizations that lacked strong internal accountability mechanisms might drive an insurmountable wedge between leaders and members (*ibid*: 111). Moreover, "by using NGOs as channels to implement programmes (*sic*) and channel aid, donors can in fact weaken these organizations as representative and accountable institutions within civil society" (*ibid*: 121). A plausible inference is that in this context, donor interference can be even more destabilizing, a hypothesis that the chapters in this collection explore.

A further concern has been that NGOs have made little impact on the international order; they have failed to encourage Western publics to make government take global inequality seriously, and they have failed to address the question of living standards and consumption patterns (Hulme and Edwards 1997 and Pearce 2000). As the Marxist critique suggests, they have become reduced to creating "safety nets" for the poor, no longer fulfilling a transformative function. In the words of Commins (2000), they have become "ladles in the global soup kitchen."

The crisis of confidence in the NGO sector induced by these reflections has stimulated two broad, though by no means mutually exclusive responses. Firstly, there has been a "technocratic" response. This often takes the form of detailed analytical elaboration and enumeration of all the problems besetting NGOs and their interrelations with donors and the state. This is sometimes accompanied by the drawing of complicated diagrams and charts, presumably as a means of helping NGO workers think their way through these predicaments, but more likely for the sake of their ritual effects.[15] This type of response very much fits the description of "normal science," or "problem-solving" within a prevailing paradigm. The development machine is perceived not to be working so attempts are made to fix it. The assumption that such a machine is needed is rarely subjected to scrutiny.

The second response has been to make bold aspirational statements about revolutionizing the form of global cooperation. Michael Edwards has argued that NGOs need to return to the "grassroots," at the same time as lobbying for new discursive, co-operative, democratic arrangements at global level. There are also recommendations that NNGOs begin to do development work in northern communities, in which SNGO workers are involved as participants (Bebbington and Riddell 1997). These are fine ideas indeed, but the development community has historically thrived on the marriage between utopian development visions and worn-out means of development practice. The ultimate goals of development, indeed development itself, remain unquestioned in this optic. "The challenge for the future is not an intellectual one thinks Edwards, we already know the principles of project success" (cited in Pearce 2000: 32).

In this respect the NGO self-critique has the character of an internal conversation utterly oblivious to the challenges of communitarian or post-development thinkers. While the literature spawned by NGOs is replete with anxieties about NGOs becoming businesses, about them cozying up to government and about them losing touch with the grassroots, thereby constraining their ability to attack poverty, there is rarely any discussion of what "poverty" is, whether it can be realistically eradicated, and what negative transformations might be required in order to do so. Hulme and Edwards (1997: 17) hint at problems of cultural dissonance in their observation that, "a criticism made by commentators from the South is that the whole debate on NGO performance, accountability, legitimacy and cost-effectiveness is framed exclusively in Western (liberal) terms" but they admit that their volume, while recognizing this "important criticism," is effectively deaf to it.

The narrowness of this auto-critique misses a crucial perspective on African NGOs: the ways in which the actors concerned conceptualize the problems at hand, how they perceive their own roles, how they construct their worldview.

---

15. For an example of the former, see the diagram in Hulme and Edwards, "Ngos, States and Donors: An Overview," 12, and of the latter, the stupefying table in Harry Blair, "Donors, Democratisation and Civil Society," in *Ngos, States and Donors: Too Close for Comfort?*, ed. David Hulme and Michael Edwards (Basingstoke: Macmillan Ltd. with Save the Children Fund, 1997), 34–36.

Furthermore, how do these conceptualizations influence action and the outcomes of NGO interventions? These perceptions and processes are something that the ethnographic method is uniquely equipped to reveal.

Toward an Ethnography of NGOs and Civil Society in Africa

NGO Myths and Normative Perspectives

As the previous sections illustrate, one of the central challenges faced by NGO researchers in Africa is to penetrate the normative discourses and myths surrounding African NGOs. In the words of Kenyan NGO researcher, Njuguna Ng'ethe (1989: 1):

> What is known about NGOs is too often clouded by what is believed about them. Theoretically it should be relatively easy to distinguish fact based knowledge from belief based articles of faith. In practice, however, such analytical distinction is extremely difficult. The reason is that in the current sociology of knowledge of NGOs, and the accompanying epistemology of knowledge, NGOs, as principal sources of this knowledge have tended to generate and target this "knowledge" in a way that creates some myths about themselves; a feat that is often achieved by blurring the line between fact and belief.

All of the authors whose work appears in this volume have struggled to come to terms with normative discourses surrounding African NGOs, and have tried to understand their implications for the institutions and processes they were observing in the field. This is evident from the number of times the words "fiction" and "myth" appear in their chapters.

What we have also learned, however, is that penetrating these normative notions is no easy feat. First of all, the ideas that NGO researchers may be trying to dispel are often "necessary fictions" (Bornstein this volume). As Dorman (this volume) points out, these types of ideas are set out by donors, because they reflect their own views of how the African NGOs they are funding should behave. This situation has been reinforced by research methodologies that revolve around the desire of donors to understand how well African NGOs "fit the demands set before them, with respect to their efficiency, participation levels, and transparency." Furthermore, donors, NGO leaders, government officials, and even local people may perpetuate these myths for a variety of "practical reasons" (Challinor this volume). In some cases they may do so cynically, in others they may do so because they wholeheartedly embrace them. In any case the ideas and discourses surrounding African NGOs may continue to persist even in cases where they are demonstrably false.

Furthermore, it is not enough simply to dispel the normative discourses surrounding African NGOs, as they effectively become part of the terrain in which these organizations operate. As Rawlence (this volume) points out, these discourses "may have a questionable purchase on local realities but...despite this they have nevertheless played a crucial role in shaping the environment in which NGOs are highly valued." NGO researchers therefore face a slippery challenge of revealing the ways in which such discourses fail to accurately portray "local realities," while simultaneously documenting the ways in which they may ultimately come to shape those realities. Such a challenge calls for an intensive empirical investigation of African NGOs that can only be provided by an ethnographic approach.

Ethnographic Approaches

Traditional ethnographers sought to live amongst isolated exotic people and then write systematic accounts of their cultures. Today ethnographers are far more aware of the integration of the world's people into global networks of institutions, ideas, and money. Rather than describe discrete cultures, they are more inclined to describe the impacts of this integration on people's lives in specific local contexts. All of the articles in this volume reflect this contemporary approach to ethnography, by using African NGOs as a window for understanding the articulation of African communities into these global networks. Two aspects of the ethnographic approach make it especially amenable to understanding African NGOs: (1) long stays in specific communities; and (2) participant observation.

Bronislaw Malinowski (1922, 1929, and 1930), one of the pioneers of ethnographic fieldwork, advocated the importance of the ethnographic approach for finding solutions to practical problems. He argued that ethnographers were better equipped to understand the nature of these problems than other "men on the spot" (colonial administrators and missionaries). In contemporary terms, ethnographers tend to avoid the types of biases outlined by Chambers (1984): urban, tarmac, dry-season, and people. While they obviously are not immune to these biases, they are likely to spend extended periods of time outside of urban areas, visit areas away from paved roads, live in rural communities year round, and spend time talking to non-elites. This approach stands in stark contrast to the situation described by Temudo (this volume) in which consultants and NGO leaders arrive in rural communities at mid-morning and hope to depart the same afternoon. In the words of a Tanzanian NGO leader, "These donors already know what they want to know, and they're in a hell of a hurry." Under such conditions, it is not surprising that normative discourses are frequently substituted for empirical realities.

It is important to note that being "on the spot" is only part of what ethnographers have to offer the study of African NGOs. Most ethnographers come to the field with the ability to speak local languages, if not they almost certainly can by the time they leave. Ethnographers are also participant observers. They attend NGO meetings, participate in workshops and trainings, keep minutes, share information, help write funding proposals, and offer advice. They also live in the communities served by the NGOs. If they become an accepted part of that community they will learn about NGOs from a variety of perspectives—from those who are enamored to those who consider themselves to be victims of NGOs and their activities.

This type of experience allows ethnographers to penetrate the normative discourses surrounding African NGOs. They see the NGO offices standing vacant while NGO leaders are off pursuing other activities. They witness the internal politics of specific organizations and the struggle for NGO resources (Bornstein, Challinor, Dorman, Docking, and Rawlence), as well as the resistance of local people to NGO interventions (Temudo). They observe the opportunistic pursuit of donor money by NGO leaders (Jackson, Rawlence, and Temudo), and they are on hand when NGO leaders brief their constituents in how to mouth the rhetoric of donor-driven paradigms (Challinor). Most importantly, ethnographers are frequently involved in the grassroots social movements that gave birth to specific NGOs. They are therefore able to provide perspectives on how these movements have been transformed into formally registered NGOs (Dorman, Docking, Igoe, and Pommerolle).

Finally, as Dorman (this volume), points out ethnographers are in a unique position to provide "thick description" of African NGOs. Coined by Clifford Geertz (1973), the idea behind "thick description" is to reveal the cultural meaning behind institutions and events. Bornstein (this volume) uses "thick description" to reveal the ways in which Zimbabwean NGO leaders imagine their mission through the discourses of Christian doctrine, especially the idea that they were "transcending" the politics of the Zimbabwean state. Temudo (this volume) documents a telling belief held by rural people in Guinea-Bissau. Her informants explained that scientists and other western experts were luring the spirits of their homeland to Europe by offering them a higher standard of living. Pommerolle (this volume) describes how Kenyan activists have linked the question of human rights to the question of land rights by invoking the Mau Mau uprising of the middle 1950s. This type of "thick description" is essential to NGO interventions, as interventions that fail to account for the perceptions and beliefs of NGO leaders and local people are likely to misfire.

Civil Society

Clearly the ethnographic approach taken by the authors in this volume goes a long way in penetrating the myths and normative discourses surrounding African NGOs. In the process they also penetrate myths and normative discourses surrounding African civil society, and therefore offer an important contribution to the growing theoretical literature on this topic. Because of the pervasive assumption that NGOs equal civil society in Africa, all of the authors in this volume have found it necessary address this concept in some capacity. Most of them make some attempt to speak directly to civil society theory, including the works of Bourdieu (Challinor), de Tocqueville (Docking, Dorman, and Igoe), Foucault (Bornstein, Igoe, Jackson, and Temudo), Gramsci (Igoe), and Hegel (Docking).

Because of the explosion of civil society literature in the 1990s, a detailed discussion of this concept need not detain us here. For the purposes of this introduction, it is sufficient to note that civil society is usually conceptualized as a socio-political space between the household and the state. This is the putative space in which the NGO revolution occurred and within which the authors in this volume conducted their ethnographic fieldwork. All the articles in this volume make some reference to this space, which opened in the wake of retreating African states. In the case of Jackson's study of NGOs in eastern Congo, "the state didn't even exist." In the case of Docking's study of cotton farmer's unions in Southern Mali, the state steadfastly refused to abandon the space of civil society. In most cases, however, Structural Adjustment programs reduced the role of state actors in civil society, but the impacts of these processes were complicated by the fact that the line between the state and NGOs was becoming increasingly blurred in many contexts.

Of course the studies in this volume present a very different picture of African civil society than that employed in the normative discourses of western donors. In development and governance circles, the scaling back of African states was seen as an important first step in the creation of a "new policy agenda," which would neatly divide the world into three sectors: (1) states, (2) markets, and (3) NGOs—each with a different function (see Edwards and

Hulme 1996). States would ensure the political stability and protection of private property necessary for economic growth. Markets would be the engine for this growth. NGOs would instill citizens with a sense of political efficacy, so that they might hold the state to account and ensure that it fulfill its function of creating an "enabling environment" for free market capitalism and economic growth. They are also meant to deliver social services previously delivered by the state.

This three sector paradigm revolves around the market—with the other two sectors having essential roles in supporting its growth. It is interesting, therefore, that the question of markets is conspicuously absent in this volume. Only two studies make explicit mention of markets. Docking describes how the politics of Malian unions were closely tied to struggles over the promotion of free markets. Bornstein describes how Zimbabwean NGO leaders use the discourse of markets (along side of the discourses of Christian doctrine) in establishing their claims that they have transcended the realm of politics. In all of the other studies, however, the market is overshadowed by the aid sector. This is consistent with Challinor's discussion of Cape Verdean officials who talked about the difficulty of convincing foreign investors that their country had a viable economy. As noted in the first part of this chapter, most African countries are so dependent on foreign assistance that opportunities to gain access to aid money commonly overshadow any market opportunities that might exist.

In the studies presented in this volume, African civil society appears as a much murkier space than the three sector model would imply. Arguably there are still three sectors: (1) the state; (2) foreign aid; and (3) NGOs. However, the relationships between these sectors are obscured in a variety of ways, making it nearly impossible to assign a normative function to each. The role of donors in African civil society is obscured by the fact that officially they have no role. They provide funding and promote good governance, but never should they have a vested interest in the outcome. In the language of development, donors are rarely defined as "stakeholders" and most would reject such a label. Furthermore, the line between states and NGOs is frequently difficult to draw. Certainly, the relationships that currently exist between states and NGOs in Africa are fundamentally different than that envisioned by the normative three sector model. Because the prevailing assumption in development circles is that NGOs equal civil society (Challinor, Dorman, Igoe, and Jackson), this makes the parameters of African civil society especially difficult to define.

The idea that donors stand outside African civil society usually revolves around assertions that they cannot interfere in the internal affairs of sovereign governments. The reality of the matter is starkly different, however, since donors interfere in the internal affairs of African countries all the time. In Mali (Docking) western NGOs and western governments have meddled in the internal affairs of the Malian government in order to promote the privatization of the cotton industry. In Tanzania (Igoe) the Canadian Government has taken an active role in local civil society in Hanang District and the direction of indigenous NGOs operating there. In Kenya (Pommerrolle) the Moi administration accused human rights NGOs of being puppets of western donors. Almost anyone who has worked in development and/or governance in Africa could mention numerous other examples.

Another important aspect of the relationship of western donors to African NGOs is the degree of dependency that the former has on the latter. This is closely related to the lack of market opportunities, which make it very difficult for African NGOs to ever become economically autonomous (the notable example being the human rights NGO studied by Pommerolle in Kenya). Even in cases where African NGOs started out by rejecting donor agendas, the imperative of institutional survival frequently changed their minds over the long haul (Igoe). Temudo (this volume) argues, African NGO leaders frequently resemble the leaders of Melanesian cargo cults, with an "if-we-build-it-they-will-come" mentality. The major difference, of course, is that some times with NGOs the cargo does materialize.

A similar phenomenon can frequently be seen in the institutional transformation of African NGOs themselves. In order to be regarded as legitimate—and therefore eligible for funding—these organizations need to take on institutional forms that western donors recognize and are comfortable with. These transformations are commonly referred to as "professionalization" in the NGO literature (Challinor, Docking, Dorman, and Pommerolle). An increasingly common critique of this process is that it moves African NGOs away from the "grassroots," as western donors and their agendas become their new constituents.

Dependency on donor money frequently brings African NGOs in direct competition with African states. "Weak and desperate" African states often covet the resources of the NGO sector. Some states have responded by creating oxymoronic GONGOs (Governmental Non-Governmental Organizations) as in the cases of Congo (Jackson) and Guinea Bissau (Temudo). In other cases, African officials have started up NGOs while keeping their positions within the government. Often the line between governments and NGOs becomes exceedingly blurred in the process (Challinor, Temudo, and Rawlence). Government officials may also seek to take credit for the achievements of

NGOs in specific local contexts (Bornstein, Igoe, and Rawlence). Finally, there are a few rare instances in which NGOs are dependent on African Governments for funding, and therefore must abide by state (as well as donor) agendas (Challinor and Docking).

In addition to the local blurring of states and NGOs in Africa, increasingly African governments are insisting that NGOs should be nothing more than an extension of the state—that it should be the function of NGOs to carry out state development policy. Therefore, NGOs should be directly "accountable" to African states (Bornstein, Challinor, Dorman, and Igoe). By extension this also means that NGOs should not become involved in politics. Most organizations abide by this imperative to avoid deregistration or other negative consequences (Bornstein, Challinor, Dorman, and Igoe). In rare cases, however, NGO leaders do insist that they have a role to play in the political transformation of their societies. The most notable example in this volume is the director of a Kenyan human rights NGO who played a key role in the constitutional reform of the Kenyan state (Pommerolle).

These accounts reveal that African civil society is a complex and contested space, which is different in many ways from the normative vision of mainstream—and even critical—civil society theory. In spite of their complexity, however, these accounts have thus far revolved around a very limited cadre of individuals—African NGO leaders, government officials, and western donors. Conspicuously absent are "the people," these individuals claim to represent. This is especially ironic, since the current popularity of African NGOs is closely linked to a perception that they are closely linked to the grassroots.

This brings us what is arguably the greatest challenge facing NGO researchers in Africa: understanding the relationship of African NGOs to their constituent communities, while capturing the complexity of the communities themselves. The difficult nature of this challenge is captured in the words of a Cape Verdean NGO leader, interviewed by Challinor (this volume). This NGO leader explained that western NGO leaders wanted to fund "the people" directly, but then added with a smile "But the people do not exist."

Considering the imperative of African NGOs to working with "the people," this is an especially poignant statement. Clearly, this statement is not literal. People do exist. But who are "the people?" This question is exceptionally difficult to answer. Traditionally, "the people" are described as being at the bottom of a "top-down" hierarchy—with western donors and African elites suspended far above them. From this disadvantaged position, "the people" are out of the loop—they exist on the margins of the global system—with very little knowledge of, or control over, the institutions and processes that affect their daily lives. Challinor (this volume) quotes James Ferguson from a book edited by Vincent and Nugent (2004), in which he encourages us to reconsider this paradigm:

> Can we learn to conceive, theoretically and politically, of a "grassroots" that would not be local, communal, and authentic, but worldly, well-connected, and opportunistic?

This way of thinking about African NGOs is useful, since in many cases they have clearly bypassed African states completely. In many cases, African NGOs provide a direct institutional interface between "the people" and global systems of institutions, ideas, and money. All of the chapters in this volume make some attempt at describing this institutional interface, and how it operates in a variety of local contexts.

While this institutional interface is clearly unprecedented, it is probably premature to speak of a "grassroots" that is "worldly, well connected, and opportunistic." In spite of the proximity of African NGOs to their constituent communities, they are still oriented outward to western donors and the funding they provide. As Docking cleverly points out in his concluding statements (this volume) African NGO leaders frequently "think locally and act globally."

As the work presented in this volume illustrates, this orientation distances NGO leaders from "the grassroots"—both literally and figuratively. This raises a question that Challinor astutely poses in her chapter—whether or not NGO leaders are still part of their own communities. This is a question to which there is no easy answer. Even local people themselves are not clear on this matter. In many cases, local people view NGO leaders as having been lost to the community. The position of many African NGO leaders in their home communities is an ambivalent one. It is important to note, however, that NGO leaders may also bring important benefits to their communities, empowering local people in the process.

It is often the case, however, that many people at the community level are still left out of the loop. They are not "worldly and well connected." Rather they are mystified and disconnected from the new institutions that have emerged in their midst. Who are they for? What does it do? Why do donors give money to them? What do the people in charge do with that money? Ironically, these questions are frequently posed to NGO researchers working in Africa by local people wondering about ostensibly local NGOs.

The relationship between "the people" and African NGO leaders is perhaps best captured by the Bourdieuian perspective employed by Challinor. Successful NGO leaders have mastered the habitus and discourses necessary to capture support from western donors. They also know how to effectively play the game of state elites (and may even be state elites themselves). Their constituents, meanwhile, are "mired in doxa"—lacking the habitus and knowledge necessary to make the system work for them. Due to their knowledge of "how to play the game," NGO leaders are able to accumulate economic, social, symbolic, and cultural, capital. They are then able to use this capital to bolster their position *vis-à-vis* the "grassroots." Their constituents, meanwhile, remain on the margins. This is not to imply, however, that local people may not benefit in the process.

The situation described in the previous paragraph is in many ways a product of the "rock-and-a-hard-place" relationship of NGO leaders to western donors and African states. Many African NGOs emerged from popular grassroots movements, only to be transformed into mini "grassroots" bureaucracies. In order to survive in the highly competitive environment of the development industry, African NGO leaders needed to maintain their connections to "the people." In this context, however, the idea of "the people" became a reified concept of marginal communities waiting to be "empowered" by NGO interventions—and worthy of these interventions by virtue of being "local, communal, and authentic." These reified imaginary (as opposed to imagined) communities have become important symbolic capital for African NGO leaders and their western donors. Connections to "the people" are an essential justification for any development intervention in African today, whether it revolves around the protection of rare birds or the establishment of civil society.

The unfortunate outcome of this arrangement is that local people—reified as "the people"—are in danger of becoming commodities of a global NGO industry, rather than participants in real processes, programs, and institutions that might actually improve their quality of life. Understanding this phenomenon—in the context of Africa's emerging NGO sector—is essential to the improvement of NGO interventions. After all, without engaging "the people" it is unlikely that African NGOs will ever become the foundation of a vibrant civil society. The studies in this volume represent a drop in the bucket; many more NGO ethnographies are needed. Hopefully, however, they are pointing in the right direction.

Conclusion

The standard critique levelled at ethnographic critiques of development is that they are long on analysis and short on solutions. Part of the reason for this problem is that it is impossible to propose simple solutions for complex problems. There is no formula that will solve the problems outlined in our studies, and it would be disingenuous to imply that there were. This being said, all of the authors in this volume are committed to the idea that their observations and ideas should inform new types of policy and action that would strengthen African NGOs in ways that would benefit African communities. In the conclusion of this volume, therefore, each of us offers our own recommendations on possible ways forward for African NGOs. Before moving to solutions, however, we invite you to explore the ethnographic case studies that are at the heart of this volume, since our recommendations would be essentially meaningless without supporting case material.

Works Cited

Abrahamsen, R. 2000. *Disciplining Democracy: Development discourse and good governance in Africa*. London: Zed Books.

Allen, C. 1995. Understanding African politics. *Review of African Political Economy* 65: 301–20.

Bangura, Y. and P. Gibbon. 1993. Adjustment, authoritarianism and democracy: an introduction to some conceptual and empirical issues. In *Authoritarianism, Democracy and Adjustment*, edited by Y. Bangura, P. Gibbon and A. Ofstad. Uppsala: Nordiska Afrikainstitutet.

Barry, A., T. Osborne, and N. Rose, eds. 1996. *Foucault and Political Reason: Liberalism, neo-liberalism and rationalities of government*. London: UCL Press.

Bates, R. 1981. *Markets and States in Tropical Africa: The political basis of agricultural policies*. Berkeley: University of California Press.

Bebbington, A. and R. Riddell. 1997. Heavy hands, hidden hands, holding hands: donors, intermediary NGOs, and civil society organizations. In *NGOs, State and Donors: Too close for comfort?*, edited by D. Hulme and M. Edwards. Basingstoke: Macmillan Ltd and Save the Children Fund.

Blair, H. 1997. Donors, democratisation and civil society. In *NGOs, States and Donors: Too close for comfort?*, edited by D. Hulme and M. Edwards. Basingstoke: Macmillan Ltd. with Save the Children Fund.

Bratton, M. 1989. The politics of Government-NGO relations in Africa. *World Development* 17 (4): 569–87.

Bratton, M., and G. Hyden, eds. 1992. *Governance and Politics in Africa*. Boulder CO: Lynne Rienner.

Bratton, M., and D. Rothchild. 1992. The institutional bases of governance in Africa. In *Governance and Politics in Africa*, edited by M. Bratton and G. Hyden. Boulder CO: Lynne Rienner.

Brodhead, T. 1987. NGOs: in one year and out the other. *World Development* 15 (supplement): 1–6.

Callaghy, T. 1988. The state and the development of capitalism in Africa. In *The Precarious Balance: State and society in Africa*, edited by N. Chazan and D. Rothchild. Boulder: Westview Press.

Chambers, R. 1984. *Rural Development: Putting the last first*. New York: Longman.

Charlton, R. and R. May 1995. NGOs, politics, projects, and probity: a policy implementation perspective. *Third World Quarterly* 16 (2): 237–55.

Chazan, N. 1988. Ghana: problems of governance and the emergence of civil society. In *Democracy in Developing Countries: Sub-Saharan Africa*, edited by L. Diamond. Boulder CO: Lynne Rienner.

———. 1982. The new politics of participation in Tropical Africa. *Comparative Politics* 14: 169–89.

Clark, J. 1991. *Democratizing Development: The role of voluntary organizations*. London: Earthscan Publications Ltd.

Commins, S. 2000. NGOs: ladles in the global soup kitchen? In *Development, NGOs and Civil Society*, edited by D. Eade. London: OXFAM GB.

Diamond, L. 1987. Class formation and the swollen African state. *Journal of Modern African Studies* 25 (4): 567–96.

———. 1988. Introduction: roots of failure, seeds of hope. In *Democracy in Developing Countries: Sub-Saharan Africa*, edited by L. Diamond. Boulder CO: Westview Press,.

———. 1994. Rethinking civil society: toward democratic consolidation. *Journal of Democracy* 5 (3): 4–17.

Edwards, M. and D. Hulme 1996. Introduction: NGO performance and accountability. In *Beyond the Magic Bullet: NGO performance and accountability in the post-Cold War world*, edited by M. Edwards and D. Hulme. West Hartford, Connecticut: Kumarian Press.

Farrington, J., A. Bebbington, K. Wellard, and D.J. Lewis, eds. 1993. *Reluctant Partners? Non-governmental organizations, the state and sustainable agricultural development*. London: Routledge and Overseas Development Institute.

Ferguson, J. 2004. Transnational topographies of power: beyond 'the state' and 'civil society' in the study of African politics. In: *A Companion to the Anthropology of Politics*, edited by J. Vincent and D. Nugent. Oxford: Blackwell.

Fisher, W. 1997. Doing good? The politics and anti-politics of NGO practice. *Annual Review of Anthropology* 29: 436–34.

Foucault, M. 1977. *Discipline and Punish*. London: Allen Lane.

————. 1982. The subject and power. In *Michel Foucault: Beyond structuralism and hermeneutics*, edited by H. L. Dreyfus and P. Rabinow. London: Harvester Wheatsheaf.

————. 1991. Governmentality. In *The Foucault Effect: Studies in governmentality*, edited by G. Burchell, C Gordon and P. Miller. London: Harvester Wheatsheaf.

Fowler, A. 1988 *Non-Governmental Organizations in Africa: Achieving a comparative advantage in relief and micro-development*. Discussion Paper 249. Nairobi: Institute of Development Studies.

Fukuyuma, F. 1989. The end of history? *The National Interest*, Summer Issue: 4.

Geertz, C. 1973. Thick description: towards an interpretive theory of culture. In C. Geertz, *The Interpretation of Cultures: Selected essays by Clifford Geertz*. New York: Basic Books.

Government of Tanzania 1994. *National Policy on the Promotion of NGOs in Tanzania*. Dar es Salaam, mimeo.

Hanlon, J. 1991. *Mozambique: Who calls the shots?* London: James Currey.

Hearn, J. 1998. The U.S. democratic experiment in Ghana. In *Africa and Globalisation: Towards the millennium*. Volume 1 of the collected papers of an international conference from the African Studies Unit, the University of Central Lancashire, Preston.

————. 2000. Aiding democracy: donors and civil society in South Africa. *Third World Quarterly* 21 (5): 815–30.

Hudock, A. 1999. *NGOs and Civil Society: Democracy by proxy?* Cambridge: Polity Press.

Hulme, D. and M. Edwards. 1997. NGOs, states and donors: an overview. In *NGOs, States and Donors: Too close for comfort?*, edited by D. Hulme and M. Edwards. Basingstoke: Macmillan Ltd in association with Save the Children Fund.

Hyden, G. 1980. *Beyond Ujamaa in Tanzania: Underdevelopment and an uncaptured peasantry*. Berkeley: University of California Press.

————. 1983. *No Shortcuts to Progress: African development management in perspective*. London: Heinemann.

————. 1997. Civil society, social capital, and development: dissection of a complex discourse. *Studies in Comparative International Development* 32 (1): 3–30.

Igoe, J. 2003. Scaling-up civil society: donor money, NGOs, and the pastoralist land rights movement in Tanzania. *Development and Change* 34 (5): 863–85.

Kelsall, T. 1998. Donors, NGOs, and the state: the creation of a public sphere in Tanzania. Paper presented at the ASA Africa and Globalization Conference, University of Central Lancashire (24–27 April).

Leys, C. 1994. Confronting the African tragedy. *New Left Review* 204: 33–48.

Malinowski, B. 1922. *Argonauts of the Western Pacific.* London: Routledge.

———. 1929. Practical Anthropology. *Africa* 2: 22–38.

———. 1930. The rationalization of anthropology and administration. *Africa* 3: 405–30.

Manji, F., and C. O'Coill. 2002. The missionary position: NGOs and development in Africa. *International Affairs* 78 (3): 567–83.

Masoni, V. 1985. Nongovernmental organizations and development. *Finance and Development* 22 (3): 38–41.

Maren, M. 1997. *The Road to Hell: The ravaging effects of foreign aid and international charity.* New York: The Free Press.

Mercer, C. 1999. Reconceptualizing state-society relationships in Tanzania: are NGOs making a difference? *Area* 31(3): 247–58.

Ng'ethe, N. 1991. *In Search of NGOs.* Nairobi: Institute for Development Studies.

Olukoshi, A. 1998. Economic crisis, multipartyism, and opposition politics in contemporary Africa. In *The Politics of Opposition in Contemporary Africa*, edited by A. Olukoshi. Uppsala: Nordiska Afrikainstitutet.

———. 2002. Governing the African development process: the challenge of the New Partnership for Africa's Development. Occasional Paper. Copenhagen: Centre for African Studies.

Pearce, J. 2000. Development, NGOs and civil society: the debate and its future. In *Development, NGOs and Civil Society*, edited by D. Eade. Oxford: Oxfam GB, 2000.

Poulton, R. and M. Harris, eds. 1988. *Putting People First: Voluntary organizations and third world organizations.* London and Basingstoke: Macmillan.

Salamon, L. 1993. The Global Associational Revolution: The rise of the third sector on the world scene. Occasional Paper no. 15. Baltimore: Institute for Policy Studies John's Hopkins.

Sandberg, E. 1994. Introduction. In *The Changing Politics of Non-Governmental Organizations and African States*, edited by E. Sandberg. Westport, Connecticut: Praeger.

Sandbrook, R. 1985. *The Politics of Africa's Economic Stagnation*. Cambridge: Cambridge University Press.

Sandbrook, R. and R. Cohen, eds. 1975. *The Development of an African Working Class: Studies in class formation and action*. London: Longman.

Saul, J. 1997. For fear of being condemned as old fashioned: liberal democracy versus popular democracy in Sub-Saharan Africa. *Review of African Political Economy* 73: 339–53.

Tandon, Y. 1991. Foreign NGOs, uses and abuses: an African perspective. *IFDA Dossier* 81: 67–78.

Tendler, J. 1975. *Inside Foreign Aid*. Baltimore: Johns Hopkins University Press.

———. 1982. *Turning Private Voluntary Organizations into Development Agencies: Questions for evaluation*. Evaluation Discussion Paper no. 10. Washington D.C.: U.S.A.I.D.

United Nations Development Program. 1996. *Human Development Report*. Oxford, UNDP.

———. 2000. *Human Development Report*. Oxford, UNDP.

Vakil, A. 1997. Confronting the classification problem: toward a taxonomy of NGOs. *World Development* 25 (12): 2057–2070.

Vivian, J. 1994. NGOs and sustainable development in Zimbabwe: no magic bullets. *Development and Change* 25: 181–209.

Williams, D. 2000. Constructing the economic space: the World Bank and the making of *Homo Oeconomicus*. *Millennium-Journal of International Studies* 28 (1): 79–99.

———. 1993. Review Article: liberalism and development discourse. *Africa* 63 (3): 419–29.

Williams, D. and T. Young 1994. Governance, the World Bank, and liberal theory. *Political Studies* XLII: 84–100.

Williams, G. 1985. Taking the part of peasants: rural development in Nigeria and Tanzania. In *The Political Economy of Contemporary Africa 2nd Edition*, edited by P. Gutkind and I. Wallerstein. Beverley Hills: Sage Publications.

———. 2002. Reforming Africa: continuities and changes. In *Africa South of the Sahara* 31st edition. London: Europa Publications.

World Bank. 1981. *Accelerated Development in Sub-Saharan Africa: An agenda for action*. Washington DC: World Bank.

———. 1989. *Sub-Saharan Africa: From crisis to sustainable growth*. Washington DC: World Bank.

———. 1997. *World Development Report 1997: The state in a changing world*. New York: Oxford University Press.

———. 2000. *Can Africa Claim the 21st Century?* Washington DC: World Bank.

Young, T. 'A project to be realised': global liberalism and contemporary Africa. *Millennium-Journal of International Studies* 24 (3): 527–45.

CHAPTER 2

STUDYING DEMOCRATIZATION IN AFRICA: A CASE STUDY OF HUMAN RIGHTS NGOS IN ZIMBABWE

Sara Rich Dorman[1]

School of Social and Political Studies, University of Edinburgh
sara.dorman@ed.ac.uk

Introduction

Since the late 1980s, social scientists, donors, and development workers in East and Southern Africa have devoted much time and resources to the question of "democratization." Yet, it is not clear how this concept of "democratization" has helped us to understand African politics or if donor support for "democratization" has been successful. There are both methodological and conceptual problems with the way democratization is used to explain processes as varied as the de-racialization of South Africa, the post-civil war effort to rebuild Mozambique, and the different patterns of change to multi-party politics in Kenya, Zambia and Malawi.

Many accounts of these processes of democratization are a-historical, or decontextualized from their historical and cultural situations. Secondly, in-

---

1. This chapter is based on material included in my DPhil thesis "Inclusion and Exclusion: NGOs and Politics in Zimbabwe" (Oxford, 2001). The argument benefited from presentation to Development Studies MPhil Core Course at Queen Elizabeth House, Oxford in 1999 and 2002, and on-going discussions with Tim Kelsall, Gavin Williams, Tina West and Tom Young.

stitutions which are thought to enable democratizations—like churches and NGOs—are poorly understood and little studied. Assumptions, rather than empirical evidence, dominate current studies of democracy. Such partial understandings of the societies and institutions under observation leads to inappropriate policy responses by bilateral and multi-lateral donors eager to support "democratization."

In this paper I explore the ways in which the development industry has adopted and used concepts of "democratization" and "civil society" and the problems inherent with this process. I focus on the role of local or "indigenous" NGOs as recipients of donor aid and potential agents of democratization. In order to understand why NGOs are assumed to contribute to a process of "democratization" we need to examine both what donors think NGOs are, and the relationship of NGOs with the state, as well as how this plays out in practice. In particular, we need to examine the changes that have resulted from the increased resources made available to the NGO sector. A case study of a prominent Zimbabwean Human Rights NGO, ZimRights, will be used to illustrate the problems caused by growth and expansion. First however, I want to examine the methodology and conceptualization of "democracy" as used by donors.

Methodological Issues

Studies of NGOs in Africa are usually based on interview research focusing on a wide number of organizations within a particular sector (Dicklitch 1998; Kiondo 1993; Tripp 1992; Semboja and Therkilsden 1995; Anheier and Salamon 1997). Zimbabwean NGOs are amongst the most studied, but these studies still conform to this tendency (Moyo 1992; Moyo, Makumbe, and Green and Matthias 1997).[2] This method prevents detailed study of individual NGOs, making it less easy to interrogate certain aspects of NGO behavior, such as internal decision making. Neither the history of the NGO, how it interacts with the history of the country or region, nor the people within the NGO are ex-

---

2. See also Ann Muir with additional material by Roger C Riddell, *Evaluating the Impact of NGOs in rural poverty alleviation*, ODI Working paper 52 (London: ODI, 1992); Diana Conyers, "Report of a study of existing NGO activity in Zimbabwe" November 1991 [study undertaken for ODA and the British High Commission in Zimbabwe]; Marleen Dekker, "NGOs in Zimbabwe: Developments and Changes since 1990" Livelihood and Environment Working Paper, August 1994.

amined, except as background detail. Thick description of how NGOs function is sidelined in the interest of labeling and categorizing them.

Methodology has to some extent been dictated by the research agenda of donors and international institutions. In the 1980s, official aid was increasingly channeled not to bilateral partners, but through northern NGOs to local communities or local NGOs (Smillie 1999). Local NGOs were seen in the 1980s and 1990s as "apolitical" development organizations. As a result of this emphasis, most early studies of NGOs were undertaken for donors with particular sets of questions, such as how well NGOs "fit" demands set before them, with respect to their efficiency, participation levels, and transparency, although Tvedt argues that these values are actually rarely measured (Tvedt 1998: 99–100). Within this agenda, NGOs were understood to be engaged in technical development practices such as health provision, rural development or poverty-reduction (Theunis 1992: 265–76; Wellard and Copestake 1993: 15–86). The interview methodology, with its emphasis on data collection, met the donor's need to assess their expenditures. However, it failed to position NGOs within a more political or historical setting, and to explain how they relate to the state, donors, and each other.

This decontextualization became problematic as donors and researchers took on the idea that NGOs might also contribute to expanding agendas of good governance and democratization. The landmark 1989 World Bank report, *Sub-Saharan Africa: from crisis to sustainable growth* called for economic reforms to "go hand-in-hand with good governance." (WorldBank 1989: 6–61). As part of what came to be known as the "governance agenda," NGOs were expected to go beyond being service providers and become active participants in policy-making (Bratton and Hyden 1992). NGOs and civil society were integrated into previously apolitical conceptions of human development (UNDP 1992). Development organizations were to be "turned into" activist or advocacy organizations: "financing NGOs in Africa as potential agents of democracy should be at the top of donor agendas in the 1990s." (Fowler 1991). While interview and survey-based research helps explore *what* NGOs are doing, it is less useful in explaining *why* or *how* they become (or don't become) involved in democratization-related activities (Moyo 1992).[3] In

---

3. See also Sam Moyo, *Non-governmental Organisations in Zimbabwe: Context, Role and Relationships* Working Paper December 1990; Sam Moyo, "Towards and Understanding of Zimbabwean NGOs" Paper prepared for the NANGO/MWENGO Self-Understanding Workshop, November 1995; Alan Thomas, "Does Democracy Matter? Pointers from a comparison of NGOs influence on environmental policies in Zimbabwe and Botswana" Open University DPP Working paper 31; GECOU Working paper 4. June 1995.

order to do this, I propose that we need to study NGOs from *inside*, using techniques such as participant-observation that enable us to create detailed, descriptive case studies. This methodology has the benefit of positioning NGOs more clearly against the political backdrop of the country and the institutional history of the organization studied.

Democratization = Civil Society = NGOs?

The dominant thinking about democratization in Africa—and especially that which has contributed to policy and aid decisions by western donors—has focused around what Gordon White called a "developmental panacea"—the issue of "strengthening civil society" (White 1996) Civil society is cited as the "missing key to sustained political reform" (Harbeson 1994: 1–2) and is often operationalized as non-governmental organizations. Thomas Carothers' useful account of American promotion of democracy abroad notes that:

> the current keen interest in this…almost forgotten concept was stimulated by the dissident movements in Eastern Europe in the 1980s [which] fostered the appealing idea of civil society as a domain that is nonviolent but powerful, nonpartisan yet prodemocratic, and that emerges from the essence of particular societies, yet is nonetheless universal (Carothers 1999: 207).

Civil society is understood as formally organized groups, ideally with democratic structures and pro-democratic norms (Kasfir 1998: 6–7). For aid bureaucrats, supporting civil society was a low-cost alternative to unsuccessful and expensive attempts to reform state institutions (Carothers 1999: 157–206). The practical difficulties of funding grass-roots organizations means that most donor-support goes to "…professionalized NGOs dedicated to advocacy or civic education" (Carothers and Ottaway 2000: 11; Carothers 1999: 210–211). These groups are visible and accessible. With university educated staff, it is relatively easy for them to interact with donors and provide the desired skills of accounting and report-writing.

Normatively and programmatically, civil society is advocated by the development community and donors who propose that funding civil society (*i.e.* support to non-state sectors) is both an end in itself and a means to an end of democratic governance. Carothers and Ottaway's (2004: 4) critical examination of donor funding states:

In the eyes of many donors and recipients, and even of many demo-cratic theorists, the idea that civil society is always a positive force for democracy, indeed even the most important one, is unassailable. An active—"vibrant" is the adjective of choice—civil society is both the force that can hold governments accountable and the base upon which a truly democratic culture can be built. There follows from this assumption the related idea that promoting civil society development is key to democracy-building.

The Ford Foundation, for example, has a unit dedicated to "Governance and Civil Society" whose goal is "to strengthen the civic and political partici-pation of people and groups in charting the future of their societies."[4] The of-ficial American development agency, USAID, funds "civil society organiza-tions" as one of its four democracy sectors because:

> The hallmark of a free society is the ability of individuals to associate with like-minded individuals, express their views publicly, openly de-bate public policy, and petition their government. "Civil society" is an increasingly accepted term which best describes the non-governmen-tal, not-for-profit, independent nature of this segment of society.[5]

Similarly, Sweden's International Development Agency explicitly states that Sweden funds NGOs because of:

> ....its aim of contributing to democratic development of society. A large number of organisations which, between them, represent vari-ous interests and parties is viewed as a guarantee of democracy. [6]

Activists in the developing and developed world echo this usage and there has been a remarkable consensus within development and aid circles across sec-tors and ideologies. To quote White (1996: 180–81):

> Neo-populist development theorists and practitioners extol the virtues of grass-roots non-governmental organizations....Economic liberals [emphasize] how these policies contribute to the emergence of business interests to counter-balance and discipline wayward states. Treasury-based cost-cutters see devolution of government finance to voluntary organisations as an ideologically palatable way of reducing state ex-

---

4. <http://www.fordfound.org>.
5. <http://www.usaid.gov>.
6. <http://www.sida.se>.

penditure. Conservative thinkers see it as a way of preserving traditional social solidarities...Radical socialists zero in on the potential role of social organizations...in transforming society.

However, it also became clear to academics and practitioners that NGOs may lack the capacity to "bring democratization," carry out advocacy activities, or "build civil society" and tend instead toward "gapfilling" or supplementing the state's agenda. On one level, this merely recognizes that most NGOs in developing countries are dedicated to the provision of development goods, often in co-operation with government ministries. NGOs are encouraged to go beyond this sort of gap-filling, to "...take a more pro-active, empowerment role toward democracy and development in Africa." (Dicklitch 1998: 176) "Strengthening civil society" is declared to be a " deliberately designed and targeted activity of aid." (Fowler 1991: 78). As a result, development NGOs are increasingly funded to "network" and "develop civil society" in addition to their more mundane development tasks.

These "capacity critiques" propose that while NGOs don't do advocacy very well, they can be funded to do so. Donors assume that the problem is how to program, fund, organize or otherwise catalyze democratic or participatory structures. The ready-made assumption is that NGOs want to engage in advocacy work, but merely lack the resources to do so. Questions of attitude or viability are rarely raised.

Like welfare organizations, churches, and informal markets, NGOs were "discovered" by academics and donors disenchanted with the state in the 1980s. In a rush of enthusiasm, the origins of these non-state organizations or what influences accounted for their formation, their policy goals, their activities were little studied. As Kassimir (1988: 57) notes in relation to churches, civil society approaches "decid[ed] in advance that civil organizations are principally independent variables and assign[ed] them a role rather than analyzing it." This holds also for NGOs. Clark (1997: 47), for instance, talks of NGOs "overcoming their inhibitions and seeking closer collaboration with their governments." NGOs which get too close to their own states are "co-opted" — no longer "real" NGOs nor part of civil society but "defined out" because they do not fit pre-defined notions (Beckman 1997). In proposing that we must distinguish between "true" and "false" NGOs, Clark (1991) demands that organizations fit the definitions of donors and researchers, rather than *vice-versa*. Our research should instead ask questions such as: Who works for NGOs? Why? What ideological or moral convictions do they have?

The NGO literature seems to assume that NGOs spring into being fully-formed and without political ties or links, unless they are run by civil servants, MPs or Presidential wives in which case they are pathologized as Government-NGOs (GONGOs). Yet, in reality, NGO-state relations are better understood as a continuum. NGOs may have cabinet ministers as board members; staff members may be related to government officials; the President or first-lady may be a patron. NGOs which challenge the state at the local level may have excellent relations at the center, or *vice-versa*. Linkages exist between all NGOs and power-brokers which change over time, and differing relations may exist with different levels of the state.

These linkages are often enhanced by material but also by cultural and social connections between élites, as NGO staff often come from or seek to join the same relatively small bourgeoisie. NGOs may use their personal connections with politicians and civil servants to increase their profile and enhance their ability to accomplish their goals. School ties, church adherence, and time spent in exile, in the liberation movements, or in prison may all link NGO staff and politicians. They may also receive or be keen to receive funding from the state.[7]

Problematizing Voluntarism and Professionalization

The NGO sector is presumed to be based on the Tocquevillean principles of voluntary action and charitable assistance. However, the majority of NGOs do not operate on voluntary principles. Indeed, "voluntary association" as the term was originally used to describe African colonial-era institutions was based on a distinction between traditional ascriptive associations and new, often urban, organizations which included churches, savings groups, burial societies, and sports clubs. As Wallerstein noted, they are "voluntary" in that no one's membership was fore-ordained at birth, or automatic.[8]

Donors and policy-makers are rarely explicit about how exactly the "voluntary sector" promotes democracy. Michael Bratton has elucidated these points in some detail. At the risk of making a straw-person of his argument,

---

7. See Jessica Vivian and Gladys Maseko, *NGOs, Participation and Rural Development* Discussion Paper 49 (Geneva: UNRISD, 1994), 34.

8. Wallerstein, "Voluntary Associations," 322.

I will take his contribution to the influential Carter Centre report on Governance to illustrate ideas that often remain implicit in donor discourses.

On an institutional level, it is assumed that encouraging NGOs to do advocacy and policy-related work strengthens "civil society" by providing "alternative structures to the monopolies of the state.....voluntary organizations can empower like-minded members to articulate a collective interest and take collective action."[9] A more "indirect" route to democracy-enhancement presumes that the interactions of the voluntary sector lead to the natural development of a vocal society, in what Carothers (1999: 222) has called "the benevolent Tocquevillean vision underlying US assistance to civil society...." To quote Bratton again, "voluntary organizations can promote a democratic political culture....they offer a training ground for democratic practices of governance."[10] These ideas were further reinforced by the publicity surrounding the 1993 publication of Robert Putnam's *Making Democracy Work* which advocated the importance of "civic" associations for the consolidation of democracy (Putnam, Leonardi, and Nanetti 1993).

Civil society theory, as implemented by donors, is predicated on the assumption that voluntary organizations have the capacity and desire to both *mobilize* and *socialize* their members and the wider society (Kassimir 1998: 56). Voluntary organizations are reified in this construction because their voluntary nature is the key to socialization, while their membership is presumed to be available for mobilization. Donors and others endeavoring to strengthen civil society have increasingly used this justification for channeling funds into the NGO sector.

But is it really this straight-forward? Are NGOs necessarily based on voluntary action? The increased funding, in particular, further complicates these assumptions. With access to large amounts of donor funding NGOs become "professionalized," functioning instead as implementing agencies. To quote Marcussen (1996: 415):

> With increased funding has come increased demands for accountability, professionalism, and demonstrated impact of activities. As a result, many NGOs have begun to transform themselves, reducing the voluntary part of their activities in favour of staff being trained as professionals and having explicit professional qualifications.

---

9. See Michael Bratton, "Enabling the voluntary sector in Africa: the policy context" in Carter Centre, *African Governance in the 1990s* (Atlanta, Carter Centre, 1990) 104.

10. Bratton, "Voluntary sector" 104.

The implications of this shift from voluntary to professional staff can be profound, but has not yet been taken account of by donor agencies and mainstream researchers. An ODA report which engages specifically with the issue of the impact of external funding and professionalization on local NGOs considers only half of the problem. The researchers recognize that NGOs are particularly vulnerable to internal crisis and personnel turn-over after their first tranche of major funding. In this case, professionalization is a trend in which older, volunteer members are replaced by younger, professional staff (Moore and Stewart 1998).[11] However, professionalization also occurs when members *become* the professionalized staff, a particularly volatile combination where both the government and private sectors are less attractive career options. This group of staff not only feels "ownership" of the organization, but they are also seen as "professional" experts—a potent and heady combination.

Impact of Professionalization and Growth on ZimRights

In the case of ZimRights, the growth of the organization and the steady progression of members becoming staff led to very serious organizational conflicts, and the collapse of the NGO. An examination of the broader history, impact of donor funding and organizational development of ZimRights helps us to understand the organization's vulnerability to external and internal challenges.

ZimRights was founded in 1992 by a group of prominent professionals and activists.[12] It was Zimbabwe's only significant NGO dedicated explicitly to human rights issues. As such, it was perhaps inevitable that ZimRights was both visible and controversial within Zimbabwean politics. Indeed, since its founding ZimRights has rarely been out of the headlines, ironically, most often providing the story itself, rather than uncovering human rights abuses.

ZimRights was both a membership organization and a professionally-run NGO. Its offices provided membership services and coordinated donor-funded programs. The latter included projects run by the Education, Information and Legal departments. The Education department organized civic education workshops in peri-urban and rural areas. The Information office, staffed by a steady stream of foreign interns, mainly issued press releases and published the membership newsletters. The Legal Desk, which came into being in May 1996, gave legal advice to members and clients, as well as the organization.

---

11. For more detail see ODA, " The Impact of External funding on the capacity of Local NGOs." Final Report Number R5968 N.D, *see especially* 40–52.

12. "New Human rights organisation formed" *Herald* 22 May 1992.

The grass-roots of ZimRights were its estimated 14,000 members. Member-ship gave ZimRights a particular cachet with donors, who want to work with grass-roots organizations. Further, the existence of ZimRights' members gave a certain weight to its pronouncements in the press. Yet a membership survey which I carried out in 1997 suggested that most members felt they had nei-ther been adequately informed nor involved in the organization.[13] Indeed, membership lists, which would enable members to at least receive newsletters, have tended to be sketchy and addresses frequently incorrect. Relatively few members ever actually received the publications of the information desk. The Gweru chair claimed that none of the 300 plus members of his branch ever received a ZimRights publication.[14]

In contrast, ZimRights' élite is the Advisory Board—composed of well-known public figures who lend prestige to the organization, such as Sir Garfield Todd, the former Prime Minister of Southern Rhodesia, Enoch Dum-butshena, a former Chief Justice, Chenjerai Hove, the award-winning author, and Morgan Tsvangirai, the trade unionist. Members were represented through a structure of regional committees, known as Regional Councils, the chairs of which were automatically members of the National Council, the main policy-making body, to which others were also elected at the AGM. Councils did not exist consistently in all provinces, but have tended to reflect the existence of donor-funded projects, which catalyze membership and or-ganization. Some regional councils were quite actively involved in nationally-driven activities such as workshops and election-monitoring, while others pur-sued local human rights cases brought to their attention. In rural areas, some regional council members were involved in complaints relating to land tenure, for instance attempts to remove squatters, disputes over land ownership or water usage rights. More recently, they also supported communities displaced by political violence.

In between the membership and the Advisory Board is the National Coun-cil which used to oversee much of the day-to-day management of the organ-ization, but since 1994 the Executive Director and staff took on increased re-sponsibilities and the Council met less frequently. This was a matter of regret for some older members who remembered the old "activist" days fondly. In-evitably there was been conflict between Council and staff, as many of the older members believe that they had more commitment to the issues than the

---

13. ZimRights, "Self-evaluation report" March 1997.
14. Memo from the Gweru Chair of ZimRights to the National Director, 16 December 1996.

new, younger, staff. Council members, especially those based in Harare or Bulawayo, did continue to exercise some authority until 1996, as they sat on committees which supervised particular areas or programs. However, these "activist" council members tended to demand input into day to day management, leading to staff complaints of interference. In reaction, committees were abolished, except on an "ad-hoc" basis, further reinforcing staff control over decision making.[15]

Many older council members—those who recall the "good old days"—suggested that the people employed by ZimRights were not "activists" like those who started the organization. The current staff were thought to be influenced by "nine-to-fiveism" and expected to be paid for the time they put in outside regular office hours, although this reflects a wider attitude in the Zimbabwean NGO community, reinforced by the dire economic situations of many. However, ZimRights did not see a simple withering of the Council. Former Council members formed the backbone of the secretariat as well—of the twenty-four employees in 1997, six were former National Council members, and these were often in particularly powerful positions within the organization.

As more staff were hired divisions between staff and membership became blurred. When ZimRights was formed, all the staff of ZimRights were volunteers, who were paid allowances and eventually given salaries. Subsequently, ZimRights has expanded immensely, moving from two part-time staff in 1993, to three full-time staff members in 1994, to eight in 1995, eleven in 1996, twenty-four in 1997, and forty in 1998. External evaluators in 1997 recommended the decentralization of the secretariat which resulted in the opening of regional offices all requiring their own staff. This might have contributed to ZimRights strengthening its membership base and diminishing the power of the Harare central office, but at the same time it strengthened the Secretariat.

In addition to the six former National Council members who became staff members, other positions were filled by ZimRights members and/or volunteers who turned voluntary positions into paid ones. While it is difficult to be conclusive, my research suggests that at least half the secretariat from 1996 onwards were members or volunteers who had fundraised and created full-time jobs for themselves.

Indeed, for some, being active in an NGO like ZimRights is only possible when unemployed, but it is also seen as a "job" in so far as it occupies one's

---

15. Issues raised at Institutional Development Workshop, 5–6 April, 1997, see Thoko Ruzvidzo and Alice Zinyemba, *Report on ZimRights Institutional Development Workshop*, 5–6 April, 1997, n.d. esp. pp. 18–19.

time, inspires respect in the community, and brings in some remuneration. It is not insignificant, perhaps, that a listing of National Council members for 1999–2001 identifies 8 out of 20 as "unemployed"—although some of them might dispute this label, preferring to be described as self-employed or retired.[16] The saliency of this issue is most strongly revealed in the dependence on "per diems" given to members for attending meetings. Theoretically, per diems cover out-of-pocket expenses, recognizing that receipts are rarely available on informal-sector transport. In reality, though, the money is an incentive to attend, or at least a reward for attending. For Harare based participants, 1997 AGM transport expenses were unlikely to have been higher than ZWD 30 (USD3), for transport from most suburbs to the city centre, where transport was organized to take delegates to the conference centre in an outlying suburb. However, all delegates received ZWD100.00 (USD10.00) attendance allowances per diem, which grew to ZWD200 in later years.

Most ZimRights' activities were organized by the staff and not the membership. They tended not to emphasize human rights *per se*—instead they resembled civic education and legal aid projects run by other NGOs throughout the country. While the membership structures did channel some grass-roots concerns to the national level, most staff were occupied with relatively uncontroversial donor-funded "projects." Occasionally, the ZimRights information office responded to current political events by issuing press releases. While many of these were picked up by the government and independent media, reference to particularly sensitive incidents provoked attack from the ruling party.

Within a month of its formation, ZimRights was forced to defend the inclusion on its board of former Chief Justice Enoch Dumbutshena, denying any link with Dumbutshena's Forum for Democratic Reform Trust, which went on to become the Forum Party.[17] And then, at the official launch, Garfield Todd, the former Southern Rhodesian Prime Minister, attacked the state press, comparing their editors to the three monkeys who see no evil, hear no evil and speak no evil. In the racially charged environment, this was interpreted in the worst possible way by the state-controlled *Sunday Mail*: "Zimpapers editors are monkeys."[18] And, in the same speech, he also criticized the decision to promote Perence Shiri, former commander of 5 Brigade, to Air

---

16. ZimRights. "ZimRights National Council, 1999–2001 April".

17. We are not Political, says ZimRights. *Weekend Gazette*, 5 June 1992, 5.

18. Zimpaper editors are monkeys, says Todd. *Sunday Mail*, 30 August, 1992, 1.

Force Commander, which led to another acrimonious exchange in the media, in which Defence Minister Moven Mahachi challenged Todd's record on human rights while Prime Minister of Southern Rhodesia.[19] ZimRights was again targeted in the official media in November 1995, in the aftermath of a rally protesting police brutality. While pursuing petty criminals, police officers accidentally shot and killed three by-standers. The protest march organized by ZimRights, degenerated into rioting and looting. In an inflammatory speech, President Mugabe labeled ZimRights "ZimLooters" and a "gangster organization." ZimRights denied that the rioting and looting had any link at all to their protest, suggesting that the march had concluded and dispersed long before the riots, and that ZANU(PF) youths were responsible for the violence.[20]

In 1996, ZimRights also came under attack in the government-controlled media, for their support for a sustained and damaging strike by doctors and nurses. ZimRights provided the striking workers with sanctuary and access to telephones and faxes. On their own front, ZimRights issued several press releases to the media about the need to resolve the strike issue, and in particular, appealed to MPs to find a solution, which led to a very critical discussion of the issue in Parliament.[21] ZimRights was attacked for this very visible and public support of the nurses and doctors in both a *Herald* news story and an editorial, which claimed that the strike was "hardly normal" and alleged outside interference. The editorial claimed that ZimRights had been used as a conduit to transfer ZWD 2 million from "foreign well-wishers" to the nurses and doctors, although this was firmly denied.[22]

A more pro-active project was undertaken in 1996 when it was proposed that ZimRights conduct research on the controversial and little-known human rights abuses in Matabeleland with the intention of publishing a book. Although donor funding was forthcoming, and the ZimRights leadership supported the book project, it was bogged down in in-fighting and turf-disputes.

---

19. Fifth Brigade—Mahachi replies Todd. *Sunday Mail*, 6 September 1992, 1; "Don't point accusing finger—ZimRights" *Herald* 9 September 1992, 3.

20. Mugabe labels Zimbabwe Human Rights Activists Gangsters. *Reuters* 13 December 1995.

21. *Junior Doctors and Nurses Strike: Report to ZimRights Advisory Board and Council*, 6 December 1996.

22. Fired Nurses Await Pledged Cash. *Herald* 24 December 1996, 1; "Editorial: Nurses and Doctors Strike was Hardly Normal. *Herald* 25 December 1996, 4; ZimRights Press release, The Herald Xmas Day Comment" 27 December 1996.

Publication was delayed for two years after the election of a new National Council which demanded to read and consider the draft. Those with personal knowledge of the Matabeleland conflict wanted their experiences included and were concerned that it missed events they considered significant. Eventually, the text was judged to conform with the demands of the National Council, giving them a sense of ownership over the project. In February 1999, the book was again deemed ready for printing. Publication was delayed until October, however, because of controversies between staff and council members about the title of the book and responsibility for the foreword. In the end, the Executive Director wrote a foreword and the book was released in October 1999 nearly two years after its text was finalized.[23] By this time, discussion of the Matabeleland conflict had become less sensitive owing to widespread media discussion and the acceptance of culpability by some party and army officials.

The Matabeleland book was probably the most controversial project undertaken by ZimRights between 1992 and 1999 and was both a product and a victim of ZimRights' organizational culture. The informality of ZimRights' office life allowed an American intern to get approval for the book from the Executive Director and Chairman:

> Chimhini [the director] was initially very supportive because he wanted the organization to be seen to be doing "serious work" like other NGOs that publish books and document abuses…Matchaba-Hove [the chairman] appeared to be most concerned about what the donors would think and how they would react…he did not want the project to jeopardise funding for the organization by being too controversial, but once the donors lined up with funding, then he showed some support.[24]

However, their commitment to the project was passive, because there were more potential costs than benefits to such a controversial project and publication was easily delayed once the newly elected Council members expressed concern. The book's eventual publication, with which staff members credit Director David Chimhini, was probably influenced by donors who wanted the organization to account for the expenditure of their funding.

---

23. ZimRights, *Choosing the Path to Peace and Development*: Coming to terms with Human Rights Violations of the 1982–1987 Conflict in Matabeleland and Midlands provinces (Harare: ZimRights, 1999); "ZimRights releases report on '80s atrocities" *Financial Gazette*, November 11, 1999; "ZimRights launches book on civil strife" *Herald* 5 November 1999.

24. Personal Communication, Charles Cater, 7 August 2001.

As this account suggests, ZimRights did come under attack from the state and its intelligence operatives, but it suffered more grievously from internal conflicts arising from the blurred distinction between members and staff. To date, these have been little considered in accounts of ZimRights' troubled history, which either ignore ZimRights problems, or blame them all on malicious infiltration.

ZimRights' first Secretary-General was the former director of the Catholic Commission for Justice and Peace (CCJP) Nick Ndebele, who, it is widely believed, had been forced to resign from the CCJP in 1991 owing to accusations of financial mismanagement.[25] These allegations made Ndebele an ambiguous figure, but many continued to respect his championing the cause of those tortured and brutalized in Matabeleland in the 1980s. Ndebele "...with no thought for his own safety, had traveled through the troubled areas of Matabeleland and the Midlands interviewing people who had been the victims of atrocities."[26] He did not escape unscathed. As previously discussed, Ndebele was arrested and detained under the Rhodesian-era Law and Order Maintenance Act. He and his family were also been traumatized during the conflict, in which several relatives were detained, tortured or killed.[27]

In 1992, after serving as Secretary-General of ZimRights for only a few months, Ndebele was replaced by Ozias Tungwarara, after further accusations of financial irregularity—charges he always strenuously denied, but which were lodged by the highly respected Zimbabwe Project, which had been providing offices and access to phones for ZimRights, as well as "banking" their monies. They claimed that cash advances had been requested by Ndebele, of which the Council had remained unaware.[28] Ndebele later claimed that his dismissal was because in 1992 he had again highlighted issues around the Matabeleland massacres—alleging that human remains found near a CIO building were linked to the Matabeleland disappearances.[29] Nevertheless, as a member of the organization, Ndebele continued as chair of the human rights

---

25. "Catholic Commission director quits," *Sunday Mail*, 31 March 1991, 3.

26. Auret, *Reaching for Justice*, 162.

27. Auret, *Reaching for Justice* 161–62; ZimRights, *Choosing the path to Peace and development* (Harare: ZimRights, 1999), section 4.3; Lawyers Committee for Human Rights, *Zimbabwe: Wages of War* (New York, Lawyers Committee), 28.

28. Anonymous National Council Member, "A case study of ZimRights" 8; "ZimRights man replaced" *Herald* 4 November 1992, 1; Interview, Nick Ndebele, 27 November 1996; Interview, Nick Ndebele, 27 September 199.

29. Interview, Nick Ndebele, 27 September 1999.

education committee, and, as we shall see, was given a full-time job organizing human rights education in 1994.

After this initial controversy, ZimRights grew gradually and relatively smoothly from 1993 until 1995 under Tungwarara's leadership. Programs and budgets had expanded and ZimRights acquired new staff members and moved in 1995, from cramped city-center offices to a spacious, if somewhat run-down, house on the outskirts of the Central Business District. In the tenser political environment of 1995, which was an election year, ZimRights began to feel they were being targeted by a "destabilization" campaign, typified by Mugabe's labeling them "ZimLooters."[30] This feeling of attack intensified in late 1995 when a document was circulated accusing Tungawarara of sexual misbehavior. ZimRights has always claimed that this was planted by the CIO. Despite support within the organization, he left soon afterwards. He was replaced by David Chimhini, a ZimRights member and former employee of the Zimbabwe Teachers Association.

Despite his dismissal as Secretary-General, Nick Ndebele had remained a member of ZimRights, and he had returned as a paid employee of ZimRights, in 1994, working as education officer until 1996. When Tungwarara left, Ndebele applied for his job: "as the second most senior employee" Ndebele felt that he was the "obvious" successor to Tungwarara.[31] However, when asked in his interview how ZimRights should relate to the CIO, Ndebele says he answered that it was best to make information available to the CIO, so as to "clear misunderstandings."[32] Soon after this, a story appeared in the respected weekly *Financial Gazette* saying that Ndebele had admitted to being a CIO agent, and the job went to David Chimhini.

Ndebele lost his job as Education Officer with ZimRights the next year, when Ford Foundation funding for the project expired. But soon after, a new department for civic education for community theatre, funded by Norwegian People's Aid (NPA) was opened and therefore the new civic education officers were hired, who had both worked in the Zimbabwe Association of Community Theatre (ZACT).[33] Ndebele claimed that the new director, David Chimhini, had manufactured the move from Ford Foundation funding to the

---

30. ZimRights, "Minutes of the ZimRights 3rd AGM, 27–28 April 1996," 4.

31. Interview, Nick Ndebele, 27 September 1999.

32. Interview, Nick Ndebele, 27 September 1999. This is, I suspect, standard practice for most NGOs in Zimbabwe, as many other Zimbabwean NGOs report similar relations to the CIO.

33. Interview, Emma Chiseya and Cousin Zilala, 8 October 1996.

NPA project as an excuse to get rid of him. The claims that Ndebele was a CIO informant continue to reverberate, despite an apology made by Reginald Matchaba-Hove for the rumor at the 1997 AGM.[34] Many of Ndebele's former close associates steered clear of him and concerted efforts were made within the organization to prevent him holding an elected office at either regional or national levels, though these proved unsuccessful.

Nevertheless, despite these internal conflicts, ZimRights grew even more rapidly under Chimhini's guidance. The numbers of staff more than doubled between 1996 and 1997, and then doubled again between 1997 and 1998. Similarly, membership doubled from a claimed 3,000 in both October 1995[35] and April 1996,[36] to 6,000 in May 1997,[37] to 10,000 in 1997, and 14,000 in 1998.[38] This growth served to exacerbate internal tensions further. Unemployed, and smarting from rejections, Nick Ndebele had made no attempt to hide his interest in either the Directorship or the Chairmanship. He was unsuccessful in his bid to win control of the Harare Regional Council in 1997 but was subsequently elected to represent Harare on the National Council.[39] In 1999, he was unexpectedly elected Chair of the Council. When Reginald Matchaba-Hove resigned the Chair in 1999, the anti-Ndebele faction felt sure that they had guaranteed the election of academic Charles Nhachi as Chair and Paul Nyathi as Vice-Chair.[40] Indeed, they have accused Ndebele of unfairly influencing "naive, rural" voters into voting for him as an anti-élite candidate.[41]

It was clear from the outset that, despite protestations to the contrary, David Chimhini, who had presided over Ndebele's departure as education officer, would be unable to work with Ndebele, and *vice-versa*. Ndebele began

---

34. Research notes, ZimRights AGM, Adelaide Acres, 10 May 1997.

35. ZimRights, Director's report to the 2nd AGM October 1995, 1.

36. ZimRights, Report of the 3rd AGM, 27–28 April 1996, 8.

37. ZimRights, National chairman's report to the 4th AGM, 10 May 1997, 2.

38. ZimRights, 1998 Annual Report, 18.

39. Research Notes, ZimRights Harare Regional Council AGM, 19 April 1997.

40. Much of the following is based on interviews with: Munyaradzi Bhidi, Acting Director 13 September 1999; Peter Maregare, Legal Officer, 13 September 1999; Paul Themba Nyathi, former National Council Member, 16 September 1999; Weston Kwete (member) and Never Gadaga, former Information Officer, 24 September 1999; David Chimhini, [Former] Director, 4 October 1999; Interview, Reginald Matchaba-Hove, Zimbabwe Human Rights Association, 8 October 1999.

41. Interview, Paul Themba Nyathi, Zimbabwe Human Rights Association, 16 September 1999; Interview, Reginald Matchaba-Hove, Zimbabwe Human Rights Association, 8 October 1999.

to articulate political positions which were very much at odds with the attitudes of most other NGO élites. Influenced by a particular strain of radical Africanism, he wrote a letter of support to President Mugabe over Zimbabwe's intervention into the Congo War.[42] Similarly, he backed campaigns against the white judges, who Mugabe was also attacking.[43] He later tried to pull Zim-Rights out of the National Constitutional Assembly framework, just as it was squaring up to the government.[44] At a time when politics in Zimbabwe was becoming more and more polarized, the closeness of policy between Zim-Rights and the President's pet projects was interpreted by observers as complicity. Council members might not agree with statements being issued by Ndebele, but they had no formal sanction. They were dispersed across the country and communication with them was not always possible, nor was it feasible to arrange *ad-hoc* meetings. Unlike Matchaba-Hove, who was on the Faculty of Medicine at the University of Zimbabwe and kept up a profitable private practice, Ndebele was unemployed or periodically self-employed and quite prepared to become a full-time Chair.

Over the next months, the conflict between Ndebele and Chimhini degenerated into rival allegations of sexual, financial and administrative misdeeds, carried out through the press and the courts, as Ndebele first stage-managed Chimhini's dismissal, and was later forced to resign himself. The toll of this conflict was to be extremely damaging for ZimRights, the organization. Staff members, caught in the middle of this conflict, fled to more stable jobs. Donors began removing their financial support soon after Ndebele's election as Chair, in response to letters from Chimhini.[45] Lack of donor funds, and court costs, forced ZimRights to sell its headquarters to settle its debts.[46]

Understanding ZimRights' Collapse

ZimRight's demise had a number of causes. These included: a protracted and unequal confrontation with the Zimbabwean state, the internal dynamics

---

42. Basildon Peta, "ZimRights fumes over chairman Ndebele's praise letter to Mugabe," *Daily News,* 11 May 1999.

43. Interview, Nick Ndebele, 27 September 1999.

44. ZimRights Unhappy with NCA Decision. *Chronicle,* 26 July 1999, 9.

45. Interview, Clare Morris and Hilary MacKay, Westminister Foundation, London, 30 January 2001; Letter from David Chimhini to unspecified donors, dated 10 September 1999.

46. ZimRights Puts Office on Sale. *Daily News,* 10 August 2001.

of the organization in a setting where NGOs become a preferred source of employment for their ostensibly "volunteer" members and the donor funding. All of these factors should lead us to be skeptical that NGOs—by virtue of their "voluntary" nature—represent a panacea for donors trying to foster grass-roots advocacy as part of some larger governance or civil-society project.

Even if one discounts assertions that ZimRights was the victim of CIO machinations, the organization was in an isolated position throughout its brief existence. Without the protection of a larger body grounded in Zimbabwean society—the CCJP, for example, was bolstered by its position within the Catholic Church—it had little protection when singled out for attack. ZimRights was also one of the only NGOs in Zimbabwe which occasionally used Moyo's oppositional tactics by issuing press releases and organizing demonstrations. No other Zimbabwean organization was so regularly attacked in the media by President Mugabe and such pressures contributed to internal tensions and suspicions. Yet, at the same time, ZimRights' only pro-active attempt to document human right abuses—the Matabeleland book—was initiated and carried through almost entirely by volunteer interns from the US, Canada, and Sweden.

Perhaps even more crucially, the resources to which ZimRights had access made it a site of even more determined contestation. Its objectives as an advocacy organization were undermined by the job-creating and resource-distributing functions it came to serve. For example, one of the issues of conflict between David Chimhini and Nick Ndebele was a proposal to remove sitting allowances for Council members and staff to attend meetings. This was a particular threat to those councilors who were unemployed, many of whom were sympathetic to the position of Ndebele, who played a populist card against the "élite."

The intra-organizational divisions are on one level merely a fight between two disparate personalities and their factions, exacerbated by both sides' willingness to use the press to press their points. One of Ndebele's relatives, Weston Kwete, became a reporter for the explicitly pro-ZANU *Sunday Mail* and leaked many of the anti-Chimhini stories. On the other hand, the independent press did publish a vituperative exchange between, on the one side, Chimhini and Matchaba-Hove, and on the other, Ndebele and the former ZimRights' information officer, with the dubious, but high-profile, backing of Jonathan Moyo.

While this reveals the dangers implicit in hiring councilors as staff it also reflects the ability of a large, professionalized secretariat to alienate membership. Ndebele has always described himself as the founder of ZimRights and feels that he deserved more respect from the organization. ZimRights under

Chimhini's leadership had gained a high profile and large increases in donor funds, all of which had merely led to the organization distancing itself from its roots. Donors developed particularly good relations with Chimhini, who is articulate and speaks their language well.

This conflict between advocacy and employment was, ironically, aggravated by the donor funding, upon which ZimRights came to depend. Many donor-dependent organizations go through similar explosive spurts of growth, often accompanied by crisis. ZimRights was clearly a case of the "flavor of the month" syndrome in that it was so popular it rapidly raised money from multiple sources. While Oxfam is reported to have a rule that an annual budget increase of more than 25% is likely to lead to organizational difficulties,[47] ZimRights, in just one of the years studied, is reported to have multiplied its budget nearly five-fold.[48]

Whether or not NGOs are "naturally" voluntary, the increased funding throughout the 1990s has made this claim less and less relevant. The collapse of ZimRights, at a time when human rights observers were particularly needed is an extreme example. The people who have lost out are the Zimbabweans, especially those displaced by the recent violence, who have need of both documentation of their rights and protection from those abusing them. ZimRights members too, still have great faith and hope in their organization. Donors, on the other hand, have merely transferred their funds to other, perhaps equally vulnerable, organizations.

Pragmatic Decision Making

We can now turn to the implications of these multiple misunderstandings of how NGOs function and how they relate to the state. NGOs derive diverse benefits from their newly increased roles. While skeptics point to the material benefits of NGO careers—and these are not insubstantial—we should not ignore the "immaterial" yet substantive benefits which churches and mosques have long recognized when they have gained converts through the provision of health or education services (Anheier and Salamon 1997: 366–67). NGOs, like any organization, take pride in their growth and high-profiles locally and internationally and senior positions in NGOs may bring with them considerable public recognition. There is also a potential down-side to the "profitabil-

---

47. Moore and Stewart, "Corporate Governance" End-note, 3.

48. ZimRights. Executive Director's Report to the Fourth Annual General Meeting. 10 May 1997, 2.

ity" of the non-profit sector. Entrepreneurs may also form NGOs to provide employment, prestige and connections to the well-resourced development sector, rather than for any commitment to abstract ideals advocated by donors.

In Zimbabwe, it is widely accepted that NGOs use non-confrontational tactics, variously defined as entryism and inclusion, to influence various levels of state and party apparatus (Moyo 1992). My research has focussed on the efforts of a few "activist" NGOs to mobilize their colleagues to lobby the government over three policy issues: economic structural adjustment, legislation brought in to control the NGOs, and the Constitution. In every one of these cases, the activist NGOs met substantial obstacles. Other NGOs were not interested, were suspicious of their intentions, and preferred to use "non-confrontational" methods or to work through government-approved channels for expressing discontent (Dorman 2001, 2002).

Although the "beneficiaries" of NGOs are often defined simply as those whom the programs are designed to benefit, the term should probably include the entire network that relies upon NGO funding, such as employees and consultants (Stewart 1997: 24). In some cases, this wider group is seen as merely part of societal patronage networks. Leaders of NGOs are thought to seek to enhance their own prestige, rent-seeking potential, and client base (Bratton 1994). Such analyses pathologize these NGOs for abandoning the voluntarist, altruistic goals of "real" NGOs. It seems more important to think critically about the political implications of such motivations on the part of NGO staff, leaders and hangers-on. How do the incentives to work for and gain office in NGOs, the increased stakes in doing so, and the personal motivations of office-holders influence the way in which NGOs and interest organizations interact with the state?

Where the state remains relatively administratively competent, typically, all the "sticks"—closure, deregistration, investigation and coordination—and "carrots"—tax exemption, access to policy-makers and public funding—are seen as emanating from the state, while the NGOs have little, if any bargaining power (Hulme and Edwards 1997: 13). NGOs may therefore seek access to the state to influence its policies as well as to avoid conflict or secure protection (Beckman 1997: 5). As Fowler noted in his well-grounded study of Kenyan NGOs, "it appears that more can be achieved by appearing to support, respect, and improve prevailing systems, rather than openly agitating against them" (Fowler 1994: 293).[49] NGOs often initiate these interactions with states—and

---

49. A. Fowler 1994. Non-Governmental Organisations and the Promotion of Democracy in Kenya. Doctoral Dissertations, University of Sussex.

are not always "co-opted" by the state. As development organizations, NGOs exercise strategic pragmatism in order to ensure that their clients continue to benefit from the "goods" they bring. Fowler (1994: 288) extends this point and emphasizes that "providing welfare services can be an important factor allowing other, more politically sensitive, work to take place." The Undugu Society in Kenya, which both provides services to street-children and advocates for policy reform, "pursues an emancipatory agenda through a managed mix of macro and micro activities designed to reinforce each other so exploiting the limited development space that exists and the opportunities which arise within it" (*ibid*: 291). NGOs, therefore, may refrain from political activity in order not to risk their primary goal. At the same time, however, their role as development organizations also enables them to press for certain policy changes. NGOs have good reason to value harmonious relations with the state and cultural élites. At the same time, as NGOs become more professionalized, and are run by large staffs rather than volunteers, the interests of the staff may begin to predominate over those of the membership. Michels' (1962) "iron law of oligarchy" operates in NGOs as well as political parties.

Conclusion: Pathologizing *versus* Romanticizing

My critique of the romanticization of NGOs in Africa has been one of several similar projects. Amongst a plethora of writing on NGOs, a few significant studies which have emerged from research based mostly in East Africa, deserve serious consideration. Igoe (2004) and Cameron (2001), studying pastoralist NGOs in Tanzania, emphasize the ways in which donor agendas shape NGOs, and the multiple ways in which NGOs become little more than new patronage vehicles for "big men" in rural communities (Cf. Fowler 1994). In contrast, Kelsall's study of NGO operations in north-eastern Tanzania, is more interested in the attempts of NGOs to enhance communities' abilities to undertake collective action. Kelsall is profoundly critical of the liberal development agenda of NGOs, but also explores the extent to which they accomplish their ends. In his account, the NGOs are unsuccessful in fostering participation, accountability or democracy within the community because of the way in which they impose their agendas.[50] Also concerned about "liberal development," Hughes' (2001) very different methodology enables him to examine the

---

50. Kelsall, T., 2000. *Subjectivity, Collective Action, and the Governance Agenda in Tanzania.* Doctoral Dissertation: SOAS.

interaction of NGOs with local people in remote areas of Mozambique and Zimbabwe. Hughes effectively identifies not only the ways in which NGO-led participatory workshops marginalize local peoples, but also their potential to eat away at land and resource entitlements of rural groups.

All of these recent studies suggest that we are right to be critical of claims and assertions about NGO abilities: "there is no magic bullet." (Vivian 1994). Not only is there little evidence that NGOs are either more efficient or more participatory than other development schemes, but the exact opposite may be true (Marcussen 1996; Tvedt 1998). What Stewart (1997: 13) calls the "NGOs do it cheaper, better faster" argument seems to have little evidence backing it up. However, there is a new danger of donors and academics falling out of love with NGOs and descending instead into an equally problematic discourse which pathologizes NGOs, suggesting that they are nothing more than new power resources for élites. In the words of a recent, iconoclastic approach to African Politics, NGOs are, according to Chabal and Daloz (1999: 22):

> ...a successful adaptation to the conditions laid down by foreign donors on the part of local political actors who seek in this way to gain access to new resources....NGOs are often nothing other than the new "structures" with which Africans can seek to establish an instrumentally profitable position within the existing system of neo-patrimonialism....The use of NGO resources can today serve the strategic interests of the classical entrepreneurial Big man just as well as access to state coffer did in the past.

While such an account may provide a useful balance to earlier effusions, its reluctance to take NGO activists seriously betrays an equally limited approach. The authors dismiss NGOs summarily as merely saying what the donors want to hear, which is more of an *ad-hominem* attack than analytical reasoning or empirical evidence. While the romanticization of NGOs needs reconsideration, so do approaches which conclude that they fail in all capacities. Instead, NGOs need to be understood as organizations bound up in power relations on various levels.

Studying both the organizational encumbrances of NGOs and their position within the ideological sphere or political culture may help us explain their inter- and intra-organizational decisions. Situating NGOs within their political context and considering internal processes avoids both the romanticization and the more recent pathologizing of NGOs which dominate the literature. Considering the continued weight placed upon NGOs in donor discourses and funding, such an approach is not only timely, but necessary. Participant-observer research is a particularly valuable way of avoiding such pathologizations. After reading a particularly controversial case study—involving allegations of sexual harassment, financial mismanagement, and government infiltration—one of my informants said,

> Your characterization of ZimRights seems on target…a few things are left vague and unanswered, but maybe that is best after all.......It is OK not to have all the answers. In some ways it really confirms the need to take a very close look and use "thick description." If you had done an organizational analysis from a macro perspective, none of these scandals would even come up on the radar screen—and they really tell a big part of the story as far as ZimRights is concerned.[51]

Understanding intra- and inter-organizational dynamics as a participant-observer enables the researcher to make sense out of apparently incongruous evidence and guards against tendencies to romanticization and pathologization of NGOs.

This suggests a need to reconsider the methodological and theoretical basis of "democratization." The understanding of democratization as a re-configuration of state and society relations in a series of very different and complex post-colonial societies should affect our choice of research techniques. Whitehead notes in a significant re-assessment of the interaction between theory and empirical research on democratization: "the best and perhaps the only, way to grasp the dynamics of a long-term open-ended process is through narrative-construction." (Whitehead 2002: 10). If we conceptualize democratization "as a complex, dynamic, long-term and open-ended process…then the type of theory-building and hypothesis-testing that would be possible and appropriate…would be interpretative rather than demonstrative." (*Ibid*.: 1, 2). This brings us back to a more Weberian social science, where the purpose of research is " interpretative understanding of social action…and causal explanation of its course and consequences" (Weber 1968: 4).

Complex and dynamic processes are best studied using a multiplicity of methodological tools. Interview research, participant-observation, and documentary evidence reinforce each other and reflect different aspects of the process under study. Organizations like NGOs benefit from being studied

---

51. Personal communications, Charles Cater, 19 and 20 July 2001.

from the "inside" so as to generate "thick description" and capture their internal decision-making processes. Documentary evidence enables the study of changes within discourses. Interview research is a necessary, if not sufficient, tool for clarifying information, and allowing the subjects of the study to speak directly to the topic. Together, these methods provide the material through which we can construct historical narratives that enable understanding and explanation.

We need to present a much more complex and historicized vision of the role played by NGOs and churches in state-society politics. Yet at the same time, we must avoid demonizing or otherwise dismissing as "un-African" those political actors keen on reform or who work for NGOs. These are important lessons for academics and the donor fraternity, many of whom either accept at face value teleological narratives of democratization (and are then baffled by the lack of "democracy" in post-transition societies), or see Africa's political cultures as irredeemably collapsing into chaos.

Works Cited

Anheier, H. and L. Salamon. 1997. *Defining the Non-Profit Sector: A cross-national analysis.* Manchester: Manchester University Press.

Beckman, B. 1997. Explaining democratization: notes on the concept of civil society. In *Civil Society, Democracy and the Muslim World*, edited by E. Ozdalga and S. Persson. Istanbul: Swedish Research Institute in Istanbul.

Bratton, M. 1994. Micro-democracy? The merger of farmer unions in Zimbabwe. *African Studies Review* 37 (1): 9–38.

Bratton, M. and G. Hyden, eds. 1992. *Governance and Politics in Africa.* Boulder CO: Lynne Rienner.

Carothers, T. 1999. *Aiding Democracy Abroad: The learning curve.* Washington DC: Carnegie.

Carothers, T. and M. Ottaway. 2000. The burgeoning world of civil society aid. In *Funding Virtue: Civil society and democracy promotion*, edited by T. Carothers and M. Ottaway. Washington DC: Carnegie.

Chabal, P., and J.-P. Daloz. 1999. *Africa Works: Disorder as political instrument.* Oxford: James Currey.

Cameron, G. Taking stock of pastoralist NGOs in Tanzania. *Review* of *African Political Economy* 28(87). 55–72.

Clark, J. 1991. *Democratizing Development: The role of voluntary organisations.* London: Earthscan Publications Ltd.

————. 1997. The state, popular participation and the voluntary sector. In *NGOs, States and Donors: Too close for comfort?*, edited by D. Hulme and M. Edwards. London: Macmillan.

Dicklitch, S. 1998. *The Elusive Promise of NGOs in Africa*. Basingstoke: Macmillan.

Dorman, S. 2001. NGOs and state in Zimbabwe: implications for civil society theory. In *Civil Society and Authoritarianism in the Third World*, edited by B. Beckman, E. Hannson and A. Sjogren. Stockholm: Podsu.

————. 2002. Rocking the boat? Church-NGOs and democratization in Zimbabwe. *African Affairs* 101 (402): 75–92.

Fowler, A. 1991. The role of NGOs in changing state-society relations: perspectives from Eastern and Southern Africa. *Development Policy Review* 9: 53–84.

Green, A. and A. Matthias. 1997. *NGOs and Health in Developing Countries*. Basingstoke: Macmillan.

Harbeson, J. 1994. Civil society and political renaissance in Africa. In *Civil Society and the State in Africa*, edited by J. W. Harbeson, D. Rothchild and N. Chazan. Boulder CO: Lynne Rienner.

Hughes, D. 2001. Rezoned for business: how eco-tourism unlocked black farmland in eastern Zimbabwe. *Journal of Agrarian Change* 1 (4): 575–99.

Hulme, D. and M. Edwards. 1997. *NGOs, States and Donors: Too close for comfort?* London: Macmillan.

Igoe, J. Scaling Up Civil Society: donor money, NGOs, and the pastoral land rights movement in Tanzania. *Development and Change* 34(5): 863–85.

Kasfir, N. 1998. The conventional notion of civil society: a critique. *Commonwealth and Comparative Politics* 36 (2): 1–20.

Kassimir, R. 1998. The social power of religious organisation and civil society: the Catholic church in Uganda. *Commonwealth and Comparative Politics* 36 (2): 54–83.

Kiondo, A. 1993. Structural adjustment and NGOs in Tanzania. In *Social Change and Economic Reform in Africa*, edited by P. Gibbon. Uppsala: Nordiska Afrikaininstitutet.

Marcussen, H. 1996. Comparative advantage of NGOs: myths and realities. In *Foreign Aid Towards the Year 2000: Experiences and challenges*, edited by O. Stokke. London: Frank Cass.

————. 1996. NGOs, the state and civil society. *Review of African Political Economy* (69): 405–23.

Michels, R. 1962. *Political Parties: A sociological study of the oligarchical tendencies of modern democracy*. New York: Free Press.

Moore, M. and S. Stewart. 1998. Corporate governance for NGOs. *Development in Practice* 8 (3): 335–42.

Moyo, S. 1992. *NGO Advocacy in Zimbabwe: Systematising an old function or inventing a new role?* Harare: ZERO.

Moyo, S., J. Makumbe, and B. Raftopoulos. 2000. *NGOs, the State and Politics in Zimbabwe.* Harare: SAPES.

Putnam, R., R. Leonardi, and R. Nanetti. 1993. *Making Democracy Work: Civic traditions in modern Italy.* Princeton NJ: Princeton University Press.

Semboja, J., and O. Therkilsden, eds. 1995. *Service Provision Under Stress: the state, NGOs and people's organizations in Kenya, Tanzania and Uganda.* Copenhagen: Centre for Development Research.

Smillie, I. 1999. At sea in a sieve? Trends and issues in the relationship between northern NGOs and northern governments. In *Stakeholders: Government-NGO partnerships for international development*, edited by I. Smillie, H. Helmich, T. German and J. Randel. London: OECD and Earthscan.

Stewart, S. 1997. Happy ever after in the market place: NGOs and uncivil society. *Review of African Political Economy* (71): 11–34.

Theunis, S. 1992. *Non-Governmental Development Organisations of Developing Countries: And the south smiles.* Dordecht: Novib/Nijhoff.

Tripp, A. 1992. Local organizations, participation and the state in urban Tanzania. In *Governance and Politics in Africa*, edited by G. Hyden and M. Bratton. Boulder CO: Lynne Rienner.

Tvedt, T. 1998. *Angels of Mercy or Development Diplomats?* Oxford: James Currey.

UNDP. 1992. *Human Development Report 1992.* New York: Oxford University Press.

Vivian, J. 1994. NGOs and sustainable development in Zimbabwe: no magic bullets. *Development and Change* (25): 167–93.

Weber, M. 1968. *Economy and Society: An outline of interpretive sociology*, edited by C. Wittich. Vol. 1, 4. New York: Bedminster.

Wellard, K., and J. Copestake, eds. 1993. *NGOs and the State in Africa: Rethinking roles in sustainable agricultural development.* London: Routledge.

White, G. 1996. Civil society, democratization and development. In *Democratization in the South: The jagged wave*, edited by R. Luckham and G. White. Manchester: Manchester University Press.

Whitehead, L. 2002. On theory and experience in democratization studies. In *Democratization: Theory and Experience*, edited by L. Whitehead. Oxford: Oxford University Press.

World Bank. 1989. *Sub-Saharan Africa: From crisis to sustainable growth.* Washington DC: World Bank.

CHAPTER 3

Transcending Politics Through the Kingdom of God and Free Markets: A Case Study of Religious NGOs in Zimbabwe

Erica Bornstein

Postdoctoral Fellow, Society for the Humanities,
Cornell University
elb33@cornell.edu

Introduction

This chapter is about the national political-economic context of religious NGO work in Zimbabwe in the late 1990s. My research in Zimbabwe preceded the racialized political struggles of 2000–01, which included state-sponsored violence and farm invasions. Although this chapter does not account for, or explain, such violence, it does document the bubbling economic and political discontent that was pacified through NGO programs of economic development. NGOs worked in collaboration with the Zimbabwean state to offer these programs while at the same time espousing a discourse that transcended national politics. This discourse, drawing on two themes—a Christian discourse of "A Kingdom of God," and a neo-liberal discourse of "free markets"—facilitated what I call a politics of transcendence. As my ethnographic examples will demonstrate, the Zimbabwean state at this time was weak and desperate. It was heavily dependent on the welfare work of Christian NGOs to pacify a nation in economic decline.

In the late 1990s, NGOs were working to assist rural communities in becoming economically self-sufficient in the face of reduced social services resulting from structural adjustment (cf. Hanlon 2000) and other neo-liberal economic reforms that had drastically reduced welfare service for Zimbabweans (Bond 1991 and 1998). Dependent on international forms of charitable aid, the Zimbabwean state was in a precarious relationship with internationally funded Christian NGOs. The tensions rumbling during my research were evident every day in growing violence that was manifested in increased crime, mobs that publicly disrobed women for being scantily dressed, weekly riots at the University of Zimbabwe, and heavy-handed state attempts to quiet them. It was also present in the protests of war veterans, at that time organized against Mugabe, before he agreed to pay their pensions. The analysis in this chapter speaks to debates on supposed "civil society" and the state in Africa (Keane 1988; Taylor 1990; Hyden and Bratton 1992; Woods 1992; Bayart 1993; Williams 1993; Harbeson, Rothchild and Chazan 1994; Ndegwa 1994 and 1996; Williams and Young 1994; Sachikonye 1995; Mamdani 1996; Marcussen 1996; Rich 1997; Turner and Hulme 1997; Comaroff and Comaroff 1999; Maxwell 2000; Dorman 2002; and Ferguson 2002) on church-state relations (Gundani 1988; Hallencreutz 1988; Hallencreutz and Moyo 1988; Gifford 1994; Maxwell 1995, 1998, and 2000; and Dorman 2002), and on the ways that development has historically intersected with the extension of state power in Zimbabwe (Robins 1994; Makumbe 1996 and 1998; Munro 1998; Worby 1998; Moore 1999; Alexander and McGregor 2000; Rutherford 2000). It also builds on recent critiques of neo-liberal efforts (like structural adjustment programs) and their social consequences (Sachikonye 1995; Bond 1998; Potts 1998; and Hanlon 2000).

The ethnographic research that informs this paper was conducted in 1996–97 with two Christian NGOs: WV Zimbabwe (World Vision Zimbabwe) and Christian Care. Both were similar in focus—assisting rural Zimbabweans with agricultural development programs, as well as providing water, sanitation and education programs. Both NGOs also, at times, built schools and encouraged micro-enterprise development. However, their histories differed. World Vision, a transnational NGO, was founded in the United States as an evangelistic organization and began its work in Zimbabwe in the late 1970s assisting children in orphanages. It is funded primarily through child sponsorship—the process through which donors support "community development" by sending a monthly remittance targeted toward a specific child in need. Christian Care, by contrast, is the development arm of the Zimbabwean Council of Churches. An ecumenical organization, it began its work in Zimbabwe in the late 1960s, assisting political detainees from the liberation war. Its history as a political organization is particularly pertinent to the argument I present in this paper: that as much as religious NGOs in Zimbabwe in the late 1990s espoused the mercurial discourse of transcending politics, their work was entwined with the Zimbabwean state. Following the work of Ferguson (1994), who shows how the ostensibly apolitical work of development paves the way for the politics of the state, my case explores two specific discourses—of the Kingdom of God and of neo-liberal economics—that facilitate such a process. In addition, my ethnographic study of NGOs in Zimbabwe illustrates a precarious interdependence between NGOs and a desperate and volatile state.

Theorizing NGOs in Zimbabwe

Scholarly debates involving NGOs most often occur over the relationship between civil society[1] and the state. In Africa in particular, as African states are increasingly deemed corrupt by international donors, civil society has become a prescriptive arena for efforts toward democratization and development. Neo-liberal economic programs such as the structural adjustment programs of the 1990s championed this approach, funnelling donor funds through NGOs (instead of the Zimbabwean state) in an effort to decentralize the state and reduce its power, and its potential power to corrupt. Alongside the demonization of African states, NGOs have become harbingers of "good governance." Neo-liberal economic theories discursively locate civil society and the purview of NGOs outside the state (Hyden and Bratton 1992 and Diamond 1994). Others have explored how civil society is perpetually engaged

---

1. See Ferguson and Gupta (2002) for the limits of this concept for ethnographic inquiry. Gramsci (1991; also see Keane 1988) conceptualized "civil society" via Marx with the socialist goal of ending class- and ultimately state/civil society divisions. Gramscian civil society builds on Marx's idea of civil society in relation to ideology (Marx 1975 [1843]), characterized by the hegemonic interests of the bourgeoisie. In contrast, Gramsci's civil society, and the inherent potential for resistance that lies within such a category, exists in the realm of culture and cultural institutions (Hall 1986, 1988; for Gramsci's theory put in to practice see Comaroff and Comaroff 1991, Comaroff and Comaroff 1997). This point is important, for the purposes of this study, as churches and faith-based NGOs fall within the realm of cultural institutions. Using the model of trench warfare and a "war of position," Gramsci understands that cultural production involves class struggle. For Gramsci, struggles over ideas and ideals articulate hegemonic and counter-hegemonic struggles.

with the state, and yet not bound by it. For example, Guyer (1994) explores how even supposedly "local" civil society in Africa is linked to an international arena of networks and resources (see Riles 2000 and Ferguson and Gupta 2002). The "civil society" promoted by transnational NGOs is dependent upon nation-states and extends beyond them. Boundaries between state and civil society are constantly blurred as NGOs and the state simultaneously collaborate on development and compete for international resources for similar services. Binary oppositions, such as state versus civil society, are not of much analytical utility (Ferguson and Gupta 2002). Broad and abstract, these categories fail to do justice to the social complexities of NGO work in practice. In addition, writing on civil society in a binary frame ignores religion. Where do Christianity and religious NGOs fit in to the binary opposition? Are they part of local civil society? The state? International civil society? These distinctions lose their relevance when one examines the activities of religious NGOs such as Christian Care and World Vision in practice.

Scholars who use the concept of civil society to analyze the work of NGOs sometimes conceive of it as a form of grassroots resistance, rescuing societies from repressive states. This discourse attributes to civil society the normative potential, and the moral authority, to provide ethical and educative influences in resistance to the coercive ideology of the state. Civil society is thus seen as distinct from the state by its very potential to resist it (Bratton 1989a and 1989b; Taylor 1990; Clark 1995; Diamond 1994; Gyimah-Boadi 1996; Turner and Hulme 1997). The "civil society to the rescue" paradigm is often described in connection with transnational activist movements focusing on the environment, women, or other issues of supposed global concern (Keck and Sikkink 1998). Sometimes civil society itself is discussed as a global force (Walzer 1995). One analytical limitation of the use of civil society in the case of NGOs is that the category of "NGO" is ambiguous (Fisher 1997 and Vakil 1997): there are multiple types and variations inherent to the category. The "non" of "non-governmental" could just as easily refer to grassroots resistance to national governments as to an international civil society. NGOs are represented by two conceptually distinct applications of the state-versus-civil-society paradigm. NGOs as civil society either appear in a nationalist and autochthonous sphere of grassroots political advocacy (Clark 1991; Moyo 1991; Mararike 1995; Ndegwa 1996; Weisgrau 1997), or in an international sphere of humanitarian aid (Tendler 1975 and Clark 1995).

In the realm of international civil society, criticism of NGOs stems from insider reports of aid agencies (Hancock 1989 and Maren 1997). These accounts take on foreign aid as a massive and evil business linking governments to "corrupt" African politicians at the expense of poor Africans. Such analyses accuse NGOs of exacerbating problems that humanitarian assistance is presumed to ease or solve. Foreign aid itself is portrayed as a monstrous bureaucracy in support of nothing but its own perpetuation, a "self-serving system that sacrifices its own practitioners and intended beneficiaries in order that it may survive and grow" (Maren 1997: 11). In this scheme, even when it does not name the state, the state appears as a consuming and predatory (ergo corrupt) forum, as opposed to a productive and protective one.

Other scholars argue that the work of NGOs in international civil society threatens the sovereignty of states. NGOs are able to cross national boundaries and "have created direct and independent forms of non-governmental diplomacy through networks of their own" (Clark 1995; Hanlon 2000; Kilby 2000). Conflicts arise in issues of international versus national governance when, for example, international demands voiced by NGOs for human rights and environmental conservation compete with state control over citizens and natural resources. NGOs have specialized agendas, and tackle arenas that states tend to ignore. Moreover, NGOs use International Governmental Organizations or IGOs (such as the UN) as channels to assist in lobbying efforts to alter government positions. These channels of influence are also found in NGO networks of international civil society and self-created inter-governmental arenas (Riles 2000). As NGOs have access to international financial and volunteer resources that supersede states, they bypass states in both global and local arenas. In the process, African states are becoming increasingly dependent on NGOs for the implementation of development and other social programs. Theoretically, NGOs glean increased strength from this dependence and therefore have more opportunity to press for far-reaching political and economic policy changes (Bratton 1989a; Farrington *et al.* 1993).

Scholarship on civil society conceived as a local practice (bounded by national borders) emphasizes small, local, voluntary organizations to argue that the NGO sector has advantages over governments in addressing poverty. NGOs are seen as the "natural partners of the rural poor" (Riddell and Robinson 1995), privileging small-scale projects and a base of voluntarism. In this literature, NGOs fit into the "associational life that occurs in the political space beyond the state's purview" (Bratton 1989a: 411). It is a local civil society distinct from the state. For these scholars (Bratton 1989b; Farrington et al. 1993; and Riddell and Robinson 1995) the center of political gravity has shifted in from the state to civil society. NGOs are portrayed as advocates of civil society in their struggles against repressive states (Bratton 1989a and 1989b; Clark 1991; Farrington *et al.* 1993; Wellard and Copestake 1993; Mararike 1995; Riddell and Robinson 1995). Through local civil society, NGOs challenge the state

(Ndegwa 1996; Rea 1962) and locally interpret state development programs (Weisgrau 1997).

In contrast to the above-mentioned perspectives, this chapter builds on scholarship that questions the category of civil society. Tracing the logic of the term to a neo-liberal project that conceals its own use of massive state power and defines civil society in its own image, some scholars have noted how the concept of civil society ignores existing forms of civic organization in favor of those that match the agenda of free-market democracy (Woods 1992; Beckman 1993; Eyoh 1996; and Williams 1993). They argue that liberating civil society from the hegemonic grip of the state is a critical component of the neo-liberal economic project, and caution that the concept should not be applied without regard to specific social, economic, and historical circumstances. Chatterjee's (1990) critique of Taylor's use of the term "civil society" is a notable example. He uses Hegel to argue that civil society is a western European concept that cannot be released from the particular relation of states to the bourgeoisie in early European history, something that is not applicable in other parts of the world and at other times in history—especially in contexts where the nuclear family is not dominant. Others add a critique of "good governance," arguing that it too is a conceptual product of neo-liberal ideological priorities propelled by the World Bank through NGOs (Leftwich 1994; Williams and Young 1994). Still others argue against neo-liberal concepts of democracy and civil society that divorce them from the state, and see civil society rather through the lens of social movements such as student protests and labor strikes; a theoretical middle ground—again, spatial metaphors intact—between states and local communities (Chazan 1994; Sachikonye 1995; Ferguson and Gupta 2002). In the late 1990s, Zimbabwean NGOs were neither merely part of a transnational humanitarian civil society nor did they bubble up with the spirit of democracy from local soil. NGOs were organizations whose ground could not be fixed, and this was how their power was articulated and became productive.

Ambiguous Loyalties, Categorical Uncertainties, Ethnographic Challenges

One example of the categorical uncertainty between NGOs and the state occurred at WV Zimbabwe's Annual Day of Prayer in 1997. It was a transnational company picnic where employees of each national office united to pray for world events. One of the invited speakers was Mrs. Olivia Muchena, a board member of WV International and Zimbabwe's Deputy Minister of Agriculture. Mrs. Muchena spoke simultaneously as the voice of World Vision and the voice of ZANU-PF (the ruling party): "MPs [Members of Parliament] are supposed to be legislators but we are doing development, talking about development, doing your work....One of your responsibilities is for you to pray for your leaders, us the politicians."[2] In this setting, the identity of the NGO board member troubled categorical boundaries between NGOs and the state. She was not alone. If one examines the employment histories of the staff members of both Christian Care and World Vision, one discovers that most of the NGO staff have worked for the state at some point in their careers. At Independence, the Zimbabwean civil service grew to build a new Zimbabwe.[3] Yet, during structural adjustment, World Bank initiatives demanded the scaling back of the Zimbabwean state. As a result, redundant employees from the Ministries of Agricultural Development, Information, Education, and Health and Social Welfare flooded the staff of the transnational NGOs that were pouring into the country to "help with the transition." Working for an NGO in Zimbabwe in the late 1990s was therefore prime employment for educated Zimbabweans. Hence, categorical boundaries between NGOs and the state bled into each other, a fact demonstrated by the World Vision board member who was also an MP.

This categorical uncertainty was also reflected with regard to NGOs and the communities with which they worked. For example, in the development projects of WV Zimbabwe, because of the donor structure of child sponsorship and the labor-intensive apparatus required to track sponsored children and their correspondence with foreign sponsors (Bornstein 2001), a project clerk and bookkeeper were hired from the local community to work for WV Zimbabwe. They lived at the project site and monitored the project on a daily basis. They represented the NGO as it was embodied in the local community. These individuals grew up in the rural community, and they worked for the NGO: reporting to it, monitoring development, and keeping the project "on track." They were of the community and of the NGO. A growing trend with WV Zimbabwe projects was the Area Development Program (ADP). In this development initiative, the entire NGO staff lived at the project. Hired from Harare and placed in the community, they became part of the community.

---

2. World Vision Day of Prayer, Harare, October 1, 1997.
3. Herbst (1990: 31) notes that shortly after Independence, the civil service was increased from 40,000 to 80,000. The larger civil service was an attempt by the new government to move Africans into the state.

World Vision field officers "walked with the people" the way Jesus did; the NGO was "inculturated." It "grew local roots," echoing colonial missionary boards with their native catechists. The ADP structure aimed to eliminate the NGO field officers based in Harare, along with the monthly check-ups. However, it did not eliminate the ambiguity of the relationships forged between NGOs and rural communities. Nor did it eradicate bureaucratic structures of accountability and governmentality. The ADP project staff continued to report to donors, to speak on behalf of community projects to local state representatives and donors, and to liaise with local government structures and funding bodies.

These religious NGOs were engaged in long-term projects lasting anywhere from two to ten years. While NGO field officers overseeing the development projects and reporting to the Harare office shuttled between the rural projects and urban Harare on a monthly basis, development was also monitored and in effect conducted by local development committees of village community members.[4] At monthly development meetings when field officers made their visits to "the rurals," these complex relationships between communities, NGOs, and local government generated political tensions. A project clerk mentioned how WV Zimbabwe project offices were not solely for community meetings; the state utilized the buildings as well: "Agritex teaches farmers here; whenever the District Councillor has something to say, he comes here."[5] As I will demonstrate, the lines between NGO workers, communities, and local government were in constant motion, as development became a desperate political platform for the state. In addition to the politics of individual intent—of donors, recipients and families involved in development—the work of NGOs was tightly bound up with the politics of the state. Working amidst these delicate and often competing political agendas presented constant difficulties for NGO staff.

The apparent contradictions of transcending local politics and simultaneously facilitating the operations of a weak state took particular shape in a project that I engaged in with Christian Care. Like many contemporary ethnographers, I was self-conscious about my potential to take knowledge from the

---

4. This process, although interesting, is beyond the scope of this chapter. Scholars studying rural development from the vantage of local communities focus on how local power structures of largely elder men are replicated and reinforced in supposedly democratic and participatory processes of community development. In terms of defining the "community" that is being developed (Bornstein 2003).

5. WV Zimbabwe project, Mabee.

field and to ignore my own participation in its making. I met with the Harare regional director of Christian Care and asked him how I could assist the organization. Aside from seeking some directive for daily institutional interaction, I had a vague desire to be useful. He suggested that I review the history of communication and "accountability" within the organization, and make some projections and guidelines for improving communication. There had been trouble in the past with competition between stakeholders (defined as beneficiaries, employees both paid and volunteer, donors, government, and other NGOs and churches). The trouble revolved around who had access to resources, and who had authority to distribute them. Misunderstandings had generated an internal scandal that was being addressed through an intensive organizational restructuring and evaluation.

Realizing that there were specific problems that the NGO sought to address, I reviewed relationships between three realms of the organization that I saw competing for authority: (1) the governing bodies of the NGO, including the National Council, National Executive Committee, Regional Council and Regional Committees; (2) the staff, including the National Executive Officer, and (3) external contacts and other stakeholders, including donors, media, government ministries, and beneficiaries. Churches fit in as both members of the governing bodies, and as stakeholders as the membership. My analysis was not very complex: there were frequent struggles over how much power each of the stakeholders had in the organization, and at times these struggles resulted in a lack of clarity with regard to authority and decision-making. The NGO had a decentralized structure (of regional and national offices), which was identified by many in the institution as one of the organization's strengths, as well as one of its weaknesses. Although the NGO had the potential to be in close contact with its constituency (beneficiaries), it was unclear exactly how decisions as to the allocation of resources and power were made. There were serious communication gaps between finance offices and project administrative offices that were manifest in conflicting and competing agendas between those who raised and managed the budget on the one hand, and those who worked in the field expending resources through Christian Care's projects on the other. As I interviewed employees in Christian Care, I conceptualized an organizational flow-chart that documented what I saw to be vulnerabilities in the institutional structure through which daily institutional practices were carried out.

My chart was hierarchical, with power and directives flowing downwards from the National Council, through various offices, and eventually the beneficiaries. Other stakeholders extended in octopus-like arms on the sides of the hierarchical flow. I anticipated that my project would be filed forever in a cabinet, lost or ignored. I was surprised and a bit embarrassed by how seriously it was received. Not only was my cursory analysis empowered by the strength of my outsider status, it was taken seriously by the regional director and passed on to the national director, and eventually distributed to the members of the National Council at a subsequent meeting.

The national director reflected on my analysis in the form of extensive written comments in dialogue with my recommendations. His response analyzed the limitations and potential avenues for improvement in my recommendations. His primary criticism of my analysis was its simplicity. The arrows should move in both directions, he said. My key confusion regarding NGOs and their relation to the state and to civil society (in the case of Christian Care, both the state and civil society were its "stakeholders") was a false assumption of hierarchical flow from donors, through NGOs, to beneficiaries. My analysis relied on spatial metaphors of state and civil society that posited one above the other (Ferguson and Gupta 2002). The world on the ground was far more complex.

A recurrent theme in ongoing discussions with project coordinators for World Vision and Christian Care was the complicated working relationship that NGOs had with the government (as a "stakeholder" in development). One project coordinator for World Vision said, for example, "we work very closely with the government." He described the working relationship as a process of acknowledging local power structures and local government officials. This was the theme (or fiction) of partnership. However, the fact that international funds went directly from donors to World Vision and bypassed the state was something that local government officials would not "go along with." The project coordinator said:

> I think basically what the government people want you to do, once you acknowledge their presence within a community as the leaders of the districts, and so forth, I think you would have done your job very well. All they want is for you to be given authority to work within the community and as you work to report to them about what you are doing, regularly attending their meetings and so forth and so on, its fine. But of course you will find problems, they will have their differences. You will find people in government circles maybe don't go along with your ideas because they have got their own ideas.

Officials were frustrated because World Vision's funding bypassed the state. Monies were given to the local management committee, the bookkeeper, and the staff that ran local project offices. These offices accounted for the funds, and filed reports with the Harare office. Project officers visited to check on the project, to review how the money was being used, to survey the accounting

Figure 3.1 Christian Care Communication Chart

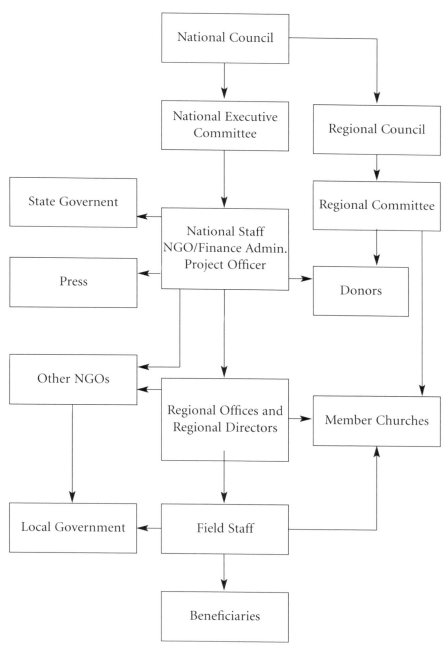

in the cashbook, vouchers, and receipts, and to guarantee there was no fraud. The government was not happy with this arrangement and it created conflict. The same project coordinator for World Vision mentioned above explained:

> So we have a problem with government in that government wants the funds to go through their office and that we are saying we give these things directly to the people. So, somehow it creates some conflict that is hidden. Because you will find some that would come out openly and say "Ok, we are not happy about the way you are doing things," and I always tell them: this is how we are supposed to be doing things. There is no way we can change, you see. Since you are a donor, you have got the money and so forth, there is no way they can say ok get out of the community. But it remains a bone of contention, to say "Ok, why is it that you are giving money directly to the communities and not through us?" Because they feel they are the rightful persons to do that kind of job. So basically that's the main problem.

These specifically local tensions were a product of the transnational context of funding in which NGOs operate. This context was highly political. As the Zimbabwean state became weaker, it depended more upon the work of NGOs to provide welfare services for its citizens. NGO workers were called upon to navigate this precarious political terrain.

Religious NGOs, Churches, and State Attempts to Control Them

When NGOs source and allocate international funds, they bypass the fiscal structures of national economies. While dollars given to the rural poor through NGOs for community development constituted a significant portion of the Zimbabwean economy at the time of this research, they did not flow through state budgets. When I asked the National Treasurer on the Executive Committee of Christian Care, formerly an employee with the Ministry of Information, how the government tracked the activities of NGOs, he replied: "The Ministry of Labor governs the Private Voluntary Organizations Act, under which NGOs have to register, but this is the extent of it—only legal issues. Perhaps in the President's office, under Rural Development, but there wouldn't be any statistics except for the registration of cooperatives [Cooperative Development]." When asked where the government recorded information, he replied, "It would be a waste of your time; these sorts of records aren't kept. Only those that want to form into cooperatives under the Cooperative Act."[6] A gentle comment by a former civil servant who was on the local governing board of an NGO. No records were kept. His experience spoke volumes about how little control African states had over the finances of NGO-driven development.

In Zimbabwe, as in other parts of southern Africa, state governments have attempted to control the efforts of NGOs through legislation (Ndegwa 1994). One dramatic example of this was the manner in which The Welfare Act of 1966 was revised without the consultation of the NGO community in 1995. A new parliamentary act called The Private Voluntary Organizations Act (PVO) sailed through parliament without debate or discussion. While the legislation required NGOs to register with the government (as had the Welfare Act of 1966), it also allowed the government to take over the management of an NGO at will. NGOs reacted to this legislation with shock and horror, especially when the government attempted to take over the Association of Women's Clubs. Religious NGOs began to protest this legislation and formed an advocacy group to change the legislation called the PVO Campaign.[7] The PVO Act was finally repealed and the regulation allowing the government to take over an NGO was removed. That this issue was taken to the supreme court of Zimbabwe, and that part of the PVO Act was repealed, received no mention in the state-controlled national press. In 1998, efforts were being made to have the PVO Act repealed entirely on grounds of freedom of speech. Between 1995 and 1997, the PVO Act was a site of a struggle between the state and NGOs over resources.

Although the PVO Act, and the Welfare Act which preceded it, did not have legislative jurisdiction over churches in Zimbabwe, religious NGOs were not outside its scope. They were some of the most vocal opponents of the legislation. Religion was conspicuous by its absence in the PVO Act. Organizations such as the Zimbabwe Council of Churches and the Catholic Commission for Justice and Peace were exempt from the strict regulations to which the NGO, Christian Care, was subject. Recall that Christian Care was created as an arm of the Zimbabwe Council of Churches, set up to handle the political tension

---

6. Interview with Christian Care national executive committee member, Harare, August 14, 1997.

7. NGOs involved in the PVO Campaign were Ecumenical Support Services and the Zimbabwe Council of Churches. Other NGOs that spoke out in protest against the legislation included senior staff from the Lutheran World Federation, the Catholic Commission for Justice and Peace, and EDICESA. For an account of the PVO Campaign, see Rich (1997).

that arose from its activities. It was an organization designed to take the political pressure off the churches. In the 1990s, PVOs (aka NGOs) were development organizations that fell under different legislation than church organizations. However, these distinctions are blurred in practice. PVOs like World Vision and Christian Care worked very closely and collaboratively with local churches. They registered with the state under the PVO Act, but merged with the activities of local, rural churches that sought development projects for their congregational communities.

Christian Care was involved in a complex manner with local churches: they were both the governing structure of the NGO and its membership. The Harare regional director felt that the interaction between the NGO, and churches in communities where the NGO worked, was not well developed. I noticed that there was no accounting of evangelism activities, or any church activities, in the annual or project reports. This had not been the case with World Vision, which supported evangelism rallies at its projects and meticulously documented attendance. The regional manager explained that it was the responsibility of the Zimbabwe Council of Churches (Christian Care's governing body) to concern itself directly with evangelism. As a field officer, he was responsible for overseeing the technical aspects of development projects. He said, "We would rather have Christian Council do the evangelism and we do the development work. This is why you probably couldn't get that message in our reports. Because I guess that is deliberate."

Although he did not consider it part of his job to evangelize per se, he worked with local churches in the field. The churches facilitated the development work of Christian Care by accommodating staff when they made visits to projects, as well as by providing the NGO with background information on communities. Church leaders knew the needs of the communities. As he said, "because they stay with the people I think they are the frontline in terms of information gathering." Churches also made communities aware of the services that Christian Care could offer. At the time of my research, Christian Care was going through a restructuring that would give more power and initiative to the churches, the "membership" of the Zimbabwe Council of Churches. Previously, only churches that were members of the Zimbabwe Council of Churches could participate in the work of Christian Care. The aim of restructuring was to provide more direct links between churches and Christian Care. The regional director explained that in the new structure, "churches have now been asked to be members of Christian Care in their own right. And I think that way I can see churches playing a more facilitatory role in determining the mission of Christian Care." This was, in a way, a return to the more political and historical relationship that Christian Care had with churches, working directly on issues of poverty and welfare. The churches, through the Zimbabwe Council of Churches, formed Christian Care in order to care for political activists who were put in jail during the liberation struggle. In addition to ministering to the detainees, there was the welfare of the families with which to be concerned. Christian Care was formed to provide welfare assistance to those who were being persecuted during the liberation struggle. The Harare regional director explained how two directives intersected, linking politically with the church to bypass the state, and promoting the Christian mission of helping the needy:

> Because Christian Care's beginnings were in the church...how would I put it? The church realized that there was injustice within the previous [colonial] government if I can call it that, the persecution of political activists, their being put in jail. The churches then saw themselves as having a role not only to minister to those who had been detained, but also to meet the needs of their families when they were out. So initially I would put it that way, so it was that fight for justice that the churches saw. Because they were observed and seen as religious groupings, they could not administer to the welfare of these people so they thought of Christian Care.

Since its inception as a political welfare organization, the focus of Christian Care had changed. In the late 1990s, it was focused on "economic injustice" as it assisted the poor. The regional director continued: "We are looking at the poor, those who cannot meet their own needs." After the liberation struggle ended, those who had been assisted by Christian Care became the politicians of the new Zimbabwe, and the policies of Christian Care were set by church leaders. They sat on the National and Regional Councils that governed the NGO. The churches were also actively involved in the development of World Vision. At rural project sites, church leaders sat on local management committees, and World Vision worked directly with churches in providing skills training for development projects (such as dressmaking classes). Both Christian Care and World Vision depended on connections to local church leaders in their development work.

In Zimbabwe, not much importance was placed on whether an NGO was religious or secular. This was perhaps due to the historical role of churches in the provision of agricultural development in the region. While I found that Christian NGOs were more overtly involved in challenging the state than secular NGOs, those that did challenge the state were not involved with economic development. Organizations like the Catholic Commission for Justice and

Peace, Ecumenical Support Services, and the Zimbabwean Council of Churches employed staff to research government policies and present critical evaluations. Christian NGOs tackled some extremely controversial topics.

Secular NGOs, by contrast, were more dependent on the government for political (local and national) support. With less rural infrastructure to rely upon (e.g. no church base), and conspicuous ties to foreign institutions such as the World Bank and the IMF, secular NGOs largely kept quiet during the PVO debates. This is not as counter-intuitive as it may seem. Secular NGOs were reluctant to criticize the government lest work permits be revoked. Directors of secular NGOs told me that their job was not to get involved in local politics; they were not particularly concerned by government efforts to control the activities of NGOs. However, when I asked a field worker for Christian Care about why the Zimbabwean government was so concerned with the activities of NGOs, he said curtly, "Why try to control something if you already have control over it?" With the PVO Act, the government (ZANU-PF) took extra precautions to control the flow of foreign aid. In the midst of such efforts, Christian NGOs such as World Vision and Christian Care negotiated with the state through a politics of transcendence.

The Kingdom of God and Neo-liberal Economics

Using the religious discourse of a Kingdom of God and the neo-liberal economic discourse of free markets, World Vision and Christian Care sought to avoid threats of reprisal from a desperate and volatile state. Although categorized as non-state actors, NGOs were directly involved with the state. This contradictory relationship resembles the ambiguity of colonial missionaries as they supported and challenged the Rhodesian state (Ranger 1962 and Weller and Linden 1984). Most NGOs involved in humanitarian and development work in Zimbabwe—religious and secular—identified themselves as "apolitical." But Ferguson (1994) and others (Worby 1998 and Alexander and McGregor 2000) have shown that development agencies, even when not directly allied with political forces, have distinctly political effects. This apolitical stance of development agencies, the "anti-politics machine," paves the way for the state. Two discourses facilitated this apolitical stance in Zimbabwe: the first was a discourse of the "Kingdom of God" and the second was a discourse of "markets."

Ironically, although World Vision and Christian Care advocated a similar anti-politics, the genesis of each institution arose from highly politicized contexts. World Vision International (the parent organization of World Vision

Zimbabwe) began its work in the late 1940s and was staunchly anti-communist (communist nations did not support Christian organizations). This political agenda continued in post-Cold War attempts to target places such as the newly "free" Soviet Union. A politically "neutral" stance was officially endorsed. For example, in a World Vision interoffice memo from its California office regarding the subject "Writing for World Vision," the following guidelines were proposed: "World Vision articles should not take political positions. The agency's work transcends politics to meet human need wherever and for whatever reason it exists. Articles should not favor or criticize any Christian group, because the agency is non-sectarian and inter-denominational."[8] In email solicitations to support WV USA's international efforts I encountered the following description: "World Vision is an international Christian humanitarian organization serving the world's poor and marginalized by providing programs that help save lives, bring hope, and restore dignity. This assistance is provided without regard to people's religious beliefs, gender, or ethnic background." I will add political affiliation. World Vision insisted on presenting itself as neutral. Christian Care, as the development arm of the Zimbabwe Council of Churches, also emerged from an intensely political history (described earlier) but positioned itself as politically neutral.

The "official" discourse of World Vision International and one that many of its employees had adopted in Zimbabwe was that the NGO transcended politics via the moral order of the "Kingdom of God." The Kingdom of God transcended national boundaries and historic particularities through a universalizing Christian agenda. The Kingdom of God discourse, however, was riddled with contradictions. For instance, its monarchical model and sovereign authority stood in direct contrast to World Vision's democratic structure of a network of "partners" and its mission of "community-based" development. Nonetheless, the aim of transcending political allegiances afforded NGOs like World Vision and Christian Care a particular ease when working in the context of politically volatile situations such as famine and drought, or even with governments on the verge of collapse. One of the six points outlined in World Vision's mission statement was the "promotion of justice that seeks to change unjust structures affecting the poor among whom we work," a goal with obvious political consequences, if not political intent. Mauss (1990 [1950]) has observed that the word commonly known as "alms" is derived from an Arabic word which means "justice." This notion contains the philo-

---

8. Document dated January 4, 1991.

sophical beginnings of the social obligation to give, and of Western forms of charity. In the case of World Vision, employees were not "appeasing the Gods," but were using the implicit link between gift exchange and spiritual forces to transcend worldly political structures that restricted their mobility and made their work impossible. By placing "God as the leader of development" (a phrase repeated by WV Zimbabwe-sponsored communities as well as WV field officers), it created a transcendent sphere of operation, supposedly immune to local politics.

Although NGO employees described their work as apolitical, every employee I spoke with in both Christian and secular NGOs had something to say about politics. Opinions about political engagement varied widely among NGO staff. However, a common discursive thread was that NGO workers operated as impartial interpreters, as agents of change. They were neutral ambassadors of an international civil society. If not the Kingdom of God, then the market offered an anti-political metaphor for NGO activities. For example, the director of CARE Zimbabwe (a secular NGO) defined the mission of his NGO as "facilitating markets." In this case, the NGO transcended politics, and the state, through the neutral zone of "markets" and "choices." NGOs gave people options, the director said, "by creating systems whereby the economies can expand in the rural areas." This involved eliminating "market distortions" created by the colonial state that had restricted the economy of rural areas, and favored the development of a rural labor force for urban industry. One of CARE's primary objectives, as this director saw it, was to liberate market forces through micro-enterprise development programs that made credit more accessible. While this liberation was discussed in terms of breaking down the social and economic barriers that had been installed during colonialism, in practice it involved remaking (or unmaking) the post-colonial state. He explained how CARE was involved in efforts, funded by the IMF and the World Bank, to decentralize the state.[9] CARE was "working at the level of the government":

> The government of Zimbabwe has adopted a policy whereby they are decentralizing a lot of activities down to the district level. Well that's all fine and dandy. You've got to empower the people at the district levels with the skills, the knowledge, and the facilities to be able to make use of that decentralization power that they've just received. So, we are working at the level of the government.

---

9. Makumbe (1996; 1998); Raftopoulos (1991).

Through an apolitical politics that worked to "build local government" and to decentralize the Zimbabwean state, this secular NGO—in its very attempt to strengthen markets—was weakening the existing state. This approach was not without contest among NGO staff. Some employees of Christian NGOs that I spoke with firmly believed that their efforts should not work against the state. Others strongly felt that their mission was to be the state's moral critic. As much as some saw their work as apolitical, others in the same sphere were critical of that stance. Some, such as the Christian Witness Coordinator at World Vision, felt that "NGOs can't afford to be at loggerheads with the government," and that they should never see themselves as working in opposition to the state. If the churches were, as Mugabe proposed in a speech quoted in the local newspaper, to become the moral fiber of the nation, then Christian NGOs were also engaged in taking its moral temperature. There was a symbiotic relationship between churches, Christian NGOs involved in development, and the state. To work in collaboration with the state was the official position of World Vision and Christian Care, as well as every secular development NGO I encountered.

As an example, I offer a picture of a World Vision development project office. Each WV Zimbabwe development project site had an office, consisting of a cement-block house with a desk, chair, bookkeeping ledgers, and a wall with a photomontage. Displayed on heavy construction paper, with visual and textual narratives accounting for the boreholes drilled, latrines dug, and school-blocks built, these montages were evidence of industry and accomplishment. They visually manifested the products of development. In one photo, the national director of WV Zimbabwe resembled a politician campaigning for office, smiling while shaking hands with villagers. This realm of rural development project sites was where local communities worked with local government and NGO field officers to plan, monitor, and conduct "development." The interaction between local government officials and NGO officials commenced during the initial stages of a project. One of the first rituals of an NGO field officer's visit to a rural development site was to stop by the local government office to see either the Rural District Councillor or the District Administrator. This respectful visit garnered permission to continue what NGO staff repeatedly described as "a partnership with local authorities." Indeed, this was a recurring part of an NGO field officer's responsibility. Nonetheless, when I asked members of local development committees at rural project sites how the state, in the form of local government, participated in their development efforts, my question was often met with laughter. Groups of men said "aaaaaaa," and laughed at the ridiculous nature of my enquiry. One group said: "We communicate information to the [District] Councillor, but no response." Another, in the same region, said, "The Rural District Councillor comes through once a month. The MP came once. They convince us with their sweet tongues. At the district level, the council is 60K from here and the MP is in Harare."[10] The state was without resources for development. The "partnership" was a necessary fiction.

This fiction of peaceful partnership and collaboration with the state differed from the more challenging and advocacy-oriented approaches of other Christian NGOs, such as Ecumenical Support Services and the Catholic Commission for Justice and Peace (Dorman 2002; Ndegwa 1996). Notably, NGOs involved in advocacy were not involved in programs of economic development. What was it about development that was both extremely political and required the denial of political engagement? While churches like the Catholic Commission for Justice and Peace were actively challenging some government policies, many churches and Christian NGOs were involved with development work that the government depended upon. This was the contradiction of Christian development NGOs, a contradiction of being on the forefront of politics and striving to transcend it.

Despite the discourses of the Kingdom of God and liberal markets that framed the work of Christian NGOs as politically neutral, the development work of religious NGOs was intensely political. Indeed, in the late 1990s their work was a rather desperate platform for party politics. Due to the impacts of structural adjustment, the state had limited development funds. NGOs, on the other hand, provided access to resources but relied on permission from local state officials to carry out their projects. NGO employees described their work as being "in collaboration" with local government officials. This dynamic set up a series of tensions in which the state was so weak that it begged NGOs to continue their development work, and simultaneously tried to take credit for it. To illustrate this precarious and political dynamic, I offer three ethnographic examples.

The first example took place in March of 1997, when I travelled with two field officers from Christian Care to visit projects in Hurungwe, north-western Zimbabwe. After stopping by the farmer-cooperatives that the NGO had assisted, the field officers attended a meeting with three regional officers from Agritex (the Ministry of Agricultural Extension and Rural Resettlement). During the meeting, local government officials asked Christian Care for funds to support a regional plan that would, as they explained, "outline well-planned villages." They said, "The government wants to create well-planned villages. Planning gives direction to everybody." The meeting was a sad affair.

---

10. WV Zimbabwe projects, Maparaidze and Chirariro.

The Agritex officers spoke of how the state lacked resources for national level planning, and that the state was broke. The three Agritex officers had not been reimbursed for their petrol expenses in months. The Christian Care staff were accustomed to such requests from the state, but could not meet its demand, their funding was allocated for small-scale projects, not national planning. The NGO employees delicately expressed their regrets to Agritex. In this setting, the state was not only unable to pay for "planning"; it was precariously feeble. Despite these weaknesses, however, the state attempted to look strong.

Attempts by state actors to appear strong are clearly visible in my second example, which is a graduation ceremony at a World Vision project in northwestern Zimbabwe. Along with speeches, there were praise songs, and a parade of final projects designed by dressmaking students. As each proud graduate-to-be modeled their tailoring, the audience sang, clapped, and danced. Husbands danced their wives down the aisles. Certificates were distributed to graduates. The students, dressed in blue and white uniforms and clustered on one side of the room, formed a dressmaking choir. They sang Shona praise songs about Jesus and dressmaking.

As a pastor began her sermon, a truck-full of ZANU-PF representatives raced through the door in a dramatic entrance. They came late and stole the show, pulling up to the door in a white Jeep with ZANU-PF stencilled on its side. As they piled out of the truck, their presence was loud and official. The dressmaking choir switched the words of their songs to praise ZANU-PF as the five representatives of the state paraded in and took seats facing the large audience. Embodying the state, the Rural District Councillor introduced the ZANU-PF party member, the construction officer, an Agritex officer, the District Chairman for ZANU-PF, the District Administrator, and a woman representing the chairwoman of the ZANU-PF Women's League who could not attend. Three government representatives stood up to make speeches; each speech took credit for the development work of World Vision, which was planning to pull out of the project in the coming months. This transition, a passing on of development from the NGO and community to the community and state, was dangerous in its liminality. Local government officials begged the church collaborating with World Vision to stay, and took credit for the development work of the NGO and community. An Agritex officer stood up and encouraged people to cooperate with donors and projects to "raise themselves up." She encouraged the community to believe in God, to work together, and to work with the churches. She spoke of how the district used to be "the most poor in the country." After two years of the dressmaking classes "we are more developed," she said. The ZANU-PF district representative begged World Vision not to leave. His speech was framed in distinctly moral terms, as he urged the community to work with the church, to concentrate on development (in contrast to gossip), and to work in harmony to make money:

> To World Vision I am saying: Don't leave us. We are begging you to keep on helping us, and to [the church]: to keep on helping us and bringing us to God. In the community we need not to gossip but to concentrate on development. Not on this and that which are bad words....I love people who live in harmony. If you are not sick, if you are not in prison, if you are not in bad mental health, there is nothing to stop you from making money.

Harmony and moneymaking, these were the possibilities that NGOs such as World Vision offered. The district representative made promises that extended beyond the confines of the classroom block. After promising to bring the development concerns of the community to the attention of parliament, and to encourage the building of a factory in the area that promised new jobs, he asked World Vision to stay, again, so that he could be re-elected:

> I am going to ask parliament to come and see what you are doing. Even donors will source more funds to help people who are doing so well. I am going to tell your MP to make a factory here, and to encourage your MP to come and see how things are starting to move... World Vision should remain here in the province so I will also be able to remain here as the district head.[11]

The development work of World Vision, in collaboration with a local church, was a key resource for the state. Yet NGO workers spoke of their work as transcending local politics to alleviate poverty in allegiance with the Kingdom of God. This politics of transcendence, distinctly apolitical, facilitated interaction with the state.

My third example is a case in which the anniversary celebrations of Christian Care became a desperate platform for state politics. Christian Care's 30th anniversary celebrations were held in October of 1997 at rural project sites. The rationale for setting the celebrations at project sites instead of in an urban area was to emphasize that development was for the people being developed. One field officer explained it to me as bringing development back to the peo-

---

11. WV Zimbabwe project, Kasonde.

ple. Aside from the 200 or so community members who came for this particular event, which incidentally involved a free meal, the state was on parade. In attendance were the following local authorities: a Member of Parliament (MP), Chief Seke, the District Administrator, several Agritex officers (from the Department of Agricultural, Technical and Extension Services, Ministry of Agricultural Extension and Rural Resettlement, Government of Zimbabwe), someone from ARDA (Agricultural and Rural Development Authority), a representative from the Ministry of National Affairs and Cooperative Development, two representatives from the Ministry of Health, a woman from the Ministry of Information, and the District Councillor. How, I wondered, was this placing development in the hands of the people?

The local MP, from the central committee of ZANU-PF, arrived two hours late with big fanfare; the agenda of the celebrations had been rearranged in anticipation of his arrival. He dressed formally in a full suit and yellow tie on this hot day. His cell phone rang conspicuously during his speech. He began his speech with party slogans: *"Pamberi ZANU-PF, Pamberi President Robert Mugabe"* ("Forward with ZANU-PF, forward with Robert Mugabe"). Christian Care was "complementing government efforts," he said, and spoke of the challenges of finding markets for the products of the cooperative. Then he began making promises. He promised that 1/4 tons of poultry or pig feed would be given to the co-op. He said he had written to a number of organizations for donations, and handed out bank brochures for the National Credit and Savings Society, in anticipation of all the money the community would ostensibly be making. He said donors from the USA would be installing electricity and building houses in the area in December. "From 100 houses will be increased to 150 at Christmas time. Tiles will be manufactured locally so they will place a big order. There will be training for tile makers." The MP was full of promises of good fortune: he positioned himself as a saviour. Following this speech, a Christian Care staff member gave him a T-Shirt with "Christian Care 30 Years of Hope" printed across the front. The invited church choir sang a song whose words translated as "those people who are lazy, they can join cooperatives."[12] The choir sang thanking Mugabe for his support. They sang to thank the MP, the Councillor for the area, Christian Care, and all the government ministries that supported them. Development in this context was more of a theater for politicians than "for the people." The politicians took credit for the work of the NGO and the community, and used the celebration

---

12. I also heard this song sung at World Vision projects.

as a platform for campaigning. Chief Seke was the only individual who was publicly critical of the project. He criticized the cleanliness of the livestock pens, and commented on the small profits that had been reaped.

Conclusion

In his essay, *The Poor*, Georg Simmel (1994 [1908]) describes how charitable giving serves to support the status quo. He writes, "the motive for alms then resides exclusively in the significance of giving for the giver. When Jesus told the wealthy young man, "Give your riches to the poor," what apparently mattered to him were not the poor, but rather the soul of the wealthy man for whose salvation this sacrifice was merely a means or a symbol" (153). He elaborates that assistance is a symptom and necessity of socio-structural inequities: "the goal of assistance is precisely to mitigate certain extreme manifestations of social differentiation, so that the social structure may continue to be based on this differentiation" (155). The social aim is consequently to maintain a status quo. The haves constitute the needs of the have-nots; poverty as a social phenomenon is defined by those who attempt to alleviate it. When giving is institutionalized, it is abstracted and removed from its sensate form. When giving becomes the obligation of states and institutions (such as NGOs) instead of individuals, the poor are removed from the functional means-ends teleology of maintaining the status quo.

Giving through states or NGOs may not be styled as giving at all. For example, in the early socialist era of independent Zimbabwe, development (and social welfare) was an entitlement. In the neo-liberal paradigm of the late 1990s, however, development had once again become a charitable act. While welfare states speak of entitlements, NGO discourse, in contrast, has moved toward a charity model. In this model, NGOs act as agents of the political and funding initiatives of wealthy nations, or "international civil society" (cf.Hanlon 2000). The relevance of Simmel's point to the work of NGOs in Zimbabwe is that once giving is institutionalized it is no longer about human suffering. The effect is that the status quo is reified for those who are giving assistance. The poor, the recipients of aid are simultaneously within and without the group. Akin to Simmel's concept of the stranger—an outsider who is nevertheless an integral part of the collectivity by his very alien status—the social poor are no longer those who lack means or "suffer specific deficiencies and deprivations, but those who receive assistance or should receive it according to social norms" (Simmel 1994 [1908]: 175). It is in this way that categories such as "beneficiaries," "civil society," and "the state" are reified and taken for granted.

This was clearly expressed during one rather boring interview about development with a projects officer in the Church and Development Program of the Zimbabwe Council of Churches, the NGO employee made a startling assertion about the importance of Christian development for keeping Zimbabweans peaceful. He said, "Without such assistance, it will be difficult: socially, politically. Our government alone cannot support these projects. If there are no water projects, aspects like hygiene, diversification, micro-projects...If people don't have the basics that will spill into riots, social commotion will result in civil wars. A lack of basic infrastructure and commodities will create gaps in classes and at the end of the day it will cause social repercussions, problems." The development of Christian NGOs was a form of charity funded by donors in other nations, not an entitlement of Zimbabwean citizens.

Perhaps such charity did serve to maintain the status quo, and keep people from rebelling against the state. In the late 1990s, it was in the interest of the Zimbabwean state to appear to have strong national development, a strong economy, and a sector of small-scale farmers who were peaceful and harmonious. When members of this sector had food in their bellies, they were less likely to riot for food, to complain about government, and to threaten the social order. Perhaps the contemporary land question in Zimbabwe echoes early post-independence discourses of development that expressed a more radical (and political) agenda of social equity and redistribution of wealth. As an ethnographer, I also found it difficult to navigate the terrain of politics that must be transcended. In the field I did not see myself as apolitical, although I was not sure where my allegiances lay. In discussions with NGO employees I often brought up politics. Yet I was also aware that the subject was delicate and dangerous. NGOs were in a precarious relationship with the state. In order to continue my research, I too had to frame my work as transcendent and neutral. I too, alongside the NGO employees I worked with, soon faced the realities of this impossibility. I was seen by rural communities as part of the NGO staff: rich, white, and able to help, although I was not. Perhaps this simultaneous helplessness and political engagement could only be expressed through a discourse of transcendence.

Works Cited

Alexander, J. and J. McGregor. 2000. Wildlife and politics: CAMPFIRE in Zimbabwe. *Development and Change* 31 (3): 605–27.

Bayart, J-F. 1993. *The State in Africa: The politics of the belly*. New York: Longman.

Beckman, B. 1993. The liberation of civil society: neo-liberal ideology and political theory. *Review of African Political Economy* 58: 20–33.

Bond, P. 1991. Geopolitics, international finance and national capital accumulation—Zimbabwe in the 1980s and 1990s. *Tijdschrift Voor Economische En Sociale Geografie* 82 (5): 325–37.

———. 1998. *Uneven Zimbabwe: A study of finance, development, and underdevelopment*. Trenton, NJ: Africa World Press.

Bornstein, E. 2001. Child sponsorship, evangelism, and belonging in the work of World Vision Zimbabwe. *American Ethnologist* 28 (3): 595–622.

———. 2003. *The Spirit of Development: Protestant NGOs, morality, and economics in Zimbabwe*. New York and London: Routledge.

Bratton, M. 1989a. Beyond the state: civil society and associational life in Africa. *World Politics* 41 (3): 407–30.

———. 1989b. The politics of government-NGO relations in Africa. *World Development* 17 (4): 569–87.

Chatterjee, P. 1990. A response to Taylor's "modes of civil society". *Public Culture* 3 (1): 119–32.

Chazan, N. 1994. Engaging the state: associational life in sub-Saharan Africa. In *State Power and Social Forces: Domination and transformation in the Third World*, edited by J. S. Midgal, A. Kohli and V. Shue. Cambridge: Cambridge University Press.

Clark, A.M. 1995. Non-governmental organizations and their influence on international society. *Journal of International Affairs* 48 (2): 507–25.

Clark, J. 1991. *Democratizing Development*. Hartford, Connecticut: Kumarian Press.

Cohen, J. and Andrew A. 1992. *Civil Society and Political Theory*. Cambridge, MA: MIT Press.

Comaroff, J. and J.L. Comaroff. 1991. *Of Revelation and Revolution: Christianity, colonialism and consciousness in South Africa. Vol. 1*. Chicago: University of Chicago Press.

Comaroff, J.L. and J. Comaroff. 1997. *Of Revelation and Revolution: The dialectics of modernity on a South African frontier. Vol. 2*. Chicago: University of Chicago Press.

———. 1999. *Civil Society and the Political Imagination in Africa: Critical perspectives*. Chicago: University of Chicago Press.

Diamond, L. 1994. Rethinking civil society: Toward democratic consolidation. *Journal of Democracy* 5 (3): 4–17.

Dorman, S. 2002. Rocking the boat? Church-NGOs and democratization in Zimbabwe. *African Affairs* 101: 75–92.

Eyoh, D. 1996. From economic crisis to political liberalization: pitfalls of the new political sociology for Africa. *African Studies Review* 39 (3): 43–80.

Farrington, J., A. Bebbington, K. Wellard, and D. Lewis. 1993. *Reluctant Partners? Non-governmental organizations, the state and sustainable agricultural development*. London & New York: Routledge.

Ferguson, J. 1994. *The Anti-Politics Machine: "Development", depoliticization, and bureaucratic power in Lesotho*. Minneapolis: University of Minnesota Press.

———. 1999. *Expectations of Modernity: Myths and meanings of urban life on the Zambian Copperbelt*: University of California Press.

———. 2002. Of mimicry and membership: Africans and the "New World Society". *Cultural Anthropology* 17 (4): 551–69.

Ferguson, J. and A. Gupta. 2002. Spatializing states: governmentality in Africa and India. *American Ethnologist* 29 (4): 981–1003.

Fisher, William F. 1997. Doing good? the politics and antipolitics of NGO practices. In *Annual Review of Anthropology* 26: 439–64.

Gifford, P. 1994. Some recent developments in African Christianity. *African Affairs* 93: 513–34.

Gramsci, A. 1991. *Selections From the Prison Notebooks of Antonio Gramsci*. Translated by Q. Hoare and G. N. Smith. New York: International Publishers.

Gundani, P. 1988. The Catholic church and national development in independent Zimbabwe. In *Church and State in Zimbabwe*, edited by C. F. Hallencreutz and A. M. Moyo. Harare: Mambo Press.

Guyer, J. 1994. The spatial dimensions of civil society in Africa: an anthropologist looks at Nigeria. In *Civil Society and the State in Africa*, edited by J. W. Harbeson, D. Rothchild and N. Chazan. Boulder, CO: Lynne Rienner.

Gyimah-Boadi, E. 1996. Civil society in Africa. *Journal of Democracy* 7 (2): 118–32.

Hall, S. 1986. Gramsci's relevance for the study of race and ethnicity. *Journal of Communication Inquiry* 10 (2): 5–27.

———. 1988. Gramsci and us. In *The Hard Road to Renewal: Thatcherism and the crisis of the left*, edited by S. Hall. London: Verso.

Hallencreutz, C. E. 1988. A Council in Crossfire: ZCC 1964–1980. In *Church and State in Zimbabwe*, edited by C. F. Hallencreutz and A. M. Moyo. Gweru: Mambo Press.

————. 1988. Ecumenical challenges in independent Zimbabwe: ZCC 1980–1985. In *Church and State in Zimbabwe*, edited by C. F. Hallencreutz and A. M. Moyo. Gweru: Mambo Press.

Hallencreutz, C. and A. Moyo. 1988. *Church and State in Zimbabwe*. Gweru: Mambo Press.

Hancock, G. 1989. *Lords of Poverty: The power, prestige and corruption of the international aid business*. New York: Atlantic Monthly Press.

Hanlon, J. 2000. An 'ambitious and extensive political agenda': the role of NGOs and the AID Industry. In *Global Institutions and Local Empowerment: Competing theoretical perspectives*, edited by K. Stiles. New York: St. Martins Press.

Harbeson, J., D. Rothchild, and N. Chazan. 1994. *Civil Society and the State in Africa*. Boulder, CO: Lynne Rienner.

Herbst, J. 1990. *State Politics in Zimbabwe*. Harare: University of Zimbabwe.

Hyden, G, and M. Bratton, eds. 1992. *Governance and Politics in Africa*. Boulder, CO: Lynne Reinner.

Keane, J., ed. 1988. *Civil Society and the State: New European perspectives*. New York: Verso.

Keck, M.and K. Sikkink. 1998. *Activists Beyond Borders: Advocacy networks in international politics*. Ithaca: Cornell University Press.

Kilby, C. 2000. Sovereignty and NGOs. In *Global Institutions and Local Empowerment: Competing theoretical perspectives*, edited by K. Stiles. New York: St. Martins.

Leftwich, A. 1994. Governance, the state and the politics of development. *Development and Change* 25: 363–86.

Makumbe, J. 1996. *Participatory Development: The case of Zimbabwe*. Harare: University of Zimbabwe.

————. 1998. *Democracy and Development in Zimbabwe: Constraints of decentralisation*. Harare: SAPES Books.

Mamdani, M. 1996. *Citizen and Subject: Contemporary Africa and the legacy of late colonialism*. Princeton, NJ: Princeton University Press.

Mararike, C. G. 1995. *Grassroots Leadership: The process of rural development in Zimbabwe*. Harare: University of Zimbabwe.

Marcussen, H. 1996. NGOs, the state and civil society. *Review of African Political Economy* 69: 405–23.

Maren, M. 1997. *The Road to Hell: The ravaging effects of foreign aid and international charity*. New York: The Free Press.

Marx, K. 1975 [1843]. On the Jewish question. In *Early Writings*, New York: Vintage.

Mauss, M. 1990 [1950]. *The Gift.* New York & London: W.W. Norton.

Maxwell, D. 1995. The church and democratisation in Africa: the case of Zimbabwe. In *The Christian Churches and the Democratisation of Africa*, edited by P. Gifford, pp. 109–29. Leiden, New York & Koln: E.J. Brill.

———. 1998. Delivered from the spirit of poverty? Pentecostalism, prosperity and modernity in Zimbabwe. *Journal of Religion in Africa* 28 (3): 350–73.

———. 2000. 'Catch the cockerel before dawn': pentecostalism and politics in postcolonial Zimbabwe. *Africa* 70 (2): 249–77.

Moore, D. 1999. The crucible of cultural politics: reworking "development" in Zimbabwe's Eastern Highlands. *American Ethnologist* 26 (3): 654–89.

Moyo, S. 1991. *NGO advocacy in Zimbabwe: systematising an old function or inventing a new role?* Vol. No. 1, *IDS Working Papers*. Harare: ZERO Publications.

Munro, W. 1998. *The Moral Economy of the State: Conservation, community development, and state making in Zimbabwe. Monographs in International Studies Africa Series No. 68.* Athens, OH: Ohio University Center for International Studies.

Ndegwa, S. 1994. Civil society and political change in Africa: the case of non-governmental organizations in Kenya. *International Journal of Comparative Sociology* 35 (1–2): 19–36.

———. 1996. *The Two Faces of Civil Society: NGOs and politics in Africa.* Hartford, Connecticut: Kumarian Press.

Potts, D. 1998. Basics are now a luxury: perceptions of structural adjustment's impact on rural and urban areas in Zimbabwe. *Environment and Urbanization* 10 (1): 55–75.

Raftopoulos, B. 1991. *Beyond the House of Hunger: The struggle for democratic development in Zimbabwe.* Harare: Zimbabwe Institute of Development Studies.

Ranger, T. O. 1962. *State and Church in Southern Rhodesia 1919–1939.* Salisbury, Southern Rhodesia: Historical Association of Rhodesia and Nyasaland.

Rea, W. F. 1962. *The Missionary Factor in Southern Rhodesia.* Salisbury: Historical Association of Rhodesia and Nyasaland.

Rich, S. 1997. The state of NGOs in Zimbabwe: honeymoon over? *Southern Africa Report* 12 (3): 17–20.

Riddell, R. and M. Robinson. 1995. *Non-Governmental Organizations and Rural Poverty Alleviation.* Oxford: Clarendon Press.

Riles, A. 2000. *The Network Inside Out.* Ann Arbor: University of Michigan.

Robins, S. 1994. Contesting the social geometry of state power: a case study of land-use planning in Matabeleland, Zimbabwe. *Social Dynamics* 20 (2): 91–118.

Rutherford, B. 2000. Learning about power: development and marginality in an adult literacy center for farm workers in Zimbabwe. *American Ethnologist* 27 (4): 839–54.

Sachikonye, L. 1995. Democracy, civil society and social movements: an analytical framework. In: *Democracy, Civil Society and the State: social movements in Southern Africa*, edited by L. Sachikonye, Harare: SAPES Books.

Sachikonye, L. 1995. From 'equity' and 'participation' to structural adjustment: state and social forces in Zimbabwe. In *Debating Development Discourse*, edited by D. Moore and G. J. Schmitz. New York: St. Martin's.

Simmel, G. 1994 [1908]. The poor. In *On Individuality and Social Forms*, edited by D. N. Levine. Chicago: University of Chicago Press.

Taylor, C. 1990. Modes of civil society. *Public Culture* 3 (1): 95–118.

Tendler, J. 1975. *Inside Foreign Aid*. Baltimore & London: The Johns Hopkins University Press.

Turner, M. and D. Hulme. 1997. *Governance, Administration and Development: Making the state work*. Hartford, CT: Kumarian Press.

Vakil, A. 1997. Confronting the classification problem: toward a taxonomy of NGOs. *World Development* 25 (12): 2057–70.

Walzer, M., ed. 1995. *Toward a Global Civil Society*. Providence, RI: Berghahn Books.

Weisgrau, M. 1997. *Interpreting Development: Local histories, local strategies*. New York: University Press of America.

Wellard, K. and J. Copestake. 1993. *Non-Governmental Organizations and the State in Africa: Rethinking sustainable agricultural development*. New York: Routledge.

Weller, J. and J. Linden. 1984. *Mainstream Christianity to 1980 in Malawi, Zambia and Zimbabwe*. Gweru: Mambo Press.

Williams, D. 1993. Review article: liberalism and development discourse. *Africa* 63 (3): 419–29.

Williams, D. and T. Young. 1994. Governance, the World Bank and liberal theory. *Political Studies* XLII: 84-100.

Woods, D. 1992. Civil society in Europe and Africa: limiting state power through a public sphere. *African Studies Review* 35 (2): 77-100.

Worby, E. 1998. Inscribing the state at the "edge of beyond:" danger and development in North-Western Zimbawe. *Political and Legal Anthropology Review* 21 (2): 55-70.

CHAPTER 4

Leader in the Human Rights Sector: The Paradoxical Institutionalization of a Kenyan NGO

Marie-Emmanuelle Pommerolle
Centre d'Etudes d'Afrique Noire, Bordeaux
mepommerolle@free.fr

Introduction

Academics tend to dismiss human rights NGOs as donors' marionettes, while African states often accuse them of being foreign agents; however, there are rather few concrete studies of African NGOs, and even fewer of human rights NGOs. The research conducted on such actors tends to be either normative or focused on the international dimensions of transnational human rights diffusion (Welch 1995; Ambrose 1995; Risse, Ropp, and Sikkink 1999; Schmitz 1999). More generally the paradigm of *dependency* which dominated studies on the African state in the seventies has returned to explain the emergence of actors such as NGOs in the nineties. The emphasis on external factors can be explained by the fact that most NGOs have been born out of or helped by donors' will and funding, in a context of externally encouraged democratic change. Yet NGOs deserve to be analyzed in the same way as any other social or political group, and the individual trajectories and moral views of the actors inside them need to be taken into account if we are to understand their organizational logic and their differential impact on the political environment (Dezalay and Garth 2002).

In order to understand the strengths and weaknesses of any particular NGO, it is necessary to situate it in historical context. In the Kenyan case, it is important to explain the legacy of past authoritarian regimes and the strategies of resistance to them, as well as the strategic move by individuals to situate the role of newly created pressure groups within that legacy. That is what I will do by studying the KHRC, a "second generation" human rights group whose present is determined by past trajectories of opposition and by the capacity of its members to mobilize such history and to transcend and shape it to their advantage (Kibwana 1998).

The Kenya Human Rights Commission (KHRC) was registered in Kenya in 1994 to promote and defend human rights in that country. From the beginning, it has had to negotiate a field of opportunities and constraints that is shaped, on the one hand, by its dependence on foreign funds, and, on the other, by its vulnerability to attacks by the Kenyan state. This chapter will argue that it has managed these conflicting demands with some success. Far from being considered a puppet of either donors or the state, this NGO has become a well-respected group in Kenyan civil society, a feared lobby by the government, a think tank where foreign and Kenyan researchers collect information, and a base for alternative political leadership. This is the result of efforts by the diverse members of the NGO to gain autonomy and to accommodate external pressures with their own perceptions of their work and ideals.

The first section of this chapter provides a brief history of Kenyan opposition, its people and its struggles, from where human rights activists of the 1990s originate. Their distinctive oppositional culture has a wide impact on today's strengths and contradictions of the NGO. Born out of political struggle and openness, and out of fresh and early donors' money, the KHRC will indeed have to reconcile this oppositional culture embodied by different generations of opponents with its relationships to foreign actors and the state. The second part deals with the internal struggles and organizational dynamics stirred by those tensions. I will show in a third part that the success of the NGO has been achieved via its capacity to root its claims in local political discourse and to adapt to external injunctions. While stressing the KHRC's success, I will also look briefly at the new challenges posed by the victory of its political allies in December 2002, and its new stance toward the state which has been, all along, its intimate enemy.

A Sociology of Actors:
Successive Generations of Opponents

Over the past half century Kenya has given birth to succeeding generations of political opposition. In the 1950s, Mau Mau guerrillas fought against the structures of colonial rule (Lonsdale and S. Odhiambo 2003); after independence, the ruling party KANU fractured into a left and right wing, leading to the formation of a breakaway party, the Kenya People's Union; in the 1970s politicians within parliament criticized the government for abandoning the ideals of the Mau Mau struggle; in 1982 dissent and opposition moved to the university and underground; in the mid-80s public defiance of the regime was expressed by professional communities—most notably lawyers and religious leaders—in face of arbitrary detentions and further manipulation of judicial and political rules (Dauch 1983; Widner 1992: 177–78; Ross 1992; Maupeu 1995). It is the generation of dissidents from the bloody struggles of the 1980s who have been at the heart of the NGO movement. Lawyers, in particular, have used a human rights discourse to critique the regime.[1] Strengthened by international links, these groups have denounced human rights abuses by the regime, and become, with the support of foreign embassies, the main proponents of the reintroduction of multipartyism, which occurred in 1991 (Throup and Hornsby 1998).

In 1992 five Kenyans, two of whom were in political exile, created the KHRC in North America.[2] Lawyers, academics, and journalists, their aim was to counter the pro-Moi lobby in Washington. When it was registered in Kenya

---

1. The human rights argument was developed in the legal community by the International Commission of Jurists (Kenya-section) created in 1952, and vocal from the mid-1980s. Human rights were also enunciated by individual lawyers, and expressed by the *Nairobi Law Monthly*, also from the mid-80s. During the 1990s, a number of legal associations worked on human rights, and the Law Society of Kenya, dominated by liberal lawyers, became also vocal on the issue.

2. The five were: Makau wa Mutua, a former student leader at the University of Nairobi, doctor in law, and employee of the Lawyers Committee for Human Rights (USA); Maina Kiai, masters student in law in Harvard, intern in Transafrica and organizer of demonstrations against the Kenya regime in Washington; Peter Kareithi, former journalist at the *Weekly Review*; Kiraitu Murungi, a lawyer who had to flee Kenya facing detention without trial; Willy Mutunga, former lecturer at the University of Nairobi, writing his law doctorate in Toronto. See, Muntunga, W., *Constitution-making from the middle. Civil society and transition politics in Kenya 1992–1997*, SAREAT (Nairobi, Mwengo, Harare, 1999), pp. 68–69.

two years later, these leaders decided to focus on denouncing human rights abuses, as they had already started to do with their first publications in 1992 and 1993.[3] Funded from the beginning by the FORD Foundation and the Swedish Foundation for human rights, it also enjoyed support from fellow lawyers in Kenya from whom it received moral and material support.[4] Two of the KHRC leaders had been prominent teachers at the University of Nairobi in the 1970s.[5] In the 1990s this gave them notoriety among their former students and among the liberal lawyers. Besides links with the legal profession, the KHRC leaders also had relationships with former underground activists. Mutunga, and Mazrui had themselves spent time in prison, and Mutunga was a member of the December 12th Movement.[6]

When the need for research and administrative staff arose, these men hired younger opposition activists who had been prominent in the 1980s. According to some of them, this was a deliberate move by activist members of the Board who wanted to diversify and politicize their HR struggle: "Who else could I hire? Only these guys had shown any commitment to HR and nobody else could employ them".[7] Some of the new hired staff had spent time in prison and had been in exile elsewhere in East Africa. Engaged in political and student activism in the 1980s and then imprisoned, some of them were not able to finish their education and found most employers reluctant to hire them given their well known opposition past. Their work in the KHRC was a good opportunity for them to find employment and to continue their struggle against the regime. As I shall show later, the presence of these activists had a strong influence on the way the NGO initially carried out its activities and balanced the legal inflexion of its main partners and founding members. The 1980s activists were joined by a new generation

---

3. KHRC, *Haven of repression: a report on the University of Nairobi and academic freedom in Kenya* (Nairobi, 1992); KHRC, *Slow torture: a report on the deprivation of medical care to the treason four in Kenya* (Nairobi, 1992); KHRC, b *The fallen angel: a report on the performance of Amos Wako in promoting human rights and democracy as Kenya's Attorney General* (Nairobi, 1993); KHRC, *State of human rights in Kenya: a year of political harassment* (Nairobi, 1993).

4. When it settled in Nairobi, the KHRC was hosted by Kamau Kuria and Kiraitu Murungi Advocates, two famous human rights lawyers.

5. Mutunga was a lecturer of law and Mazrui a linguistic professor.

6. See Mutunga, W., "About the author", in Mutunga, W., *Constitution-making from the middle. Civil society and transition politics in Kenya 1992–1997*, SAREAT, Nairobi, Mwengo, Harare, 1999.

7. Electronic interview, March 2002

made of students who engaged in politics through student unions and associations at the beginning of the 1990s and wished to continue it. This last group brought knowledge and combined technologies of struggle with original artistic repertoires of action. As non-lawyers with a history of directly confronting the state, these successive generations developed an activist and highly visible image for the KHRC on which it still trades, in rhetoric if less so in reality.

A Sociology of Action: External Shocks, Internal Struggles and Changes of Strategies

More recently, the activist core of the KHRC has been joined by an influx of "professional" NGO workers, partly as a result of donor demands. The Board of the NGO decided to introduce a new internal structure and a change of strategy. It welcomed people from different backgrounds, especially from the "private sector", and it introduced what one staff member called a "manager mentality". This led to "ideological differences" between the Board and the activist staff. After an internal audit and a reorganization of work in 1998 and 1999, the most radical officers of the KHRC were progressively sacked on the grounds of their "inefficiency".[8] Professional people, whose careers have started in NGOs, and who see themselves not as activists but as "human rights defenders" replaced them.[9] While these different kinds of personnel were still cohabiting, there were strong tensions between them. Eventually, the professionals stayed, and the activists left. Donors approved this move and believe that this change in recruitment is the reason for KHRC's current success: "Now they do less advocacy, they sing and dance less in the streets, and are more professional".[10]

The struggle within KHRC is part of a broader trend in the human rights sector, which has responded to the increased availability of donor funds with rationalization and professionalization. Although most old members of the human rights struggle understand this move, they blame it for declining morale and honest commitment to the struggle. A member of Release Political Prisoners, a human rights pressure group closely related to the KHRC, where donor funding came after years of voluntary work, stated that before:

---

8. Interviews with two of these former staff members, Nairobi, 2001 and 2002.
9. Interview with a staff member hired in 1998, Nairobi, 2000.
10. Interview with a donor, Nairobi, August 2001.

everybody gave a contribution. But then when we received funding there were problems. As soon as there is money, there is a problem: "who gets hired, who doesn't."[11]

Another member stated that:

"Since donors started giving us money, people are more worried about keeping time and about their files. Activism in the streets and in the communities came to a slow down; before you were doing it from your heart and just because a program officer is not available did not mean you cannot work. Now, nobody will go anywhere if there is no allowance. Not even the members".[12]

In KHRC, one staff member finds it difficult to "find a balance between the level of commitment of professionals and activists".[13] The dedication in work from the "activist members" who stayed has declined while everybody was asked to nurture "the culture of excellence, hard work." According to the 2001 strategic Plan, the KHRC "has failed sometimes miserably in meeting crucial deadlines. The culture of doing more work than assigned still remains a dream since I cannot finish what has been assigned in time." Thus, the new strategy is accompanied by a system of rewards, because "We cannot build a dedicated, professional and skilled staff if we do not reward excellence".[14] This new approach of professional commitment is clearly different from the moral commitment of former staff who expected rewards in terms of successful HR achievements.

These conflicts were illustrated in a tragic episode, when Father Anthony Kaiser, an American priest engaged in human rights in Kenya, was found dead on a road on August 24, 2000.[15] This news saddened and angered the human rights community which used to work in cooperation with this outspoken man who defied the most powerful and corrupted men of Moi's regime.[16] The press was soon claiming that he had been assassinated and some KHRC members decided to rouse the human rights Network (HRN), a loose group of NGOs working in the field, to strongly demand the truth about this death. The NGO members thought it would be a good idea to take part in Kaiser's funeral. During the two meetings to prepare the HRN contribution to the fu-

---

11. Interview, Nairobi, August 2001.
12. Interview, Nairobi, August 2002.
13. Interview, Nairobi, August 2000.
14. KHRC, Strategic Plan (Nairobi, 2001).
15. I was then an intern in the KHRC (July–August 2000).
16. *Daily Nation*, "Outspoken priest died as he lived," 26 August 2002.

neral, strong divergences arose between different generations and types of activist. In addition to the cleavage between the Catholic representatives and the rest, and between the generalist NGOs and the legal ones, there were strong discussions between "activists" and "professionals". The former wanted to demonstrate strongly their defiance of the regime by organizing a demonstration around Kaiser's coffin on the way to the Church, and by burning Moi's effigy in front of the President's offices (which they eventually did in front of stunned police). They refused to be told by "wiser activists" that they had to respect Kaiser's dignity, because in their opinion they had always acted with dignity. For them, it was the police and hired thugs who created violence, not them. At the same time they expressed their fear of being abandoned on the day of the demonstration. They suspected that the "heads" of the NGOs would not keep their promise to come. Within KHRC, the staff were divided. Only the "activists" took part in the event. For them, this kind of action, advocacy and rapid response to human rights abuses, should be their only activity because that is what they know how to do.

Confrontation or Cooperation

The question of knowledge and strategy is now at the center of internal conflicts in the human rights group. It is moreover determined by external injunctions from donors and the State. A good example of this is the shift in advocacy toward police abuses, which has been a permanent target of the KHRC, and which highlights the constraints, adjustments and contradictions faced by the Kenyan organization throughout its ten-year history.

The KHRC started its denunciations of police abuses by bringing the issue to public light through alternative and original collective action. In 1997, one of the first public advocacy campaigns was launched over police extra-judicial killings. Though not a new issue, the *Quarterly Human Rights Reports* of the KHRC counted close to a thousand killings from 1994 to 2000.[17] Disappointed by the unsatisfying responses by the Attorney General, the KHRC decided to organize demonstrations where people would carry the coffins of victims of extra-judicial killing. The reaction of the press and the government was mixed as they claimed the practices were "weird" and contrary to "African tradition".[18]

---

17. KHRC, *Quarterly human rights Report*, vol. 2, N°2, April–June 2000 (the Quarterly was formerly entitled *Quarterly Repression Report*) (Nairobi, 2000).

18. Citizens "discover" a new form of protest, *East African Standard*, 28 April 1997 and "Demo with corpse halted," *Daily Nation*, 12 April 1997.

However, the demonstrations were appropriated by people and the press eventually reported them without any comment.[19] Imitating practices seen in South Africa, the initiators succeeded in attracting attention and renewing the form of demonstrations, which became a "routine" of protest in Nairobi from the beginning of the 1990s. However, if these demos led to a public debate in the Press about extra-judicial police killings, the main target of these pressures, public authorities, did not take much more action. The KHRC progressively engaged the state in a public discussion about the causes of these police killings. Debating their frequency, the profile of their authors, the working conditions of the police forces, the KHRC eventually succeeded in making the government recognize extra-judicial killings as a major problem. Whereas in 1995 the government had accused the human rights group of being a foreign agent, it came to accept its own failures and to endorse the human rights discourse on the police. This move has not occurred without ambiguities. Indeed, President Moi more than once encouraged the police force in their violent behavior. It is however clear that the problem has been identified and that both sides have engaged in a dialogue which has replaced street confrontations (on this particular subject)(Ruteere and Pommerolle 2003).[20]

Moreover, the KHRC has now moved to a kind of cooperation with the police. A symbolic example is the *"Kenya Police Human Rights Training Manual"* to which the KHRC contributed. More importantly, it started projects of "community policing" the goal of which is to make people and police cooperate in preventing crime and resolving security problems. KHRC cooperated with the Vera Institute, and imported new technologies of community policing. The move to a "community based" approach, focused on education and work with ordinary citizens has developed in the KHRC from the vision that the group needs to establish a "grassroots" legitimacy. One of the tactics of the state has always been to deny any representativeness to the NGO. Hence, the more the NGO has become visible in the public sphere, the more the need to speak in the name of "people" has arisen. In this light the new program appears to be a strategic move in building KHRC visibility and capacity. It has worked together with police in establishing downtown police booths, and with

---

19. KHRC, *Mission to repress, torture, illegal detentions and extra-judicial police killings by the Kenyan police* (Nairobi, 1998).

20. Major police reforms target crime and greater motivation, *Saturday Nation*, 30 June 2001. Government of Kenya, *Human Rights in Kenya: the way it is* (Nairobi, 1995). "Police officers: why I shoot to kill," *Sunday Nation*, 12 August 2001. British Council, *Kenya Police human rights Training Manual* (Nairobi, 2001).

the police and the local community in Kangemi, one of Nairobi's slum areas.[21] In a departure from its oppositional instincts, the KHRC now finds itself working in tandem with an institution which is mired in criminality and which has been commonly used as an instrument of political oppression. Its projects in Kangemi have been vulnerable to hijack by local elite interests.

The move to this kind of imported project can also be explained by the change in KHRC staff. It is the result of the progressive departure of the activists, whose history makes them neither competent nor willing to go to the grassroots. Their history has been to confront the state, not to educate communities nor make people cooperate with the police. Even if not officially stated, the turn to the grassroots has clearly replaced the activist work. And this move has been deplored by some staff, stating that: "the move to the CBOs is a big mistake because KHRC has no competence for this particular work".[22] If the lack of competence has been filled by hiring more community based staff, the change in strategy, from confrontation to education, remains true. For the same staff member, the move to the grassroots was meant to "remove KHRC from hot political issues". In any case, it is true that a more "professional" view of the advocacy work entered the KHRC with its new staff. Yet, this interpretation of linking professionalization of the organization and more neutral activities is partial. Discussions with the KHRC executive director put a different light on this new community based approach. Far from withdrawing from the political sphere, he claims that this "agenda is overtly political. It can lead to the contestation of power, because the people empowered could then vie for councilors' or MPs' positions". It is an "alliance of a middle-class and a people-class project".[23] Once more, this discourse, far from supporting the neoliberal view of a politically neutral community approach, is more subversive and political than expected.

A Sociology of Ideas:
Nationalizing Human Rights and
Asserting Political Independence

Far from being a marionette in the hands of donors, the KHRC has been able, from its beginning, to gain autonomy by defining its own legitimacy,

---

21. Interview, August 2001.
22. *Ibid.*
23. Interview, August 2001.

and, progressively, its own means of action. In particular, the NGO has been able to adjust its discourse to external actors (donors, the state and the Kenyan public) as well as to fit with the main social and political representations of its members. In the following paragraphs I highlight these ideological adjustments that combine different views and are rooted in Kenyan political culture, and which have led, in my opinion, to the strength of KHRC. I will then turn to more practical aspects of the NGO's autonomy which assure its progressive institutionalization in the Kenyan public sphere.

Defining the Cause

"Human rights" is often perceived as a universalistic orthodoxy, which is spread via international groups and donors, which channel funds to local NGOs. On this ground the relevance of the human rights issue in Africa is largely debated (Shivji 1989; An-Naim and Deng 1990). However, this orthodoxy is far from fixed. NGOs have had to adapt their own programs and fields of action to the changing priorities of international human rights "prophets". For their part, African governments often deny the legitimacy of human rights discourse, because of its "foreign" origins. African NGOs have to steer a course between these conflicting pressures.

Following the Western agenda while having some normative purchase on the Kenyan government are thus two necessities for the KHRC. The members of the NGO have been able to adapt these injunctions to their own perceptions of struggle, locating them within domestic intellectual and political traditions. The most striking proof of this voluntary adaptation is the intellectual work performed by its leaders, notably Makau wa Mutua (1994, 2002), who has published a number of pieces debating the local relevance of the human rights struggle. This academic input however has few direct effects on the NGO's activities. Such "subversive" ideas, if they highlight the intellectual independence of the KHRC, remain far from the day-to-day work of the NGO. It is on the basis of programs and concrete activities that I will show how the NGO is able to escape constraints, or at least appropriate the injunctions.

The first example lies in the way the KHRC has moved, along with the donors, to widen its agenda to economic and social rights while associating them with indigenous political representations. At the moment of its creation, the KHRC confined its claims to political and civil rights. This was the result of donor priorities, the focus of which was multipartyism and "democratic transition". It was also due to the "legal bias" of some founders whose interest was mainly in strengthening institutions and achieving the "rule of law". And, according to Willy Mutunga, "in a backward regime, the so-called 'bourgeois' freedoms were revolutionary". "Also, we could mobilize the international community on this discourse".[24] Internally and externally, this restriction to one aspect of recognized rights was accepted as sufficient and efficient.

Subsequently, the International Vienna Convention in 1993 changed international perceptions of human rights. After the end of the Cold War and the pressures of non-state actors, the Second Covenant on social and economic rights was recognized as important as the first one.[25] In this international context, the KHRC is now able to claim social and economic rights more strongly. To show its commitment to follow international standards, it links its programs on social and economic rights to the "integration of human rights" claimed by the Vienna Convention. But for some KHRC staff, the struggle for economic and social rights sounds more like a return to their first activist and intellectual positions grounded in materialist theory. Defending "social democracy" as the ideology of KHRC, the executive director actualizes the old discourse of Kenyan leftists on economic nationalism and the fight against neo-imperialism.[26]

The KHRC started to engage with socio-economic rights with the release of a research report on the struggle of rice farmers working for a public company, emphasizing the interconnectedness of poverty and authoritarian government.[27] The aim of this report was to highlight a "popular" struggle and to point out the contribution of the Kenyan political structure to poverty. It denounces the farmers' deplorable working and living conditions as "a symbol of the continued dominance of the colonial ideology of power in post-colonial Kenya".[28]

This first attempt to tackle social and economic rights was followed by two campaigns defying multinational companies. The first one challenged Del Monte Kenya which owns a pineapple plantation and a plant in Thika. Trade unions, in coordination with an Italian Catholic leftist lobby, placed workers'

---

24. Interview with the W. Mutunga, Nairobi, August 2001.

25. The International Covenant on civil and political rights and the International Covenant on social economic and cultural rights have been both signed in 1966.

26. See Mutunga, W., Mazrui Al A., "Rights Integration in an institutional context," unpublished paper, 1999.

27. KHRC, *Dying to be free. The struggle for rights in Mwea* (Nairobi, 2000).

28. *Ibid.* 40.

rights back on the political agenda (Ngunyi and Gathiaka 1993; Maupeu and Lafargue 1998). After a boycott of Del Monte products in Italy and two years of threats and negotiations locally, the government and the firm accepted to sign a broad agreement which addresses the issues of social development, workers' rights and trade union rights, environmental rights, health and safety, and wages and benefits. The new dispositions are guaranteed by a monitoring committee.[29] Strengthened by this first success, the KHRC launched the same kind of investigations and denunciations concerning flower plants, one of the most lucrative businesses in Kenya.[30] The reluctance of firms to accept such external control show the contradictory interests of workers' rights and business in a country where such issues have long been marginalized in face of the rise of a successful indigenous capitalism on one hand, and the acuity of exactions by an authoritarian regime on the other.

Here the KHRC draws on a strong leftist tradition of critiquing the colonial and neo-colonial exploitation of Kenyan wealth (Anyang'Nyong'o 1989). Indeed, the issue of land, foreign farms in the Highlands and lack of redistribution after Independence have been a bone of contention between the regime and its opponents. Expressed first by the "leftist" branch of KANU led by Jaramogi Odinga in the 1960s, this issue has been embodied by diverse characters (Odinga 2001 (1967)). The "populist" MPs in the 1970s, and notably JM Kariuki (whose assassination remains mysterious), agitated for a more equal distribution of wealth in the country (Dauch 1982). This issue was then publicly raised by academics and especially by novelist Ngugi wa Thiong'o, whose theatre plays and books denounced artistically the colonial attitude of the post-colonial regime (Thiong'o 1977). Subsequently, this issue moved to the underground and was debated, for instance by Mwakenya, whose manifesto deplores that "the most productive land is owned by private landlords—a few rich Kenyans, individual foreigners and transnational corporations".[31] In light of this, the KHRC struggle for social and workers' rights and against the "paternalist authoritarianism" of the government and foreign firms seems to fit very well with one side of Kenyan political representations, and especially some of the KHRC members whose intellectual trajectories flowed

---

29. See "Lobbies call off products boycott", *Daily Nation*, 18 March 2001.

30. See *La Lettre de L'Océan Indien*, N°988, 16 March 2002 and N°1002, 29 June 2002, and the letter of the chairman of the Kenya Flower Council denouncing the human rights NGOs attacks against its industry: "Concerted attacks on the flower industry harmful to economy," *Daily Nation*, 27 September 2002.

31. Mwakenya, *Draft Minimum Program*, (Nairobi, September 1987).

through these leftist streams. This intellectual congruence is clearly expressed when Mazrui and Mutunga insert their human rights struggle into broader ideological objectives:

> "the KHRC and other HR organizations have been operating within a shared framework of western liberal democracy which, as argued earlier has been sufficient for effective advocacy for political and civil liberties. The case is obviously different within economic, social and cultural rights: rooted as they are in national and global capitalism, and in specific class relations, these still exist in the terrain of intense ideological contestation and struggles. (…)And what we have identified as entry-points projects of KHRC are, in fact, contexts within which grassroots forces can be galvanized and from which a concrete social democratic consciousness can begin to emerge and be sharpened over time".[32]

The second example of KHRC' s attempt to insert human rights into a Kenya-specific context is the use of nationalist symbols and myths. The reference to the Mau Mau struggle in KHRC's publications and discourse is a way of legitimizing its current struggle by using strong symbols of indigenous opposition politics. Indeed, as many authors have shown, the memory of Mau Mau has been an object of dispute between government and opposition since Independence (Clough 1998). But, however disputed it is, the Mau Mau past seems now to operate as a

> usable political language (…) a commonly understood set of symbols that sum up, by allegory, myth and metaphor, the core values that ought to, but seldom do, govern the always disputable relationships between individuals and any society in their provision of future, which is implicit in the way in which they reproduce the present out of the past (Lonsdale 1992: 204).

It could be surprising that the memory of Mau Mau, described also by Lonsdale, as a "Kikuyu nationalism" anchored in economic, social and political problems of a particular group in the 1950s, be today used as a universal flag bearer (Lonsdale 1992). Of course, the Mau Mau memory is still used as a stake of internal Kikuyu politics. But Lonsdale also shows very well the dif-

---

32. Mutunga, W., Mazrui, Al., "Rights Integration in an institutional context", unpublished paper, 1999.

ference between a "political tribalism" and a "moral ethnicity" shared beyond the Kikuyu group and based on a collective will to make leaders accountable, and considered as "the nearest Kenya has to national history and a watchful political culture" (Lonsdale 1992: 467). As such, the two issues raised by the Mau Mau struggle—the quest for land and freedom—interpreted and debated by political or academic commentators are understood by the majority of Kenyan citizens and has been used since the start of the democratic claims at the beginning of the 1990s.

For instance, in 1992, mothers of political detainees demanding the release of their sons compared them to freedom fighters and their fight to the Mau Mau struggle against oppression (Sabar-Friedman 1995; Tibbets 1994). This movement, which gave birth to Release Political Prisoners (RPP) continues to link its claims to the memory of freedom fighters. By the same token, references to the Mau Mau struggle as the source and the symbol of human rights struggle can be located in the diverse products and discourse of KHRC. A preface to one their reports pays tribute to "thousands of patriotic Kenyans who died during the Mau Mau war fighting for land and freedom".[33] Even in the 2001 Strategic Plan, the introduction reminds that "our demand for self-determination has been the same one that Me Kitilili, Waiyaki, Koitalel, Markan Singh, Pinto, the Land and Freedom Army led by Kimathi, among other movements, made at different periods of our history". More explicitly, the KHRC and RPP carried a petition to the British High Commission in 1997 and 1998 demanding that the British government exhume the remains of Dedan Kimathi, a Mau Mau leader hung by the British in 1956, and hand them over to the Kenyan government for a decent burial.[34] Today the KHRC gives legal support to a recently created "Kimathi Movement" still demanding the decent burial of the freedom fighter. Arrested several times while attempting to mark a site for a new burial, the young members of the Movement have succeeded in attracting media attention and in gathering some support.[35] Mutunga and Mazrui explain the relevance of this project regarding human rights struggle as a symbol of the integration of rights, raising at the same times the issue of the death penalty and the "questions of land appropriation and national sovereignty that had triggered the independence strug-

---

33. KHRC, *Beyond the Curtain* (Nairobi, 1996).

34. *The People*, 27 March 1998 – 5 March 1998 and interview with the former coordinator of Kimathi Movement, July 2002

35. See, for instance, *The People*, 26 February 2001, *The East African Standard*, 19 February 2001 and 20 February 2001.

gle in the first place and their continuing effects on the economic and social being of the people".[36] Clearly then, the human rights struggle is a continuation of Mau Mau ideas, and the human rights activists style themselves as the inheritors of the unfinished work of Dedan Kimathi.

Using Mau Mau names and glorifying its heroes is a way to inscribe the human rights discourse in Kenyan national and opposition history. It is a way to indigenize human rights and to make sense of it. This work is aimed at legitimizing the discourse, at "nationalizing" a universal paradigm, and at legitimizing the KHRC. This process highlights the constructed nature of any cause, be it a defense of narrow selfish interests or of a moral and universal one. In constructing it, the KHRC has been successful in digesting international standards and formulating them in a national language. Donors and state constraints have both been bypassed.

Institutionalization and Politicization

Not only has the KHRC managed to develop a relevant discourse on human rights, it has also gained organizational autonomy and political independence. Indeed, in spite of the tensions outlined above, which highlight the interdependence of the KHRC with its external environment, I want to show that the major trend characterizing the NGO is its autonomization, and, hence, its institutionalization. The KHRC is able to define its own rules of functioning and the norms it wants to spread as a pressure group. Moreover, the group has sufficient independence to be politicized. Whereas such politicization could be considered a sign of dependence on a partisan group, it is claimed here to be a deliberate and independent choice. This apparent paradox of institutionalization and politicization is what I want to explain now.

A first sign of its internal autonomization is the financial arrangement the KHRC has put in place with its donors and its attempts to secure autonomous finance.[37] The donors have indeed accepted to secure financing for strategic plans of four years guaranteeing a middle-term working program for the group. Before this, the activities depended on the changing will of donors. For instance, in August 1998 when most of them disapproved the radical stand of the NGO in the constitutional review process they cut the funding endangering the sustainability of its activities. This "package deal" with donors has been

---

36. Mutunga, W., Mazrui, Al.A., "Integration," op.cit.
37. See KHRC, Operational Plan, internal document (Nairobi, 2001).

made possible by the smooth change of leadership[38] and KHRC leaders' reputation for integrity, as well as members who enable it to exercise some room for manoeuvre vis a vis donors.[39] Moreover the KHRC is trying to become "institutionally and programatically sustainable" by managing an "endowment fund" which would also allow it to finance other human rights structures. This managerial dimension resembling American foundations, indicates an advanced institutionalization compared to many groups in civil society, said to be waiting for donor funding in order to operate.

A second feature of this organizational development is its new membership structure. Following the community centered approach, the KHRC wants to open its board to members of human rights communities and to a wider range of partners. Actually, it wants to open to its social environment and to emancipate from the board of directors, which decided its organizational orientation. This move is however ambiguous in its concrete set up. The fear of becoming vulnerable to "badly intentioned" members made them erect a financial barrier. In addition, each small human rights community is supposed to have only one representative as will any wealthy individual wanting to be a member. The contradictions of opening up and wanting to remain in charge will lead to deep debates.

A last aspect of this autonomization is the diverse partners the KHRC works with and its progressive assertion as a "natural leader" of the human rights sector in the country. I showed previously that since the beginning its staffs has come from various ideological and professional backgrounds. I stated that the group has taken the path of professionalization, but, far from conforming to one standardized view of human rights work, the KHRC remains open to any group sharing its goals and strategies. Whereas the first major partners of the KHRC were legal groups and some pressure groups like RPP, it now works closely with less high profile groups like hawkers' groups, trade unions, and community based groups, and gives legal cover or support to more activist groups. Relevant with its stand for the whole gamut of human rights and its will to challenge social and economic status quo, this diverse cooperation is also a sign of its independent capacity to choose its partners. Its capacity to deal with so many issues and groups has progressively made it become a "leader" among human rights NGOs in Kenya. Ten years after the opening of

---

38. In 1998, Willy Mutunga, former chair of the board replaced Maina Kiai as the executive director of the KHRC. He has been re-elected in 2003 to complete a second mandate until 2006.

39. Interview with a donor, August 2001.

the regime and a high presence of foreign donors, the human rights sector had diversified and specialized, with organizations working only on one issue or on medical, legal, or social aspects of this field.[40] This widening of the human rights field has created tensions (expressed by schisms in NGOs, for instance) but also a reasonable degree of coordination between groups, especially inside the loose Human Rights Network. Thus, when needed, KHRC plays the role of the leader, as was the case after the death of Father Kaiser when actions were decided and coordinated in KHRC offices. Concerning the issues raised, the KHRC sets the agenda on human rights issues. Its relationships with the press help also setting this agenda and disseminating it. Sometimes ironically designated as "hegemonic", its leadership seems far from authoritarian and rather open to diversity: its own scope of action ranges from specialized lobbying on parliamentary bills to the setting of theatre plays in Korogocho (a marginalized slum area of Nairobi).

In the same vein, the KHRC leadership has chosen to express political opinions in the name of the group. From the beginning, it is very clear that the organization, because of the nature of its work, opposed the Moi government. For a staff member, and this view is shared, activism in Kenya can't be disconnected from politics. Indeed,

> in the West, human rights developed in a context of relative freedom whereas in Africa the human rights struggle is part of political change. It is difficult to draw a line between political activism and human rights activism. For instance, Koigi [wa Wamwere] was struggling for the same thing as Amnesty but not with the same language of human rights.[41]

However, the entry of KHRC to the political debate started really in 1996 with the constitutional review process.[42] The KHRC, with other groups, was one of the main organizers of the mass action of 1997 through the National Convention Executive Council, the organizing committee of the constitutional reform movement and the political branch of civil society. This involvement in politics has been rationalized by the current director who has developed a "theory" of civil society partisanship, where he states that civil society, far from

---

40. In 2002, the National Council of NGOs counted 45 NGOs registered under the section "Human rights, social justice (including education for democracy, refugees and displaced persons)."

41. Interview, August 2001.

42. For a subjective review of the Constitutional review process, see Mutunga, W., *Constitution-making from the Middle*, op. cit, 1999.

remaining neutral and apolitical, should take a strong role in the political sphere.[43] In spite of the apostasy of most political parties during the Inter-Parliamentary Party Group talks of November 1997, where they accepted a compromise with government in order to stand for elections, the KHRC has continued its involvement in politics, especially through the constitutional debate, but also more directly by taking part in party politics (Harbeson 1998). The issue of the constitutional process is another interesting political distortion of what could be seen as a mere legal arrangement, another application of the "rule of law" supported by neutral donors. They managed to make it a very political issue and to produce mass action, compelling every political actor to take a stand on the issue. Since the first actions in 1997, the questions are still pending, raising very sensitive debates about who has the legitimacy to shape a new constitution and to adopt it.[44]

The KHRC leadership has also been deeply involved in party politics, trying to strengthen the opposition. From the beginning, the KHRC has been close to the "young Turks", those lawyers or opponents to the regime who took part in the struggle for multipartyism with long standing opponent to the regime, Jaramogi Odinga, and who then entered politics (Throup and Hornsby 1998). In 1994, some of the board members entered the board of the Mwangaza Trust, a development group and a kind of springboard for some of the young Turks. After its disbanding by the regime, SAFINA was created and a KHRC board member became its treasurer. After the 1997 failure in the constitutional process, the need to rebuild a credible opposition encouraged Mutunga to set up a political lobby movement called "Mageuzi wa Muungamano" and then a "Third Force" opposed to the regime and to the official opposition.[45] The initiative failed but Mutunga is said then to have been crucial in building the National Alliance of Kenya, a group of three major opposition parties, and then the National Rainbow Coalition (NaRC), which won the 2002 elections (Anderson 2002; Anderson and Maupeu 2003). The KHRC even called Kenyan citizens to vote for Mwai Kibaki and NaRC candidates through a press release.[46]

---

43. See different written statements of Mutunga in Mutunga, Mazrui, op. cit., KHRC, "Integration," op. cit., and KHRC, *Human Rights and Politics*, op. cit.

44. For a recent account of such debate, see Onyango, D., "Threat of slip over the Ghai proposals after poll victory," *Daily Nation*, 2 February 2003.

45. Interview with Mutunga, August 2001 and KHRC, *Human Rights and Politics* (Nairobi 2003).

46. See KHRC, "Why and how to bring about regime change in Kenya," October 2, 2002, published in KHRC, *Eyes on the prize* (Nairobi, 2003).

This claim of partisanship is the result of a very political vision of the human rights struggle. In the case of KHRC, as I have shown, human rights has been seen as another way to play politics not a mere opportunity to get funds from external donors.

Conclusion: Remaining Autonomous When One's Allies are in Power

The KHRC is now facing a new challenge: remaining independent from the new rulers it has chosen, and getting out of the constraint of complacency that could endanger, in another way, its newly gained autonomy. Indeed, having been involved in political bargains in the 2002 elections, and with many of its allies now members of the government or of public administrations, the KHRC needs to redefine its position in the face of a more "human rights friendly" government. This political change does not mean that human rights abuses have ceased, as a relevant Human Rights Watch report warned just before the fall of KANU.[47] While the new rulers seem to have wanted to make positive signs to human rights defenders through symbolic and important gestures, such as opening torture chambers and addressing the question of Kimathi's grave,[48] burning issues remain. KHRC expresses its independence in different ways and is eager to show that it has never sacrificed it.[49]

Works Cited

Ahluwahlia, P. 1998. Human rights in Africa: a post-colonial perspective. *Human Rights Quarterly* 38 (1): 21–37.

---

47. Human Rights Watch, *Kenya's unfinished democracy: a human rights agenda for the new government* (December 2002).
48. See "Torture victims visit monument of shame", *Daily Nation*, 12 February 2003; "Victims remember the dark days," *Daily Nation*, 12 February 2003.
49. See the texts compiled in KHRC, *Eyes on the prize*, op. cit., justifying KHRC political positions and challenging the new government on Human rights issues. See also "human rights group rallies to Moi's defense," *Daily Nation*, 5 May 2003, where KHRC's director defends publicly the right of former President Moi to speak publicly when some would like to shut him up.

Ambrose, B. 1995. *Democratization and Human Rights in Africa*. London: Praeger.

Anderson, D. 2002. Kenya's elections: the dawning of a new era? *African Affairs* 102 (2): 331–43.

Anderson, D., and H. Maupeu. 2003. Kenya, la succession de Moi. *Politique Africaine* (90): 5–17

An-Naim, A., and F. M. Deng, eds. 1990. *Human Rights in Africa: Cross-cultural perspectives*. Washington: Brookings Institute.

Anyang'Nyong'o, P. 1989. State and society in Kenya: the disintegration of the nationalist coalition and the rise of presidential authoritarianism, 1963–1978. *African Affairs* 88 (351): 229–51.

Clough, M. 1998. *Mau Mau Memoirs: History, memory and politics*. Boulder, CO: Lynn Rienner.

Dauch, G. 1982. J. M. Kariuki ou l'éthique nationale du capitalisme. *Politique Africaine* 8: 21–41.

———. 1983. L'université et le pouvoir au Kenya. *Politique Africaine* (12): 80–98.

Dezalay, Y., and B. G. Garth. 2002. *The Internationalization of Palace Wars: Lawyers, economists and the contest to transform Latin America*. Chicago: Chicago University Press.

Harbeson, J. 1998. Political crisis and renewal in Kenya: prospects for democratic consolidation. *Africa Today* 45 (2): 161–83.

Kibwana, K. 1998. Constitutionnalisme et démocratie au Kenya, 1990–97. *Politique Africaine* 70: 74–83.

Lonsdale, J. 1992. African pasts in Africa's future. In *Unhappy Valley: Conflict in Kenya and Africa*, edited by B. Berman and J. Lonsdale. London: James Currey.

Lonsdale, J., and A. E. S. Odhiambo (eds.). 2003. *Mau Mau and Nationhood*. London: James Currey.

Lonsdale, J. 1992. The moral economy of Mau Mau: wealth, poverty and civic virtue in Kikuyu political thought. In *Unhappy Valley: Conflict in Kenya and Africa*, edited by J. Lonsdale and B. Berman. London: James Currey.

Maupeu, H. 1995. Eglises et transition démocratique au Kenya. In *Démocratie et Développement*, edited by G. Feltz and M. Esoavelomandraso. Paris: Karthala.

Maupeu, H., and J. Lafargue. 1998. La société civile Kenyane: entre résilience et résistance. *Politique Africaine* (70): 61–73.

Mutua, M. 1994. Domestic human rights organizations in Africa: problems and perspectives. *Issue* 23 (2): 30–33.

———. 1994. Human rights and state despotism in Kenya: institutional problems. *Africa Today* 41 (4): 50–56.

————. 2002. *Human Rights: A political and cultural critique.* Philadelphia: University of Pennsylvania.

Ngunyi, M.G., and K. Gathiaka. 1993. State-civil institutional relations in Kenya in the 1980s. In *Social Change and Economic Reform in Africa,* edited by P. Gibbon. Uppsala: Nordiska Afrikainstitutet.

Odinga, J. O. 2001 (1967). *Not Yet Uhuru.* Nairobi: East African Educational Publishers.

Risse, T., S. Ropp, and K. Sikkink, eds. 1999. *The Power of Human Rights: International norms and domestic change.* Cambridge: Cambridge University Press.

Ross, S. D. 1992. The rule of law and lawyers in Kenya. *Journal of Modern African Studies* 30 (3): 421–42.

Ruteere, M., and M. Pommerolle. 2003. Democratizing security or decentralizing repression? The ambiguities of community policing in Kenya. *African Affairs* 102 (409): 587–604.

Sabar-Friedman, G. 1995. The Mau Mau myth. *Cahier d'études Africaines* 37: 101–31.

Schmitz, H. P. 1999. Transnational activism and political change in Kenya and Uganda. In *The Power of Human Rights: International norms and domestic change,* edited by T. Risse, S. Ropp and K. Sikkink. Cambridge: Cambridge University Press.

Shivji, I. 1989. *The Concept of Human Rights in Africa.* Dakar: CODESRIA.

Thiong'o, Ngugi wa. 1977. *Petals of Blood.* Heinemann: London.

Throup, D., and C. Hornsby. 1998. *Multi-Party Politics in Kenya.* Oxford: James Currey.

Tibbets, A. 1994. Mamas fighting for freedom in Kenya. *Africa Today* 41 (4): 27–48.

Welch, C. E. 1995. *Protecting human rights in Africa: Strategies and roles of nongovernmental organizations.* Philadelphia: Pennsylvania University Press.

Widner, J. A. 1992. *The Rise of a Party-State in Kenya: From* harambee *to* nyayo. Berkeley: University of California Press.

CHAPTER 5

POWER AND FORCE IN TANZANIAN CIVIL SOCIETY: THE STORY OF BARABAIG NGOS IN THE HANANG COMMUNITY DEVELOPMENT PROJECT

Jim Igoe

University of Colorado at Denver, Department of Anthropology
james.igoe@cudenver.edu

NGOs, Civil Society, and the Ethnography of Anti-Politics in Tanzania

This chapter explores the relationship of Tanzanian NGOs to transnational donors and the Tanzanian state in the context of community-based development, and analyzes the implications of these relationships for the emergence of Tanzanian civil society. The dynamics of these relationships, as revealed in the case study of this chapter, are essentially different from the scenarios imagined by the neo-Tocquevillian paradigms of civil society that have pervaded development and governance initiatives throughout Africa since the Soviet collapse.

The assumptions of these neo-Tocquevillian paradigms are revealed in HCDP (Hanang Community Development Project), a project funded by CIDA (The Canadian International Development Agency) to promote civil society and economic development in Hanang District in the latter half of the 1990s. Like so many other development and governance programs implemented in Africa during this period, the discourse of the HCDP revolved around assumptions that local voluntary associations would become a training ground for democratic practice, imbuing local people with a newfound sense of political efficacy. A further assumption of this paradigm is that this process will create a counterbalance to corrupt and inefficient African states (Kelsall 1997), thereby promoting western liberal democracies and free market economies throughout Africa (Harbeson 1994). So pervasive were these assumptions during my time in the field (1993 to 1997) that I came to know them just by listening to donors talk.[1] During the final stage of my fieldwork I could often predict what donors were going to say at workshops and community meetings.

Whether donors knew it or not, the ideas they were espousing were derived largely from Alexis de Tocqueville's *Democracy in America*, in which he observed that voluntarism and voluntary associations were crucial to the success of American democracy in the first half of the nineteenth century. The revival of Tocquevillian thought in the latter part of the twentieth century revolved around ideas that the global proliferation of NGOs following the Soviet collapse was a groundswell of voluntarism, similar to what de Tocqueville witnessed during his visit to the United States in the 1830s (Salamon 1993). It quickly became a common assumption in governance and development circles that NGOs equal civil society (Hyden, 1995; Edwards and Hulme 1996; World Bank, 1997; Kelsall 1998; and Abramson 1999), and that funding these organizations equals building civil society (Chabal and Daloz 1999:22).

Ironically, the brand of Neo-Tocquevillian thought circulating in Africa at the end of the millennium ignored important nuances of de Tocqeuville's analysis, nuances that were crucially significant to the experiences of millions of Africans under economic and political liberalization.

First, de Tocqueville observed that American democracy, including voluntary associations, excluded and marginalized two ethnic minorities: African Americans and Native Americans (he could also have added women). In order for this system to work effectively in the future, he argued, this problem would need to be rectified. Secondly, de Tocqueville also warned that America's sys-

---

1. At this point in my career I had no formal training in social theory or the classic works of civil society. It was from hearing donors talk about civil society that I became interested in the topic, and came to study it extensively in the years immediately following the completion of my Ph.D.

tem of laissez-faire capitalism, with its emphasis on individualism and competition, was having a dangerously isolating effect on the American people. In the long run, he argued, there was a danger that this tendency might weaken the American penchant for voluntary collective action, and the spirit of mutual cooperation. Economic liberalization and the proliferation of NGOs in Tanzania has contributed to similar problems, benefiting some groups at the expense of others and undermining the effectiveness of voluntary initiatives at the grassroots level (Igoe 2000 and 2003b).

The HCDP, and indeed development interventions around the world, have effectively concealed these fundamentally political processes by recasting them as "development" problems, amenable to technical solutions. The best-known work on this phenomenon is of course Ferguson's (1990) *Anti-Politics Machine*, in which he uses Foucauldian analysis to document the depoliticizing effects of development interventions in Lesotho. The idea of "anti-politics" has since come to pervade studies of development and governance. Brosius' (1999) study of rainforest conservation in Sarawak Malaysia, documents how it was gradually redefined from a political struggle by local indigenous peoples to technical a problem that could be solved by the involvement of transnational environmental NGOs. Referring "anti-politics" to the question of NGOs and the global associational revolution, Fisher (1997) maintains:

> Just as the "development apparatus" has generally depoliticized the need for development by treating local conditions as "problems" that require technical and not structural or political solutions, it now defines problems that can be addressed via mechanisms of NGOs rather than political solutions.

Development theorists drawing from this Foucauldian perspective argue that the discourses of a global "development apparatus" defines its own "suitable targets of intervention." These discursively constructed targets may be as large as the entire "third world" (Escobar 1995), slightly smaller like the country of Lesotho (Ferguson 1990), a group of people like the Maasai (Hodgson 2001), or culture bound individuals who need to become universal producers and consumers (Berthoud 1988). Their problems are not defined with reference to structural inequities or political power struggles, but as inherent to the targets themselves. They are fettered by "traditional attitudes" and/or inadequately integrated to the global economy. The interventions implied by these discourses are designed to transform these targets in ways that facilitate the penetration of global capitalism and/or the expansion of state control.

The discourses of HCDP support the idea of "anti-politics" and the construction of "suitable targets of intervention." The Barabaig, who are the central targets of this intervention, have been the subjects of "anti-political" discourses since the colonial period, and continue to be today. The discourses of the HCDP continue to invoke elements of colonial development discourses, which portrayed the Barabaig, and most rural Africans for that matter, as responsible for their own poverty. This perspective ignores the fact that the poverty of Barabaig communities is largely the product of the wholesale appropriation of their grazing land by the Tanzanian Government for wheat farms funded by the Canadian Government.

While a Foucauldian "anti-politics" paradigm goes a long way in explaining the apparent discrepancies between the rhetoric and reality of the HCDP, the relationship of this type of intervention to actual events occurring within African civil society are usually difficult to pinpoint. The central issue this chapter addresses is the ways in which these discourses manifest themselves through particular interventions and in effect become reality. Is this, as Ferguson (1990: 21) suggests, an "unauthored" process? As the details of this case study will illustrate, the question of authorship is a sticky one, but one that is crucially important to the study of African NGOs and their putative relationship to the emergence of African civil society.

As Foucault (1980: 95) himself emphasized, it is important to avoid confusing intentionality with authorship; power relations are simultaneously "intentional and non-subjective." As he succinctly put it, "People know what they do; they frequently know why they do what they do; but what they don't know is what they do does" (quoted in Dreyfus and Rabinow 1982: 187). Even though actors may have specific intentions in specific contexts, the overall "directionality of power relations in society" will be well beyond these intentions and their contexts (*ibid*). [2]

Foucault admitted, however, that the relationship between intentionality and outcome was closely tied to questions of scale. In the context of local politics, there may be a much closer relationship between intentionality and outcome than at the level of "society" (*ibid*). This is an important point for ethnographic studies of African NGOs, since NGO politics frequently take place in the context of local politics. In the case of the HCDP, for instance, there was

---

2. Thanks to Erica Bornstein for calling my attention to this crucially important distinction, and for numerous other comments and suggestions on the theoretical aspects of this chapter. Her insights on Foucault, Gramsci, and Althusser helped me to think more clearly about theories of power.

a close relationship between intentionality and outcome. The "anti-politics" of HCDP was not an "unauthored" side effect, but a meticulously authored objective. Two powerful individuals had interests in "displacing the political" in Hanang: the Canadian High Commissioner and the Prime Minister of Tanzania. While these actors had different reasons for wanting the HCDP to succeed, both had an interest in erasing the decidedly political history of dispossession and human rights abuses that their respective governments had previously visited upon the Barabaig.

In order for these two individuals to achieve their objectives, however, it was first necessary to elicit the cooperation of key community members, especially the leaders of Barabaig NGOs. From this perspective, civil society in Hanang looked less like a neo-Tocquevillian training ground for democratic practice than a Gramscian sphere of action in which "consent is manufactured." Certain aspects of the Gramscian paradigm are particularly amenable to the ethnography of "anti-politics" in Hanang. Of particular importance to this study is the way in which organic intellectuals, who are members of marginal subaltern groups, seek to resist the hegemonic discourses of the ruling elites, constructing credible counter-hegemonic discourses in the process. Such ethnography can also reveal the ways in which elites coerce the intellectual subalterns to comply with the terms of their hegemonic discourses, even if they never fully accept or internalize them.

In the context of these struggles, local NGOs closely resemble Althusser's (1971) "Ideological State Apparatuses," which are "not only the stake, but also the site" of struggles between ruling elites and members of subaltern classes (147).[3] Althusser also carried forward the Gramscian insight that consent and force are inextricably woven together. "Ideological state apparatuses function massively and predominantly by ideology, but they also function secondarily by repression, even if ultimately, but only ultimately, this is attenuated and concealed, even symbolic" (*ibid*: 145). If Ferguson's "anti-politics machine" is a feature of African civil society, then its inner-workings should be visible in local interventions like the HCDP and its related struggles over the ideological state apparatuses of Barabaig NGOs. This study seeks to demystify the "anti-politics machine" by revealing the details of "anti-political" processes from an ethnographic perspective in the context of local politics.

Since this ethnographic analysis revolves around the analysis of discourses that are a-historical in nature, it is necessary to include an account of the socio-historical processes leading up to the planning and implementation of

---

3. Again, credit for this insight must be given to Erica Bornstein.

HCDP. The following section provides a historical overview of the appropriation of Barabaig grazing land by the Tanzanian State and the emergence of Barabaig NGOs, with special attention to the discourses of development and governance that accompanied these processes. Section III discusses the HCDP as a product of the involvement of the Canadian Government in these historical processes. Section IV is an ethnographic account of the "anti-political processes" in the HCDP. The conclusion of this chapter addresses the theoretical implication of the HCDP for NGOs and civil society on the African continent.

A Socio-Political History of Barabaig NGOs and Civil Society in Hanang

The implementation of HCDP is premised on the involvement of local NGOs, especially those of the Barabaig ethnic group. The contemporary Barabaig are a remnant of the larger Datooga ethnic group, which was decimated by punitive expeditions, interethnic wars, and the introduction of new disease vectors, all of which accompanied European contact at the turn of the twentieth century (Wilson 1952, Kjaerby 1979, and Lane 1993). Today the Barabaig number only about 40,000 people, but they have gained international recognition through their involvement in the global indigenous peoples' movement. The Barabaig have two NGOs. The first is KIPOC-Barabaig, which is the local branch of a larger Maasai NGO called KIPOC (Korongoro Integrated Peoples' Oriented to Conservation – also a Maasai word meaning "We Shall Survive). The second is called Bulgalda (a Datooga word meaning "Dry Land).

Today both KIPOC-Barabaig and Bulgalda play an instrumental role in the local politics of Hanang District. Representing the Barabaig, who are an ethnic minority in the district, they are also an important element of local civil society. Because of the circumstances under which these NGOs emerged, they also have important relationships to the Canadian Government, through CIDA, and a Canadian NGO called CUSO (Canadian University Services Overseas). The involvement of CUSO initially revolved around the culpability of the Canadian Government in the displacement of the Barabaig by the Hanang Wheat Complex. By the time of my departure from the field in 1997, however, this situation was beginning to change. Even CUSO was moving overtly toward more politically neutral issues of technical development. As they have become increasingly influenced by these relationships, and increasingly integrated into the HCDP, both Barabaig NGOs have been moving steadily toward a service delivery agenda. These organizations began, however, as an institutional expression of local social movements that can be traced to Tanzanian independence in the early 1960s.

Understanding the contemporary position of the Barabaig NGOs, as well as the local social movements from which they emerged, requires a brief historical overview of development interventions in the area that is now Hanang. The unfavorable position of the Barabaig in the district can be traced in part to the earliest interventions in the area, which took the form of punitive expeditions by German troops at the turn of the twentieth century. The central objectives of these expeditions were tax collection, forced labor, and the conscription of African troops into the colonial army (Kjaerby 1979: 11). When direct resistance to these interventions proved unsuccessful, the Barabaig responded by moving beyond the sphere of German influence (*ibid*: 12). When the British took over the Tanganyika Protectorate from the Germans at the end of WWI, the Barabaig were living in widely dispersed multi-ethnic communities. This situation did not fit well with British expectations that Africans lived in clearly bounded, culturally exclusive, "tribes" (cf. Vail 1989, Igoe 2000, and Hodgson 2001).

The British policy of indirect rule required that administrative units of Tanganyika Protectorate be established along ethnic lines, with each tribe having its own territory and Native Authority. Because of their relatively small numbers and dispersed settlement patterns, the Barabaig did not fit well into this ethnic bureaucracy. Ultimately they became a sub-chiefdom of the larger Mbulu chiefdom (Wilson 1952). The Mbulu is another name for the ethnic Iraqw, who were far more numerous than the Barabaig, and therefore far more visible to British administrators.

This bureaucratic arrangement marked the beginning of a systematic discrimination against the Barabaig in favor of the Mbulu, which has remained a central problem for the HCDP and civil society in Hanang District. Significantly, this discrimination was informed by British development discourses, elements of which have also remained an important part of HCDP. Unlike the Barabaig, who were bellicose and prone to ritual murder, the Iraqw were peaceful and productive agro-pastoralists (cf. Wilson 1952). While the Barabaig resisted paying their taxes and selling their cattle, the Iraqw appeared eager to do both. During the 1930s and 1940s, British administrators encouraged Iraqw farmers to settle on Barabaig grazing land, and appointed increasing numbers of Iraqw elders to the offices of the Barabaig sub-chiefdom. The central objective of these interventions were that the "civilized" Iraqw would have a "moderating" influence on the "ungovernable" Barabaig, who would also settle down and become productive members of colonial society (Kjaerby 1979: 13).

The colonial emphasis on development for specific ethnic groups ended with independence in 1961, when ethnicity was condemned as a hindrance to Tanganyika's emerging spirit of national unity. Accordingly, President Julius Nyerere dissolved ethnically based native authorities in favor of the ruling party of TANU.[4] Ironically, this major policy shift did not bring an end to discrimination against the Barabaig in Hanang, which if anything increased. The discourses accompanying this discrimination did change in keeping with the rhetoric of Nyerere's official policy of African socialism. However, the idea remained that the Barabaig were an impediment to economic development and government administration. Instead of being an impediment to the colonial project, however, they were now an impediment to the national unity of the independent socialist nation of Tanzania.

Under African Socialism colonial biases toward semi-nomadic pastoralists increased as members of predominantly agricultural groups took the reins of the ruling party.[5] The virtues of agriculture became one of the central tenets of the ruling party, enshrined in the slogan *Kilimo ni Uhai* – Agriculture is Life. It would be through agriculture, Nyerere argued, that Tanzanians would become a self-sufficient socialist nation and break the bonds of neo-colonialism. Not only did subsistence-oriented pastoralism threaten this vision, the mobility of groups like the Barabaig impeded the implementation of African Socialism at the community level. Two of the central principles of African Socialism were education and the delivery of social services. Neither of these things would be possible with people who simply refused to sit still. Furthermore, party leaders wanted Tanzanian citizens to organize themselves into local cells of TANU. Because of their experiences under colonialism the Barabaig were not well organized to do this. The Iraqw, on the other hand, had ample experience with administrative responsibility. Consequently, they continued to dominate local government, while the Barabaig remained un(der)represented (cf. Lane 1993). This is a problem that has continued up to the present day.

---

4. TANU stood for the Tanganyika African National Union. In 1964 the newly independent country of Tanganyika merged with the island nation of Zanzibar to become Tanzania. In 1977 TANU merged with Zanzibar's Afro-Shirazi Party to become CCM (*Chama cha Mapinduzi*—The Party of the Revolution). CCM remained the ruling party of Tanzania until the introduction of a multi-party electoral system in 1991.

5. The major exception to this process was a young Maasai politician named Edward Sokoine. Sokoine became Prime Minister of Tanzania and was widely acknowledged as the most viable presidential candidate when Nyerere decided to stand down. He died in a mysterious car accident in 1984. Foul play is still widely suspected.

By far the biggest problem facing pastoralist groups under African Socialism was the appropriation of their traditional rangelands for national development projects. The rationale for this appropriation was that pastoralists were a numeric minority and contributing little to the national purse. Large-scale development projects, by contrast, were being undertaken for the national good. They would ultimately benefit all Tanzanians; even the Barabaig if they were willing to make some changes to their lifestyle and embrace the party's ideals of progress and national unity.

The appropriation of Barabaig grazing land by the central government was informed by the notion that Hanang would become the breadbasket for Tanzania and other newly independent African countries. By the time of independence a small group of modernizing elites had organized themselves into agricultural cooperatives and had successfully established several mechanized wheat farms. The productivity of these farms captured the attention of officials within the Ministry of Agriculture, who reasoned that larger farms run by the central government would be even more productive, and benefit the nation that much more. In 1967, a newly established parastatal corporation called NAFCO (National Food and Agriculture Corporation) established the first of several large mechanized farms in Hanang. These pilot farms incorporated the established wheat farms of the local agricultural cooperatives. Between 1967 and 1980, NAFCO expanded these pilot farms to establish the Hanang Wheat Complex, which encompassed over 100,000 acres or 12% of the total land area in Hanang District (Lane 1993).

Most of the land taken over by the Hanang Wheat Complex represented the best pasture and water resources in the traditional Barabaig herding regime (for full details see Lane 1993 and Igoe 2000). In 1985, a fact-finding mission from the University of Dar-es-Salaam's Legal Aid Committee visited Hanang. According to its report (Shivji and Tenga 1985: 1):

> Peasant after peasant told us during our research visit to Mulbadaw (a village within the Hanang Wheat Complex) that they had been reduced to paupers as a result of their evictions. Their cattle, which had no access to water because the NAFCO farms had surrounded and cut off their former water sources, were dying of thirst. Pasture was scanty, and cattle in search of grass on stony slopes often slipped and died. A rough survey of ownership of cattle of some of these families indicated that their herds had been halved since 1979, mainly due to deaths.

The social impacts of these socio-economic changes have been felt throughout Barabaig society. Growing numbers of Barabaig youth have moved to the district headquarters of Katesh, and some have moved to more distant urban centers like Babati and Arusha. Barabaig NGO leaders repeatedly expressed concerns that Barabaig women were engaging in prostitution at local bars and guesthouses. An even larger number of Barabaig have moved away from the area altogether. While census data is unavailable, everyone I met could name several households that had relocated to other parts of the country (cf. Galaty 1988). It is likely that they number in the thousands. In many cases informants had not heard from these people for several years. The members of this exodus are for the most part beyond the reach of Barabaig NGOs and the potential benefits of HCDP, which is ostensibly being implemented for their benefit.

But the socio-economic impacts of the Hanang Wheat Complex are only half the story. During this period, the Tanzanian Government also targeted the Barabaig for a series of repressive actions. In 1967, and again in 1976, the Barabaig were subject to collective punishment following conflicts with neighboring ethnic groups. The power of the Tanzanian president to administer collective punishment is derived from a colonial law that has remained on the books. This law clearly violates Nyerere's doctrine of national unity, and the notion of equality for all Tanzanians regardless of ethnic status. Hundreds of Barabaig youth were arrested and incarcerated without trial solely on the basis of their ethnicity. The national police confiscated thousands of Barabaig cattle, which were sold by local officials. In spite of official inquiries into these operations, an accurate account of what happened to this money has never been produced.

The second of these collective punishments coincided with the ruling party's national villagization campaign, which displaced millions of rural Tanzanians in the middle-1970s. The local version of this villagization campaign was known as *Operation Barabaig*. In this operation, local militias used cattle fines and house burnings to force the Barabaig to relocate into nucleated villages. A Barabaig village official recounting these events stated that "people were beaten like donkeys" in the course of this relocation (Lane 1993: 50). Barabaig NGO leaders, and other Barabaig elders, felt that *Operation Barabaig* was particularly repressive because it was a final effort by the ruling party to effectively control the unruly Barabaig. They also pointed out that the operation systematically removed people from areas that were then taken over by NAFCO for the Hanang Wheat Complex.

The social movements that gave birth to the Barabaig NGOs were a direct resistance to NAFCO and these human rights abuses. One of the prime movers behind the Barabaig resistance to the Hanang Wheat Complex was a community leader named Duncan Getanod. Duncan was one of the local elites who started agricultural cooperatives to grow wheat in the 1950s. He saw himself as an example to other Barabaig whom he expected would follow his example by settling down and becoming commercial producers as well. He was disabused of this notion when NAFCO took over his cooperative's wheat farm and ranching schemes, and government officials refused to hear his grievances. Duncan then decided to organize Barabaig elders to defend their customary land tenure rights.

Through the end of the 1960s, local people engaged in acts of direct resistance against NAFCO and the Hanang Wheat Complex. These included attacks on farm workers, destruction of NAFCO tractors and other farm equipment. Some of the most vociferous protestors were Barabaig women, who stood in front of the NAFCO tractors and refused to move.[6] The national police put down these activities by the early 1970s, but acts of covert sabotage have continued to the present day. Even after public resistance to the farms had ended, animosity between NAFCO authorities and the Barabaig continued. Throughout this period, local people were subject to a variety of human rights abuses at the hands of NAFCO employees, district officials, and the local police. These included assault, rape, the burning of their homesteads, arbitrary arrests, and the confiscation of their livestock (Kisanga Commission 1993).[7]

In 1978, Duncan approached Maasai MP Edward Sokoine with a document outlining the grievances of the Barabaig people against the Tanzanian State. He also oversaw the registration of forty-four Barabaig villages, in the hopes that this would prevent further alienation of Barabaig land. In the following year, however, NAFCO began a massive expansion of the Hanang Wheat Complex. In February of 1981, regional officials and parliamentarians came to investigate Duncan's allegations of human rights abuses in Hanang. They saw the burnt houses, and agreed that people should be compensated. The

---

6. That Barabaig women should be so actively involved in this resistance is consistent with their traditional role in Barabaig society. According to anthropologists George Klima (1965), Barabaig women are the custodians of Barabaig social order. When this order is threatened, usually within the domestic sphere, they have the power to convene a council to resolve the problem. During his fieldwork, Charles Lane (1991: 254) found that women's councils were being called to deal with issues such as land grabbing, corruption of village officials, and the distribution of food aid. These councils are a public demonstration against forces that threaten Barabaig social order. It is only logical, therefore, that Barabaig women should have responded in a similar fashion to the Hanang Wheat Complex.

7. Kisanga Commission. 1993. *Report on the Commission on Violation of Human Rights in NAFCO Wheat Farms Hanang District.* Dar-es-Salaam: mimeo.

complainants were each given four acres by NAFCO on which to grow wheat. NAFCO employees used modern equipment to prepare, plant, and harvest the farms. After paying NAFCO's expenses, the farm owners would get the remaining profits. In most cases, however, there were none, and some of the Barabaig "farm owners" even wound up in debt to NAFCO as a result of this intervention.

Suspicious that this was yet another ploy to take more land, Duncan and a multi-ethnic group of elders organized to sue NAFCO in the High Court of Tanzania (cf. Shivji and Tenga 1985), as well as to bring international attention to the plight of the Barabaig. In 1983, the courts ruled in favor of the local people. However, an executing order for the return of the land was never issued. In 1985, a higher court overturned the original decision on the basis of several bizarre technicalities and found in favor of NAFCO (Tenga and Kakoiti 1993; Lane 1993; and Shivji and Kapinga 1998). With the support of the Legal Aid Committee of the University of Dar-es-Salaam, and funding from CUSO and several other international organizations, Barabaig leaders opened another round of court cases against NAFCO and the Tanzanian State. None of these have gone in favor of local people, the last being settled in 2002 in favor of the defendants.

The advocacy activities around the NAFCO land cases brought Duncan and other Barabaig leaders together with indigenous groups involved in similar struggles. In 1988, several Barabaig elders attended a workshop on pastoralist land tenure problems with pastoralist leaders from Tanzania, Kenya, and Uganda. Among them was Moringe ole Parkipuny, a Maasai MP and founder of the NGO KIPOC. Over the next two years Duncan traveled to KIPOC headquarters in Loliondo to attend meetings of the organization. In 1990 he established his own branch in Hanang, known simply as KIPOC-Barabaig. Duncan became executive secretary and a local official named Daniel Murumbi became program coordinator. According to accounts of both these individuals, the NGO began having problems right away. District officials were afraid that KIPOC-Barabaig would give Duncan too much power. National officials were sensitive about the negative attention that his activities had brought to the Tanzanian Government. Shortly after KIPOC-Barabaig opened its office in Katesh, Duncan received a letter from the District Commissioner of Hanang instructing him to "end all KIPOC activities in the district until further notice."[8] Seeing that the organization would never operate effectively

---

8. Duncan Getanod provided the author with a copy of this letter.

as long as he was in charge, Duncan voluntarily resigned in 1992 and formally withdrew from further advocacy.

Even after Duncan's departure from the NGO scene, KIPOC-Barabaig remained dormant for a further four years. Murumbi and other Barabaig leaders had decided to start their own NGO, which would be independent of KIPOC and the Maasai NGO movement. In 1993, twenty Barabaig elders came together to establish this new organization, which came to be known as Bulgalda. The organization was officially registered the following year. Bulgalda main activity was land tenure advocacy, which continued to revolve around the court cases and NAFCO. Bulgalda leaders continued to work with the Legal Aid Committee to internationalize their grievances. Most significantly, they petitioned the UN Sub-Commission of the Prevention of Discrimination and Protection of Minorities to Intervene on their behalf. However the effectiveness of Bulgalda in carrying out these activities was limited by conflicts within the organization. These conflicts were finally resolved in 1997, during this same year a group of young educated Barabaig revived the dormant KIPOC-Barabaig. These events coincided with the initiation of HCDP (see Igoe 2000 for a more detailed version of this history).

The history briefly described in this section reveal that Barabaig NGOs emerged from socio-historical processes that were decidedly political. It also belies the a-historical discourses of HCDP, which describes the emergence of these organizations and other local NGOs as an "indicator of the dynamism of Tanzania's democratization process, which began a few years ago" (www.habari.co.tz/hpdf/forums.htm). Clearly the democratic impulse and grassroots social movements that finally gave birth to Barabaig NGOs in the early 1990s have been going on for at least thirty years. During the first twenty-five years of Tanzanian independence, which were dominated by large state-sponsored development programs, this type of grassroots democracy was of little concern to CIDA and the Canadian Government, who worked through the one-party socialist state of the Republic of Tanzania.

In the wake of the Soviet collapse, however, these social movements were able to gain institutional legitimacy through officially registered NGOs. NGOs and civil society simultaneously became organizing concepts within the global apparatus of governance and development of which CIDA is a constituent part. Barabaig NGOs were now an important element of Tanzanian civil society, which CIDA could only support. Unfortunately, they were also calling attention to CIDA's role in a thirty-year development fiasco. Their activities were besmirching the good name of the Canadian Government in Tanzania, at home, and with the international community. Consequently, CIDA came under pressure to compensate local people who had been displaced by the Hanang Wheat Complex, while officially denying that the Canadian Government was directly responsible for these problems. Additionally, Canadian officials needed to accommodate powerful Tanzanians who were adamant that there would be no development intervention that would benefit the Barabaig exclusively. This would constitute a type of ethnic discrimination that the Tanzanian Government officially forbade. The HCDP was a product of all these, often conflicting, pressures.

CIDA, The Hanang Wheat Complex, and HCDP

CIDA's initial involvement with the Hanang Wheat Complex reflected predominant discourses that informed development interventions around the world throughout the 1960s. Foremost among these were modernization and dependency paradigms. While opposed to each other in many ways, these two paradigms were premised on the idea that development was a process of macro-transformation, whereby entire populations of people would be brought out of a state of relative ignorance and deprivation to a higher standard of living. In both paradigms, the state was treated unproblematically as the prime mover behind these transformations.

The modernization perspective drew heavily from W.W. Rostow's *Stages of Economic Growth*, in which he described the process of modernization as moving away from a traditional "pre-Newtonian" state to a state of "high mass consumption." This transformation would occur as people shed their traditional attitudes (colonialism often being an essential catalyst) and began to industrialize. Dependency theory, informed by thinkers like Andre Gunder Frank and Walter Rodney, denied that "traditional attitudes" were the primary impediment to development. Rather, these theorists argued, it was the historical exploitation of poor countries by wealthy European empires that was the primary reason for their poverty. These poor countries would only develop by becoming less dependent on their links to these former imperial powers, and by establishing autonomous domestic economies. In most dependency paradigms, however, these changes would still revolve around a process of industrialization.

African Socialism in Tanzania incorporated elements of both these theories. Nyerere supported the industrial transformation of the Tanzania economy à la modernization theory, but was wary of his country's position in the global economy. He advocated, therefore, that industrialization in Tanzania should build on the agricultural sector, which was the strongest economic sector in the country. Large-scale mechanized wheat farms would transform Tanzania's agricultural sector, thereby making the country less dependent on imported food. The wheat grown by these farms would be used to feed a growing urban population, which would become the workers in Tanzania's growing industrial sector. An article by a Canadian volunteer currently working in Tanzania describes the moment thusly (Harker 2002):

> It began when two of the world's finest statesmen at the time put their heads together and came up with what they felt was a great idea. Julius Nyerere, President of the developing nation of Tanzania and Pierre Trudeau, Prime Minister of Canada had much in common; they were both brilliant, they were visionaries and they were disinclined to let practical matters deter them from attempting to achieve an idea that they felt was a good one. Canada was willing to provide substantial aid to Tanzania but it had to be in a manner that helped the country and that would be self-sustaining. After some study, it was felt that a large and seemingly unused area in central Tanzania could be used to grow wheat. The soil was good, the land was flat, the sun was warm and the rainfall adequate. The fact that Tanzanian's staple diet was based on corn flour was not considered a serious drawback. City dwellers of the future would no doubt begin to enjoy bread and any wheat that was not consumed within the country could be exported to obtain much needed foreign capital. Nyerere and Trudeau, together with their advisors felt they had hit on a first rate idea and so began the project known as the Canadian Hanang Wheat Project.

While this revisionist account ignores the socio-historic problems outlined in the previous section, it does an excellent job of capturing the prevailing development attitudes at the time that the Canadian Hanang Wheat Project was established. By supporting the project, CIDA was fostering progress and industrialization, while simultaneously empowering a progressive socialist government to define the terms of its position in the global economy. And what government was better suited to undertake this project than the Canadian Government? If there was anything Canadians understood it was how to grow wheat. The Hanang Wheat Complex was overtly modeled after the large-scale mechanized wheat farms of Saskatchewan and Manitoba. CIDA was actively involved in the Hanang Wheat Complex from 1967 to 1989, when it began to look for "exit options."

The profitability of the Hanang Wheat Complex was never clear. While the farms produced 51% of the country's total wheat production, total domestic consumption never reached 10% of the total population (Walsh 1996).[9] Furthermore, transportation and input costs were extraordinarily high. The farms needed fertilizers, imported seeds, mechanized equipment, and spare parts, all of which needed to be imported at the expense of Tanzania's foreign exchange reserves (*ibid*). Considering the low levels of domestic wheat consumption, and the high costs of domestic wheat production, it would probably have made more sense for the country to import wheat, freeing up the resources invested in the farms for other projects. Like any other large-scale development program, however, there were a number of powerful people who were profiting from the continued existence of the Hanang Wheat Complex. Canadian technicians and development consultants were employed in the project. Tanzanian elites used NAFCO equipment to farm large tracts of land for their own personal accumulation. A confidential letter from the Canadian High Commissioner to NAFCO's director of planning suggests that the farms were as much as 30% larger than the official figures given by NAFCO.[10]

These conditions may have passed unnoticed except for the efforts of Barabaig activists to internationalize their cause. With the assistance of an Australian anthropologist named Charles Lane, a group of Barabaig elders drafted an "Open Letter to the Canadian People" in 1989. These elders had been selected by the Barabaig community to investigate the details of the NAFCO farms and to speak on their behalf (Lane 1993). The letter appeared widely in the Canadian Press in November of 1990. It outlined the grievances of the Barabaig and emphasized the role of CIDA in establishing the Hanang Wheat Complex. It ended with a plea to all Canadians "to use whatever means are available to resolve this conflict in the name of justice."[11] Duncan was slated to read this letter in front of the Canadian Parliament, but was denied a passport by the Tanzanian Government. He asked Lane to read it on his behalf.

The impact of the "Open Letter" was strengthened by an independent investigation of the Tanzanian Government headed by Chief Justice R.H.

---

9. Walsh, S. 1996. *CLWR Review of the Hanang Community Development Project, January 4 – January 22 1996*. Ottawa, CIDA: mimeo.

10. Mourneau, Y. 1987. *Confidential Letter (04/12/87) to Mr. Fabiano Shempemba Director of NAFCO, Regarding the Hanang Wheat Complex*. Dar-es-Salaam: mimeo.

11. This quote is taken from a Xerox of the original letter, which bears the thumbprints of five Barabaig elders, "on behalf of the Barabaig people of Hanang District, Arusha, Tanzania."

Kisanga. The Kisanga Commission substantiated Barabaig claims of human rights abuses at the hands of NAFCO employees. It also acknowledged that the Wheat Complex had been expanded illegally and that powerful individuals within NAFCO had profited as a result. It stopped short, however, of suggesting that any land actually be returned to the Barabaig, suggesting instead that they "be made to engage in agriculture as an alternative method of livelihood and income" (Kisanga 1993). Prior to these events it was nearly impossible for the Barabaig to communicate directly with Canadian officials, because the party-state claimed a monopoly right to represent the Tanzanian people to transnational donors. Following these events, however, the Canadian Government began to take an active interest in the plight of the Barabaig, and lines of communication between Barabaig leaders and Canadian officials were gradually opened.

The HCDP was a direct response to the "Open Letter" and the Kisanga Commission Report, although its architects envisioned from the beginning that it would be low key and non-controversial. The project would clear the good name of the Canadian Government by providing technical services to those who had been negatively affected by the "social problems arising from the (NAFCO) farms and the inevitable clash between pastoralists and sedentary farmers" (CIDA 1994: 1).[12] Project documents emphasized the Kisanga Commission's conclusion that abuses committed against local people were isolated acts of individuals, and in no way sanctioned by NAFCO (Walsh 1996: 6). This position implicitly exonerated the Government of Canada since according to the discourse of HCDP most of these acts were the unfortunate byproduct of a socialist system in which "checks and balances" were sadly lacking (Harker 2002: 2). That the Canadian Government enthusiastically supported this socialist system for many years is conveniently forgotten. The HCDP seeks to address the question of corruption by promoting "anti-corruption culture" in Hanang, which will have taken root by 2025 (www.habari.co.tz/hpdf/forums.htm).

Unlike previous technical development interventions undertaken during the socialist period, the HCDP is much more explicitly geared toward social engineering. In addition to promoting "anti-corruption culture," the project seeks to foster "a community with a developmental mind-set and culture, which cherishes human development with respect to all people at all levels

---

12. CIDA. 1994. *Hanang Community Development Project, Concept*. Dar es Salaam, CIDA: mimeo.

and gender. Hanang residents in the year 2025 will be imbued with the following positive attributes: professionalism, ingenuity, entrepreneurship, innovativeness and creativity, hard work, self-reliance, community spirit balanced by individual initiative, responsible parenthood, continuous learning, honest and trustworthy behavior, rejection of all forms of corruption" (*ibid*). This promotion of civil society through development, or development through civil society as the case may be, implies that the problems of Hanang are largely mindset problems. Instead of addressing the structural inequities created by the Canadian Hanang Wheat Project, it focuses on changing people's attitudes through forums and workshops. Within this framework the promotion of civil society is reduced to an exercise in group therapy.

In addition to erasing the politics of the Hanang Wheat Complex, this discursively constructed vision of civil society in Hanang creates suitable "targets of intervention" for HCDP. The extraordinary complexities of Hanang District are reduced to problems that can be solved within a "logical framework analysis," with "expected results," "performance measurements," and "risk indicators." Like development interventions in the socialist period, which sought to implement "technical fixes" for complex socio-economic problems, more recent interventions like the HCDP appear to revolve around the implementation of "institutional fixes" to complex socio-economic problems. The goals of the project are achieved by bringing together the right mix of "stakeholders," so that every sector of civil society in Hanang is adequately represented. In the case of HCDP, these stakeholders make up the Project Development Group, and include representatives of CIDA and the Canadian High Commission, representatives of local and national government, a representative of the Hanang Wheat Complex, a representative of the business community and an influential member of the private sector at the national level, representatives of local NGOs, representatives of local religious organizations, and representatives of "traditionalist communities" (www.habari.co.tz/hpdf/whatis.htm). The negotiations of these various "stakeholders" are "mediated" by a Canadian development anthropologist who also acts as project manager.

The concept of "stakeholders" also has an "anti-political" effect, since it assumes that all vested interests are equally valid and that all participants are equally empowered. The historical grievances of the Barabaig are no longer an issue, while the Barabaig themselves are transformed from a marginalized ethnic minority to one of several stakeholder groups. Two NGOs and a representative of their "traditionalist community" represent their interests in the Project Development Group. The job of these representatives is to promote economic development by holding government officials to account and fostering the right kinds of attitudes among their constituents. They are also eligible to apply to the HCDP for funding for small-scale technical development projects, just like all the other "stakeholders" in Hanang. This vision is exemplary of the neo-Tocquevillian paradigm outlined in the introduction to this chapter. It also imagines a way in which the social, political, and economic problems of Hanang District can be solved with a few million Canadian dollars. In order for this vision to be institutionalized in HCDP, however, it was first necessary to gain the consent and cooperation of Barabaig NGO and community leaders.

Consent and Coercion: Barabaig NGOs as State Ideological Apparatuses

The Neo-Tocquevillian vision of civil society embodied by HCDP is constructed on web sites and project documents, but it could only be institutionalized through complex interventions by Canadian and Tanzanian officials in the actually existing civil society of Hanang District in the mid-1990s. Empirical accounts of these interventions reveal that this actually existing civil society was a public sphere between the household and the state, as envisioned by the neo-Tocquevillian model, but it was more importantly a sphere in which "consent was manufactured" in keeping with the Gramscian model. An ethnographic account of these processes reveals how the "anti-political" effects of HCDP were made to work at the community level.

The difficulty that representatives of CIDA faced in "manufacturing consent" in Hanang was revealed early on at a CUSO-sponsored planning workshop. In addressing a CIDA representative at this workshop, community members made the following statements (CUSO 1994: 2–3):

> **Madai Sakesta:** We are the people who in the future would not have a place. We are losing our land to the rich. Since I was born, I have never heard of a father who robs his children of everything as the government has done to the Barabaig. What kind of father is this?
> **Amuye Asmeida:** I am very happy that one person from the organization that helped NAFCO steal our land (CIDA) is here. Is there anything she can tell us? Does she have any idea of our problems? As a human being has she ever been hurt the way we have suffered? Does she have emotional feelings that we are also human beings?

Nakai: The Tanzanian Government has placed a fire near our homes. I hope the woman who gave them the fire is here. Can she help me since my farm is burned? The Canadians have left. The NAFCO people have not left. You lit the fire. How will you prove to us that you are not still supporting the (Tanzanian) government? Prove it by helping. We should request CIDA, not CUSO, because it was CIDA who burned our homes. The father of the child who burns someone's home has some responsibility to remedy the situation. That is why I am looking to CIDA more than to CUSO.[13]

Representatives of CIDA quickly made it known that this community priority would not be addressed by HCDP. Elders who attended community meetings with CIDA representatives repeatedly brought up the issue of land, but were told that this was a matter to be settled by the Government of Tanzania, not the Government of Canada. One of the first activities of HCDP was to fund a program of village demarcation and registration for the ostensible purpose of protecting Barabaig land rights. Since development interventions for specific ethnic groups are forbidden in Tanzania, however, the program was officially designed to benefit all citizens of Hanang. Since the most powerful citizens of the district tended to be farmers, it came as no surprise to my informants that long-standing biases against Barabaig herders continued to be part of this latest intervention (cf. Gabba and Green 1993: 29).[14] The Barabaig soon found themselves victims of a gerrymandering campaign, which favored the ethnic Iraqw at the village level.

This situation intensified in 1995, when the MP for Hanang, Fredrick Sumaye, was elected to the office of Prime Minister. During his time in Parliament, Sumaye made numerous public statements that he was not a representative of the Barabaig and that he represented his own people, the Iraqw, first and foremost (*ibid*: 35 and Walsh 1996: 17). Ironically, he labeled Bugalda as a "tribalist" organization. Following his election to Prime Minister, Sumaye was very keen to see HCDP go forward, as he was now the official liaison between the Government of Canada and the communities of Hanang (CIDA 1996: 17). The project presented him with tremendous opportunity to bolster his political support in his home district. The only fly in the ointment was that the Government of Canada had agreed to release the project funds only if all the NGOs in Hanang agreed to participate in HCDP.

---

13. CUSO. 1994. *Barabaig Community Development, Workshop Report*. Arusha, mimeo.

14. Gabba, A and M. Green 1993. *Report on Hanang District Project Development Exercise*. Arusha, CUSO: mimeo.

Barabaig NGO leaders and representatives of CUSO saw this situation as an opportunity to reintroduce the historical grievances of the Barabaig into the agenda of the HCDP. They threatened to withhold their support for the project until Sumaye addressed the problems of the Hanang Wheat Complex and worked on returning some of the traditional Barabaig grazing lands. According to Barabaig NGO leaders and CUSO personnel, Sumaye trumped this move by threatening to deregister Bulgalda if they continued to impede HCDP. Meanwhile CUSO underwent major restructuring, replacing a confrontational Kenyan coordinator with a more moderate British one. One of his first moves was to disassociate CUSO with the politics of the Hanang Wheat Scheme. Barabaig NGO leaders decided that it was their responsibility to get what they could for their constituents from HCDP. With the consent of these key "stakeholders" HCDP was finally ready to move forward (for a more detailed discussion see Igoe 2000).

During this period (Spring of 1996) I attended a meeting between Sumaye, the Canadian High Commissioner, and NGO leaders of Hanang. The purpose of this meeting was to outline the visions of HCDP and where the NGO leaders would like to see their district in the year 2025. It was also an opportunity for the Canadian High Commissioner to become acquainted with local NGO leaders. Barabaig NGO leaders expected that this meeting would be an informal round table between themselves and the Canadian High Commissioner. During the meeting the Canadian High Commissioner mentioned that this was also her expectation. Instead, the Prime Minister carefully orchestrated the meeting, keeping interactions between local NGO leaders and the High Commissioner to a minimum.

In a speech to local NGO leaders, Sumaye decreed that everyone was going to have to work together to make HCDP a reality. He said that local NGOs would have a dual role in this process: 1) to promote development; and 2) to foster national unity. He went on to say that no one hated organizations that helped orphans, and that the Tanzanian Government loved NGOs. That is, the Tanzanian Government loved NGOs as long as the NGOs did what the government wanted. He emphasized that NGOs should implement government policies and deliver services that the government cannot deliver itself. In order for this to work, NGOs would need to be transparent and keep the government apprised of all their activities and agendas.

The Prime Minister concluded by reiterating that he did not want NGOs doing anything that the government wouldn't like. If one or two NGOs did something like that, then everyone else would have to tell them, "we don't agree with you." After all, they couldn't let the ideas of a handful of radicals spoil this unique opportunity to finally bring development to the long neglected district of Hanang. He carefully avoided mentioning who these individuals might be, but stated emphatically that he was prepared to take it upon himself to ensure that no one undermined the successful implementation of HCDP. Finally, he assured the assembled NGO leaders that there would be plenty of money, stating literally "*hela za nje hazina mwisho*" (money from outside has no end – donor money is an infinite resource). Therefore, he playfully exhorted, there would be absolutely no reason for anyone to fight over funding.

This entire speech was made in Swahili, and it was unclear how much the Canadian High Commissioner actually understood of it. When Sumaye was finished, she rose and added some words of here own. She began by saying that she saw "radical and revolutionary" change taking place in Tanzania, both political and economic. She said that she expected that there would be a lot more Canadian investment in the country as a result. She proclaimed that Tanzania was entering a bold new era, in which an exciting new relationship would develop between the state and civil society. She called for more transparency both within the government and NGOs. She concluded that she was happy to be able to say that the Canadian Government no longer has any development projects in Tanzania. Their new role was now to support the development initiatives of Tanzanians. Some day in the future, it would doubtless come to pass that even this kind of support would no longer be necessary.

When she finished, she asked the assembled NGO leaders to briefly outline their vision for the future of Hanang. Each rose in turn and emphasized that they hoped that the funding for HCDP would not be too much longer in coming. The High Commissioner agreed that there had been enough talk and that now was the time for action. Now that all the key "stakeholders" had reached a consensus, it was time for the project to go forward. The meeting ended abruptly as the High Commissioner and the Prime Minister departed to the singing of a pro-government song. They drove away without further interaction with NGO leaders. HCDP had the official blessing of the local community, including the Barabaig.

In spite of all this fanfare and emphasis on community participation, HCDP appears to have become the latest in a series of development interventions and government policies that have facilitated the alienation of Barabaig land, while ostensibly compensating the losers with technical development projects. Local development trends, which seek to replace pastoralism with "modern" production systems, continue unabated. Simultaneously, anti-tribal rhetoric and neoliberal ideology has justified extending the benefits of HCDP to a variety of local players, all of whom have been designated as "stakeholders." It has also benefited a number of well-placed outsiders, who were descending on Hanang to offer their services as it became clear that HCDP would actually materialize. During my time in Hanang, I encountered a number of representatives of national and international NGOs who had come to offer their services to local NGO leaders. These services usually consisted of the provision of workshops geared toward institutional capacity building, and assistance with drafting grant proposals. The exorbitant fees for these services would be written into the proposals themselves. The building of civil society, as envisioned by CIDA and the Tanzanian State, had become a profitable enterprise attracting a significant number of transnational investors and entrepreneurs.

These developments have stacked up against the original political direction of the Barabaig NGOs and the social movements that gave birth to them. The courts have provided no relief for their grievances against NAFCO, and their only transnational supporter, CUSO, has pulled the plug on further advocacy programs. Meanwhile, one of the top-ranking government officials in Tanzania has made it clear that he will deal decisively with these organizations if they allow their human rights agendas to interfere with the smooth implementation of HCDP. Within the context of the HCDP, Barabaig NGOs need to design sound technical development projects if they wish to compete with other local NGOs for their share of the CIDA money. While the younger leaders of KIPOC-Barabaig readily accepted this arrangement, the older leaders of Bulgalda stated that they would continue their commitment to cultural autonomy and land rights for the Barabaig.

This commitment notwithstanding, it appears that the Barabaig land rights movement has now been overtaken by events. On my last day in Hanang I asked Bulgalda leaders what they would do in the unlikely event that land from the NAFCO farms was ever returned to the Barabaig (this scenario is even more unlikely as the farms become privatized as part of economic liberalization). Who would be in charge of the land? How would it be divided up, and what about the members of the Barabaig community who have moved so far away that they are unlikely to ever return? Bulgalda leaders responded that if they ever won the land back from NAFCO that they would continue to cultivate wheat there. The profits from this collectively owned Barabaig farm would go to Bulgalda, which would use it to initiate technical development projects on behalf of their constituents (who they could no longer officially claim were exclusively Barabaig). In the political economy of civil society in Hanang all roads appear to lead to technical development and service delivery.

Conclusion

The experience of Barabaig NGOs in HCDP supports Ferguson's notion of "the Anti-Politics Machine," in that a fundamentally political history has been transformed into an a-political question of development and governance, in which key "stakeholders" work together to create a "development culture," which is beneficial to everyone in question. Like Ferguson's "Anti-Politics Machine" HCDP has also facilitated state control in a particular local context, as well as specific development interventions by transnational institutions.

Understanding how these processes actually unfold, however, depend on detailed ethnographic description. The ethnography of "anti-politics" in Hanang reveals the inner-workings of local civil society as a sphere where consent is manufactured and the interests of ruling elites are promoted. It also reveals how powerful individuals like the Tanzanian Prime Minister and the High Commissioner of Canada actively "authored" these "anti-political" effects in the limited context of the HCDP. The details of this ethnography illustrate that coercion and consent are never far apart in the production of anti-political politics.

Like other studies of power and governmentality in Africa, however, this study is plagued by the difficulty of applying theories to contexts they were never meant to address. Gramsci's ideas of the subaltern, for instance, were derived almost exclusively from his knowledge of Italian workers and peasants. Althusser's notion of state ideological apparatuses is derived from a Marxist analysis of western class relationships, which are of questionable relevance in most of Sub-Saharan Africa. Foucault loudly asserted that he was uninterested in establishing a general theory of power, and discouraged other theorists from applying his ideas about power in specific contexts to power in new and different contexts. Nevertheless, social scientists doggedly persist in reworking these theories and others to explain relationships of power in Africa. Since I am clearly guilty of this offense, I conclude this chapter with some preliminary observations about the application of western theories of power to African civil society.

The case of the HCDP suggests that a modified Gramscian perspective may be fruitfully applied to the question of NGOs and civil society in contemporary Africa. Civil society in contemporary Hanang is similar to Gramsci's paradigm of civil society in a period of hegemonic crisis. Subaltern intellectuals, in the person of Barabaig NGO leaders, had resisted the hegemonic discourses of the ruling elite, and even constructed a credible counter-hegemonic discourse. The counter-hegemonic ideas of these subaltern intellectuals resonated with the experiences of other subalterns leading to collective action that threatened fundamental changes in local power relations and the distribution of resources. From a Marxist perspective, the struggle of the Barabaig threatened the reproduction of relations of production, especially with regards to the question of who could legitimately control the means of production. As in much of Sub-Saharan Africa, the means of production at stake were land, other natural resources, and development aid.

What remains open to question, however, is the exact nature of hegemony in the context of African civil society, if such a thing can be said to exist at all. Gramsci defined hegemony as a situation in which members of the subaltern classes comprehensively embrace the ideas of the ruling elites. As Shivji (1991) observes, however, this type of hegemony is probably not possible in Africa, where the ruling classes represent an insignificant portion of the total population, and one that is heavily dependent on support from transnational interests. Gramscian hegemony is further impeded by the inability of the state to effectively reach every part of the country, and the experience of the vast majority of Tanzanians belies the idea that their country is in the process of "developing" to the benefit of all. Most people are simply not taken in by elite discourses, as their lives are clearly not improving (cf. Ferguson 1999).

And yet the idea of "development" in Tanzania contains some elements of what Gramsci called hegemony. It is a concept that is widely accepted, even though most people are only vaguely aware that it has to do with improvement in their standards of living. I have never interviewed anyone who said that development was a bad idea, and accusations that a specific group of people is trying to "block development" are a powerful coercive strategy that I have often seen employed by Tanzanian politicians and NGO leaders. Because of the colonial history of state formation in Africa, however, ideas of development are usually employed to control relatively small groups in specific local contexts, instead of representing a national ideological hegemony.

Foucauldian ideas seem tailor made for addressing the diffuse nature of power in Africa. After all, Foucault explained that power has no center. It is everywhere and nowhere, pervading all relationships. The problem with applying this perspective to Africa has less to do with the diffuseness of power as with the relationship of discourse to relationships of power in specific contexts. In his earlier works, Foucault argued that discourse alone shaped reality by creating rules, unknown to the actors involved, that "regulated and governed all of their serious speech acts" (Dreyfus and Rabinow 1982: 102). In his later works, however, he revised this position, arguing that the role of discourse in shaping reality is only "intelligible as part of a larger set of organ-

ized and organizing practices in whose spread the human sciences play a crucial role" (*ibid*: 103). Here of course we are speaking of disciplinary techniques
and technologies of discipline as outlined by Foucault in what is probably his
best known work, *Discipline and Punish* (1977).

It almost goes without saying that techniques and technologies of discipline
are not nearly as pervasive in sub-Saharan Africa (with the possible exception
of South Africa) as they are in the global north. For instance, Biolsi (1995: 28)
documents the ways in which the United States Office of Indian Affairs internally pacified the Lakota people of South Dakota by constructing new kinds
of "knowable and recordable individuals." In the body of the article, Bilosi outlines administrative practices on the part of the Office of Indian Affairs, which
he calls after Foucault "modes of subjection." These practices included the imposition of property ownership, demonstration of competency, registration
of Indian "blood quanta, and recording genealogy." They required complex
and expensive administrative intrusion into the lives of the Lakota people.
Most African states, by contrast, lack the resources and the political will to engage in the same types of surveillance and classification projects as their northern counterparts, especially recent projects like the U.S. Department of Homeland Security's Total Information Awareness System. Consequently, the types
of "modes of subjection" described by Bilosi in are far less likely to come into
play in most African contexts than they would in developed countries.

The same argument can be applied to a lesser extent to Althusser's (1971:
43) ideological state apparatuses, which include churches, schools, trade
unions, political parties, the legal system, the press, and electronic media. He
argues that the most important of these apparatuses are schools, since these
have the function of inculcating almost everyone in society with the ideologies of the prevailing relationships of production. Foucault also saw schools
as an important site for the production of "knowable and recordable subjects,"
additionally he saw them as having an important normalizing effect. Clearly,
such an argument cannot be applied easily to sub-Saharan Africa, where funding for schools has all but disappeared in the wake of IMF sponsored structural adjustment programs. In many areas schools no longer exist, in areas
where they do exist many people do not allow their children to attend.

Admittedly some institutions do fill the role of ideological state apparatuses
in Africa, as well as providing sites for disciplinary technology and practice.
Political parties and electronic media, for instance, still pervade the every day
lives of most African people. Bornstein (this volume) illustrates the importance of churches and religious ideology to African civil society. Docking (this
volume) demonstrates that trade unions still have an important role to play

as well. Almost all of the articles of this volume outline the importance of NGOs as both the stakes and the sites of ideological struggles. It is possible that they are also becoming sites of disciplinary technology and practice.

It is important to note, however, that the influence of these institutions tends to be fragmented in ways that they simply would not be in the global north. Many African states, for instance, have a tenuous hold on their national territories, with some areas being completely beyond state control (Jackson this volume). In the post-9/11 world, the ideological influence of Islam may stand in direct opposition to prevailing relationships of production, the forces of globalization, and by extension African governments. The ideological influence of Christian churches is often fragmented in ways that reflect the carve-up of territories by competing missionary groups during colonialism. The ideological influence of NGOs, likewise, is often fragmented according to territorial influence. Some organizations have broader influence than others, but only a notable few can be said to have national influence.

In brief the nature of African civil society, as an analogue to weak African states, is highly fragmented and prone to the exigencies of local (as opposed to national or society-wide) conditions. This situation has been noted by Mamdani (1996) in his discussion of "decentralized despotism," in which state institutions (today one could add NGOs) wield considerable power at the local level and remain impervious to democratic reform. One of the central features of "decentralized despotism" is a frequent recourse to force or coercion. In the case of the HCDP, for instance, Prime Minister Sumaye allegedly used state power to trump Barabaig NGO leaders with the threat of deregistration. Although it is more difficult to document, transnational actors (both governmental and non-governmental) are tacitly (and sometimes explicitly) involved in this coercive approach to development and governance, a stunning irony in light of their discourses of participation and democratization.

The pervasiveness of coercion in local politics has important implications for theories of African civil society. While Althusser has noted that consent and coercion are never far apart, both Gramsci and Lenin warned that too much force is likely to have self-defeating consequences. Foucault went further by arguing that "where there is force, power is not" (Barrett 2002: 67). People may respond to force, as Barabaig NGO leaders certainly have. However, they have not been disciplined as much as they have been brought into line. For the past thirty years the Tanzanian government has worked to bring the Barabaig into line, and it has been an expensive and difficult process. While Barabaig NGO leaders have now chosen to cooperate with the HCDP in the absence of other viable options, this is a situation that will doubtlessly change as the HCDP winds down. Barabaig NGOs' resistance to the Tanzanian state may yet be rekindled.

Returning to Althusser (1971: 166), the relationships outlined above have an important material foundation, since ideology is always embedded in institutions and their practices. In Africa this relationship is complicated by the historical orientation of African institutions to a global system of institutions, ideas, and money. The ideas and institutions of this global system are in a state of constant flux. The money, on the other hand, appears fairly constant. The influence of this global system is clearly visible in Hanang, where struggles between the Barabaig and the Tanzanian government have shifted in meaning over the past thirty years. What began as a struggle over the meaning of development was transformed into a struggle over the meaning of democracy. This shift in meaning was accompanied by an institutional shift, away from the state toward the NGO sector. Significantly, the emergence of NGOs as a new type of ideological apparatus presented Barabaig leaders with new opportunities to recast the meaning of their struggle by giving them access to the necessary funding and institutional support. It took some time for state elites to regain the upper hand in this new institutional arena.

Again the source of power in this context had to do with a monopoly control over flows of funding from global sources to local institutions. As the HCDP became the only game in town, for reasons outlined in the body of this chapter, Barabaig NGO leaders became correspondingly less powerful. They were reduced to clients of the Tanzanian Prime Minister and the Canadian Government. This brings us to the central importance of prebendalism to African politics, and by extension African civil society (Bayart 1993). Both African officials and NGO leaders use their institutional position to "seek rents" from transnational sources, which in turn are used to build loyal client networks. Chabal and Daloz (1999) have labeled this phenomenon *neopatrimonialism*, and argue that it represents the underlying logic of contemporary African political systems. While the impacts of prebendalism on African civil society are undeniable, two important points must be made here. First, although Chabal and Daloz argue that corruption and disorder actually "work" as political instruments, they also are extraordinarily inequitable and have profound human and financial costs. Second, transnational donors frequently blame "corrupt" African governments for the failure of development and governance interventions, when in reality prebendalism is not an inherently African problem. Rather it is a historical product of African encounters with a global system of institutions, ideas, and money. Western donors are as much to blame for prebendalism as their African counterparts (see Igoe 2003a and 2003b).

While these observations in no way add up to a comprehensive theory of power and governmentality in Africa, they do offer some tentative guidelines for the study of African NGOs and their role in civil society. To begin with, it appears that neo-Tocquevillian paradigms of civil society are largely misplaced in Africa. African NGOs are a training ground for a lot of things, but not often for democratic practice in the western liberal tradition. Secondly, western theories of power, *à la* Foucault and Gramsci, are definitely relevant to the study of African civil society. It is essential, however, to be clear about the specifics of these theories and what their purchase on specific African realities may be. Detailed ethnographic studies are indispensable to this project. In the highly decentralized context of African civil society, what Foucault referred to as the "local cynicism of power" looms large. This has important implications for anti-politics. In the case of the HCDP, for instance, it appeared that the "serious speech acts" of Barabaig NGO leaders were governed less by discourse rules, than by fear of having their organizations deregistered. Further ethnographic study of African civil society will doubtlessly reveal more about the interplay of power and force in the production of anti-political politics. It should also illuminate the ways in which differentially empowered actors negotiate a constantly shifting terrain of institutions and discourses in pursuit of the material resources necessary to support their livelihoods, interests, and worldviews. Finally, it is essential that such analysis account for institutional incentive structures and the pervasiveness of prebendalism in African political systems. This type of ethnography will inform theories of civil society, as well as our understanding of the actual effects of contemporary governance and development interventions in Sub-Saharan Africa.

Works Cited

Abramson, D. 1999. A critical look at NGOs and civil society as a means to an end in Uzbekistan. *Human Organization*: 58: 240–50.

Althusser, L. 1971. *Lenin and Philosophy and Other Essays*. London: Monthly Review Press.

Barrett, S. 2002. *Culture Meets Power*. London: Praeger.

Bayart, J-F. 1993. *The State in Africa: The politics of the belly*. London: Longman.

Berthoud, G 1992. Market. In *The Development Dictionary: A guide to knowledge as power*, Edited by W. Sachs. London: Zed Books.

Biolsi, T. 1995. The birth of the reservation: making modern individuals among the Lakota. *American Ethnologist* (22) 1: 28–53.

Brosius, P. 1997. Green dots and pink hearts: displacing politics from the Malaysian rainforest. *American Anthropologist* 10 (1): 36–55.

Chabal, P. and J-P Daloz. 1999. *Africa Works: Disorder as political instrument.* Oxford: James Currey.

Dreyfus, H. and P. Rabinow. 1982. *Michel Foucault: Beyond structuralism and hermeneutics.* Chicago: University of Chicago Press.

Edwards, M. and D. Hulme. 1996. NGO performance and accountability. In *Beyond the Magic Bullet: NGO performance and accountability in the post-cold war world,* edited by M. Edwards and D. Hulme. London: Earthscan Publications.

Escobar, A. 1995. *Encountering Development.* Princeton, New Jersey: Princeton University Press.

Ferguson, J. 1990. *The Anti-Politics Machine: Development, depoliticization, and bureaucratic power in Lesotho.* Cambridge: Cambridge University Press.

———. 1999. *Expectations of Modernity: Myths and meaning of urban life in the Zambian copperbelt.* Berkeley: University of California Press.

Fisher, W. 1997. Doing good? The politics and anti-politics of NGO practice. *Annual Review of Anthropology* 26: 439–64.

Foucault, M. 1977. *Discipline and Punish: The birth of the prison.* New York: Vintage Books.

———. 1980. *The History of Sexuality, Volume One.* New York: Pantheon Books.

Gramsci, A. 1999. *Selections from the Prison* Notebooks, edited and translated by Q. Hoare and G. Smith. New York: International Publishers.

Galaty, J. 1988. Pastoral and agro-pastoral migration in Tanzania: factors of economy, ecology, and demography in cultural perspective. In *Production and Autonomy,* edited by J. Bennet and J. Bowen. Lanham, MD: University of Maryland Press.

Harbeson, J. 1994. Civil society and political renaissance in Africa. In *Civil Society and the State in Africa,* edited by J. Harbeson, D. Rothchild, and N. Chazan. London: Lynne Reinner Publishers.

Harker, C. 2002. Canada: an image soiled and repaired. *Waves* 1: 5.

Hefner, R. 1998. On the history and cross-cultural possibility of a democratic ideal. In *Democratic Civility: The history and cross-cultural possibility of a democratic ideal,* edited by R. Hefner. London: Transaction Publishers.

Hodgson, D. 2001. *Once Intrepid Warriors: Gender, ethnicity, and the cultural politics of Maasai development.* Oxford: James Currey.

Hyden, G. 1995. Bringing voluntarism back. In *Service Provision Under Stress in East Africa*, edited by J. Semboja and O. Therkildsen. London: James Currey.

Igoe, Jim. 2000 *Ethnicity, Civil Society, and the Tanzanian Pastoralist NGO Movement: The continuities and discontinuities of liberalized development*. PhD. Dissertation, Boston University.

———. 2003a. *Conservation and Globalization: A study of national parks and indigenous communities from East Africa to South Dakota*. Wadsworth Publishing, Riverside, CA.

———. 2003b Scaling up civil society: donor money, NGOs, and the pastoralist land rights movement in Tanzania. *Development and Change* 34 (5): 863–86.

Kelsall, T. 1998. Donors, NGOs, and the State: the creation of a public sphere in Tanzania. Paper presented at the ASA Africa and Globalization Conference, University of Central Lancashire.

Kiondo, A. 1993. Structural adjustment and non-governmental organizations in Tanzania. In *Social Change and Economic Reform in Africa*, edited by P. Gibbon. Uppsala: The Scandinavian Institute of African Studies.

Kjaerby, F. 1979. *The development of agro-pastoralism among the Barabaig of Hanang District*. BRALUP Research Paper #56. University of Dar-es-Salaam.

Klima, G. 1970. *The Barabaig: East African cattle herders*. New York: Holte, Rhine, and Winston.

Lane, C. 1993. The state strikes back: extinguishing customary land rights in Tanzania. In *Never Drink From the Same Cup*, edited by H. Veber et al. Copenhagen: CDR-IWGIA.

———. 1996. *Pastures Lost*. London: International Institute for Environment and Development.

Mamdani, M. 1996. *Citizen and Subject: Contemporary Africa and the legacy of late colonialism*. Princeton: The University of New Jersey Press.

Salamon, L. 1993. *The Global Associational Revolution: The rise of the third sector on the world scene*. Occasional Paper no. 15: Baltimore: Institute for Policy Studies, Johns Hopkins University.

Shivji, I. 1991. The politics of liberalization in Tanzania: notes on a crisis of ideological hegemony. In *Tanzania and the IMF: The dynamics of liberalization*, edited by H. Campbell and H. Stein. Boulder, CO: Westview Press.

Shivji, I. and W. Kapinga. 1998. *Maasai Rights in Ngorongoro, Tanzania*. Nottingham: Russell Press.

Shivji, I. and R. Tenga. 1985. Ujamaa in court. *Africa Events* 1 (2): 18–21.

Sundet, G. 1997. *The Politics of Land in Tanzania*. Oxford: DPhil. Dissertation.

Tenga, R. and G. Kakoti. 1993. The Barabaig Land Case. In *Never Drink From the Same Cup*, edited by H. Veber et al. Copenhagen: CDR-IWGIA.

Vail, L. 1989. Introduction: ethnicity in Southern African history. In *The Creation of Tribalism in Southern Africa*, edited by L. Vail. London: James Currey.

Williams, G. 1960. The concept of egemonia in the thought of Antonio Gramsci: some notes of interpretation. *Journal of the History of Ideas*: October–December: 586–99.

World Bank. 1997. *The State in a Changing World*. New York: OUP.

Wilson, G. 1952. The Tatoga of Tanganyika. *Tanganyika Notes and Records* (33): 35–47.

CHAPTER 6

NGOs and the New Field of African Politics: A Case Study from Zanzibar

Ben Rawlence
Foreign Affairs and Defence Adviser to the Liberal Democrats in the British Parliament
benrawlence@hotmail.com

Introduction

There has been much effort over the last decade to build what is called "civil society" in Africa. The language and the resources attached to this effort have opened up new political spaces outside the purview of the state. The practical manifestation of the liberal discourse is the liberalization of social and economic state regulations; the loosening of state control over society, and the encouraging of transnational linkages with the local; relationships that bypass central authority. This process has far-reaching consequences for the nature of politics in Africa. But the consequences are largely unintended and, in the case of Zanzibar, lie in direct contradiction to the liberal ideal that civil society is supposed to serve.

This chapter examines social and political changes in one village in Zanzibar in the context of the "civil" development discourse and analyses how the reality amongst NGOs on the ground has become divorced from the liberal rhetoric espoused by foreigners assisting the village and articulated in the practices of donors. Interventions by foreign donors and individuals often have unintended consequences and what looks like civil society from outside may often be something quite uncivil. The donor-recipient relationship in this case is thus a "working misunderstanding" as each party, consciously or not, recognizes the other as something other than it is. Donors see the NGOs in the village as expressions of liberal autonomy, separate from the state whereas in fact they are populated by people whose authority is derived from the state. NGOs in their turn, do not see the donors as partners or facilitators of political autonomy, rather as resource providers, with all the problems of sustainability that that entails. In this case, an effort to build civil society has in fact led to the strengthening of the power of unelected elites, a very unliberal outcome.

The real picture needs to be better understood if a truly shared vision between partners on both sides of the development fence is to evolve, and especially if liberal donors are to be able to speak with any honesty about what they are actually achieving in Africa and elsewhere. While in this case study the delivery of resources to the village was undoubtedly beneficial and was delivered in a surprisingly equitable way, success was inadvertent. Moreover, over the long term such a fundamental misunderstanding about the basic nature of African societies risks undermining the security of African communities and the possibilities for liberal democracy itself.

By opening up political spaces outside the state which are less amenable to regulation or state control, the accumulation of political, social and financial capital becomes linked to informal networks and power brokers. In many ways these conflicts are the same ones that were traditionally situated in the realm of the formal state bureaucracy. But as informal organizations become the vehicle for the capture and distribution of funds, these conflicts instead take on the form of wars between NGOs. This results in the politicization of everyday life in African communities, and, as these spaces assume transnational dimensions, the atomization of communities. They no longer look to the state for legitimacy or resources (or political direction). This actually flies in the face of the liberal project by undermining the relevance and importance of national politics for people's welfare. Local solutions are pursued in direct contradiction to national ones. Such a movement can only further fracture any nascent national polity that might hold states to account.

Discourse

With structural adjustment programs in the 1980s and 1990s the withdrawal of the state from service provision opened up a huge market for nongovernmental alternatives. NGOs, indigenous and foreign, were seen as suited to "humanizing" the implementation of structural adjustment programs (Fowler 1991: 55–56).

In addition NGOs fitted neatly into the new market-oriented political economy of the 1980s and 1990s. Where governments were considered inefficient by donors, as Fowler shows, NGOs have come to

> embody a number of comparative advantages over governments for improving the lot of the poor: to be more cost effective in service delivery, to have a greater ability to target the poor and vulnerable sections of the population, to demonstrate a capacity to develop community-based institutions and to be better able to promote the popular participation needed for the sustainability of benefits (Fowler 1991: 56).

With such a broad based mandate and such high expectations it is easy to see how indigenous NGOs have been taken to exemplify an expanding and strengthened civil society...[which] may be influencing African politics (Fowler 1991: 57).

Briefly, this logic can be summarized as follows. African governments are seen as inefficient and perhaps even moribund. Structural adjustment has hastened this process by cutting state spending especially on social services. NGOs have been the main beneficiaries of this realignment of funding priorities, as the Danish government's strategy for development cooperation acknowledges: in pace with the gradual reduction in the role of the state, the number of registered national and international NGOs has increased considerably. Donors have established a specific coordination group to liaise with NGOs (Danida 199: 1).[1] Insofar as the distribution of development resources is necessarily political, they now constitute a political force in Africa. Such that Nyang'oro (1993: 27) can conclude the relationship between the state and NGO may define the scope of development in Africa for some time to come. [2]

But the rise of alternative forms of social organization to the state brings with it questions of sovereignty. Nyang'oro (*ibid*) claims, "in no way does the emergence and proliferation of NGOs suggest a retreat by the state". However, at the same time "the construction of development organizations is an unavoidably political act" (*ibid:* 28). And even more so in a fledgling multiparty system where some see NGOs as "potential agents of democracy" (Fowler 1991; Hyden 1997).

---

1. Danida Annual Report 1999 available at <http://www.ing.dk/danida>.
2. Nyang'oro, J. 1993. Civil Society, the State and African Development in the 1990s. Nairobi: All African Conference of Churches, 1993.

These are issues of governance. The governance agenda as it has come to be known rests "on the belief that the experience of social and economic development in Africa has been disappointing because African populations have not been adequately represented in government...As a remedy to these problems, it is argued that new arrangements for institutionalizing norms of reciprocity and accountability need to be found" (Kelsall 2000: 1).[3] In this process proponents of the governance agenda see "civil society as a crucially important factor at every stage of democratization" (Larry Diamond, cited in (Fowler 1991: 56). Fowler (1991) thinks NGOs exemplify civil society. Ultimately though both terms are rendered inoperative by the insoluble paradox of power relations in Africa originally outlined by Ekeh (1975): there are "two publics," the formal and the informal coexisting in an interdependent relationship.

Ekeh provides perhaps the most pertinent insight as far as Jambiani is concerned and it is mirrored by Fowler (1991: 54): "Africa's pervasive webs of affective relations, with their own social logic of reciprocity, render Western normative institutional distinctions between the government, the party, commercial and voluntary sectors and civil society, an inadequate analytical basis for understanding politics or government on the continent". The line between state and society in Jambiani has been blurred since colonial times and remains indistinct. Power crosscuts realms; leadership patterns in civic and state organizations in Tanzania have overlapped since independence.

Ekeh's conceptualization seems best to describe what is happening in Jambiani, nevertheless Western norms have still shaped the political space in the village because, "governance and civil society have come to be central operational concepts in the policies of Western governments and International Financial Institutions" (Young 1996: 537). The point with reference to understanding the changes taking place in Jambiani is that, while theories of governance may have a questionable purchase on local realities, they have nevertheless played a crucial role in shaping an environment within which NGOs are highly valued. The liberal universalist tendencies of this position are self-evident. But, as Tsing has shown in Indonesia, by coercing local realities into global categories, Third World actors are "produced as representatives by outsiders' standards of representation" (Tsing 1999: 167). This, of course, is a two

---

3. Kelsall, T. 2000. *Subjectivity, Collective Action and the Governance Agenda in Arumeru East*. Oxford: University of Oxford, QEH Working Papers 42.

way process as indigenous NGOs learn the language of political survival in the global economy of the new millennium.

Thus, in the liberalized economy increasing numbers of tourists come to Jambiani, a multinational company encourages the growth of seaweed as a cash crop, and local NGOs can encroach on state responsibilities such as maintenance of the school and provision of medicines to the clinic by appealing to the mandate of the governance agenda. Local NGOs have direct links with tourists and western NGOs independent of the state.[4] This is the basis of a new field of politics in which government bureaucracy is not the only "organizing principle of ambition" (Bayart 1986). This bears out Nyang'oro's claim about the salience of the NGO-state relationship, and this is exactly the relationship that will determine the future of development in Jambiani. However, the histories of both the Zanzibari state and the NGOs in Jambiani are not as distinct as the above formulation makes out. Ekeh's two publics are still at large, although this is an analysis that the liberal agenda ignores.

The Historical Formation of Authority in Jambiani

The practice of attempting to improve standards of living in Jambiani has in recent years been conducted by several organizations; Western and Tanzanian, governmental and non-governmental. These very typologies are rooted in a Western discourse that is at the heart of the "working misunderstanding" that allows the development project to function. The Tanzanian personnel involved with development in the village defy categorization according to Western typologies of "governmental" or not, as members of "civil" society or as "uncivil" agents. They operate in many roles at once. It can be argued that a failure to take African social structures on their own terms has led to a misrecognition on the part of the donors involved with Jambiani: what donors broadly label "civil society" may in fact be a reworking of old patterns of state/party hierarchies, perhaps even less pluralistic in nature.

Since the Arusha Declaration in 1967 Tanzania followed a policy of socialist self-reliance and communalism. Under the villagization policies of Julius

---

4. The most recently formed local organization has received money from the Ford Foundation and two British NGOs (Charles Musiba pers. comm 1999).

Nyerere (the first President) *maendeleo*[5] became the organizing principle of social life and many people were forcibly moved to government villages. Hyden pointed out the rationale, "the peasants cannot conceivably be at the forefront of the route to a modern society, as such a development is bound to be at their expense" (Hyden 1980: 16). According to Bayart, for the developmental state of the postcolonial era, "the aim [was] to administer society even against itself, and to order it according to the explicit, ideal canons of modernity" (Bayart 1986: 113). As Tsing has shown in Indonesia (Tsing 1999) "development" in this context has been synonymous with "politics" for quite a while. Therefore, "provision of social amenities became the principle on which legitimacy was constructed" (Fowler 1991: 62).

During the period of Arab rule in Zanzibar the local representatives of the Sultan were *masheha* (ward chiefs), appointed from among the local population. Under the British a familiar form of indirect rule was initiated into which the office of *sheha* fitted neatly (Middleton and Campbell 1965: 30). Although not formal government employees under the British, *the masheha* enjoyed "considerable unofficial influence" (*ibid.*). The same can be said today where they are responsible for land allocation and dispute resolution.[6]

The Current Situation

In terms of formal authority, the area has a member of parliament who has little say over the day-to-day administration of Jambiani. There is a district commissioner too. However, the two most concrete examples of the government's presence in the village are the clinic and the school. The government's ability to support social services is severely limited. According to the teachers at the school even salaries were hard to come by during the 1990s. A decade earlier the Tanzanian government asked the Danish government for assistance "to repair and maintain Tanzania's secondary schools and train local staff to maintain the buildings"(Danida 1992: 14).[7] Danish assistance thus became linked to the government's ability to fulfill the needs of its citizens. The school was the largest and most politicized government project in the village and,

---

5. *Maendeleo* translates as "development" in English.
6. M.Simai pers comm. 1997.
7. Danida 1992. Evaluation of the School Maintenance Project. Available at <http://www.ing.dk/danida/1992-7/tx>.

with the help of Danida, the one area where the state was actually making improvements.

The project was introduced to Zanzibar in 1986 and Jambiani was one of ten schools targeted. The project, observed in Jambiani, had a number of unintended effects. Still, it succeeded on many levels. It was the precursor to structural transformation in the village by creating new structures of opportunity for the villagers. Local involvement of this sort by Danida was the practical expression of Campbell's (1997: 67) point that, where "society at the national level is seen as abstract and unrealistic, the region, the province and/or district are viewed as real and pragmatic alternatives". By becoming involved at a local level Danida created a structure of opportunity that led to the struggles described in this paper.

Danida administered the project in Zanzibar in conjunction with the Ministry of Education until 1991, when the project was formally handed over to the Government of Tanzania with funding from Danida. The representative of the Ministry in the village is the Assistant District Education Officer. The initial plans for repair covered five areas; roofs, water, sewerage, electricity and burglar-proofing. The school in Jambiani like many others in Tanzania was suffering from overcrowding and disrepair as a result of government underinvestment.

The project was established to repair and maintain buildings. However, Danida's objectives were swiftly capitalized on. Danida would roof any building that needed it. A group of four teachers quickly realized the potential of Danida's assistance and set up the School Extension Group in 1993. Since roofing in Zanzibar is "the costliest and most time-consuming" (*ibid: 25*) part of any construction work, they mobilized communal village labor and built as many "shells" as they could (i.e. four walls without a roof). They could do this because the materials for building walls are locally available: coral rag and lime. On four occasions Danida came and erected roofs on classrooms built by the SEG. In addition the SEG began digging wells at the school and planning a library in 1995.

These advancements were in themselves not unwelcome but the existence of the SEG meant that the state no longer had a monopoly on the provision or direction of resources. The community was beginning to mobilize for its own benefit. As such the SEG had the potential to threaten the state. It is easy to see in such an environment that "the construction of organizations at least in the development field is an unavoidably political act" to quote Nyang'oro (1993: 28) again. By laying claim to development resources one is also claiming political capital. Therefore a lack of development resources would leave the state politically vulnerable.

The School Extension Group had the potential to threaten the monopoly of the Ministry of Education, represented by the Assistant District Education Officer, on the means of development. Two other events increased this potential to the point where the SEG was eventually disbanded by the government.

Firstly, the growth of the tourist industry in Jambiani had created a ready market for charitable donations. In 1985 there was one government guesthouse. By 1995 there were 13 privately owned establishments. In 1997 the owner of the largest hotel in the village estimated that there were 100 visitors a day passing through Jambiani (Vuai Sahihi pers comm 1997). The SEG was quick to realize the potential again. In 1994 it had collection boxes in each hotel and by 1995 it was offering guided tours of the school and a history of its development efforts. The result was an expanding financial stream in the form of donations and links with western organizations such as War on Want and partnerships with several schools in Europe. This increase of resources at a local level reflected the shift at the policy level in the 1990s away from state-sponsored development.

Secondly, Danida withdrew its support from the government of Zanzibar after the 1995 elections that Denmark viewed as unfair. The minimal purchase that the Ministry of Education had over the development of the school infrastructure thus evaporated. It had virtually no resources of its own and no access to foreign funds in the wake of the disputed election.

The SEG had control of the supply of foreign resources. The Assistant District Education Officer had no means of garnering funds from tourists in the name of the government. In this sense the SEG was an example of the way in which, "communities have to adopt organizational forms and project designs that the donor can recognize if they are to have access to project funds, even if those forms do not reflect community traditions" (Escobar 1991: 676). Tourists were unlikely to donate money to the Government for the upkeep of the school. It would have been a task which they, rightly, assumed should be universally provided. However, the SEG, four plucky teachers, making the case in the language of voluntary and charitable work, were very successful.

The dominance and success of the non-governmental format can in many ways be seen as a reflection of the "changing shape of allegiances in the wider world" (Guyer 1994: 215). Regardless of the allegiances though, the assumption behind Guyer's argument is that patterns of social organization in the South will respond to the ideological trends of the North. This same point is made more explicitly by Escobar, that "the development encounter…amounts to an act of cognitive and social domination" (Escobar 1991: 677).

In so far as the ideological parameters of the relationship are concerned this is true, but Escobar underestimates the innovative ways in which African communities are working within such constraints. The SEG responded creatively to the presence of Danida in their village. Further, the way in which "the state" responded to the simultaneous challenge of the SEG and the decline of its own resource base is another good example of such innovation.

As mentioned above, "the state" is a problematic concept in Africa. The *masheha* are not government officials but are most definitely part of the established elite. The teachers are on the government payroll, and the ten-cell *maskan* (mobilization points during the single party era) still dominate the village landscape. It was not long ago (1992) that the ruling party was the only party and every authority figure was a party member. Far from the seat of central Government, the niceties of multiparty democracy had not yet penetrated Jambiani by the mid nineties. A dozen disaffected individuals supported the opposition Civic United Front (CUF). But otherwise, the ruling CCM party held sway.

The SEG threatened the authority of the local government representatives: the district education office. It also elevated the four teachers who were involved to an enviable position of control in the school and the headmaster was not among them.

Where control over development resources is the sine qua non of community politics, what should the elite (i.e. those for whom the party and the government performed an authorizing function at some level whether now or in the past) do in a situation such as that described in Jambiani in order to maintain control over the means of development? Given the foreign and ideological tenor of the governance agenda, the answer is simple – start an NGO. In this case however, there was already one in existence, the SEG.

In early 1996 the Ministry of Education transferred the four teachers of the SEG from the staff of Jambiani School to other schools in Zanzibar, far from the East Coast, on the recommendation of the headmaster and the Assistant District Education Officer. A new organization was formed in its place: the *Kamati ya Maendeleo ya Jambiani* (Jambiani Development Committee). The JDC took over the fund-raising responsibilities of the SEG and a whole host of other functions besides. There are two interesting dynamics at work: the demography of the members of the board and the role that the committee assigned for itself.

The Assistant District Education Officer chaired the committee. There were twelve other members: the headmaster and two teachers, a retired government official, and eight *masheha*, (ward chiefs). Apart from the teachers and the Education Officer none of these individuals is on the government payroll. However, between them they represent the symbolic power of the state as an authorizing realm. Thus, the committee might style itself as non-governmental but in fact, a theoretical separation between state and society is not possible in Jambiani. This is neither a new nor an isolated observation. Nyanpan and Vaa noticed that TANU[8] positions and traditional village leadership positions were held by the same people (cited in Chitere 1994). Hyden (1980: 28) too describes "an 'invisible' economy of affection that provides opportunities for social action outside the framework of state control". The point is that the historical formation of structures of authority created formal and informal institutions which are closely intertwined. Power crosscuts realms and therefore it is impossible to take the JDC on its own terms as "non-governmental."

This is even more apparent when examining the activities of the newly formed NGO. Not only is it pursuing infrastructural expansion for the school and the clinic but also it has asked for contributions from the hotel owners and from the producers of the local cash crop, seaweed. It is in effect levying taxes in the name of development.

Thus to warn that "civil society leaders may be tempted to become men of the state" (Hyden 1997: 14) or that "civil society may ultimately become part of the state" (Allen 1997: 336) is to miss the point. In this case the state might have become civil society but the history of both is intertwined. What is really needed to understand the political economy of development in this context is an analysis of the historical and ideological basis of authority in the village. Since, "historically pre-existing institutional patterns…ultimately determine what class will be in the best position to take advantage of available opportunities" (Nash 1981: 399). In Jambiani this means those who have been consistently relied upon by the administration, whether Arab, British or CCM, to represent central government authority in the village. In the last stage this involved a very comprehensive influence over forms of social organization in Jambiani. Therefore although teachers and *masheha* may have no representative function viz a viz the Zanzibari government at some level they draw their status from an association with the powers that be. This is clearly evidenced by the pre-eminent influence within the JDC of a former civil servant who used to work in the ministry of defence.

---

8. TANU stands for Tanganyika African National Union and was the first party to govern Tanzania, it later became CCM.

The JDC appears not as the beginning of civil society in the village but rather as the latest expression of state control over associational life. The state in such a formulation is understood not merely as the formal institutions of the Zanzibari government but as a quantum of authority stretching from the President downwards. Although on the surface then, the defeat of the SEG by the JDC may appear as a fight between NGOs, the state is in fact still at large.

Yes, the state is still at large but it has been redefined again. The JDC enjoys a monopoly on the distribution of resources from non-governmental sources to the school and the clinic and other projects. Such resources are considerably greater than the government spends. From 1996–98 it had a monthly income of approximately $100. But it is not the official representative of the government in the village. Because of its non-governmental status it has in fact given respected elders and teachers a chance to participate in the real decision making process; something difficult to achieve within the formal bureaucracy.

An irony needs to be elaborated here. One only needs to examine the members of the JDC to see that they drew a lot of their authority from their association to the formal and informal "state": the ruling party of the single party era, ward chiefs, state employees past and present. Now however, they do indeed have an independent economic base from which it would be quite possible to launch policies with the support of the village which are at variance with those of the central government. The next section will address this potential and the implications for development brought by this new field of politics.

Uncivil Society

Opportunities have come thick and fast for the JDC since it conforms well to what many donors see, following Hyden[9], as a community taking democratic responsibility for its own welfare independent of the state. The Ford Foundation sent two members of the JDC to a conference organized by the University of Florida (Gainesville) to discuss their plans for conservation of

---

9. Hyden defined civil society thus: "civil society evolves in response to the inability of the state to meet the needs or demands of its citizens" (1997: 20). From this perspective it is easy to see the JDC as a panacea.

the village's coastline.[10] The JDC is also co-operating with two British NGOs.[11] None of these relationships are negative as such; in fact they bring many positive benefits to the inhabitants of Jambiani in terms of increased inward investment and improvements in the standard of living. However, the premises on which such relationships exist are highly suspect and have far reaching implications. Direct articulation between foreign donors and communities allows the liberal universal project of development plenty of "new objects of emancipatory purification" (Young 1996: 531). At the same time though it takes the JDC to be representative of community interests while reinforcing its authority over the community.

This situation may not necessarily be detrimental to the progress of development in the village. On the one hand decision making is being implemented at a lower level than the national state, one that is closer to the people towards whom the funding is directed. On the other, such decisions will continue to be made in an undemocratic fashion by people who designate themselves members of the JDC. Such an arrangement may well function to the benefit of the residents of Jambiani (and so far the progress made by the JDC is remarkable),[12] however, it can only do so in so far as the members of the JDC are benign. The JDC is not legally accountable to anyone. Its real contribution to the development of the village is based on an invocation of older historical authority. Is this really "development"?

To the residents of Jambiani it may be, but to the adherents of the governance agenda it probably is not. Democracy and legal accountability (described above as failings of the JDC) may well be of little concern to local residents for whom the historically evolved patterns of decision-making in the village carry their own norms of reciprocity and redistribution. Critics, such as Bayart (1986: 120), who point out the limits of civic action in Africa would agree, seeing the JDC as an example of the "plural invention of modernity". But for the Ford Foundation and the British NGOs such an outcome may be contrary to their aims. They are encouraging civic participation by promoting a particular set of elites. The donors involved with Jambiani misrecognize

---

10. The conference entitled "Conservation and Development Forum 1997" was held in Turkey. Mention is made in the Ford Foundation Annual Report 1997 of a grant of $50,000 to the University of Florida, where Hyden teaches, to "increase participation" in its conference.

11. Charles Musiba pers comm 1999.

12. The JDC had built five classrooms, a doctor's residence and installed a telephone line by 1997, one year after it was formed.

the JDC for an opaque ideal, the particular for the universal, their own definition of "uncivil" for "civil."

A Working Misunderstanding

This misrecognition is not necessarily harmful to the achievement of development as defined by the residents of Jambiani. Instead it is the basis for a working misunderstanding that allows western development organizations such as the Ford Foundation to co-operate with local communities.

The practical reality of the misrecognition is that "foreign and domestic interests become intrinsically joined in civil society organizations" to quote Jane Guyer (1994: 222). A closer look though at these interests suggests that a narrow agenda is being served by this partnership in the name of "development." Community Organizations according to Guyer (1994: 223) can "become a means to attracting foreign investment and thereby create international linkages." Such claims are perhaps not unimaginable but they make light of huge barriers to participatory development that are rooted in processes of class formation in former colonies outlined above. As a result of the "discriminatory nature of the local process of development, access to the means and benefits of development is selective....the process tends to ensure a self-reinforcing accumulation of privilege for special groups" (Sunkel cited in Nash 1981).

With a few exceptions, this is exactly the case in Jambiani. The make-up of the JDC is a coalescence of overlapping hierarchies that have pre-, post- and colonial histories: Arab, British and state socialism.

This is not to say that the JDC is a throwback to a network of primordial ties, rather it is the innovative creation of a particular set of elites. It is certainly the case that "the dynamic of development is towards the establishment and use of international linkages" (Guyer 1994: 223). In Jambiani these linkages are part of a discourse of elites, in this case the amorphous elites of the village rather than the bureaucracy of the national government. Moreover, the JDC is only legitimated in so far as colonial and post-colonial positions of authority and historical associations with the state still hold status value. In terms of democracy it is a step backwards. The JDC is not an example of "international civil society," the growth of which "is both reflected and bolstered by the groundswell of NGO participation in international conferences. It has introduced a new dynamic of embryonic participatory democracy to the global community and to the shaping of international law" (Otto 1996). Rather in this case, public power is falling into private hands.

So long as norms of redistribution and social obligation function to bring the benefits of international linkages to the rest of the community the privatization of the state is benign. Bypassing the national state may well in fact ensure that more resources go to where they are intended by donors. But by funding communities directly liberal donors compromise the ideals of the development project as a whole because " 'setting aside' loyalty to communities is what the liberal project [international civil society] is all about" (Young 1996: 538).

Atomization and Negative Liberty

The setting aside of loyalties is not occurring in Jambiani. Instead the impact of the effective decentralization of political power is that the national is increasingly obscured. By supporting organizations such as the JDC donors could be contributing to the atomization of African states: "There is little evidence to indicate a coalescence of community-level bodies into politically significant networks and broader independent associations. If anything the trend is the opposite." (Fowler 1991: 73). This is exactly case in Zanzibar.

However, NGOs are seen as custodians of a new form of politics: a challenge to the hegemony of the state in developing countries. According to the Ford Foundation "in civil society our goal is to strengthen the civic, political and economic participation of people and groups in planning the future".[13] But the picture that emerges from Zanzibar is one of parochialism, of NGOs competing with each other, not an emerging "international civil society" (Otto 1996: 140).

By emphasizing civil society as an expression of local empowerment such an agenda may even increase fragmentation rather than global integration. The atomized nature of global linkages mean that at present Jambiani receives far more resources from Europe, in the form of tourist receipts and aid donations, than from the Tanzanian mainland or even the Zanzibari government. In addition other villages have started their own development organizations and compete for the same funds.

Mobilizing the community behind these development efforts often takes a certain ethnic turn. Zanzibaris born in Jambiani but now living in the capital have formed an urban branch of the JDC. Meetings of the JDC in Jambiani and elsewhere are pointedly conducted in *KiJambiani*, a dialect of Swahili that

---

13. Ford Foundation Mission Statement (1999). Available at http://www.fordfound.org.

is a variation of the Southern Zanzibari dialect of *KiKae*. Both dialects are un-intelligible to native speakers of Swahili. This is not to suggest that villages are literally on the road to war with each other. However, all such associations in-hibit the growth of a nationally conscious polity with the ability to hold a na-tional government to account. Whether a national focus is good for African communities is beside the point, it is nevertheless what theories of civil soci-ety aspire towards. Yet in the case of Jambiani the practice engenders the op-posite; the JDC is an expression of parochialism.

Conclusions

So what of the future? Many commentators are pessimistic. Does this ap-parent process of atomization represent, in the words of Thomas Callaghy (1995 #97: 145), "yet another intense re-negotiation of powerful older polit-ical rules?". Is it a case of "Africans…returning to their roots?" (Rapley, 1996 #116: 138).

An analysis of the way in which power has changed hands in Jambiani has shown that the renegotiation of authority has not been a regression. Instead, the older political rules have, as ever, found expression in foreign institutional format. The implications and possibilities of this new format are the interest-ing focus for analysis and not the facile recognition that the more things change, the more they stay the same.

From this perspective African NGOs like the JDC are still a force for change although not quite in the sense that Fowler and others imagine. The potential of the JDC as an empowering agent is circumscribed by its locally understood legitimacy which may not conform to liberal democratic norms. The JDC thus does have the potential to instigate "a strategic realignment of the other actors on the development stage—governments and communities"[14] but this poten-tial lies in an ironic resolution of the meeting between the governance agenda and the Zanzibari government.

The discourse of civil society shaped the way in which entrenched interests within the community (authorized by the state at some level) recaptured con-trol of development resources. However, having done so the JDC is now in the position of meeting the needs of the community independently of the na-tional government: it levies pseudo taxes and collects contributions from

---

14. Nyang'oro, op. cit., 29.

tourists in the name of "development" which, as mentioned earlier, is in effect synonymous with political administration. The community at a local level may not in fact need the national state in any economic sense at all. Whether the JDC will have the desire or the ultimate ability to assert further autonomy is the question that will decide the political future of Jambiani.

Farrington (et al. 1993: 194) recognizes this as the crucial issue also: "whether NGOs attempt to take advantage of this scope to re-negotiate by interacting in collaboration with government will depend on how they assess the wider situation and the potential returns...In turn this response will be influenced by the history, background and strategy of the NGO and the key decision makers within it". Taking into account the history and background of the JDC and its members it seems unlikely that it would challenge central government policy. Still, with a resource base derived from elsewhere its potential in this regard is undiminished. As Miyoshi (1995: 744) says, "the fragmenting and fragmented units in these sites of contestation in the world are newly awakened agents not for the construction of autonomous nations but for the abandonment of the expectations and responsibilities of the politico-economic national projects".

The implications of this potential described in Miyoshi's analysis are quite sinister. Jambiani might not build itself into an autonomous nation but the incentive to participate at a national level is certainly reduced. In the absence of operative links to an international level body (like the UN) decentralized political power in Jambiani might result in local empowerment but global marginalization.

Increased autonomy does not mean that the nation state is dead, it is not a zero-sum relationship. What is important though is that the emerging political landscape will necessitate new forms of political organization: how can the residents of Jambiani influence the activities and decisions of the JDC as the key institution for the administration of development resources in the village? And is the JDC a vehicle for the representation of their interests at a national or international level? The question that remains is one of access to decision making at whatever level. The governance agenda may have contributed to an increased focus on local government (although nominally non-governmental) at the expense of the national but to shrink the playing field is not to win the game. And the game remains the same: development is a political process.

The essence of the new field of politics is: who controls the international relationships? And, how do they influence the position of the village in relation to the Zanzibari government? In terms of development the JDC's capacity to deliver will be determined by this relationship with the government:

whether or not it is perceived as a threat, and whether or not the government can do anything about it. On the other hand the organization's willingness to deliver is a function of locally understood norms of legitimacy and accountability. Where the reach of global influences is so extensive an appreciation of the anthropology of local areas becomes imperative. As Nef (1994: 10) says, it is important "in the analysis of regimes to ascertain who governs, since real power structures are not always formalized".

The lesson for those that would help the JDC in the achievement of its aims is that it does not conform to western notions of democratic accountability. This might very well provide the kind of administrative unit that is exceptionally responsive to the needs of the community but donors should be aware of compromising their own ideals. As Kelsall (2000: 15) points out, "At the heart of the governance agenda lies a liberal fiction: the idea that promoting a prescribed model of action and personhood can be squared with injunctions to respect other cultures and provide at all times for their participation." Sponsoring undemocratic NGOs that respond to local discourses of authority may be a good way of channeling resources to those who need it in the short-term, but it is in the long term interest of the donors and the recipients that they know this is what they are doing.

Works Cited

Allen, C. 1997. Who needs civil society? *Review of African Political Economy* (73): 329–37.

Bayart, J-F. 1986. Civil society in Africa. In *Political Domination in Africa: reflections on the limits of power*, edited by P. Chabal. Cambridge: Cambridge University Press.

Callaghy, T. Back to the Future? In Diamond & Plattner (eds.), *Economic Reform and Democracy*. Baltimore: Johns Hopkins University Press.

Campbell, A. 1997. Ethical Ethnicity: a critique. *Journal of Modern African Studies* 35 (1): 53–79.

Chitere, O. 1994. *Community Development: Its conceptions and practice with emphasis on Africa*. Nairobi: Gideon S. Were Press.

Ekeh, P. 1975. Colonialism and the two publics in Africa. *Comparative Studies in Society and History* 17 (1): 91–172.

Escobar, A. 1991. Anthropology and the development encounter: the making and marketing of development anthropology. *American Ethnologist* 18 (4): 658–82.

Farrington, J., A. Bebbington, K. Wellard, and D. Lewis, eds. 1993. *Reluctant Partners? Non-governmental organisations, the state and sustainable agricultural development*. London: Routledge.

Fowler, A. 1991. The role of NGOs in changing state-society relations: perspectives from eastern and southern Africa. *Development Policy Review* (9): 53–84.

Guyer, J. 1994. The spatial dimensions of civil society in Africa: an anthropologist looks at Nigeria. In *Civil Society and the State in Africa*, edited by N. Chazan, J. Harbeson and D. Rothchild. Boulder CO: Lynne Rienner.

Hyden, G. 1980. *Beyond Ujamaa in Tanzania: Underdevelopment and an uncaptured peasantry*. Berkeley and Los Angeles: University of California Press.

———. 1997. Civil society, social capital, and development: dissection of a complex discourse. *Studies in Comparative International Development* 32 (1): 3–30.

Kelsall, T. 2000. Subjectivity, Collective Action and the Governance Agenda in Arumeru East. Oxford, QEH Working Papers No. 42.

Middleton, J., and J. Campbell. 1965. *Zanzibar: Its society and its politics*. Oxford: Oxford University Press.

Miyoshi, M. 1995. A borderless world: from colonialism to transnationalism and the decline of the nation state. *Critical Inquiry* (19): 726–51.

Nash, J. 1981. Ethnographic aspects of the world capitalist system. *Annual Review of Anthropology* 10: 393–423.

Nef, J. 1994. *Human Security and Mutual Vulnerability: Some conceptual and empirical observations about global issues*. Ontario: University of Guelph.

Nyang 'oio, J. 1993. Civil society, the state and African development in the 1990s. Nairobi: An African Conference of Churches.

Otto, D. 1996. Non-Governmental Organisations in the United Nations system: the emergence of international civil society. *Human Rights Quarterly* 18 (1): 107–41.

Rapley, S. 1996. *Understanding Development*. Boulder, CO: Lynne Rienner.

Tsing, A. 1999. Becoming a tribal elder and other green development fantasies. In *Transforming the Indonesian Uplands*, edited by T. Li. Amsterdam: Harwood Academic Publishers.

Young, T. 1996. 'A project to be realised': global liberalism and contemporary Africa. *Millennium-Journal of International Studies* 24 (3): 527–45.

CHAPTER 7

"The State Didn't Even Exist": Non-Governmentality in Kivu, Eastern DR Congo

Stephen Jackson
Conflict Prevention and Peace Forum,
Social Science Research Council
jackson@ssrc.org

> "Civil society is therefore not to be taken, primarily or fundamentally, as an aboriginal nature which repels and contests the will of government: it is…a 'réalité de transaction', a vector of agonistic contention over the governmental relation" (Gordon, 1991: 23).

> "Meanwhile, we didn't sit there with our arms crossed…" [Kivu NGO worker to author, Goma, 1999]

From Leviathan to Social Contract in an Afternoon

Three months after the outbreak of the DR Congo's "Second Liberation War"[1] in 1998, NGO representatives in Goma, capital of North Kivu Province

---

1. In which newly installed President Laurent-Désiré Kabila, who had deposed President Mobutu Sese Seko, was now threatened by a new rebellion from the east, effectively partitioning the Congo (formerly known as Zaïre). Kabila was subsequently assassinated. After brief uncertainty, he was succeeded by his son Joseph.

on Congo's eastern border with Rwanda, convened "two days of reflection." As the first day wore on the conversation became despairing: how to chart a way forward amidst political upheavals if participants could not agree on how to explain the society in which they had been living? Finally the facilitator, a Congolese priest trained as an anthropologist, intervened. He moved to the blackboard and quickly sketched two figures: an upwards-slanting line and a circle. With the first, he explained Leviathan: a vertical chain of command and control ending in an absolute ruler, Maréchal Mobutu, Congo's deposed President for life. With the other he explained interdependence. "The essentially good man," the facilitator explained, "fundamentally corrupted by his desire to possess, produces inequality through pursuing his desires at the expense of others; but the emergence of a social contract between ruler and ruled limits this possibility through the enforcement of law and rights. The circle is complete." He then posed two questions: "which one of these two worlds are we living in, and how do we get to the one we want to be in?"

Theoreticians of civil society in Africa and elsewhere currently wrestle with the same questions. What kind of relationship do newly emergent NGOs have with the state? Do these institutions represent the consolidation of a democratic bulwark against predatory state power as the optimistic neo-liberal paradigm would have us believe (Ndegwa 1994), or are they merely a continuation of the "politics of the belly," resource capture by the same old political elites by new means and with new disguises as pessimistic neo-Gramscians charge (Bayart 1993 and Fatton 1992)? Distilled, these debates rehash the argument between Rousseau and Hobbes, social contract versus Leviathan (Whaites 1996).

Examining the emergence and subsequent trajectory of a raft of local NGOs in the eastern DR Congo over the last fifteen years, and inspired by Foucault's (1991) inquiries into "governmental rationality" ("governmentality" for short), this chapter moves away from analytical polarities concerning the State. Instead, as Gordon (1991) suggests, I view Kivu's associative movement as a dimension of the "vector of agonistic contention over the governmental relation." Over almost two decades, different contingent coalitions have briefly, opportunistically, and somewhat incoherently acted in the name of either "the state" or "civil society," contending turbulently and sometimes violently to test the limits of political agency. In the process, Kivu's NGOs dealt with radically shifting power configurations deploying the vocabulary and impedimenta of statehood through four distinct periods: 1) slowly atrophying Mobutiste authoritarian rule (mid 1980s–1991); 2) relative political autonomy (1991–97); 3) abruptly curtailed (and always contested) reconstruction under Laurent Kabila's AFDL (1997–98); 4) and finally violent military repression under the Rwandan-backed RCD rebels (1998–present). During each period, but for differing reasons and in varying fashion, there was a gulf between state rhetoric and the reality of power. Self-consciously, and often strategically, NGOs both contended and transacted with those acting in the name of the "state," all the while redefining what it means to be a "non-state" actor. In short, this chapter is haunted by an overriding question: what can it mean to be "non-governmental" when the state is not a state?

Governmentality and Non-Governmentality

Kivutien NGOs constantly contended with state actors over what Foucault's interpreters gloss as "a way or system of thinking about the nature of the practice of government" (Gordon 1991: 3). Foucault's neologism splices "government" and "rationality"; but one could substitute "mentality" for rationality: a collective cast of mind shaping how government is enacted (or not). For Foucault government is "a form of activity aiming to shape, guide or affect the conduct of some person or persons" (*ibid*: 2), and a set of ideas and assumptions, enacted through concrete practices (the "how" of governing), which guide "the conduct of conduct." These ideas and assumptions must be shared to some extent by governing and governed alike. They must, in principle, be both thinkable and practicable.

Foucault was interested in transformations, radically ruptured and/or smoothly shifting, of power/knowledge configurations in the centuries preceding European modernity. He identifies a transition beginning in the sixteenth century from Macchiavellian circularity, in which the purpose of sovereignty was to preserve the sovereign relation, to an "art of governing" in which "the finality of government resides in the things it manages and in the pursuit of the perfection and intensification of the processes which it directs" (Foucault 1991: 95). Rule concerns the sovereign dominance of territory and populations whereas government becomes about the proper order of "things": populations in relation to resources, structures and institutions, customs, habits, climate, demography and epidemics, and many other facets of human existence. Economy also enters the frame: the ends of good government concern proper husbandry of resources (*ibid*: 93).

By drawing our attention also to the "how" of governance (including governance of the self), Foucault directs us to multiple actors and relations within the governmental field and away from an "excessive value attributed to the problem of the state" (1991:103). The state's subjects, however, continue to fetishize the state as a unitary, central actor (Taussig 1993):

> The state, no more probably today than at any other time in its history, does not have this unity, this individuality, this rigorous functionality, nor, to speak frankly, this importance; maybe, after all, the state is no more than a composite reality and a mythicized abstraction, whose importance is a lot more limited than many of us think. Maybe what is really important for our modernity—that is, for our present—is not so much the *étatisation* of society, as the "governmentalization" of the state (Foucault 1991:103).

Foucault was predominantly concerned by the emergence of the modern European state. But with colonialism, governmentality goes to the tropics, integral to the power/knowledge of imposed European rule. Its teleology and its future-orientedness became more accentuated:

> In contrast to sovereignty, government has as its purpose not the act of government itself, but the welfare of the population, the improvement of its condition, the increase of its wealth, longevity, health, etc (*ibid*:100).

This is colonization in the mode of Kipling's "White Man's Burden": uplift of the tropics not merely through enforced Christianization, but in the duty to "modernize" tropical economics, demography, and civil politics, transforming pre-colonial governmental relations and guiding the conduct of the colonized toward progress.

From the colonial period through the end of the 1970s, the governmental relation in Sub-Saharan Africa was conceived centrally around the state as planner and deliverer of development. In the wake of the Reagan/Thatcher revolution and the Soviet collapse, however, there was a rapid western re-orientation toward Africa, away from "containment" and toward "democratic opening," enacted in abortive national democratization processes in Benin, Zaïre and elsewhere.

Indeed, Congo/Zaïre tracks much of this history. However, neither the neoliberal perspective nor the neo-Gramscian one accurately describes the Congolese case. It is more accurate to take Foucault at his word and track the birth and growth of NGOs as a "réalité de transaction," a "vector of agonistic contention over the governmental relation" (Gordon 1991: 23). As the nature of

political power invoking the state ("governmentality") shifted amidst two tur-
bulent decades of Congolese politics, so too did the organizational configurations and collective identities of those invoking the non-state prerogative.

This is what I label "non-governmentality": a new cast of mind, emerging
in the 1980s and consolidating itself in the 1990s, which believes that the welfare of the population and the improvement of its condition can best be served
by "non-state" actors. It deploys the vocabulary of popular participation, self-
reliance, "community-based development" from the "bottom up" and hooks
into an apparatus of grassroots associations, local development initiatives,
projects and programing coordinated by NGOs acting as the new funnels for
western aid money.

Needless to add, the state did not simply cease to exist in this period. Perhaps a few postcolonial states "failed." Many more, however, suffered a kind
of arrested development and a hollowing out, as the organs of resource starved
states became resources to be picked over by elite actors. This is the "crimi-
nalized state" with the "routinization, at the very heart of political and governmental institutions and circuits, of practices whose criminal nature is
patent" (Bayart et al. 1999a: 16), the "felonious state" which forms a thin governmental mask for predation.

In this new Africa, there is not just one public space but several, "each having its own logic yet liable to be entangled with other logics when operating
in certain contexts; hence, the postcolonial subject has to learn to bargain in
this conceptual marketplace" (Mbembe 2001: 104). Neither exactly resisting
nor collaborating, but colluding and conniving with power, the postcolony is
a transactional world. The complex twists and turns in the history of Congolese NGOs bear this point out, showing how the conceptual and organizational components of both governmentality and non-governmentality are
pressed into agonistic contention over the governmental relation.

Genesis in Exodus: Non-Governmentality Emerges in a Contracting State?

Around 1985, or 1987, there were already peasant and women's organisations in Kivu which began to behave like NGOs: *Solidarité
Paysanne*, UWAKI [*Umoja wa Wamama wa Kivu*—the Union of
Kivutien Women]. At that time as well, various groups of people
grouped together because they were concerned by particular social or
economic problems *à la base*.

"It was a difficult time for the population. Salaries weren't being paid, and there was more and more of an abandonment of local structures. Until 1990, Mobutu was still making some efforts to keep things going, but after 1990 he was obsessed with his own survival. So people said 'we have to take this responsibility on ourselves'..."
We had to conscientize the people as to how they could resolve their problems by themselves.

"With Mobutu withdrawing, the NGOs moved in: repairing roads for example, or in other sectors that we identified as abandoned [by the State]."

Between 1997 and 2002, I interviewed a host of personnel, senior and junior, from Congolese NGOs, large and small, old and new.[2] Consensus dated the first emergence of formalized non-governmental organs to the atrophying of state power in the Kivus throughout the 1980s and early 1990s, opening up new space into which new non-governmental actors could move. This space was at first humanitarian, welfarist, but ultimately economic and political (cf. Ndegwa 1994). The state's retreat created both need and opportunity. With vital social functions undelivered, local people would go it alone, taking on the responsibility themselves, in solidarity with one another:

Solidarity is a fetish word; I say this because people adore the word in our way of thinking, from our African perspective it is a word and a behavior. You want to get out of something and you need the help of someone else...This awakens certain behaviour, certain attitudes. You see, solidarity, it's not just a simple thing! At a certain moment it was a word which ran frequently on the lips of intellectuals here and that led to the creation of the NGOs. In this way that I can say that development started as a vague notion here but became more and more defined.

The Kivu provinces were the "cradle" of the NGOs in Congo. Kivutien activists proudly describe an entrepreneurial energy and openness to the outside that galvanized associative energies:

Kivu has always been special because of its climate, its fertility. It's always been the richest in some ways...There is an economic dynamism here that is different from elsewhere...And yet we have been left to

---

2. Unless otherwise specified, all quotes henceforward are drawn from conversations or interviews with NGO staff in the Kivus.

ourselves by Kinshasa…It is our opening to the outside [to the east] that is the factor. Orientale [Province] is never visited by anyone from outside. But with our geographical location, we are open to the neighboring countries and from there to Europe…And there is such a mixing of peoples here.

Whether exporting slaves in the nineteenth century (Fabian 1986) or minerals in the twentieth century (Vwakyanakazi 1991) Kivu has looked economically eastwards for well over a century.[3] Kivutiens see themselves historically as having followed a different trajectory from the rest of the DR Congo, one in which the Kinshasa state perennially failed to consolidate control.

Who founded Kivu's NGOs? Most were university-trained. Zaïrean universities were still teaching despite the economic crisis of the 1980s, and a considerable cadre of educated Kivutiens became involved in the NGOs. Also, there were those who had studied together at universities in Burundi, Belgium or France. Though many were originally from rural backgrounds, they had begun to form the new Zaïrean middle-classes. But the University experience, at least in Zaïre, was also an education in how to make due:

> There was no food. We had to grow it ourselves in small plots. Or our families would try to send us something.

Many of these students were women. They represent a significant proportion, though by no means a majority, of middle-ranking NGO professionals in Goma. Women's associations at the grassroots are strong, and have been so since early in the Mobutu years (the story of how, or indeed whether, they emerged from nationalist/postcolonial political/state movements would require an article in itself).

Kivutien NGO personnel describe a "conservation of social energy" (Hirschman 1984) in which personnel migrated from one non-governmental initiative to another as the associative momentum increases:

> I was amongst the pioneers. The point of departure was the cooperative movement, established in part by the religious missionaries. After independence, the legislation introduced was too restrictive for those who did not understand management. Many cooperatives went under. But the people involved always had a tendency to get back in-

---

3. That they are presently politically dominated from the east, as a result of invasion and occupation by those same two neighbors, has, I argue elsewhere, induced a collective schizophrenia of identity (Jackson, 2001).

volved. Kinshasa did set up an institute, a training center for social affairs, women's issues, literacy, and so on. But then the state dropped abruptly out of the question, suddenly provided no support. However, the various other institutes—ISDR (*Institut Supérieur du Développement Rurale*) and others in Bukavu [provincial capital of South Kivu]—continued to produce large numbers of cadres. This was in the prosperous early 1970s. Then from 1973–84 it became difficult: that was the time of Zaïreanization when Mobutu chased out all the foreign businesses and gave it all to his friends. He also cracked down on the religious—there were no more youth religious movements. But these cadres had to make due [*se débrouiller*] somehow—this was a period of economic crisis, no salaries were being paid by the State, war was going on in Shaba [formerly Katanga province]. A process of becoming self-aware [*prise de conscience*] was taking hold here [in the Kivus]...The associative energies were trying to be reborn. *Solidarité Paysanne* started in Bukavu, it was the very first [NGO]. It was a support organisation [*organisation d'appui*], a structure formed from amongst those who intervened at the level of the community organisations [*organisations de base*], such as the cooperatives, the unions, the federations. It had a kind of a monopoly at first, but then there started to be internal problems and there was a kind of fission and other organisations emerged taking the form of NGOs: CAB, UWAKI, FERACOB, GEAD and so on, all born out of this same moment, in 1987 or so. Now there was something of a legal vacuum for these organisations, frankly. All there was a law for not-for-profit organisations dating from 1965, so that was what was used...And that wasn't really appropriate: after all, the cooperatives had economic goals and were membership organisations whereas these had developmental goals and were essentially private groups that targeted the general population.

This distinction between broad-based membership organizations and NGOs as functional service deliverers of development has elided through donor pressure and NGO self interest. Donor fashion sees local NGOs as the embodiment of "civil society," while NGOs, with an eye to the main chance, have "grabbed" the civil society concept (Whaites 1996). This, suggests one activist, misses a whole stratum of Kivutien associative life:

> Whereas in Europe, one can think of civil society as broadly equivalent with NGOs, because there it is natural enough to have an office,

computers, staff and so on, this is a big mistake for Congo because it tends to exclude much activity that is hidden from that kind of world. It creates an unhealthy reflex that before anything can be achieved you have to put together structures, organise offices, purchase equipment and thus look for external funding.

By the early 1990s, several hundred formalized local organizations of various types were registered as members of the CRONG (Conseil Regional des ONGs au Kivu Nord), which in turn interacted with literally thousands of *organisations de base*. By then,

> Mobutu couldn't object to our existence: *the state didn't even exist* to object at that point…It couldn't respond to the needs of the people.

Throughout this period the much-vaunted Congolese ethic of *débrouillardise* (fending for yourself) was raised to an art form (MacGaffey 1991; De Boeck 1999; and Jackson, 2002). The trickery needed to survive was celebrated as a social value, the pursuit of prestigious lifestyles as an aesthetic in itself (Bayart et al. 1999a). However, "Système-D"[4] did not just remain an individualistic ethic of getting by. It hybridized energetically with, on the one hand, a community-development ethic of participation and self-reliance, and, on the other, with neo-traditionalist visions of African solidarity at the village level:

> Considering an NGO as an organisation of people who want to take responsibility for themselves, no, it is not entirely a Western imposition. Because even in deepest Africa, there existed movements of solidarity either for constructing a hut, harvesting or cultivating a field.

From this heady mix, Kivus' NGOs improvised a non-governmentality: a system of thinking about the practice of self-government, of getting along without a central administration. State-centered theories of political agency were countered by theories of popular agency. Mobutu's rallies had employed *animation politique*: fervent, organized exhortation of popular support through praise songs and dances for the leadership. Now the NGOs organized *animations* of their own. Conscientization sessions in community workshops used Freirean techniques of popular pedagogy (e.g. role play, codes and proverbs, story telling, but also the curricula of international human rights, adult literacy and group psychology) to encourage the peasantry to "take con-

---

4. Other inventive Congolese epithets for this "getting-by" were "the 11th Commandment" and the "Article 15" [of the Constitution].

science" of their position and agency. Community water committees, village women's associations, peasant cooperatives and the like supplanted the atrophying structures of state agencies. These collective projects produced extraordinary results adding up to "development without a state" in Kivu (Streiffeler 1994). While central government managed to block an initiative in northern North Kivu to finance a hydro-electric plant on the River Semuliki, resilient "development substitution" was on display across a variety of sectors (*ibid*:67):

> Collaboration ensured the construction of a small airport at Butembo...the construction of one new hospital and the rehabilitation of another, the establishment of rural areas with local clinics and "birth stations," the equipment of villages with water pipelines, with mills and finally with storage facilities for agricultural products. Bulldozers for the building and maintenance of roads are parked in front of the Bishop's residence at Butembo.

As Kassimir (2001: 99) notes, this kind of activity adds up to more than welfare provision. It produces localized forms of governance, power and control:

> The enactment of "state-like" functions such as service delivery by NGOs is directly linked to the politics within these organizations, the determination of who is recognized to speak for and lead members, and what members must do in order to gain access to resources and services that the organization may provide.

The multifarious development activities in this period were realized almost entirely without international assistance. Zaïre's post-independence history of aid has been one of freeze/thaw (Jackson 2003). It had been amongst the largest recipients of U.S. aid in Africa (Lancaster 1999: 94), a supposed bulwark against Marxist Angola next door. During the 1980s, it was the twelfth largest recipient of World Bank lending (*ibid*:86) with Mobutu paying lip service to Structural Adjustment. ODA declined in the late 1980s with post-Cold War disenchantment, and then climbed to an all-time high of $1.4 billion in 1991 as Mobutu seemed to open Zaïre to the "winds of change." His subsequent derailment of democratization (of which more below) was the last straw, and most donors suspended all but humanitarian assistance. The EU suspended assistance in 1992; by 1993 aid from principal donors (USA, France, Germany and Belgium) was down to about $25m each, much of this channeled through international NGOs, in theory bypassing the accountancy black hole of Mobutu's state apparatus altogether. Finally, in 1994, the World Bank pulled out.

In short, a new collective mind-set, which I dub non-governmentality, saw a profound shift from an externally financed state as centralized agent of development to non-state actors as facilitators of self-supported development from the ground-up. Key to this conception was "*la base*," a term that evades easy translation. Literally "the base," "*la base*" fulfills something of the same function in Kivutien NGO-speak as do terms like 'community' and 'population' in English: the unspecified mass of "people at the grassroots" on behalf of whom the NGOs work. It is a floating ideological signifier, a "*point de capiton*" ("quilting point") in Zizek's sense masking a "lack": an over determined term, with the ideological potency to foreclose further discussion (Zizek 1989). The term "quilts" together a variety of contradictory discourses about populations, circumstances, needs, and necessary actions. It is shorthand that everyone seems to understand, and yet for which everyone has their own interpretation. Thus, for certain Kivutien NGOs, actions which might bring them into political collision with state actors are justified because they merely represent voices "*à la base*" expressing their reactions to their circumstances:

> We represent our base. If I denounce that the base can't breathe, I'm not saying something political. I am doing my duty. But the problem is that [those in power] won't understand. But everything depends on how you do it. We don't attack Kinshasa. We find a polite, strategic way of doing it, of choosing our words.

"*La base*" is, in this sense, the constituency who cannot represent themselves and thus, who must be represented, the source for whom the NGOs work and from whom they draw their legitimacy:

> We are people who are disposed to accompany the peasants, to orient them, to animate them, to begin approaches for *responsibilisation*[5], for self-promotion of the peasants.

As objects of development, those that constitute *la base* are envisioned in the way that Kearney (1996:36) charges anthropology with having imagined the category of the "peasant": "defined as half-developed and half-underdeveloped," liminally suspended between the primitive and the modern. But in Kivutien NGO discourse, they are also development's subjects: those who take themselves in hand and assume responsibility for their own development

---

5. A French-language neologism for development pedagogy to foster community self-reliance.

through self-reliance and collective action. With solidarity as the "fetish word," Kivus' NGOs substituted themselves for a receding state.

Many of the *organisations de base*, whether cooperatives, ILDs ("local development initiatives") mutual assistance organizations, peasants' or women's associations, in fact sprung originally from state programs. Orphaned by the state's retreat in the late 1980s, the NGOs then assumed a coordinating role. In some cases new NGOs emerged organically upwards; in most, however, they imposed themselves on those structures lower down the political pyramid, staking a claim to be representative structures of coordination. Subsequently, the legitimacy of representative structures would become another vector of contention, with rival NGO coordination platforms competing with each other for supremacy. This mode of self-development represents a powerful challenge to the retreating state. As Ferguson (1994:19) notes:

> The outcomes of planned social interventions can end up coming together into powerful constellations of control that were never intended and in some cases never even recognised, but are all the more effective for being "subjectless."

Development projects deal in the technocratic dimensions of social change and, thus, are supposedly non-political. But as Congolese NGOs recognize

> When an NGO engages in a water pipeline project in a rural area where the political authorities have never set its foot or never been concerned, you see the responsibility of the NGO for that population vis-à-vis the authorities. At that level, they have to know well how to manoeuvre in order not to create unprofitable tensions; but equally, they must know how to profit from their popularity in order to consolidate their position.

Representation is a source of political power, and one that can be used tactically:

> We don't really consider that we concern ourselves with politics capital-P. But if, in the course of enacting our development, there is a detrimental political environment which handicaps this, well, if we tickle or scratch them a little where is the problem?...Today, the people are coming down with Kwashiorkor [protein malnutrition] at adult age, because the politics is so bad; would you want it that only certain people were allowed to speak of that, people who perhaps don't even know what they are talking about? We, we live with the

population, and they can tell us things that they can't speak of to the political powers.

Water projects, perhaps, only indirectly threaten a retreating state. But by the early 1990s, Kivutien NGOs were emerging with overtly political agendas and approaches, and these did awaken ad hoc reactions:

> With the start of multipartyism in our country, new NGOs were born for the promotion of democracy and civic education. You see? These were NGOs who had discovered, who felt a real need to educate the population about exactly what democracy consisted of. For all those years of the dictatorship we knew no other form of managing the state but that one…Well, when the animators of these NGOs conducted their animation, well… even though Mobutu had liberalized politics, he continued to crack down here and there…And so when the [animators] began to express themselves in this kind of way, well it was perceived as a political tendency one way or another, and that the members of the NGOs were doing these things for their own propaganda, even though their was no question of that.

Mobutu had been under heavy pressure, both externally from donors and internally from civil society, to democratize. Appearing to relent in 1991, he invoked a conference bringing together delegates from government, civil society, and political opposition to deliberate on political liberalization. He then deftly manipulated it to set the contending forces against each other:

> During the period of the *Conférence Nationale Souveraine*, civil society, in the beginning, played a very important role. There were no positions being taken, at the beginning. Civil society was like a judge, not an advocate. It was only later, when the politicians discovered "Oh no! There is a really terrible pressure group emerging here that threatens to overturn us!" that they tried to politicise everything, the conference, civil society…And it was at this point for the first time that we knew division [within the NGOs].

Mobutu's major tool to divide and rule the NGOs was "*géopolitique*"—a politics of geography which decreed that CNS representation would reflect Zaïre's differing "demographic weights" (de Villers and Omasombo Tshonda 1997: 60). In other words, CNS delegates could only represent provinces to which they were "indigenous." The CNS was immediately hamstrung by bitter squabbles about who did and did not represent legitimate indigenous interests. A month was swallowed in wrangling (Nzongola-Ntalaja 2002: 190).

The NGOs, like the political parties, emerged profoundly polarized and weakened. It furthered a tendency, already inherent from their community-basis, for them to be ethnicized:

> Many of the NGOs here are "colored." When they speak of GEAD here, they know it is Bahunde or Banyanga. When you speak of ACORDERI, then you know you are speaking of [a prominent Tutsi figure] and everyone knows what that means...And everyone limits themselves to that—you speak of [him] as if that is sufficient. If you mention ACOGENOKI then someone will say...[aping how someone would carp] "oh, XXX, he's just a Mututsi."

Again, accusations and counter-accusations of ethnic bias commonly fly between NGOs, and also persist as a vocabulary through which state actors can criticize non-governmentality.

Mushroom NGOs

The CNS proved a temporary return to form by Mobutu. As the 1990s wore on, his attention focused on clinging to power in Kinshasa; the NGOs were largely left to their "development without a state." However, Mobutu's long-standing manipulation of inter-ethnic tension was charged to explode: it did so in 1993, with the "Inter-Ethnic War," killing, injuring or displacing tens of thousands of Kivutiens. Then, in 1994, events next door triggered a sudden deluge of international aid. Genocide in Rwanda precipitated the flight of one million Rwandan refugees (genocidal killers amongst them) into Kivu.

International aid arrived, late as always, a massive humanitarian operation by international NGOs which bypassed the local NGOs (and population) completely, in what became known locally as the "HCR economy":[6]

> One million dollars a day was spent on the refugees, in total disproportion to the Zaïreans. There were three hospitals for the refugees, nothing for the locals...The vehicles of the [international] NGOs were like Brownian motion amongst the refugees.

At first, the damage to local NGOs was a predictable "braindrain" as key staff members were lured to international agencies by better salaries and conditions. But in a later phase:

---

6. Named for UNHCR, the United Nations refugee agency.

The local NGOs were made to crumble by this tidal wave of emergency aid.

As the international presence started to wind down, agencies, adjoined by donors to seek local partners for reasons of program "sustainability," competed for partnership with established local NGOs or, more often, caused new ones spontaneously to self-create.

> Once the funds started to diminish again, they started to say to their local staff "OK, you will have to quit, we don't have anything for you, but we do have funds for projects so if you organise yourselves out there and you propose something to us we will be able to finance it for you…" This itself contributed to the creation of tension, to the creation of what we call *ONGs Ponctuelles* ["well-timed" or "of the moment" NGOs].

More senior Kivutien NGOs use other dismissive epithets to discredit these NGO opportunists. They are "mushroom NGOs" [*ONGs champignons*] which spring up over night to avail of the manure [money] thrown over them; "momentary" [*ONGs momentanées*], "spontaneous," "occasional," or "hobby NGOs" responding to economic signals thrown out by the international community, "prostitute" or "fictitious" NGOs, "satellite NGOs" [which hang from the international agencies and depend solely upon them], NGOs "*à la mode*" and just plain "phony" [ONGs *bidonnes*]:

> Take UNHCR for example: If HCR has some seed to distribute, then some guys will create an association so that they can become distributors of this aid. Because FHI [Food for the Hungry International] has seed to distribute, or FAO [the UN Food and Agriculture Organisation] has seed to distribute, because Agro Action Allemande has seed to distribute, there are organisations like this that spring up at any particular moment…but a program for development, a work plan, an office, they don't have any of these things. There will probably be state agents involved. If the state is not paying them, then now, in order to get access to the international donors, they create development NGOs…But it's a trap: they suddenly spring up and then disappear again…The international community must not let itself be trapped by this kind of thing!

Around the "HCR economy" and after, local NGOs propagated exponentially:

> With HCR, all some people had to do was lay their project documents on the table and the money would emerge like peanuts.

The proliferation damaged everyone. New expatriate NGO personnel arriving in the Kivus, staff turnover being rapid in emergency situations, often regarded all local NGOs as "in it for the money." Except, that is, for ones with which their international agency had a history (i.e. the ones it itself had created). After 1994, organizational authenticity increasingly became the battleground on which increasingly bitter fights were fought out over the rights to channel dwindling international aid and a diminishing stock of "civil society" legitimacy.

Solidarity Between Ourselves

Then suddenly in late 1996, a bloody cross-border Rwandan military strike against remaining genocidal insurgents from 1994 continuing to launch their attacks from within Kivu's massive refugees camps, turned overnight into a full-scale rebellion. In just six months it marched right across country, deposed Mobutu, changed the country's name back to Congo, and installed an obscure 1960s guerrilla leader, Laurent-Désiré Kabila, as the new President, all under the hastily assembled banner of the *Alliance des Forces Démocratiques pour la Libération du Congo-Zaïre* (A.F.D.L.).[7]

The rebellion was far from bloodless. Untold numbers of genuine Rwanda refugees from the 1994 camps died, as did Kivutien citizens caught in the crossfire. For the most part, however, the reaction of Kivutiens was the same as that of other Congolese citizens: initial bewilderment giving way to gratitude for the end of *Mobutisme* and optimism for a Congolese renewal.

The attitude of Kivu's NGOs, however, was more guarded. First, many strongly opposed the impunity being granted Kabila's new government for the camp killings. When Kabila consistently blocked investigations into the massacres by the UN-appointed Special Rapporteur Roberto Garreton, Kivutien NGOs used secret channels to funnel information to his team.

Second, and perhaps more importantly, Kabila and the NGOs mutually resented each other's claim to governance. For the NGOs, the A.F.D.L. rebellion was inauthentic, one which deployed national liberation rhetoric but lacked

---

7. The rebellion uneasily united several former opposition tendencies (including Kabila's), Congolese Tutsi militias and Rwandan and Ugandan military. Many questions still remain mysterious: did the rebellion begin with the objective of overthrowing Mobutu or acquire this goal along the way? Who selected Kabila? How many were killed in the camps?

the popular mandate from "*la base*" that they themselves had so carefully cultivated. They viewed Kabila as a joke figure, someone who had through force of arms stolen the Congo at the very moment when their quiet resistance had so softened Mobutu's dictatorship that it would have fallen like a ripe fruit into anyone's lap.

Kabila meanwhile criticized the NGOs for having colluded with the dictatorship for many years. Where had the NGOs been when his *maquis* were fighting Mobutu all these years from their bases in the forest? Lining their pockets and feathering their nests while spouting empty promises of democratization from the ground-up. Only the AFDL had had the courage of their convictions. These debates reprised the contraposition between a non-governmentality of participatory democracy "from beneath" versus state-based development and regime change through revolution. At the very beginning of the Kabila government's tenure, there was some evidence that cabinet members at least had not made up their minds about civil society and donors were encouraged to promote rapprochement between government and NGOs.[8]

However the NGOs remained deeply suspicious. Kabila's talent for the business of government was proving limited. His agents were going through the motions of governing, enacting the semblance but not the substance:

> In terms of the non-existent Congolese state...nothing had changed. The moment of optimism in 1997, for me at least, lasted for only six months. For me, by December 1997 it was already clear that it was over ...After the taking of Kinshasa in June 1997, I was part of a civil society meeting in Kinshasa as an animator, and it was interesting, with a lot of optimism, but there were also people saying that the return of dictatorship is always still possible. Then there was the Provincial [i.e. governmental] meeting on reconstruction, and everything was broken there. The problems were already visible. There were arguments, with the Ministry of Planning, of Reconstruction...And then everything was annihilated by Kabila. And to say two years for elections, well that wasn't thought through either. So by Dec, we saw the first signs of a conflict coming...I knew it wouldn't end well.

---

8. USAID Congo Assessment Team. 1997. *Transition in the Democratic Republic of the Congo: Opportunities and Pitfalls*. Congo Assessment Team Report August 1997. Washington D.C.: USAID.

Moreover, Kabila's instincts were not democratic. Before even taking Kinshasa, his movement had established "village committees" which were in reality a network of political and security cells monitoring and informing upon the behavior of ordinary people. And paradoxically, it was perhaps the very speed with which the AFDL succeeded militarily, dislodging Mobutu in just six months, which left it so undeveloped politically. Arriving in the capital in mid 1997, it had not elaborated a political program and its reflex was to repress opposition rather than engage with it. Kabila's new government was composed of former Mobutistes, émigrés and co-opted representatives of almost every political and ethnic group in the country. Neither of the latter two groups had independent power bases of their own and were thus completely dependent on Kabila.[9] Shortly, he proceeded to eviscerate the AFDL as a political structure, leaving it as a mask for the power of his own PRP (Partie de la Révolution Populaire). All other political parties were suppressed. Meanwhile, the AFDL's military forces remained extremely heterogeneous, their loyalty to Kabila uncertain.

Congo's NGOs were unequivocal, asserting that despite all its faults, the *Conférence Nationale Souveraine* of 1991 remained the only legitimate expression of the popular will and that the re-foundation of the Congo must spring from its spirit. This view was strongly expressed at a June 1997 conference, co-organized by Synergies Africa, the International Human Rights Law Group and CNONGD, the national council of development NGOs, in which Kivu's NGOs, and Kivutiens based in Kinshasa, were strongly represented. While welcoming Mobutu's overthrow, the 250 NGO delegates, in a vociferous final declaration, voiced their "fears and preoccupation relating to safeguarding national and social peace, fundamental liberties and finally safeguarding the democratic process as a whole" and complained of an absence of political dialogue, the continued manipulation of ethnic antagonisms in the country, "increasing violations of human rights as well as violations of the fundamental liberties of free association, opinion and expression," "the absence of a clear separation between the army on the one side and justice and police on the other" and the absence of "a constitutional framework providing principles and sign posts for government action during the transition phase."[10]

---

9. International Crisis Group. 1999. *How Kabila Lost His Way: The performance of Laurent Désiré Kabila's government.* ICG Democratic Republic of Congo Report Nº 3, 21 May 1999.

10. Synergies Africa. 1997. Final Declaration of the Meeting of the Civil Society of Democratic Republic of Congo, Kinshasa, 16–20 June 1997. Unpublished. Kinshasa.

The Kabila government's response was equally uncompromising. Replying at the same conference, Minister for Planning Etienne Mbaya "'reminded participants that the actions of civil society had to be inscribed in the spirit and priorities established by the government."[11] He also made it clear that by contrast with the Mobutu period of non-governmental intervention in the health, education and infrastructure sectors, the new government intended re-assuming all such responsibilities. The autonomy of "development without a state" was thus directly challenged. One senior NGO participant recalls:

> Behind Mbaya's speech was the idea that, OK, you guys could get away with doing stuff then because the state didn't exist…But now that it does, you are out of a job!

Initially this challenge was less direct than it had been with political parties. Civil society activity was to be "inscribed" within the parameters of the State, not outlawed by it. But the attempt to control political dissent backfired. The NGOs, in a sequence of follow-up conferences, passed ever-stronger declarations. In turn, the Kabila regime started to crack down. Activists fled or were jailed. Follow-up encounters agreed upon between NGOs and the state were cancelled. Attempts were made to pass legislation obliging NGOs to register their work formally with the Ministry of Justice. Donors were pressured to channel their reconstruction aid via the Government rather than, as in the latter Mobutu years, directly to the NGOs.

NGOs became more and more the target of a crackdown. As Special Rapporteur Garretón (1999) later reported, NGOs (particularly those with a clear orientation toward human rights)

> have been ransacked, threatened, suspended, banned and their leaders attacked and imprisoned. On 16 January [1998] the Minister of the Interior maintained that some people did not understand the liberation and were obstructing it by creating NGOs, which were actually banned political parties. He threatened that anyone who violated the ban would be tried before the military courts. He stressed that only AFDL, the movement of all the patriotic forces in the Congo, was capable of leading the country to democracy. On 20 February the Council of Ministers debated the situation of NGOs, accusing them

---

11. International Crisis Group. 1999. *How Kabila Lost His Way: The performance of Laurent Désiré Kabila's government.* ICG Democratic Republic of Congo Report Nº 3, 21 May 1999.

of giving arms to the rebels (meaning the opposition, since there was no rebellion).[12]

Finally, recognizing the popularity of the NGO formula the Kabila government tried to copy it. In May 1998 Congolese Decree-Law 071 gave "civil personality to the NGO '*Solidarité entre Nous*' [SEN, or 'Solidarity amongst Ourselves'], to channel humanitarian assistance to the Congolese people, coordinate the activities of national NGOs, and to report on the granting of permission for them to operate and to guide their work." At the same time it established another "NGO" called the "Congolese Union for the Defence of Human Rights," responsible for "identifying for the Government human rights violations and cases of external manipulation." In both cases, the government saw itself as "countering Western propaganda [delivered] via NGOs."[13] Congo's NGO activists were incensed:

> The NGO Technical Coordination Commission is directed by the [North Kivu] Governor's nephew; now SEN is to be directed by the Governor's big brother. This is blurring things...' 'SEN? Oh, it's not serious. You can't have an NGO that is simply set-up and named by the President. This is just another bit of harassment, just one more. A "governmental non-governmental organisation"? Can you imagine that? And reporting directly to the President? It had the mission to place all of our free associations under the control of one body. We immediately issued declarations against SEN. Our movements were movements of social change, so it would have been stupid of us to deal with something designed to reduce our freedom of action. We considered ourselves part of the democratic struggle, not just "little" humanitarian actors.

Kivutiens read these events exactly the way Hibou (1999:99) would, as:

> an instance of the "privatization of development. The concept of civil society, difficult to define at the best of times, becomes infinitely ma-

---

12. Garretón, R. 1999. *Report on the situation of human rights in the Democratic Republic of the Congo, submitted to the United Nations Commission on Human Rights by the Special Rapporteur, Mr. Roberto Garretón, in accordance with Commission resolution 1998/61. E/CN.4/1999/31 8 February 1999.* New York: United Nations Economic and Social Council.

13. ASADHO (Association Africaine de Défense des droits) 1998b. "République Démocratique du Congo: Le pouvoir à tout prix: Répression systématique et impunité. Rapport Annuel 1998."

nipulable. The promotion of NGOs leads to an erosion of official administrative and institutional capacity, a reinforcement of the power of elites, particularly at the local level, or of certain factions, and sometimes a stronger ethnic character in the destination of flows of finance from abroad. In many cases, these NGOs are established by politicians at national or local level, with a view to capturing external resources which henceforth pass through these channels on a massive scale.

Although SEN was nationally established, the fight over SEN was personalized and local. As a senior representative of a Western donor organization recalls,

> It came down in the end, as it always does, to a fight between Kivutiens.

SEN was spearheaded by Emannuel Kambali, a former civil society activist hailing from North Kivu. He had been working for UNICEF in Kinshasa before being plucked by Kabila (and Etienne Mbaya) to coordinate relations of the new government with domestic and international NGOs. Amongst other roles Kambali played was AFDL liaison with the UN Garreton mission of inquiry into the violence of the AFDL takeover.[14] Meanwhile, the top ranks of NGO coordinating structures in Kinshasa, such as CNONGD, were also filled with Kivutiens. These led the fight against SEN. Local NGOs issued strongly worded declarations about the sanctity of civil society space and marshalled international influence against SEN. In particular, Robert Garretón, aforementioned UN Special Rapporteur, singled out SEN for criticism in his reporting.

These cumulative criticisms had effect. Kambali eventually resigned, leaving SEN as little more than an administrative shell in Kinshasa, directed by his successor Charles Lundjwire (also from Kivu, also a former civil society

---

14. And thus charged with defending the consistent non-cooperation of the new government with that mission. Typical of this role was the following, posted on the UN Information Service Website IRIN in their "Weekly Round-Up" of April 3, 1998: "KINSHASA DENIES PROBLEMS: A senior DRC ministry official in charge of liaison with the UN team, Emmanuel Kambali, said the investigation was going on unfettered. "I have not heard of problems that the team may have encountered in Goma. We are in contact with our people there. If there was a problem, we would know. What they [the UN] are saying is not true," Kambali told Reuters by telephone. Minister of Planning Etienne Richard Mbaya accused the team of refusing to travel with their liaison officers or informing the provincial governor as previously agreed, according to Agence congolaise de presse."

activist with one of the first Kivutien NGOs, ADIKIVU).[15] After the outbreak of a new war, Kambali became "Humanitarian Coordinator" for the RCD rebels in their capital of Goma, again dealing with querulous local and international NGOs on behalf of a rebel movement acting like a state.

In sum, the Kabila period saw a brief, maladroit, and abruptly curtailed attempt by a fragmented and hastily assembled coalition of political actors to invoke rhetoric about the governmental centrality of a quasi-authoritarian state against the gains in room for manoeuvre achieved by NGOs during the waning days of Mobutism. NGOs were not to enjoy a separate, contrary role but to inscribe their actions within the logic of a paternal state. Above all else, they were to confine themselves to strictly non-political roles in the broadest sense; the Kabila government was quicker than many academic analysts of civil society to note the payoffs in terms of political legitimacy, power and control, to NGO "service delivery."

Everyone for Peace and Development

In eviscerating the AFDL, Kabila also distanced himself from his Ugandan and Rwandan patrons. Just over a year after his installation as President, they deemed him to have gone too far. In August 1998, a looped radio broadcast interrupted a quiet Sunday evening in Goma to announce a takeover by a new rebel movement the RCD (Rassemblement Congolais pour la Démocratie) mounted by his former allies. Like the AFDL, the RCD was an unstable coalition of dissident factions. It cobbled together AFDL fighters marooned when the rebellion broke out; ex-FAZ (Mobutu's old Zaïrean army); Congolese Tutsi fighters; and even some "reintegrated" Hutu militias, ordinarily arch-foes of the Tutsi. All fell loosely under Rwandan military control.

The RCD intended to take the country from Kabila as rapidly as he had taken it from Mobutu. However Kabila enlisted the support of other regional powers, principally Angola and Zimbabwe, and the assault was blocked. A bloody stalemate entrenched, enduring to the present, partitioning the country East/West, the RCD's stranglehold on the East perpetually harassed by Kabila's "asymmetric war" via proxy militias striking from rural areas of Kivu.

---

15. Though as of 2003, an NGO with the same name was still operating from Kinshasa, giving 1996 (not 98) as its date of birth, and receiving international assistance for programming to "encourage and support solidarity movements capable of weaving together new alliances for unity and peace between the populations."

The RCD domination of the East was despised by the ordinary population, interpreted as "foreign occupation" and greatly adding to the resentment of the minority Congolese Tutsi population as mere "Rwandans" (Jackson 2001). Precipitously launched, once again a Congolese rebel movement presented itself as the legitimate political claimant to the mantle of the state but advanced no programmatic strategy for capturing the support of "*la base*":

> [The RCD] don't have any project for society. When there is a meeting or a speech given or something, all they can ever find to say is "we will fight until victory" or "Kabila must go" or something like that. These are their only slogans: "after Kabila, it is we who will rule." They have never said "we will help you to build hospitals, we will help you to rebuild the roads" or anything like that.

This is an analysis of both moral and strategic political failure. In giving no thought to the developmental needs of the ordinary people, the NGO perspective is that the RCD displayed the emptiness of their claims to government and their thoughtlessness about the popular support crucial for real victory. Hastily assembled to mount a coup that quickly failed, the RCD had no time to develop a cohesive ideology, still less a program of popular *animation* to dynamize support *à la base*. Fundamentally a military insurrection, the RCD at first grafted on veterans of the independence-era Left such as Ernest Wamba-dia-Wamba and Jacques Depelchin to "buy in" political legitimacy. Quickly, however, these leaders were marginalized, and then expelled. The RCD would undergo four changes of Presidency in as many years, revealing itself more and more as a superficial cover for Rwandan interests for forcefully occupying Kivu. Splits proliferated, and RCD "wings" multiplied.

As the national military stalemate embedded, violence in Kivu heightened dramatically, in a tit-for-tat of attack and reprisal between militias and military, the population (and the NGOs) were caught in the crossfire:

> The Tutsis [RCD or Rwandan Army indistinguishably], when they come, they accuse the local population of having conspired or collaborated with the Mayi Mayi [militias]...Then you're done for. They burn the villages, they catch the people, and they slit their throats like goats...The Mayi Mayi, when they go into a village, if the Tutsis have already been through and the villagers have now come back from the bush, the Mayi Mayi will say to them, "you have collaborated with the Tutsi, so you are complicit with them, no question, we will have to execute you as well."

For the NGOs developmental goals became unimaginable: international donors once more suspended support, populations became unreachable, the future unpredictable and violent. Some converted to humanitarian assistance roles. Others inhabited an ambiguous space of activity somewhere between civic education, democratization and local-level reconciliation on the one hand, and human rights advocacy on the other. Behind the scenes, many activists were linked to anti-RCD resistance. Some resistance was peaceful: organizing "Ville Mortes" [literally "dead towns," or general strikes] or issuing calls for peace demonstrations. Increasingly these approaches were suppressed by the RCD. Less peacefully, some NGOs were linked to the militia movements, and "dans les coulisses" [behind the scenes] prepared and circulated anonymous tracts boasting of armed resistance. Many tracts were venomously anti-Tutsi.

Meanwhile, the RCD administration in Kivu made noises about governance and development in the name of the Congolese people and State. "Popular expressions" of support were organized for Independence Day and other days of significance; at formal ceremonies relayed via closely controlled local media, Vice-Governors would make a show of recognizing exceptional local teachers or students; and from time to time the RCD would make hint of grandiose plans for the welfare of all citizens. But it only half-heartedly donned the garb of governmentality; it had neither the competence nor the commitment to deliver on these dreams. As one NGO worker bitterly cracked, "they are at the dance but they don't know the steps!"

Recognizing, as the AFDL had before it, that the NGOs did know the steps and danced them pretty well, the RCD vacillated between suppressing the NGOs altogether, and trying to co-opt their political capital. But in both directions, the RCD's attempts were more extreme than that of the AFDL. Large numbers of NGOs, including some of the most venerable, were forced to close. Activists were frequently arrested, not least for the "crime" of remaining in contact with civil society colleagues in Kinshasa. Detention was often accompanied by torture. In January 2000, for example, two very well known leaders of the Congolese Women's Movement were arrested in Goma, and during interrogation about their organizing a cross-Congo peace movement, were whipped with pieces of tire. After an internationally coordinated campaign for their release, several fled to international refuge.

Equally blunt and largely ineffectual attempts were made to capitalize on the political legitimacy the NGOs carried in relation to the ordinary people. One approach was to try formally to incorporate the NGOs as a constituent but dependent part of RCD political structures. Senior NGOs were approached to take on a coordinating role, and firmly declined:

Last week, some representatives of the RCD came and paid us a visit [at our NGO], in order to question us, to have us give advice, to see if their RCD could...well, to see how one might organise a "civil society" depending from them, with their coordination, with their orientation. We said to them "well you the RCD, you can't even manage to reconcile yourselves to each other. How can you imagine that you could be in the business of reconciling people?"

Taking a page from the AFDL experience, the RCD then established a "governmental non-governmental organization" to achieve the same goal. This was "Tous pour la Paix et le Développement" [Everyone for Peace and Development, or TPD]. As a representative of the RCD's Justice and Conflict Resolution Department explained to me in January 2000,

There is now an NGO called TPD, a new one, which is the only one who is involved in sensibilising the [Hutu] refugees there. They collaborate even with the military. [TPD] are the only ones that are able to convince the refugees to put down their arms, by working through former combatants who can convince the population, and also those coming back from Rwanda who can say that it is OK there. We would not say that the whole of the civil society in North Kivu is anti-Tutsi, but there are many of them who are....This kind of [animosity and resentment] always happens when the political power is weak...We find we have lots of problems with the local NGOs. They say that RCD is supported by the Ugandans and the Rwandans, and that Kivu will be annexed—something which is not true—and they attempt to mount an ideology which will cause us problems in the future, saying we are foreigners as a movement. We worry that the NGOs are laying the ground for a genocide against the RCD. We have tried already to approach them, to say that that this is not the work of the NGOs. They are not there to intoxicate against us. Me, I worked in the NGOs myself once. But they are now intoxicating the population and maybe we will arrive at an uncontrollable situation. We have also thought of meeting with our compatriots who can be found elsewhere to involve them. There have been two meetings of Congolese civil society at Bonn. But that is not sufficient—we would need the political people in to that conversation too, so that they understand our goals: to defeat Kabila and his dictatorship, and that the idea of cohabitation should exist without vengeance, hostility. The others are in the process of destroying what we are trying to do.

In contrast to this glowing self-portrayal, the International Crisis Group described TPD as:

> a parastatal NGO directly linked to the Rwandan Directory of Military Intelligence (DMI), [which] was established soon after the RCD itself. It was designed to accompany counterinsurgency and answer socio-economic grievances of the local population by running local development projects. TPD works in North Kivu as an alternative political authority that vets all appointments within the territorial administration, including the RCD's military arm. It provides the backbone of the governor's authority in the province down to the lowest levels.[16]

TPD's logistics transported 10,000 or so soldiers in a private army independent of RCD command and reporting directly to Eugène Serufuli, Provincial Governor, and to the Rwandan Government. It was later central to the forced repatriation of thousands of Congolese Tutsi refugees in Rwanda.

Another attempt to approach the population was to set up Local Representative Assemblies. Always moribund, never placed on a formal legal-administrative footing, these talking shops were designed to attract membership amongst customary leadership and civil society. If NGO activists resisted, they were repeatedly pressurized, and indirectly threatened to join. From the other direction, underground tracts circulated menacing that "whoever dares to join these bloody assemblies must be punished, or their families in their stead!"

More bizarrely, some civil society figures simply found themselves appointed without their prior knowledge. One academic, with a long history in NGO circles, described how he was obliged to write a polite letter of "resignation" after he learned one morning on the radio that he had accepted an appointment to the Provincial Assembly. But other civil society figures were much less circumspect. A new term, "trampolining," was quickly coined for those who parlayed their NGO histories into rapid ascendancy within the RCD, including senior figures such as Maître Mudumbi and Maître Emungu, both former human rights advocates, who took prominent roles.

NGO relief and rehabilitation projects also provided easy pickings of political legitimacy for the RCD. In a September 2000 interview, the Adminis-

16. International Crisis Group. 2003. *The Kivus: Forgotten Crucible of the Congo Conflict.* ICG Report **No. 56**, 24 January 2003. Brussels/Nairobi: International Crisis Group.

trator of Walikale Territory, North Kivu, proudly told me how he had recently visited a potable water rehabilitation project mounted by the veteran Kivu NGO GEAD. He gave the project an official "launch," (doing some symbolic "digging," though the project was long complete) and some "sensibilisation" of the local population to the benefits that the RCD was bringing via the NGOs. Discussing this later with NGO colleagues, their sense of the Catch 22 was vivid: permission to access such needy populations was to a large extent conditional on playing into the RCD's political agenda.

In sum, the RCD recognized the NGO sector as both threat and opportunity for its governmental ambitions. The ethnopolitics of the RCD ethnicized the NGOs; its inducements to surrendering autonomy in return for formal political position thinned the ranks; its repression drove the best and brightest into exile, and drove the more extremist to go underground and engage in an increasingly violent resistance. Finally, almost complete donor disengagement meant a bitter competitive struggle for the few streams of external finance that still flowed.

Ironically, these processes may only have been accelerated by recent moves toward a Congolese "peace." Parallel negotiation tracks, one national, one regional, led in mid-2003 to an uneasy 'Government of National Unity.' Congo's four new Vice-Presidents include one drawn from "Civil Society." NGO activists describe fierce competition for such key political positions:

> Civil society has been really weakened again by the scramble for posts such as the Head of the Senate and Vice President. People have been carrying themselves just like politicians. Many civil society leaders used their roles as interlocutors in the Inter-Congolese Dialogue[17] to "trampoline" into mainstream political positions.

Meanwhile, political reconstruction at central levels in Kinshasa has been accompanied by further intensifying violence in the East. In Ituri, north of North Kivu, violence between two ethno-political factions is animated by rival "NGOs" who regularly issue genocide warnings and human rights bulletins in the non-governmental mode but which directly reflect the political concerns of their paramilitary masters, who themselves are drawn in part from former civil society activists. Much the same is true of ongoing violence in northern

---

17. The broadened discussions which brought civil society figures, rebel representatives, customary authority and the Kabila government together for talks mediated by an international facilitator in Sun City, South Africa.

North Kivu, further blurring the boundaries of what is state and what is non-state, what is governmental and what is non-governmental.

Conclusions: State of Flux

> The problem here is that the country has never been managed, not since the departure of the Belgians, anyway. Not in any of the sectors. Because Mobutu dissembled to be managing, but he managed nothing! This means that to each and everyone, it has never been the case that it was possible to say "OK, here you are, your rights limit themselves to this and your obligations limit themselves to that."

Over the last decade or so, narratives of "state failure" have increasingly dominated academic attempts to explain African crises as geographically and substantively diverse as those in Somalia, Rwanda, the DR Congo and Liberia. Other adjectives used in the copious literature include "disintegrated," "collapsed" and "imploded" (Thürer 1999:731). Symptoms of state collapse include, according to former UN Security General Boutros Boutros-Ghali (cited in *ibid*):

> the collapse of state institutions, especially the police and judiciary, with resulting paralysis of governance, a breakdown of law and order, and general banditry and chaos. Not only are the functions of government suspended, but its assets are destroyed or looted and experienced officials are killed or flee the country.

The difficulty with this analytical approach to postcolonial crisis lies not in the symptomology of the present but rather in its prelapsarian nostalgia. Bluntly, before something can be said to have "failed," it must first have existed, or have at least been a goal toward which sincere efforts were made. Undergirding arguments about the "failed state" is a modernizationist teleology presupposing that the nation-building rhetoric of the first post-independence leaders was carried through in sincere attempts to forge a nation-state out of the colonial bequest and that the emerging impedimenta of governmentality—civil services, parastatal organizations, fiscal authorities—aimed for those same goals before suddenly breaking down in the face of external pressures or internal ructions.

In reply, a heterogeneous field of analysts have questioned boom/bust narratives concerning the stock of the postcolonial African state. What if forging the state was always just that: a forgery, a *trompe l'oeil* (Bayart et al. 1999b and Braeckman, 1999) concealing, with ever decreasing effectiveness, the motives of ruling elites? What if the apparent disorder of contemporary crisis represented not a failure of strategy but highly successful tactics of instrumentalization servicing other agendas (Chabal and Daloz 1999)? What emerges from this theorizing is, crucially, not an image of chaos, not society "thrown into confusion" after an all too brief period of sense and governmentality but rather a progressive "dysorder" (Jackson 2003): a pathological order entailing enormous uncertainty but, nonetheless, a remorseless inner logic elaborated through violence, close in spirit to Duffield's (1998:51) schema:

> Rather than the developmental rhetoric of scarcity or breakdown, one has to address the possibility that protracted instability is symptomatic of new and expanding forms of political economy; a function of economic change rather than a developmental malaise. It is difficult for the development model of conflict to convey such a sense of innovative expansion.

If it is true that the state "develops" in ways that depart from the normative directions that western governmentality presupposes (good husbandry, welfare provision, the conduct of conduct, and so on), what becomes of the "non-state"? In effect, in the DR Congo, "state" and "non-state" cannot, at least thus far, be understood as two distinct and competing spheres but rather as interpenetrating discourses of politics, government and development. "State" discourse has repeatedly been deployed by different actors comporting themselves in the name of the state: first the Colonial Power, Mobutu, Kabila (senior and junior), but also the various splinters of the RCD rebels. By contrast, "non-state" discourse, proffering its non-governmental vision of political development, has been deployed by a wide variety of different actors and movements. It has also been repeatedly appropriated (to incomplete effect) by "state" actors. These discourses, as always, comprise both rhetorical and practical levels. There has been an ever increasing gulf between these levels, so that both discourses appear increasingly hollow and insincere to each other, to the ordinary population, and to the international community and its donors.

The interpenetration of the two discourses, in terms of constant frequent migration of individuals between the two, the proliferation of organizational forms that subvert easy distinctions between "state" and "non state" and the repeated attempts by one either to resist or co-opt the energies of the other is, I argue, illuminated by Gordon's Foucauldian injunction, with which this essay begins. Civil society is best understood transactionally, through histories that chart the shifts and shapes of claims and counter-claims over "the governmental relation."

Works Cited

Braeckman, C. and M-F. Clos, eds. 1998. *Kabila Prend Le Pouvoir*. Brussels: GRIP and Editions Complexe.l'Homme.

Bayart, J-F. 1993. *The State in Africa: The politics of the belly*. London: Longman.

Bayart, J-F., S. Ellis, and B. Hibou. 1999a, eds. *The Criminalization of the State in Africa*. Oxford: James Currey.

Bayart, J-F., S. Ellis, & B. Hibou. 1999b. From kleptocracy to the felonious state? In *The Criminalization of the State in Africa,* edited by J-F. Bayart, S. Ellis, & B. Hibou. Oxford: James Currey.

Braeckman, C. 1999. *L'Enjeu Congolais: L'Afrique Centrale après Mobutu*. Paris: Fayard.

Chabal, P. and J-P. Daloz. 1999. *Africa Works: Disorder as political instrument*. London: James Currey.

De Boeck, F. 1999. Domesticating diamonds and dollars: identity, expenditure and sharing in Southwestern Zaïre (1984–97). In *Globalization and Identity: Dialectics of flow and closure,* edited by Meyer, B. and P. Geschiere. Oxford: Blackwell Publishers.

de Soto, H. 2002. *The Other Path: The economic answer to terrorism*. New York: Basic Books.

de Villers, G. and J. Tshonda. 1997. *Zaïre: la transition manquée*. Paris: L'Harmattan.

Duffield, M. 1998. Aid policy and post-modern conflict: a critical review. Unpublished paper, July 1998, School of Public Policy, International Development Department, University of Birmingham.

Escobar, A. 1995. *Encountering Development: The making and unmaking of the Third World*. Princeton: Princeton University Press.

Fabian, J. 1986. *Language and Colonial Power: The appropriation of Swahili in the former Belgian Congo, 1880–1938*. New York: Cambridge University Press.

Fatton, R. 1992. *Predatory Rule: State and civil society in Africa*. Boulder, CO: Lynne Rienner.

Ferguson, J. 1994. *The Anti-Politics Machine: 'Development', depoliticization, and bureaucratic power in Lesotho*. Minneapolis: University of Minnesota Press.

Foucault, M. 1991. Governmentality. In *The Foucault Effect: Studies in Governmentality*, edited by G. Burchell, C. Gordon, and P. Miller. Chicago: University of Chicago Press.

Gordon, C. 1991. Governmental rationality: An introduction. In *The Foucault Effect: Studies in governmentality*, edited by G. Burchell, C. Gordon, and P. Miller. Chicago: University of Chicago Press.

Gupta, A. 1998. *Postcolonial Developments: Agriculture in the making of modern India*. Durham, NC: Duke University Press.

Hirschmann, A. 1984. *Getting Ahead Collectively: Grassroots experiences in Latin America*. New York : Pergamon Press.

Jackson, S. 2001. Nos richesses sont pillées: economies de guerre et rumeurs de crime dans les Kivus, République Démocratique du Congo. *Politique Africaine, No. 84 Décembre 2001 Special Issue République démocratique du Congo : la guerre vue d'en bas*.

_____. 2002. Making a killing: criminality and coping in the Kivu war economy. *Review of African Political Economy*, 93/94, 517–36.

_____. 2003. *War Making: Uncertainty, improvisation, and involution in the Kivu Provinces, DR Congo, 1997–2002*. Ph.D. Dissertation, Princeton University, Princeton NJ.

Kassimir, R. 2001. Producing local politics: governance, representation, and non-state organizations in Africa. In *Interventions and Transnationalism in Africa*, edited by Callaghy, T., R. Kassimir, & R. Latham. Cambridge: Cambridge University Press.

Kearney, M. 1996. *Reconceptualizing the Peasantry: Anthropology in global perspective*. Boulder, Colorado: Westview Press.

Keen, D. 1994. *The Benefits of Famine: The political economy of famine in south-western Sudan, 1985–1988*. Princeton, NJ: Princeton University Press.

Lancaster, C. 1999. *Aid to Africa: So much to do, so little done*. Chicago: University of Chicago Press.

MacGaffey, J. 1991. Historical, cultural and structural dimensions of Zaïre's unrecorded trade. In *The Real Economy of Zaïre: The contribution of smuggling and other unofficial activities to national wealth*, edited by J. MacGaffey. Philadelphia, PA: University of Pennsylvania Press.

Mbembe, A. 2001. *On the Postcolony*. Berkeley, CA: University of California Press.

Ndegwa, S. 1994. Civil society and political change in Africa: the case of NGOs in Kenya. *International Journal of Civil Society* 35 (1–2): 19–36.

Nzongola-Ntalaja, G. 2002. *The Congo, From Leopold to Kabila*. London: Zed Books.

Sachs, W. 1992. Introduction. In *The Development Dictionary: A guide to knowledge as power*, edited by W. Sachs. London: Zed Books.

Scott, J. 1998. *Seeing Like a State: How certain schemes to improve the human condition have failed.* New Haven, CT: Yale University Press.

Streiffeler, F. 1994. State substitution and market liberalization in northern Kivu, Zaïre. *Sociologia Ruralis,* 34 (1): 63–70.

Taussig, M. 1993. Maleficium: state fetishism. In *Fetishism as Cultural Discourse,* edited by E. Apter and W. Pietz. Ithaca, NY: Cornell University Press.

Thürer, D. 1999. The "failed state" and international law. *International Review of the Red Cross* 836: 731–61.

Vwakyanakazi, M. 1991. Import and export in the second economy in North Kivu. In *The Real Economy of Zaïre: The contribution of smuggling and other unofficial activities to national wealth,* edited by J. MacGaffey. Philadelphia, PA: University of Pennsylvania Press.

Whaites, A. 1996. Let's get civil society straight: NGOs and political theory. *Development in Practice* 6(3): 240–44.

Willame, J-C. 1999. *L'Odyssée Kabila: Trajectoire pour un Congo nouveau.* Paris: Karthala.

Zizek, S. 1989. *The Sublime Object of Ideology.* London: Phronesis, Verso.

CHAPTER 8

International Influence on Civil Society in Mali: The Case of the Cotton Farmers' Union, SYCOV

Timothy W. Docking
U.S. Department of Agriculture
tim.docking@usda.gov[1]

"All that is decided for us and without us is decided against us."

—Antoine Baba Berthé,
first president of the cotton farmer's union, SYCOV[2]

Introduction

The comprehensive transformation of African politics during the late 1980s and early 1990s were simultaneously a response to, and a catalyst for, a revolution in the way western donors interact with their African recipients. During the 1980s international financial institutions and bilateral donors advanced an agenda of economic conditionality across Africa. In addition to free trade and the adoption of economic austerity measures, African states were called upon to promote human rights, freedoms of speech and of the

---

1. The views expressed in this chapter are those of the author and do not necessarily represent opinions held by the USDA.

2. SYCOV and CIEPAC. 1995. La Longue Marche des Paysans du Mali Sud. *SYCOV Livret de formation syndical.* Bamako.

press, gender equality and the decentralization of political power. Clearly, many of these pronouncements were just that, western rhetoric that was belied by western action. Nevertheless, the rhetoric, as well as its occasional support through economic conditionalities, seemingly had a salient effect on African politics during the early 1990s as fully half the states in sub-Saharan Africa held elections during this time. At second glance however, we see that many of these "elections" were mere facades, designed by strongmen to gain international legitimacy and consolidate domestic power. Africa's "democratic revolution" of the early 1990s was thus adjudged by many a failure, as an era when nascent democracies across the continent were pushed aside by the resurgence of authoritarian leaders who subsequently established pseudo-democracies.

However, democracy did grow roots in Mali during this period; an exception among Africa's failed democracies that has not gone unnoticed by western policy makers. Indeed, Mali has become the darling of the development community, held up as an example of how good government is fundamental to national development, and supported by dozens of international agencies and NGOs that have rushed to take part in the Malian democratic "success story." But all this "support" for the Malian revolution has been a mixed blessing for Mali's nascent democratic institutions.

This chapter explores Mali's relationship with western donors during the 1990s and attempts to identify the political trends, on both sides, that have influenced and characterized this relationship. A case study of the cotton farmers' union, SYCOV, will illustrate the dramatic liberalization that has taken place within Malian society since the fall of the Second Republic in 1991 and highlight the influence of the west on Malian civil society. More specifically, it describes how well-intentioned international actors perverted the development of an organic cotton farmer's movement. At the heart of this study is an in-depth analysis of the international/local nexus in Mali at the end of the twentieth century—an important factor in the study of democratization in developing countries that scholars have until recently overlooked.

This study also illustrates the challenges facing local groups in Africa and the serious pitfalls and unintended consequences facing western agencies and NGOs as they attempt to engage with and help foster the development of civil society. The study concludes that civil society in Mali is being instrumentalized by state and international actors alike and consequently drawn away from the constituent communities that development professionals and policy makers aim to help. In short, this work suggests that just as the democratic revolution of the 1990s produced numerous artificial democracies in Africa, the international effort to strengthen civic groups is contributing to the growth of "pseudo civil society" on the continent.

The Evolution of the Cotton Farmers' Movement

Colonial Origins

Throughout the twentieth-century the farmers of southern Mali periodically resisted central government policies. Until 1991 however, peasant resistance consisted of passive forms of non-compliance, smuggling, tax evasion and participation in parallel markets. During this period farmers were able to influence rural policy through non-cooperation and other "everyday forms of resistance," but they were unable to raise their complaints beyond the village level and thus, incapable of gaining significant redress vis-à-vis the exploitative policies emanating from the colonial, and later state, cotton company (cf. Scott 1985).

Archival information indicates that French colonial officials had a mandate to spread cash-crop farming schemes, particularly the cultivation of cotton, across the French Sudan. The policy was designed to break French dependence on American cotton and to build a rural tax base for the colonial government. The French undertook two initiatives in the territory which is present day Mali in order to meet this mandate: 1) a giant irrigation scheme known to this day as the *Office du Niger*, established in the 1930s; and 2) CFDT (*Compagnie Française pour le Développement des Textiles*), established in the 1940s. Following the failure of the *Office du Niger's* irrigation scheme, southern Mali, with its relatively high population concentration, ample rains and local knowledge base about cotton farming, became the center of French efforts to turn the Sudan into an inexpensive, reliable and plentiful source of cotton for the metropolitan textile industry.

During the 1970s, with nationalist movements at a zenith across Africa, the CFDT ostensibly handed control of the cotton scheme over to the Malian government creating a Malian parastatal organization known as the CMDT (*Compagnie Malienne pour le Développement des Textiles*). The "new" state-owned company followed a course set by the CFDT of expanding cultivation throughout southern Mali in an attempt to increase production. Yet, the CFDT—as a 40% stake holder in the CMDT, as a monopoly buyer of Mali's raw cotton, and as a monopoly seller of inputs—maintained a keen interest, and de facto control over, the CMDT by extending vital technical services to the company and facilitating important financial support from the French government.

Socio-Economic Conditions Among Cotton Farmers During the Late-1980s

In order to grasp the growing discontent of Malian farmers during the late 1980s, one must first understand the economic realities they faced. During the 1970s, the statist policies of the military government came under growing pressure from international financial institutions and bilateral donors. In 1982 the Malian government agreed to internal austerity measures and signed its first structural adjustment program. But a series of economic short falls led to the non-payment of salaries to government employees and civil servants in 1985. This in turn set off a series of strikes, which threatened to topple the Malian government. At the end of this year a long simmering border dispute with Burkina Faso boiled over leading to a five-day war, from December 24–29. The wave of Malian patriotism that ensued buoyed the Traoré regime and brought a swift end to the strikes. Nevertheless, Traoré remained politically weakened by the strikes and unable to make the difficult choices necessary to stay in line with structural adjustment. By 1987 the government had abandoned the agreement.

Mali's economic conditions continued to worsen, and in 1988 the government was forced to return to the World Bank for a bailout. The economic reforms accompanying the bailout stung Malians at all levels, including the cotton farmers. As grain markets were liberalized and price controls eased, the cost of farm inputs also rose along with interest rates from Mali's National Agricultural Development Bank (BNDA). Unaware of the full ramifications of these changes, during the late 1980s many cotton farmers drew freely on credit at the start of the agricultural season only to find themselves locked into debt after their harvest had been sold. Tensions thus rose in the cotton zone as farmers felt pinched by the CMDT on one side, and corrupt local government tax collectors on the other. Indeed, under the Traoré regime Malian tax collectors timed their arrival into villages to coincide with the payment of cotton proceeds; villages unable to meet the heavy tax burdens suffered the humiliation of having their chief taken prisoner and held in the local administrative capital until accounts could be settled.[3]

---

3. I witnessed these events as a Peace Corps Volunteer living in rural southern Mali, 1989–91.

Moreover, in 1986 the CMDT negotiated a ten-year agreement with the Malian government to buy cotton from farmers for 93 CFA/kilo (or 12¢/lb. based on the 1986 exchange rate of 346 CFA = $1.) That same year, cotton traded on the world market at 365 CFA/kilo, or roughly four times what the CMDT paid the Malian farmers. Over the next five years the average price of cotton on the world market was 485 CFA/kilo (75¢/lb.). By 1989 production costs for the Malian cotton farmer had risen to 95 CFA/kilo, meaning that many farmers actually lost money on their crop (Bingen 1994: 61). Unable to repay debts to the bank and cotton company, and lacking viable alternative livelihoods, farmers were obliged to continue farming cotton.

Tensions Build in the Koutiala Area

Tensions between farmers and the CMDT were pushed to the breaking point in late 1989 when rumors circulated among farmers about an impending price hike in farming equipment, and a salary hike for rural CMDT agents. In response, angry groups of farmers began to meet informally to discuss the growing difficulty of their situation. Out of these talks arose one question: *why couldn't they demand a higher price for cotton?* Thus, by the 1989–90 agricultural season tensions between peasants and the CMDT/state were high throughout the cotton zone. But nowhere were Malian cotton farmers better organized than in south-eastern Mali, in and around the town of Koutiala. In September of 1990 a meeting was called by representatives from village associations (VAs) in the Zébala area (twenty-five kilometers east of Koutiala) to discuss perceived injustices in BNDA policies. Led by Tyro Dembélé, the group built a federation of thirty-eight VAs. In October, representatives from the Federation gathered in Zébala to discuss a response to the BNDA. At issue was a bank policy of collecting its agricultural debts directly from the CMDT before payments for cotton sales were distributed to farmers, a practice which infuriated farmers. Farmers were also enraged by a policy which prohibited reimbursement for unused agricultural inputs at the end of the season.[4] The Federation presented its complaints to numerous local officials demanding clarification of input prices and BNDA interest rates. Remarkably, in November, peasant demands were met; the farmers also succeeded, even more remarkably, in involving the state cereals board

---

4. Tyro Dembélé, Secretary General of SYCOV, interview with author, Bamako. February 6, 1998. For another account of these events see: SYCOV and CIEPAC. 1995. *Livret de formation syndicale. La Longue Marche des Paysans du Mali Sud.*

(OPAM) in the sale of area food crops, thus increasing the producer price of millet offered by Koutiala's merchants. Buoyed by their new found power, Federation leaders looked to expand their movement.

Meanwhile, in Bamako discontent with single-party rule intensified amid calls for democratic reforms. Farmers from across the cotton zone watched during the first months on 1991 as the state's central authority unravelled. As unrest spread through regional capitals and large towns across Mali the farmers saw an opening to broaden their movement and intensify their demands. During the tense days surrounding the March 1991 coup CMDT factories across southern Mali were threatened by violence from disgruntled farmers and angry youths.

While clashes were avoided between peasants and the CMDT, several state agents from the hated *Eaux et forêts*—the corrupt national forestry service which oversaw the enforcement of land management policies and the assessment of fines for bush fires and other violations—were lynched by mobs. One Union member, Tyro Dembélé, recalls that the events surrounding the March revolution emboldened the cotton farmers. "The movement picked up speed after the political events of 1991." When asked why, Dembélé adds: "Because the people were not as afraid as they had been. People were demanding justice everywhere and so did we."[5]

The Birth of SYCOV

In April of 1991, the farmers in the Koutiala area met again to discuss the problems associated with the upcoming agricultural campaign. In an effort to expand the movement throughout the region, the Federation dispatched its delegates to gather support in the countryside for a May 6th meeting in Cinzina. Again, Tyro Dembélé recalls the event:

> We organized a meeting in Cinzina (near Koutiala) and put together a list of grievances with twelve points. We did this because we were angry, primarily at the BNDA and the CMDT over the matter of inputs, but also because we did not have a voice in the policies affecting us. The government said that it spoke for us, i.e. during the contrat-plan negotiations of 1989, but it did not. [question: "Were you ever encouraged by the CMDT to organize a union?"] No, this was something we did ourselves.[6]

---

5. Dembélé, *Ibid.*
6. Dembélé, *Ibid.*

On May 8th, these demands were presented to the Koutiala regional office of the CMDT. One of the peasant leaders at the time remembers the ultimatum the farmers gave to the CMDT: "We told the director...whether you recognize us or not, you must find a solution to these twelve points or we will not plant cotton during the present season!"[7] But the regional director of the CMDT dismissed farmer complaints and refused to submit them to the CMDT national office in Bamako. Soon tempers flared in Koutiala as several hundred cotton farmers surrounded a CMDT factory and threatened to burn it down. While the sacking of the cotton gin was avoided, the CMDT was shaken by the intensity of farmer threats and quickly backed down. On May 13th, a high-level delegation comprised of a representative from the Ministry of Rural Development, the General Director of the CMDT and the President of the Chamber of Agriculture, was assembled in Bamako and sent to Koutiala to meet with the leaders of the Federation of VAs. As a result of the meeting, nine of the twelve farmer demands were met. However three demands, among the most important, remained on the table:

- an increase in the producer price of cotton;
- a decrease in the price of inputs; and
- the provision of 50% of seed cake production to farmers.

For the farmers, this settlement was unacceptable. Indeed, it was the inability to attain seed cake along with low producer prices that had been at the core of their initial grievances. In 1991 the production cost of a kilo of cotton was 40% below the 1985 cost. Although the CMDT paid the farmers an 8 CFA/kilo refund following the 1990–91 season, Malian cotton farmers remained the lowest paid in francophone Africa. Thus, on May 17th the farmers declared their non-compliance with the contrat-plan (production agreement between farmers and CMDT), reiterated their demands, and threatened a strike just as the planting season was about to begin. The Federation's tough stance elicited a response: this time an official delegation led by the Minister of Rural Development, Mrs. Sy Miamuna Ba travelled to Cinzina, "the peasants' backyard," for another meeting.[8] By the time the delegation arrived, more than a thousand representatives from VAs around the region had assembled in Cinzina. The farmers won a 10

---

7. Gaoussou Sanogo, Regional SYCOV representative from Koutiala, quoted in *Système francophone d'information agricole* (SYFIA). "*Mali: la lutte exemplaire des planteurs de coton*," Bulletin no. 33B, 1 (October 15, 1991).

8. The farmers perceived the location of the meeting ("in their back yard" vs. in Bamako or in some other neutral location) a symbolic victory.

CFA/kg refund for the coming cotton season and an assurance from Minister Ba that their final two demands would be addressed in the future.

Although the farmers failed to get everything they wanted, the agreement represented a solidifying event in their fight for justice. Moreover, this high profile meeting attracted significant national and international attention. The French Farmers' Association for International Development (*Associations des Agriculteurs Français pour le Développement International*, AFDI), had a long history of working with peasants in the Koutiala area and with the backing of the French Ministry of Cooperation, quickly provided technical and financial support to the farmers' group. Other international organizations were quick to follow, providing vital financial and technical assistance. Thus, after generations of toil and inequitable exchange under predatory policies of the colonial and national administrations, Malian cotton farmers had apparently gained a voice.

While most eyes were focused on the political changes taking place in Bamako following the March 1991 *coup d'état*, the cotton farmers movement continued to gain momentum and legitimacy. Talks continued between the state, the CMDT and the Federation of VAs. The CMDT thus decided to hold a seminar to discuss farmer demands and to consider the creation of a cotton farmers' association. In September 1991, the World Bank and the CFD (*Caisse Française de Développement*) sponsored a meeting to bring together the principal actors from the farmers' movement and the Malian Government to discuss the future of the movement and to address the problems articulated by farmers; most notably marketing and the provision of cotton seed cake for cattle.[9] The seminar was clouded by distrust on both sides. In the lead up to the meeting the CMDT had attempted to isolate the hard-line San and Koutiala leaders within the Federation of VAs, by forming a partnership with more moderate farmers representing other regions of Mali.[10] Moreover, the Federation lacked the financial means to publicize their new movement and attract new members from other parts of southern Mali. The task of finding peasant representatives thus fell in the lap of the CMDT, which gladly selected the delegates from the other three CMDT areas of Southern Mali (Fana, Sikasso and Bougouni). Nevertheless, the hard-liners successfully swayed a majority of the group to their side and succeeded in thwarting CMDT co-optation. The seminar ended with pledges from the CMDT to revise the con-

---

9. The CFD is the central banking institution for French overseas Departments and Territories (DOMs and TOMs).

10. SYCOV and CIEPAC, op. cit., 15.

trat-plan in order to give the farmers a voice in future negotiations, and to create an association of farmers in the cotton zone. More important however, were decisions made outside the formal meetings at the Segou seminar by the farmers themselves. "The decision to create a union stemmed from the September 1991 [meetings]:[11]

> At the Segou seminar, we did not designate the nature of our organization. This problem led us to realize that we risked leaving the infant to be born, to grow and to be named [by someone else]. Meanwhile, a group of peasants at the seminar decided we would become a union so that we could have judicial status and be recognized everywhere on the national and international stage.[12]

Still, few within Southern Mali had any knowledge of the strides being taken by their comrades in the East; the cotton farmers' movement was localized around Koutiala and San with the exception of a smattering of delegates—hand picked by the CMDT—from the other regions.

One farmer from Bougouni, a *cercle* town in south-western Mali, recalled the instrumental role of the CMDT in setting up the union: "The CMDT approached me because they knew I was educated and asked me to join the group. With their help I set up a local committee of cotton farmers."[13] The dependence of the Koutiala farmers' group on the CMDT during the early days of the movement effectively blurred the line between the future union and the company it had formed to fight. This ambiguous relationship between farmer activists and the CMDT was compounded when the company assumed control of the extension of the movement and the selection of farmer representatives across Southern Mali. Again, Modi Diallo remembers the nascence of the cotton farmers' "movement" in Bougouni:

> [From its beginning] the creation of the cotton farmers' association in Bougouni was all very poorly organized. For example, the CMDT would often inform me of meetings just a couple of hours in advance. This made it very difficult to get word out to the VAs in the area about

---

11. Antoine Baba Berthé, interview in Dagnon, Gaudens, Bamako, March 31, 1992, in *Regards Croises sur les Organisations Paysannes au Mali*. Tome I. *Les documents de travail de la FPH*. Paris: *Fondation pour le progrès de l'homme*, 27.

12. SYCOV delegation, interview in Dagnon, Gaudens, Paris. March 4, 1992. In *Ibid.*, 29.

13. Modi Diallo, regional SYCOV representative from Bougouni, interview with author, Bougouni, Mali. March 4, 1998.

the time and place of meetings. Moreover, the CMDT said that we had to put our village-based groups, "village coordination" groups in place throughout the *cercle* before December, 1991. This was impossible to do and thus, our work got off to a bad start.[14]

Yet, from the perspective of the CMDT, the selection of farmer representatives and the hasty assemblage of an administrative framework were part of a larger plan. The CMDT had been under pressure by foreign donors (most notably the World Bank and IMF) since the signing of the contrat-plan in 1988 to open up its capital and to devolve more responsibility to Malian peasants. Up until the May 1991 Koutiala events, however, the CMDT had taken no steps in this direction. From the perspective of the CMDT the legitimizing of peasant demands signalled a time to fulfill some of its international mandates.

During this period the Technical Director of Rural Development, and the administrator most responsible for company/farmer relations at the CMDT was Jean Baptiste Diabaté. He recalled the nascence of the farmers' movement in a different light from the account given above:

> We [CMDT] wanted the union to form. We had anticipated it and just had to move up our plans so that we could set it in place in 1991 after the farmers' revolution. Nevertheless, the creation of a national union was not the goal of the peasants in Koutiala at this time, they wanted cotton seed cake for their cattle. It was us that put all the structures into place for SYCOV. We organized them...[15]

Evidence suggests that Diabaté's perspective reflects the feelings of a majority of CMDT administrators, i.e. that SYCOV was created by the CMDT for the peasants. More significant, however, is that these same individuals discount the independence and legitimacy of the farmers' group and maintain a paternalistic attitude toward the union.

The cotton farmers resisted these efforts to take over their movement in its early stages. On January 29, 1992 the farmers' association, along with representatives from the Ministry of Rural Development, Chamber of Agriculture and the CMDT, met again in Segou.[16] The farmers elected a provisional national bureau with a delegate from Kadiolo (a *cercle* town near the Ivory Coast

14. *Ibid.*

15. Jean Baptiste Diabaté, *Directeur Technique du Développement Rural*, CMDT, interview with author, Bamako, October 16, 1997.

16. Again, local delegates from each of the six regions were transported to the event by the CMDT.

border), Antoine Baba Berthé, as president. This was widely seen as a tactic to broaden the movement to other areas of Southern Mali. The farmers also made the provocative move of declaring their organization a union, instead of a federation or cooperative as the CMDT had wished. This act of independence was perceived as insubordination by the CMDT. One of the delegates described how the cotton company quickly struck back:

> After the January 1992 meeting, the CMDT sent out a company-wide circular announcing that no company funding would be allotted for the farmers' union without prior written consent from the national office of the CMDT. But the French Cooperation and other funders chipped in to sponsor our constitutive congress later that year.[17]

Indeed by distancing itself from the company, the young union made it clear that Malian cotton farmers would no longer accept the status quo. Nor would the group accede to the CMDT's desire to use the union for its own ends of appeasing foreign donors eager to create a platform for Malian peasants. "SYCOV was put in place to achieve our demands on the CMDT and the government…SYCOVs vocation is thus not only syndical, it is political, social and economic."[18] The union clearly outlined its objectives in the spring of 1992:

1) To protect the revenues of the peasants against low cotton prices and high input costs;

2) To make available seed cake for cattle because the rains [in 1991] were poor and there is insufficient grass to feed and prepare the cattle to plow again;

3) To participate in the planning of cotton marketing;

4) To defend the peasants from *Eaux et forêts* who often [falsely] accuse villagers of setting bush fires and fine them between 100,000–250,000 CFA;

5) To participate in local government in order to insure that local tax revenues are spent on development projects in the localities where the money originates;

6) To help set farm prices at equal rates throughout the cotton zone;

---

17. Modi Diallo, interview with author, op.cit.
18. SYCOV delegation, interview in Dagnon, Gaudens, op. cit., 28.

7)   To help find solutions to credit/saving problems that exist at the village level.[19]

In September 1992, the union held its constitutive congress in Cinzina. A national administrative bureau of eighteen members was elected, with Antoine Baba Berthé remaining president, along with a central council of forty-two members (seven members from each of the five CMDT and one OHVN regions). The new union leaders approved a constitution and adopted a set of internal rules. Perhaps more importantly, however, SYCOV used the congress to again assert its independence by rejecting invitations to affiliate with two different national unions: the *Union Nationale des Travailleurs Maliens* (UNTM), composed of salaried city dwellers; and the *Syndicat national de la Production Agricole* (SYNAPRO), composed of salaried workers in agri-industrial professions, including CMDT employees. While UNTM leaders perceived SYCOV's rebuff as a signal that the union was in the pocket of the CMDT, it seems more likely that the rationale for not joining the larger urban-based groups was based on two primary reasons: 1) the almost instinctive distrust that Malian peasants feel toward non-peasants; and 2) the firm belief among farmers that salaried workers and farmers fall into two different categories with distinct interests.

The first order of business for the union was to generate an operating budget. SYCOV thus adopted a policy of selling union membership cards in the countryside. The *Carte de Membre* cost 1,000 CFA per family, per year. This plan however, was met with little success and according to SYCOV members, was subverted by the CMDT.

> We tried to raise money by selling SYCOV membership cards, but CMDT agents spread rumors throughout the villages that our union was corrupt. So, very few farmers bought the cards and joined the union. The sale of membership cards was truly a failure for SYCOV. But in reality, I knew that the membership card scheme was a bad idea. Southern Mali is as big as a country and even if someone at the village level collected the money for us, the risk of it disappearing was high. Moreover, a peasant movement is not like a workers' movement; when we are out of our fields, working for the union, we do not get paid—we don't make a salary [implication: it is costly for farmers to leave their fields to conduct union activities such as member recruitment].[20]

---

19. *Ibid.*, 29.
20. Modi Diallo, interview with author. *Ibid.*

This statement illustrates the multiple challenges facing SYCOV, and sheds light on its eventual orientation to international organizations. It also attests to the broader problems surrounding the organization of rural unions in the developing world.

International Influence on Civil Society

Unable to raise funds from its intended constituents, SYCOV turned to the west for support and found it in abundance. A number of foreign donors were eager to see the conditions laid out in the 1988 contrat-plan negotiations, giving farmers a bigger role in the Malian cotton network, finally met by the CMDT. The World Bank was quick to assist the farmers in the early stages of their movement. So too were several NGOs, the CFDT, the French Minister of Cooperation and the CMDT.

International Assistance for the Cotton Farmers' Union

The motives behind western support for the farmers were mixed. A number of small French NGOs came to SYCOV's aid early in its development, offering technical and financial support. One of the early actors to work with the peasants was CIEPAC (*Centre d'appui au développement local*), a French NGO financed primarily by the French Ministry of Cooperation. Indeed, CIEPAC is representative of the small French NGOs that came to SYCOV's aid in the early 1990s. CIEPAC director Jacques Berthomé recounted his feelings upon first learning about the farmers' movement with satisfaction:

> I recognized early that this group was unique. In twelve countries where there are cotton parastatals in Africa, this was the first cotton farmers' movement that I had ever seen. Moreover, Mali was both the biggest producer of cotton and her farmers were the lowest paid.[21]

But he also recalled that SYCOV faced serious challenges; both internal and external:

---

21. Jacque Berthomé, Director of CIEPAC (*Centre d'appui au développement local*), interview with author, Castelnau-le-Lez, France. June 19, 1997.

The union had a huge problem with internal communication, from the top to the bottom of the organization. Everything went through the CMDT: faxes, telephone calls, transportation…and while this was not appropriate, it was necessary. Nevertheless, this gave people, farmers and outsiders alike, the impression that SYCOV was not independent. Moreover, SYCOV faced a serious deficit in human capital—its membership was not educated. They were mostly young and the only thing they knew was agriculture. The president of the union Antoine Baba Berthé was thus the whole show and this made it difficult to have an internal democracy.[22]

CIEPAC's interactions with SYCOV targeted these problems. In 1992, the NGO organized the Segou seminar; in 1993 Berthomé returned to Mali to help SYCOV prepare for contrat-plan negotiations; CIEPAC bought SYCOV a car so its leaders could campaign across the region and helped the union start a newsletter to increase awareness of the union among the farmers. And in 1995, the NGO wrote a booklet on the history of the farmers' movement, distributing 5000 copies across southern Mali in French and Bambara.[23]

SYCOV Grows Dependent on Outside Aid

CIEPAC was not the only NGO working with SYCOV. The AFDI (*Agriculteurs Français pour le Développement International*), another French NGO, had a relationship with the cotton farmers that stretched back more than ten years. It was no surprise, therefore, when the organization became involved with the movement. It began by providing technical assistance: helping farmers to organize, as well as calculating production costs and cotton pricing. Later, the organization worked with SYCOV on accounting practices, educated members about the contrat-plan, and helped them strategize about negotiating higher refunds. It also sponsored excursions to France for SYCOV representatives and coached the group in public speaking.

SYCOV also benefited from cooperation with a Paris-based consortium of NGOs. Initially known as the *Réseau GAO* (or *Groupments, Associations villageoises, Organisations paysannes*), one of three groupings of French development agencies working in Africa with the financial support of the French Min-

---

22. *Ibid.*
23. *Ibid.*

ister of Cooperation.[24] One of the *Reseau GAO's* members, Denis Pesche, recalled sponsoring a conference in Bamako in 1992 for forty Malian peasants,
fifteen of whom were SYCOV members. The group discussed a number of
macro-level factors, including the political economy of Malian agriculture and
the nuances of the contrat-plan agreement. During the spring of 1992, GAO
also hosted a group of SYCOV representatives in France. "These meetings with
SYCOV went very well and we decided to follow up with a long term [two-
year] professionalization program based in Bamako. We started the program
in 1995, with SYCOV placed at the heart of our efforts."[25]

Figure 8.1: Sources and Sums of SYCOV Funding: 1993–98 [26]

Caisse Française de Développement	27,714,190 CFA	$46,190	39.2%
Comité Française de Solidarité Internationale	24,436,290	40,727	34.5
Centre Canadien d'Etudes (CECI)	6,449,924	10,750	9.1
Coopération Hollandaise	3,907,000	6,512	5.5
Coopération Suisse	3,000,000	5,000	4.2
Mission Française de Coopération	2,309,640	3,849	3.3
Cellule appui aux Organ. Professionnelles	1,850,000	3,083	2.6
Agriculteurs Française et Dév. Internat'l (AFDI)	642,610	1,071	.9
SYCOV membership cards	335,000	558	.5
TOTALS	70,644,654	117,741	100

* 600 CFA = 1 $US

In 1993 the CFDT brought fifteen SYCOV leaders to France to observe the
vertical integration of world cotton production. The group visited ports, the
French textile industry and research centers, where they discussed issues surrounding Malian cotton production. Yet, seemingly informative trips like this
one did little to improve SYCOV's image back home. The sudden prestige and
privilege that was heaped upon union leaders alienated the union from Malian

---

24. The other two groups included networks focusing on research and development
and food production strategies. In 1996, the three networks came together to form a consortium of French development organizations called the *Inter-réseaux.* Benoît Vergriette,
Director of SOLAGRAL, interview with author, Paris. April 10, 1997.

25. Denis Pesche, Director of *Inter-Réseaux,* a French consortium of NGOs, interview
with author, Paris. May 16, 1997.

26. *Assemblee Permanente des Chambres d'Agriculture du Mali. Compte Rendu de Mission: Premier* [sic]*congres du syndicat des producteurs de coton et vivrier* (SYCOV). April
14–18, 1998. Bamako, 1998. 5–6.

farmers, who already had concerns that SYCOV was becoming too closely tied to the CMDT. Nevertheless, the small group of union leaders, exhilarated by their new found stature in the international community, turned their backs on the farmers of southern Mali.

SYCOV Neglects its Base

Much of what happened at the national and international levels escaped the peasants at the local level. Indeed, few villagers in Southern Mali had ever heard of SYCOV. And even fewer knew anything about SYCOV's activities. One farmer expressed his confusion about SYCOV even though he was appointed to the SYCOV committee in his village of Sirakoro:

> A representative from SYCOV came to Sirakoro this year and held a meeting. But we have not heard from him again. [Question: did anyone buy a membership card to the union?] No. He brought three to the meeting and left them with us. But he never sent any more. No one bought a card. [Question: Did he explain the goals of SYCOV?] He said that SYCOV is a union but actually people here in Sirakoro don't know what the union does.[27]

Another leader from Sirakoro affirmed this account, "Yes, I know SYCOV, but they really have not done much here. People don't belong to the group in this village."[28] In fact, the vast majority of villagers in the southwest of Mali seem to know nothing of SYCOV. Moreover, in areas where peasants do know SYCOV, fears of corruption run high. One rural leader from the Sikasso area affirms that SYCOV is widely known there, however:

> The problem with SYCOV is that there are many rumors circulating in the countryside about the character of the group's leaders. Thus farmers are reluctant to join the union and pay dues. But this is not because of poor leadership—they face huge challenges in organizing the cotton zone—rather, it is because SYCOVs leaders are

---

27. Soloman Koné, Secretary of Sirakoro VA and SYCOV committees, interview with author, Sirakoro, Mali. May 1, 1998.
28. Satigi Koné, President of Sirakoro VA, interview with author, Sirakoro, Mali. May 2, 1998.

spread too thinly and have thus, in many cases, lost touch with their base.[29]

IFIs, Privatization and the Instrumentalization of SYCOV

The CFDT and the French connection

The problems described above were exacerbated by the fact that not all foreign onlookers wanted SYCOV to succeed. As the primary financier of the CFDT, the CFD (Caisse Française de Develppement) has also invested millions of dollars into Mali's seventeen cotton gins. The CFD is also said to be the voice of the French state and according to one French informant, has adopted a cautious attitude toward SYCOV. "The CFD has made it known that the Malian cotton farmers' union better not take its demands on the CMDT too far. By doing so, the CFD feels the union risks killing the CMDT cash cow."[30] At the start of the 1990s the CFDT and its affiliates had net revenues of approximately $450 million and interests in fifteen African countries.[31]

By the early 1990s however, the World Bank and IMF had begun promoting neo-liberal reforms with new vigor. The CFDT and Bretton Woods Institutions crossed paths in Uganda in 1993. Plagued by corruption and by a civil war, Uganda's troubled Lint Marketing Board (LMB) had failed. Seeing an opportunity to expand its network of African "partners" the CFDT entered into negotiations with the Ugandan government to take over the LMB and man-

---

29. Bakary Diarra, Permanent Secretary for the Federation of Unions and Tons in Sikasso (FUTS), interview with author, Sikasso, Mali. April 17, 1998.

30. Benoît Vergriette, interview with author, op. cit. This last point provides a good illustration of the non-monolithic nature of the French development apparatus. While on the one hand the French Minister of Cooperation has been actively supporting the efforts of liberal NGOs to help SYCOV develop as a *contre-pouvoir* and partner in the cotton development scheme, on the other, the CFD is reportedly working against the union.

31. In 1993, the *Groupe* CFDT consisted of five members: the CFDT, in charge of industrial and agricultural production of cotton; the *Compagnie Cotonnière* (COPACO), in charge of cotton marketing; the *Société de Services pour l'Europe et l'Afrique* (SOSEA), in charge of transit/import/export of cotton at l'Havre; the *Société Dépannage Export Express* (D2E), in charge of purchase and delivery of cotton; and the trimesterly review, *Coton et Développement*. The net income for *Groupe* CFDT was 1,808,924,951 FF. See: The CFDT. *Rapport Annuel*: 1993, Paris: France. 1993. 4–5.

age all aspects of the cotton production process.[32] The CFDT proposal included provisions to rehabilitate the Ugandan cotton sector and to set a minimum producer price for farmers. But the CFDT's proposal flew in the face of Bank plans to privatize the Ugandan cotton sector. Eventually the Ugandan government signed a multi-year program to liberalize the cotton sector, as part of a larger structural adjustment agreement with the World Bank.[33]

Figure 8.2: The CFDT Cotton Network in Africa[34]

Country	Company name	Percent owned by CFDT
Burkina Faso	Sofitex	34%
Cameroon	Sodecoton	30
Central African Republic	Sococa	34
Chad	Cotonchad	17
Ivory Coast	CIDT	25
Madagascar	Hasyma	29.4
Mali	**CMDT**	**40**
Senegal	Sodefitex	20
Spain	MASA	50
Zaire	Codenord	37.5

These events were a harbinger of the changes in store for the CFDT. The World Bank had set its sights on the French colonial cotton company and sought its demise. With the encouragement of the World Bank cotton parastatals in Togo, Benin, Cameroon, Ivory Coast and Senegal made moves to privatize between 1990 and 1996. In February 1996 the CFDT was shocked to see its name among French companies listed by the Juppe government as candidates for privatization by simple decree. In response to this threat at home the CFDT reportedly called on its African "friends," heads of state from sub-Saharan Africa, to lobby senators and deputies from the French-African Community in Paris to intervene in the French Senate and National Assembly on behalf of the company.[35] In particular, President Idriss Deby from Chad pledged his resistance to the dictates of the World Bank.

---

32. *La Lettre de l'Ocean Indien, Ouganda: Liberalisation de la filiere coton,* no. 583 (July 10, 1993).

33. *La Lettre de l'Ocean Indien, "Ouganda: Liberalisation du secteur cotonnier,"* no. 626 (June 4, 1994).

34. *Ibid.,* 5. The other African states in partnerships with the CFDT at this time were: Benin, Burundi, Gambia, Guinea, Guinea Bissau, Togo.

35. *La Lettre du Continent, "Lobbying aupres des chefs d'Etat africains,"* no. 254 (March 14, 1996).

Ultimately, however, the CFDT could not hold back the wave of privatization that washed over the region. In the Ivory Coast, sensing defeat and ultimate privatization of the CIDT, the CFDT attempted a "mini-privatization" *à la Française*. That is, the company entered into discussions with private French groups, such as Pinault-CFAO to avoid ceding the CFDT stake to an "Anglo Saxon" enterprise like American Continental Grain.[36] Thus, while the CFDT was helpless to stop the privatization of the CIDT, it tried to remain an actor in one of its oldest and most profitable parastatals. At a meeting discussing the liberalization of the Ivorien cotton sector, the director of the CFDT, Michel Fichet, denounced the plan and warned of the risks involved with selling-off the state cotton company (Kra 1997):

> Behind the concept of privatization, there is a risk, in our eyes, that the CIDT will be broken into pieces which will lead to the dismantling of the parastatal… [at which point] it will be difficult to avoid a wild competition between different operators.

Nevertheless, in 1997 the Ivorien government dismantled and sold off the CIDT. Surveying the CFDT's once lucrative, but now devastated, group of African parastatals at this time it became clear that the French giant would move to defend its two principal remaining West African interests: Cotontchad and its most profitable parastatal, the CMDT.

But the tide of popular opinion on the continent had clearly shifted against the CFDT. For example, the influential bi-weekly, *Jeune Afrique Economie*, ran an editorial in October 1997 highlighting the hardships of the African cotton farmer. The editorial pointed out that while Asian cotton farmers earn 90% of the price for a kilo of cotton, African farmers take home on average a mere 40%. And who is responsible for this? "It is the middle men, the CFDT and the national parastatals across the continent (Talla 1997)."

The most damning and widely publicized condemnation of the CFDT emerged in February 1998 in the form of the World Bank sponsored "Pursell/Diop Report." Written by Gary Pursell, a Bank consultant, and Mariam Diop, an economist in Burkina Faso's Ministry of Finance, the report was circulated widely in the media and the international development community. The study revealed that since 1984 national companies in Africa's francophone states have never paid producers more than 50% of the price on

---

36. *La Lettre du Continent, Adieu cacao, banane, coton…* (July 31, 1997).

the international market. By comparison, farmers in India and Zimbabwe receive 90% and 70% respectively.[37]

The Instrumentalization of SYCOV

In the face of growing pressure from abroad, the CMDT turned inward toward SYCOV. The CMDT had witnessed the privatization of the CIDT in the Ivory Coast and believed a union of Ivorien cotton farmers had played an instrumental role in the process by voting for the privatization. Recent tension between SYCOV and the CMDT as well as reports from informants inside the union's hierarchy led the CMDT to conclude that the Antoine Berthé-led leadership of the union was pro-privatization. Furthermore, at the end of 1997, the union was preparing for its second congress and the election of a new national bureau; the CMDT learned that two French NGOs (the AFDI, and *Intercoopération Suisse*) were underwriting the campaigns of hard-line union members from the Koutiala region. The perception at the CMDT was that SYCOV's president was too close to these NGOs and the IFIs, groups considered by the CMDT to be pro-privatization. The CMDT saw the upcoming elections as the perfect opportunity to put in place a more moderate (i.e. pro-CMDT) group of leaders.

The 1998 SYCOV Congress and the Co-optation of Union Leadership

The SYCOV elections were held December-January 1997/98 and its results surprised many onlookers; Berthé was unseated as a SYCOV delegate in his home town, Kadiolo. According to many within the union and NGO community, this defeat was the result of a counter-campaign waged against him by CMDT agents. Others, including members of the Malian Chambre of Agriculture and the CMDT, argued that Berthé had spent so much time outside of Kadiolo and away from his constituency that he had lost touch with his base. While there is certainly some truth to this second position, the events that followed Berthé's defeat clearly suggest the involvement of exogenous forces in the lead up to the SYCOV national congress.

---

37. Pursell, G. and M. Diop. 1998. *Cotton Policies in Francophone Africa, Preliminary Draft.* Washington, D.C.: The World Bank.

The CMDT and NGOs Battle for Control of SYCOV

In order to use the elections to mollify SYCOV leadership, the CMDT first had to identify friendly elements within the union's executive bureau. Chaka Berthé of the CMDT recalled learning of an elderly gentleman who challenged President Antoine Berthé about privatization:

> This old man named Yaya Coulibaly stood up in a meeting and told the group that he had, "seen the damage that privatization caused to the coffee sector in the Ivory Coast and refused to let the Malian state make the same mistake with the CMDT." When I heard this story I said, "this is our man." He was a real peasant too, not an opportunistic, educated, city dweller turned farmer [like Antoine Berthé][38]

The CMDT also decided that it had to counteract NGO support for SYCOV hard-liners. So the company sponsored Coulibaly's campaign, driving him around the cotton zone in company vehicles. While Chaka Berthé admits this, he rejects allegations that the CMDT gave away cash and promised favors in return for a vote for Coulibaly.

The NGOs also admitted to choosing sides in the elections and (following Berthé's defeat in his home district) financing the campaign of SYCOV hard-liners from Koutiala. They justified their involvement by arguing that it was for the good of the millions of cotton farmers who, in their eyes, have suffered commercial exploitation and severe land degradation as a result of CMDT policies. Indeed, both the AFDI and *Intercoopération Suisse* had a long history of working with farmers in the Koutiala area on conservation and food security projects. These experiences led both groups to the conviction that the CMDT had become too powerful and had to be brought in-line with pressing national development needs.

> We knew the CMDT was trying to co-opt SYCOV—the CMDT hand-picked an illiterate, elderly, Senufo farmer [Coulibaly] whom they knew was tractable. They sponsored his campaign and rigged the vote so that he won. We did not think this was in the interest of Mali's cotton farmers.[39]

---

38. Chaka Berthé, *Directeur des Programmes et du Contrôle de Gestion, CMDT,* interview with author, Bamako. May 19, 1998.
39. François Picard, Director of *Intercoopération Suisse,* Bamako, interview with author, Bamako. June 12, 1998.

In April 1998, the SYCOV congress finally took place. From its start it was clear that national delegates were split into two competing factions: 1) vociferous critics of the outgoing administration; and 2) a smaller group of administration defenders. When the elections produced a victory for the CMDT-backed presidential candidate, Yaya Coulibaly, delegates were predictably divided. One group argued that the Koutiala delegates had grown corrupt and arrogant and had to be held in check. They contended that the union needed a real peasant as president, one who could work with the CMDT and establish a cooperative relationship with the company; "without the support of the company," this group argued, "we can not accomplish a thing."[40] Delegates on the other side of the SYCOV cleavage were predictably bitter. They accused the CMDT of buying off delegates to install a puppet president. One delegate concluded, "A lot of people were promised things from the CMDT and in turn they have abandoned the cause of the farmer: SYCOV will now split."[41]

Reactions to the SYCOV Congress

Reactions from the outside were equally accusatory. Within the NGO community, the election of Coulibaly was seen as a defeat for the cotton farmers' movement.

> We have been closely tied to the Koutiala contingent of SYCOV...but they were badly beaten at the congress. The new power center within SYCOV now is Fana. Following the congress we put together a national initiative for the entire union but it was rejected by the new leadership. Only the representatives from Koutiala accepted the overture so we will continue to work with them on a regional level, trying to get them out into the village and listening to the wishes of the peasants. We don't want to cause friction or to see a break-up of the union but we think that SYCOV has a lot of work to do and needs our help. What needs to happen is that the union must go back to the beginning. They are very poorly known at the village level. They are weak. And this is because at the beginning they mixed their message; villagers never understood what their mission was and how the union

40. Yacouba Doumbia, Secretary General-elect of SYCOV, interview with author, Deh, Mali. April 18, 1998.
41. Bakary Mariko, OHVN delegate to SYCOV, interview with author, Deh, Mali. April 17, 1998.

was different from the VAs. They have obviously suffered a setback
from our point of view—they have a man in charge today that cannot read or write— but the offices will change again in four years and
things can improve.[42]

Several members of the Malian state also responded negatively to this alleged
hijacking, warning the CMDT had only made the situation worse. One well
placed informant cautioned:

> The CMDT is trying to avoid privatization but they should not fight
> the inevitable. They should work with the system and try to improve
> it. Privatization is on its way. You can't hold back the World Bank.
> The CMDT should stop meddling in the affairs of SYCOV. They will
> only complicate matters...[43]

CMDT officials predictably saw the congress in a different light. Comments
by Chaka Berthé help to place events of the congress in the larger CMDT strategy on delaying privatization:

> I think the congress went well. The leadership of the union turned
> over and is now better. There is a "real peasant" now leading the
> union and Koutiala's role has been reduced...the Koutiala group of
> SYCOV, along with some merchants, wanted to tear down the
> CMDT. They were pushing everyone toward privatization. We didn't
> get involved at all in the first election in '92 and they elected a white
> collar leader who travelled the world for five years. He was never
> home for more that three months at a time. All this time he was
> telling the world that CMDT was killing Mali's peasants, exploiting
> them, etc. When we discovered *Intercoopération Suisse* and the AFDI
> were supporting the Koutiala faction...I just couldn't sit here with
> my arms crossed.
>
> In the new contrat-plan the CMDT will sell shares to VAs and peasants.
> We will do this because we think that the farmers' interests are the same
> as ours, and because we think that this will keep the IMF off our back
> for a while. This will give everyone a chance to see the (negative) effects
> that privatization is having in our brother country, the Ivory Coast.[44]

42. François Picard, interview with author, op.cit.
43. Alpha Seydou Maiga, General Director for the Institute of Rural Economy (IER),
interview with author, Bamako. April 27, 1998.
44. Chaka Berthé, interview with author, op. cit.

Conclusion: Lessons Learned From the Case of SYCOV

While perhaps an extreme example of international penetration into African civil society, the case of SYCOV underscores some of the complex dynamics currently in play in civil society across the continent. Civil society is alive and well in Mali, yet its exact definition and character is unclear. As this study highlights, there are numerous gaps in a civil society literature that fails to explore the expanding international/local nexus in Africa. Indeed, an interface between international actors and SYCOV exists and has clearly had a major effect on the development of the union. The effects of this interaction are much too nuanced to simply dismiss as "good" or "bad," thus precluding a summary judgment. As Antoine Baba Berthé acknowledged, "foreign aid for the union is indispensable." By gaining legitimacy within the international community SYCOV was able to raise vital technical and financial support, which afforded the nascent union a degree of autonomy from an aggressive CMDT.

On the other hand, contact with international actors has proven detrimental to SYCOV in several ways. Dependence on international finances has drawn SYCOV leaders away from their constituency, opening them up to criticism by Malian farmers and CMDT officials. Informants at the village level have heard about the junkets for SYCOV leaders to Europe and Bamako and are suspicious. These same trips have sown dissension within the ranks of the union leadership itself, since only select national delegates are selected to participate. Internecine feuds and grassroots suspicion, however, are only two of the problems stemming from international interactions. The fundamental problem with SYCOV is that dependency on international financing has caused the union to turn its back on Malian farmers and focus its outreach activities on international donors. Finally, SYCOV became a pawn in a proxy war to privatize the CMDT. As the research shows, the instrumentalization of the union has had serious effects on the group, most notably causing the co-optation of the union's leadership by the CMDT at the second SYCOV Congress and the subsequent splintering of the organization.

From the standpoint of political development theory, the implications of this research are far-reaching. Indeed, this study suggests a reconceptualization of the nature of civil society in Africa is necessary. Connecting the pieces of the conceptual puzzle with the empirical data presented here is an essential next step in moving the civil society/development discourse forward. Moreover, the North clearly must reassess the nature of its interaction with Southern NGOs and civic organizations, keeping in mind the concerns raised above as it constructs and implements policies aimed at strengthening civil society and spreading democracy in Africa.

Works Cited

Bingen, R, 1994. Agricultural development policy and grassroots democracy in Mali: the emergence of Mali's farmer movement. *African Rural and Urban Studies* 1:1: 57–72.

International Monetary Fund. 1994. *International Financial Statistics Yearbook.* Washington D.C.: IMF.

Kra, Killian. 1997. Côte d'Ivoire: Un coton très dispute. *Jeune Afrique Economie.* 248: 38–39.

Scott, J. 1985. *Weapons of the Weak: Everyday forms of peasant resistance.* New Haven: Yale University Press.

Talla, B. P. 1997. Le scandale du coton africain. *Jeune Afrique Economie*, 248: editorial.

CHAPTER 9

Up for Grabs, Civil Society in a Field of Conflicting Representations: A Case Study from Cape Verde

Elizabeth Challinor
Center for the Study of Social Anthropology
echallinor@interacesso.pt

Introduction

There have been many changes in the last ten years. With the fall of the Berlin wall aid is now going elsewhere and no longer to Africa. This is because independence in the 1960s for African countries has already been achieved. Fifteen years later they said we did not deserve so much support—enough is enough. So Africans were clever and said, "OK we'll convert to democracy." Europe considered this to be Africa's second independence. Now thirty years have gone by—what reason can we give? The reason now is giving the voice to the people: women, children, the disabled, peasants, rural populations, micro entrepreneurs. The target group is now local communities and social groups.

This quote comes from a speech given by an NGO president in January 1997 at a meeting with rural associations on the island of Santiago, in Cape Verde.

The president made no attempt to conceal the donor-led nature of aid. On the contrary, he was in a celebratory mood as he catalogued Africa's history of the successful manipulation of transnational donor trends. There is also an implicit message in his words that the state is no longer the major actor in society: the "voice of the people" must now be heard through its own separate institutions: local NGOs. His words reflect the ways in which the concept of "civil society" can become a new political currency to be spent in the interests of conflicting groups.

The increasing popularity of NGOs as representatives of "civil society" amongst transnational donors in the 1990s was due, in part, to their disappointment with the past performance of African states (Farrington and Bebbington 1993:5):

> There have been economic concerns about the inefficiencies created by the state's intervention in the economy, including its implementation of development programs. Equally, there have been political concerns that many states have not been accountable to society, and indeed have been more interested in controlling and molding society to suit their own interests, than in responding to the needs of that society

Given the donor concerns expressed above, it is not surprising that the legitimacy to represent "civil society" should come up "for grabs" in a country like Cape Verde: a young democracy heavily dependent upon external aid. However, Cape Verde is by no means an isolated case. In their discussion of the role of NGOs in the development industry, Powell and Seddon (1997: 9) argue that NGOs have been so closely linked to the emergence of civil society that they have become equated with each other. A wider range of organizations and institutions such as trade unions, political parties, human rights movements and social movements has consequently been squeezed out of the picture. It is not my intention in this chapter to contribute to the debate on what constitutes "civil society" since this would entail distinguishing it from an equally problematic concept: the "state". Mitchell (1991:77, 90) describes the state as an "amorphous, multi-functional corpus of agencies with ill-defined boundaries" whilst for Abrams (1988:79) the state is "the unified symbol of an actual disunity."

Gupta's (1995:392) ethnography of the state in contemporary India is also relevant here. His analysis of villagers' everyday encounters with the state and of the discursive construction of the state in public culture challenge the reified notion of a "unitary state" by revealing multiple agencies, organizations, levels and agendas. Gupta consequently calls into question the idea of "civil society" and "the state" as two free-standing entities in opposition to each other by drawing attention to the "blurred boundaries" between the two.

In this chapter I look at the way in which international donor trends in Cape Verde were manipulated in a field of local political struggles character-ized by cross-cutting alliances between "civil society" and the "state". My aim is to explore the implications of questioning the state/civil society opposition for the anthropology of development with insights from Bourdieu's theory of practice (1977) and from Ferguson's emergent paradigm of "transnational topographies of power" in the study of African politics (2004).

Ferguson (2004: 384–85) claims that the state/civil society opposition tes-tifies to an even more pervasive way of thinking about the analytic "levels" of local, national and global that rests on an imagined "vertical topography of power." This topography constructs a "common sense state that simply *is* 'up there', somewhere, operating at a 'higher level'" than the "local" which is con-ceived as the "authentic" source of resistance:

> This imagined topography…undergirds most of our images of po-litical struggle, which we readily imagine as coming "from below" (as we say), as "grounded" in rooted and authentic "lives", "experiences", and "communities." The state itself, meanwhile, can be imagined as reaching down into communities, intervening, in (as we say) a "top down" manner, to manipulate or plan "society".

Ferguson highlights the limitations of this vertical model of state-society rela-tions. He uses examples from Zambia and South Africa to illustrate the ways in which both the "top" and the "bottom" of the model operate within a hori-zontal transnational context: the imposition of policies upon the state in Zam-bia by the World Bank and the IMF and the international sources of the fi-nancing of the activities of the Alexandra Community Organization in its fight against apartheid in South Africa. Although his examples may appear to testify to the obvious with regard to the nature of globalization, his consequent de-mystification of populist notions of the "authenticity" of the "local" constitutes a welcome challenge for the study of "local" political struggles (2004: 394):

> Can we learn to conceive, theoretically and politically, of a "grass-roots" that would not be local, communal, and authentic, but worldly, well-connected, and opportunistic?

Early studies of development as "discourse" (e.g. Escobar 1984, 1991, and 1995; Rahnema, 1990; Sachs 1992; Hobart 1993; and Crush 1995) have also rested on an imagined "vertical topography of power" with the North inter-

vening from "the top" in the affairs of the South at "the bottom". These studies have contributed towards the generation of what Grillo (1997: 20) calls the
"myth of development": the assumption that development is a monolithic,
all-powerful practice, heavily controlled from the "top" with "authentic locals"
doing their best to "resist" at "the bottom". Later studies have challenged this
"myth" (e.g. Pigg 1992; Gardner and Lewis 1996, Grillo and Stirrat 1997,
Crewe and Harrison 1998) revealing a far more complex picture. Crewe and
Harrison, for example, argue against creating a category out of those who resist development (1998: 179):

> ...creating a category out of those who engage in resistance ignores con-
> textuality and change. If it were fixed in membership, where would we
> place the farmers, potters, or stove-users who comply with project staff's
> demands on some occasions and then ignore their advice on others?

My description of the "local" political struggles in Cape Verde also testifies
against the creation of fixed categories: the "stake-holders"[1] that donors frequently identify in project appraisals. The "stakes" are far from fixed: they change
according to the logic of practical interests (Bourdieu 1977: 4). In the following
pages I focus on the dynamics of different actors looking in particular at how
they reproduced and challenged the practices of single party politics in Cape
Verde. However, this is not to argue that changes took place in a level playing
field. As will become evident below, the political capital of some of the urban
based NGOs enabled them to make the "rules of the game" serve their interests
more effectively than the rural associations many of which were "mired in doxa."[2]

Cape Verde received 116 million dollars of official aid in 1993 which is approximately equivalent to 300 dollars per person. According to the OECD
(1995) this figure constitutes the second highest level of aid per capita in the
world. The following section attempts to trace the historical roots of Cape
Verde's dependence upon foreign aid.

Constructing the "Viability" of Cape Verde

A small archipelago comprised of ten islands and eight islets, Cape Verde
is situated in the Atlantic Ocean approximately four hundred and fifty miles

---

1. My thanks to Tim Kelsall for pointing this out.
2. An expression from Jim Igoe in a personal communication which helped to clarify
my interpretation of the ethnography in the light of Bourdieu.

west of Senegal. Most historians seem to agree that unlike continental Africa, the Cape Verde islands were uninhabited when they were sighted by Genoan sailors in the mid-fifteenth century and claimed for the Portuguese Crown (Lobban 1995).

The geo-strategic location of the archipelago on the trade winds route was the Portuguese Crown's main motive for encouraging settlement which eventually turned Cape Verde into a logistical maritime support base and an entrepôt in the flourishing slave trade between West Africa, Europe and the Americas (Moran 1982:64). Slaves were also taken from the West African coast for the creation of a plantation society. With the abolition of slavery in the mid nineteenth century, the remaining slave population, still dependent upon the same landlords became locked into exploitative sharecropping/tenancy agreements. Crop failures were frequent since tenants worked on rain fed lands, cultivating crops initially introduced by the Portuguese which were unsuitable for the arid, unpredictable climate of the islands. (*Ibid.*). Moreover, the colonial government failed to take any serious preventative measures to mitigate the effects of drought and crop failure. In years when harvests were good, staples were exported instead of stored for future consumption (Bigman 1993:81). Frequent crises of drought and famine consequently swept over the archipelago taking a heavy toll on the population. Mortality rates of 40% were common right up until the twentieth century and even as late as 1950 they often reached 15% (Moran 1982:75 and Langworthy and Finan 1997:61).

In the 1950s the African Party for the Independence of Guinea and Cape Verde (PAIGC) was founded. Despite its efforts to achieve decolonization through peaceful means the PAIGC finally launched a full-scale armed struggle in Guinea for independence in 1962. The war never extended to the Cape Verde islands because their disposition and geographical location rendered them unsuitable for guerrilla warfare and their population was too poor and its level of political mobilization too low to be able to support the guerrillas (Chabal 1983: 104, 556–59). On April 25th 1974 a peaceful military coup overthrew the fascist regime in Portugal. This in turn led to the official declaration of the independence of Cape Verde on July 5th 1975. The PAIGC remained the ruling party of both Guinea Bissau and Cape Verde until 1980 when a coup in Guinea caused the Cape Verdean branch of the PAIGC to sever formal links with Guinea Bissau and to rename itself as the African Party for the Independence of Cape Verde (PAICV).

The new government inherited "an economy on its knees" (Foy 1988:108). The first priority was consequently to survive long enough to be able to elaborate a strategy for addressing Cape Verde's economic problems (*ibid*:112). In this respect it is not surprising that the Cape Verdean government should have established a one-party state and opted for a planned economy[3] The main objective during the first Republic was to retain as much control as possible over the aid process. In the words of a former government official whom I interviewed:

> We needed to be in command because we did not want to be led by the North. We wanted to manipulate our dependency which is why there was much more control.

The "manipulation" of Cape Verde's dependence upon foreign aid began with the need to convince donors of the "viability" of Cape Verde (*ibid*: 107):

> Recalling the first days of independence and the start of the process of economic recovery, Minister of Planning and Cooperation José Brito remarked to a Wall Street Journal reporter in 1986 that "The first question we had to ask ourselves was, is Cape Verde viable?"

Coming from the mouth of the man who is responsible for convincing other people—notably aid partners—that the country is not only viable but worth investing in, this is a remarkable admission. Many governments are forced to consider the wisdom of a particular policy or a specific program in the light of physical or economic constraints, but very few have to admit the possibility that the whole country may simply not be worth inhabiting, that everyone should perhaps just pack their bags and go elsewhere.

Convincing the international donor community of the viability of investing in Cape Verde also required building and consolidating the state. The political leaders of Cape Verde believed that mass participation constituted a key element of this process of state construction and that the party should be responsible for its promotion and organization. Three major mass organizations were consequently created by the party to serve the specific interests of trade unions, women and youth. Whilst these organizations were organically independent from the party they were still under its political control (*ibid*: 84,

---

3. Foy points out that in some aspects it was, nonetheless, a mixed economy. Even though enterprises were controlled by the state they were still self-financing and although the prices of the state marketing companies were fixed by the government, they were not subsidized.

104). Olivio Pires, a former PAIGC/PAICV official, offers the following justification (cited in Davidson 1989:162):

> Here in 1975 there was no political experience at all. So there wasn't
> any way, then, in which a majority could actually participate, could
> *know how* to participate. We'd come out of a long colonial night when
> no participation was as much as thinkable.

Opponents of the PAICV rejected this justification on the grounds that there
was already an autonomous tradition of political and social participation in
Cape Verde. In his book the title of which describes the one-party system in
Cape Verde as "An Assault on Hope", Cardoso (1993) argues that the party's
investment in promoting mass organizations was ultimately a means of con-
trolling or suppressing the participation of an organized civil society, which
had already manifested itself in various forms during the late colonial period.
He cites the examples of the publication of journals, newsletters and the proliferation of sport and radio clubs and the creation of the high school in Sao
Vicente (*ibid*:182). He also points out that the only institutions recognized by
the state as NGOs up until 1988 were the mass organizations. He concludes
that the objective of the colonial powers to suppress civil society was achieved
by the PAIGC/PAICV regime during the fifteen years in which it governed the
country (*ibid*:190–1).

In 1991 the Movement for Democracy (MPD) took over from the PAICV
in the first multi-party elections of the country and was re-elected in 1995.

Civil Society Comes of Age

With the change in the political regime "civil society" and "participation"
became the new buzz words in Cape Verde, bestowing a renewed legitimacy
on civil society organizations. The number of NGOs and associations increased dramatically. However, the habitus of single party state politics did
not vanish over night.[4] Given Cape Verde's history of a single party state it
is not surprising that the majority of experienced and qualified profession-

---

4. As Bourdieu (1977) points out, social and material conditions produce certain kinds
of habitus. However, there may be a lag. Social and material conditions may (in fact almost definitely will) change over time. However the habitus produced by a specific set of
social and material conditions will continue for some time after those conditions themselves no longer prevail.

als were state employees. In many cases financial restrictions prevented the NGOs from employing professionals on a full-time basis, so a large proportion of the directors and fieldworkers of the urban based NGOs retained their government positions and worked on a voluntary and/or part-time basis. These actors were consequently able to secure political capital which placed them in a privileged position to influence both "civil society" and the "state".

With the exception of a few NGOs that had been active in Cape Verde for many years, the majority of NGOs and associations had little fieldwork experience and lacked human, material and financial resources. Their legitimacy stemmed from the change in political regime. During the 1995 electoral campaign, the MPD had promised that it would "create the conditions for the subsidization of the installation and support the initial operation of civil associations" (Dow 1995:17). What were the implications of funding installations for the autonomy of these civil organizations? The parallel here with the PAICV´s creation of the mass organizations is striking: neither the PAICV nor the MPD were ready to let "civil society" go it alone.

One of the effects of the change in the political system in 1991 upon Cape Verdean society was that party political conflicts began to affect social relations between different individuals and groups. The PAICV and the MPD were the only political parties to contest the 1991 elections which resulted in a polarization of the socio-political field. (Furtado 1995:96). While five parties contested the 1995 elections, the MPD gained over a two-third majority in parliament. In spite of the opening up of Cape Verdean politics to more parties, conflicts between the two major parties continued to permeate social relations in Cape Verde. A report commissioned in 1995 for the UN on NGOs in Cape Verde states that many NGOs were often identified with the MPD or the PAICV, whichever was the party of the majority of their members (Dow 1995:14). The former mass organizations of the PAICV, for example, which had also been transformed into independent civil organizations, were still connoted with their political history although they no longer had any formal links with the party. The creation of a "plataforma" intended to facilitate collaboration between NGOs and to strengthen NGO relations with both government and donors, was affected by party politics. The president of the plataforma was also the director of the former mass organization for women and a number of NGOs refused to join on the grounds that the plataforma was associated with the PAICV.

The empirical material analyzed in this chapter derives from a period of anthropological fieldwork conducted mostly on the island of Santiago from August 1996 to August 1997. During this time, debates surrounding the issue of how to define what constituted an NGO were also intensifying, following the rapid increase in the number and range of associations. Since there was no separate law for NGOs in Cape Verde the latter were legally indistinguishable from a variety of organizations constituted on the basis of the 1987 law of associations. The different activities that these organizations promoted included: theatre, dance, sport, music, funeral savings schemes, assistance for the blind and disabled, protection of the environment and community development.

Any attempt to classify the wide range of organizations in Cape Verde is bound to be found both theoretically and empirically wanting. The concern of how to define precisely what constitutes an NGO has bedeviled academics and development practitioners for over a decade. Different ways of distinguishing between them may be: the kind of work they engage in, their management structures, who they represent and are accountable to, sources of income and ideologies. Whilst the negative terminology, "non-governmental organization", has been deemed inappropriate and unimaginative by many (e.g., Smillie 1995:22), formal independence from the government has remained the official hallmark of a broad range of non-profit making organizations for which the umbrella term "NGO" is widely used today. I have chosen to adopt the criteria of "open" versus "restricted" membership and "national" versus "local" because they reflect the ways in which Cape Verdeans contested the classification of NGOs (see table).

The director of a national development organization with restricted membership explained to me that he did not consider all of the organizations constituted on the basis of the 1987 law of associations to be non-governmental organizations for development (NGOD). Those that were created for the exclusive benefit of their members were, according to him, "member organizations" and should be differentiated from organizations such as his which had a national mandate for the professional delivery of development services. The director made a point of telling me that this distinction between NGO and NGOD was not something that he had invented but was recognized by the international development community. Taking the example of a member organization which promoted development initiatives he explained to me that it was not an NGOD according to the international interpretation of the concept because it only operated at the local level.

This distinction was contested by some of the "member organizations" in Cape Verde, which also considered themselves to be NGODs. The president of the member organization in question, whom I shall call Pedro, told me that he was not interested in transforming his "local" association into a national

Figure 9.1 Non-Governmental Development Institutions in Cape Verde
(Source: Dow 1995:13–14)

	National Organizations		Local Organizations
Organizations based on the concept of "open" association	Delegations consolidated in nearly every municipality of the country with a national network of members. For e.g. Caritas; the Red Cross and the former mass organizations transformed into independent organizations in 1991, such as the Organisation of Cape Verdean Women (OMCV).	Organizations formed on the initiative of a group of individuals from the urban elite in order to promote development at the national level. Some were expanding their network of delegations and whilst others had only recently been created and were seeking to increase their membership.	Organizations formed on the initiative of individuals from the urban elite and/or aid donors to promote development at the regional or local level. Organizations formed on the initiative of community leaders in rural and suburban areas to meet the interests of their own members which ranged from funeral saving schemes to cultural and sport activities, some of which also included local development initiatives.
Organizations based on the concept of a "restricted" association	Established by a small group of professionals to provide institutional cover for implementing projects. These organizations were not interested in recruiting lots of members.		

NGO. He knew that aid donors preferred to finance associations and to by-pass national NGOs because they believed that the use of intermediaries often resulted in the "loss" of funds. Pedro went on to add that other donors were more extreme and wanted to finance "the people" directly. "But "the people" do not exist" he concluded with a smile. The implicit message in this comment echoes that of the speech given in the meeting referred to in the introduction to this chapter: the "voice of the people" must now be heard through its own separate institutions—local NGOs. But who were these social actors and organizations that claimed the institutional legitimacy to represent "the people"? I shall now take a closer look at the interests of the main actors and organizations involved.

Setting the Scene

The attentive reader may have noted with surprise how the NGO director quoted in the introduction to this chapter included the category of the "disabled" in his example of the social groups whose voices the donors wanted to hear. The disabled do not usually appear in the traditional social categories of development jargon.[5] The explanation for their inclusion here is both simple and revealing. One of the members of an urban based association created to meet the needs of the disabled was present at the meeting. Despite the specific and limited mandate of his association, it was also a member of the "plataforma". However, some of the development NGOs affiliated to the plataforma, such as the national development organization referred to in the previous section, wished to limit the access of member organizations to those engaged in development initiatives. Others, more concerned with party politics, were eager to recruit as many organizations as possible to the plataforma, regardless of the nature of their mandates in order to challenge its alleged connections with the PAICV.

The organizations which had refused to join the plataforma were known to have close ties with the MPD. The directors of one of these NGOs held influential positions in government and worked on a voluntary basis. Early on in my fieldwork I innocently asked them in an interview what had motivated them to create their organization. Their sudden change in body language and

---

5. The most common categories include: farmers, women, the landless, the illiterate, fishermen, micro-entrepreneurs, etc.

curtness of reply, "because there was space to do so," took me by surprise. When I later became aware of the political rivalries between NGOs, it became clear to me why they had reacted so defensively. Their NGO, which I shall refer to as NGO A, was like the mirror image of the former mass organization for women: it not only had privileged access to government but women were also its targeted beneficiaries. The directors had consequently interpreted my question as an indirect probing of the rivalry between their NGO and the former mass organization for women which had been transformed into an NGO and held the presidency of the plataforma.

Most of the membership organizations from rural Santiago had never heard of the plataforma. Many had been created within the ambit of a USAID financed project in Cape Verde to promote the transfer of state run soil and water conservation works to the private sector. The associations had recently joined together to form an umbrella organization called OASIS (Organization of the Association of Santiago Island). The few organizations which were members of both OASIS and the plataforma had been created before the inception of the USAID program and were consequently more "well-connected". One of these associations was the local member organization referred to above whose president, Pedro, was also in favor of increasing the membership numbers of the plataforma. Pedro was regarded by the managing director of OASIS with suspicion for being too politically ambitious. The association members of OASIS were encouraged by the USAID program to steer clear of party politics.

The rest of this chapter analyses the political struggles characterized by cross-cutting alliances between NGOs and the government in which the legitimacy to represent "civil society" was negotiated and contested. The following section looks at how the political struggle of the plataforma to assert itself as the most legitimate representative body civil society organization constituted the doxic field of the undiscussed in a meeting for which the donor "Sahel 21" program provided the orthodox discourse (Bourdieu 1977: 168).

Speak, The Donors Want to Hear From You

The meeting with rural associations referred to in the introduction of this chapter was organized by the "plataforma" within the ambit of a regional program of the Permanent Inter-State Committee of the Fight against Drought in the Sahel (CILSS). The objective of the program, entitled Sahel 21, was to engage the civil societies of the nine member countries [6] of CILSS in a series of participatory meetings at the local, national and regional levels, in order to voice their views and reach a consensus on the desired vision for the future of the Sahel. The "plataforma" had been invited by the government to organize meetings in different localities of the Cape Verdean islands. Pedro and the Vice-President of the plataforma whom I shall call Adriano had been "allocated" rural Santiago. Pedro consequently suggested convening a meeting with OASIS.

The meeting took place in Pedro Badejo, the capital of the district of Santa Cruz. The room was full of association members who had come from all over the island of Santiago. However, before talking about Sahel 21, Adriano made an appeal to all of the rural associations present to become members of the "plataforma". He argued that they were all NGOs simply because they were not government, carefully listing all the benefits of membership and arguing that they would find strength in unity. Much discussion followed as the associations questioned whether it made sense to join another umbrella organization when they were already members of OASIS. The managing director of OASIS insinuated to me afterwards that joining the plataforma may make the associations appear "ungrateful" in the eyes of their American donors. The mixing of agendas had also caused some confusion as I noted days later when an association president told me that he was considering joining "Sahel 21". Adriano and Pedro had nonetheless managed to take advantage of this meeting to serve the "practical interests" (Bourdieu 1977) of the plataforma which were unrelated to the donor objectives of Sahel 21. Most of the associations present at the meeting were unaware of these dynamics.

The official agenda of the meeting read out by Pedro, was divided into three points: 1) what is Sahel 21? 2) why this reflection now? and 3) what are our aspirations and how can we contribute towards the reflection of Sahel 21? Some of the answers given to these questions in Adriano's speech are paraphrased below:

> In 1973 there was a terrible drought in the Sahel and lots of people and animals died. Since most of the member countries were independent they decided to create CILSS to fight against drought and desertification and CILSS was given support from northern countries, especially Europe. Cape Verde became a member of CILSS in 1976... The time for reflection has come because the amounts of aid are reducing. Northern donors think that we are not using the money

---

6. The nine member countries of the Sahel are: Burkina Faso, Cape Verde, Gambia, Guinea Bissau, Mali, Mauritania, Niger, Senegal and Chad.

properly...Studies by technicians are important but we have been told by our ministers that they are not enough because the donors are not happy with this top down approach. When donors come and see that we know nothing about Sahel 21 it looks bad. What do local farmers think should be done within CILSS? What do women think? What do the disabled think? We can't approve projects until farmers are involved because this is what the North wants. The technicians have written their reports but what do you think? We are two months behind because we have to prepare for an interstate meeting in March. So you must speak in the name of your people. The voice of women has been heard in CILSS, such as in Burkina Faso, but CILSS is not just women. There are four groups in the world that receive more money: women; poverty; aids and drugs. These are the projects that get priority funding now, remember this when preparing your projects...Now we want to gather data to produce a document...the grass roots must speak now because those who give the money say the grass roots has not been consulted. The idea is to elaborate projects and have a clear idea of what we want. It used to be the fight against desertification then it was training, now what is it? The associations have a clear vision of what they want and this is what the donors are looking for. If you don't talk now it will be a lost opportunity...We need to prepare this document by the 31 January for the national forum and then there will be a sub-regional meeting in Gambia in March...

Adriano had no problems calling a spade a spade. The "grass roots" had to be consulted because such was the wish of those with the money and the power to make decisions that would ultimately affect their lives. There was no talk of participatory democratic values or rights. Adriano's appeal was to the "practical interests" (Bourdieu 1977) of securing donor funds. The donor's demands were almost construed as whimsical: these were the rules of the game as they stood today and this was the best way to win points. The urgency of Adriano's message, speak now or for ever hold your peace, is similar to the practice of participatory rural appraisal (PRA) which also invites local people to participate together in the production of shared, "fast", palpable knowledge (see Chambers 1994). Unlike PRA, however, Adriano's invitation to speak was unstructured: there were no charts, diagrams or maps for the people to draw. It was Adriano's responsibility to produce a document based on this open consultation with the "grassroots". The first person to respond to Adriano's appeal was an association president whom I shall call Miguel who expressed his difficulty in digesting this "fast" approach towards grassroots consultations:

> Sahel 21 hasn't happened by chance. There is a lack of water, rain and food. Will the creation of Sahel 21 resolve these problems? I represent my people. I need help to motivate people about the Sahel in my watershed. Will Sahel lessen the difficulties now that you say that the people have to be consulted? As their spokesman I need to know what will make things better or worse. How can we participate?

Neither Adriano nor Pedro attempted to provide a concrete answer to this specific request. After clarifying that it was CILSS and not the Sahel that had been created, Pedro embarked upon a more general discussion of what had been achieved within CILSS at a regional level and then the discussion moved on to what was achievable in general terms in Cape Verde.

There are several points to be made here. Firstly, the transnational donor concern of the 1990s to listen to the "voice" of "the people"[7] strengthened the authority of local Cape Verdean NGOs to speak on behalf of "the people" without necessarily giving voice to those who continued to be silenced. Adriano may have replaced the international consultant but he still pursued the same objective: the production of "fast" knowledge for consumption by transnational donors. This is not to argue, however, that the whole process was donor led. The contents and celebratory tone of Adriano's speech challenge the "victim culture" (Grillo 1997: 21) produced by representations of a dominant and subjugating discourse of development by revealing the subaltern's capacity for creative manipulation. Theories of the "colonized mind" (Crush 1995) may provide misleading insights into the influence of transnational donor trends at the local level, especially if they fail to take into account the micro politics of "practical interests" (Bourdieu 1977). Increasing membership numbers constituted a pressing practical interest for the plataforma given that the government was preparing to organize the first forum between government and CSOs later on in the year.

Secondly, Adriano's capacity to manipulate transnational donor trends supports Ferguson's characterization of a "worldly, well-connected, and opportunistic" grassroots, referred to in the introduction above. The association president, Miguel, on the other hand, oblivious to the unspoken dynamics of

---

7. This trend was reflected in Cape Verde not only in Sahel 21 but in another regional program funded by the UNDP entitled the "National Long Term Perspective Study" which involved questionnaires, district held round tables, interviews, discussion groups and seminars.

the meeting, appears to correspond to the traditional rural image of the "local, communal, and authentic" grassroots. However, we should recall that Miguel was the president of an association created within the ambit of a USAID program: this apparently more "authentic" and "local" grassroots also operated within a transnational context which calls into question traditional anthropological notions of "grounded authenticity". To search for sites of local authenticity contributes to the creation of the fixed categories which Crewe and Harrison (1998) argue are unable to accommodate contextuality and change. Presuming that the president Miguel becomes more informed and gains experience in responding to donor trends are we to conclude that he is then somehow less "local" or "authentic" than when he was mired in doxa?

Government, NGOs, and CSOs Put Their Cards on the Table

This is how one of the local newspapers[8] chose to report on the first forum that took place between government and the institutional representatives of civil society in June 1997 in the capital, Praia. Given the strategies and counter strategies which I shall describe below, I would argue that some participants kept a few cards up their sleeves.

Around one hundred and fifty people from every island of Cape Verde participated in the forum, out of which about one hundred and fifteen were members of associations, co-operatives, small businesses and NGOs. Some of the OASIS affiliated associations who had attended the meeting described above were also present. Other participants in the meeting included a few transnational donors, a handful of observers (including myself) and officials from the local government and various Ministries. Some of the latter were officially present in the forum as members of their organizations and not as civil servants. However, this distinction was not always so easily made in practice, as will become evident below. Much of the debate during the forum focused on definitions: was it necessary to separate this mixed bag of organizations? If not, should the term "civil society" organizations (CSO) be adopted to include them all?

One of the opening speeches in the forum was made by the president of the Municipal Council of Praia who was also president of the Association of

---

8. Novo Jornal Cabo Verde. 11 June, 1997: 11. Forum de Concertação Nacional. Governo, ONG e OSC Deitam Cartas na Mesa. Praia.

the Municipal Councils and member of one of the local Praia based associations which had refused to join the "plataforma". During his speech, he put forward the suggestion that the associations create a strong and broad national federation. He went on to argue that this was as "an indispensable condition for a common and global intervention strategy between the government and civil society organizations."[9] For those who were "in the know" this proposal constituted a challenge to the legitimacy of the plataforma.

By establishing a single policy with a wide range of organizations the government was ultimately refusing to distinguish between them. Organizations such as drumming, carnival, theater and musical groups were consequently given the same status as organizations engaged in the promotion of development initiatives. Many of the latter were already affiliated to the "plataforma". However, if no distinction were made between the different kinds of organizations present in the forum, then the legitimacy of the representative role of the "plataforma" would be undermined and the need to create a more representative body would be established.

The government's justification for its choice of the term CSO is given in one of the preparatory documents for the forum entitled: *Regulations for the Establishment of Partnerships between the Government and Civil Society Organizations* (MCE undated: 2, my translation):

> The government would limit the participation of civil society, if it were to formulate a policy for the establishment of partnerships with civil society which were exclusively applicable to the civil associations that call themselves NGOs. Moreover, the term NGO does not have a "legal status" in Cape Verde, and is used to denominate civil entities which on the whole have the statute of non-profit making associations

Note that there is no mention in the text of the specific mandate of NGOs for the promotion of development initiatives. Many of the organizations which were engaged in development and called themselves "NGOs" believed that this mandate provided a justification for distinguishing them from other civil organizations. The government's intention behind introducing the term "civil society organization" (CSO) was questioned by an NGO member in one of the consultation meetings that took place prior to the forum:

> What is an NGO? How different is it to a CSO? Are we talking about every private association simply because it is not government? Surely

---

9. The contents of his speech were distributed in a handout.

the government does not want to regulate all of this? There is some-body here from the funeral association from the interior of Santiago. I can also see a drumming group, musical groups, carnival groups.... The government cannot hope to co-ordinate and give funds to them all. We need to restrict the associations for this law. What are the pri-ority areas? Is the fight against poverty to be given the same priority as groups involved in culture, theater, music? What criteria are you intending to use to choose some organizations rather than others? This could provoke a lot of social conflict.

The government official denied that the government was trying to put all the organizations into the same bag and justified the use of the term CSO by claiming that the government's concern was to avoid exclusion. He argued that CSOs could also implement development projects and cited the example of a sport club from Porto Novo (Santo Antão Island) which had submitted a proj-ect proposal for community development to the Ministry.

The president's suggestion that the associations create a national federation was not part of the official agenda of the forum which had been set by the Ministry of Economic Coordination. The agenda consisted of three main pro-posals submitted to the forum assembly for discussion: a new law to regulate the creation and functioning of NGOs and CSOs; an "agreement framework"[10] to institutionalize relations between the government and NGOs/CSOs and the creation of a national fund for the support of grassroots initiatives.

During the months that led up to the forum, the government had produced three or four versions of the different proposals. Each proposal was modified after a series of consultation meetings with NGOs and CSOs many of which I attended. The following section looks at how some of the struggles between government and NGOs were fought out in relation to each of the proposals.

The Proposal for a New Law

An analysis of the dynamics behind the creation of a new law for NGOs re-veals the limitations of construing the state as a monolithic entity with unity of purpose. For although in the government's proposed clauses of the law there is plenty of evidence of the "control" politics characteristic of single party

---

10. The Portuguese terminology, *quadro de concertação*, is difficult to translate. The idea behind the concept of *concertação* is basically to agree, to concert, to collaborate.

states, this evidence is not corroborated by the receptiveness of the government officials to the NGOs´ counter proposals. Whilst it may be tempting to interpret the documentary evidence of "control" politics as an indication of the endurance of the habitus of single party state politics, a closer reading of the dynamics calls for a more nuanced interpretation. My analysis of the events leads me to suggest that the political history of colonial and post-colonial Cape Verde had not provided a sufficiently fertile ground for cultivating the verbal distinction between "control" and "accountability".

A total of four versions of the proposed law were produced by a government lawyer, together with his colleagues from the Ministry of Economic Co-ordination. The NGOs' reactions to the first proposal revealed a strong concern that the government wanted to control them. A textual analysis of the document appears to support this interpretation. With regard to the legal constitution of NGOs Article 4 stipulated, inter alia, that the organizations had to have at least five years experience in their proposed activity and that they had to submit a dossier requesting "admission" to a special committee that was composed of five government representatives and one NGO representative. Article 3 identified the Secretary of State for Decentralization as being responsible for the "tutelage" (tutela) of NGOs. Article 18 stipulated that the "Ministry of Tutelage" (sic) could visit the installations and infra-structures of NGOs, in the presence of one NGO representative, giving at least one week's notice.[11]

The freedom to associate had already been guaranteed during the First Republic under the 1987 Law of Associations, which reads: "citizens...may constitute associations freely and without dependence upon any authorization" (6–7).[12] It was somewhat ironic that with the advent of democracy, the first version of the proposed new law appeared to take away rights that had already been granted during the late period of single party rule.[13] Moreover, given that the Secretary of State for Decentralization was considered to be the appropriate governmental figure to exercise "control", the lawyer seemed to be work-

---

11. Ministério da Coordenação Económica 1997a. Modalidades de Intervenção Das Organizações Não Governamentais (ONGs) e Quadro de Concertação Governo/ONGs. (Proposta de Decreto Lei). Praia: first version of unpublished proposal document.

12. Boletim Oficial 1987. 4 Suplemento, 31 de Dezembro, No.52. Lei no. 28/III/87. Regula o exercício da liberdade de associação. Praia: INCV.

13. In legal terms the proposal was also anti-constitutional. Article 51 of the new constitution of the second republic states: "The constitution of associations is free and does not require any administrative authority."

ing within the framework of the former one party state. Pedro pointed this out to the government lawyer in one of the consultation meetings which he attended:

> We must not think that the organizations are a form of decentralizing the state. The state decentralizes itself.

An analysis of the changes in the different versions of the proposed law suggests that Pedro's comment did not fall upon deaf ears. The term "tutelage", for example, was replaced in the second version with the concept of "partnership". Whilst this indicated a relinquishing of control, the second version of the document went on to state that the government was the NGOs' "primary partner and interlocutor" (Article 4:2).[14] However, following more consultations with NGOs and CSOs, the word "primary" was omitted in the third and fourth versions (1997c, Article 4:3 and 1997d, Article 5:3).[15]

Whilst these alterations constituted a "victory" for the NGOs, a closer reading of the dynamics of the consultation meetings suggests that there may have been a more nuanced issue on the government's agenda than that of control. There were a number of occasions when NGO members challenged the legitimacy of the government's attempt to control NGOs which was always denied by the government officials. Criticism of the government's restrictions upon the freedom to associate, for example, was commented upon as follows:

> One thing is partnership and another thing is to control right from the beginning the constitution of an organization…The process of constitution has to be free and cannot be conditioned. The government may decide to support one organization over another according to certain criteria, but this is a separate issue and the two should not be confused.

The lawyer's passionate denial of any intention to exercise control over the organizations prompted a defensive reply:

---

14. Ministério da Coordenação Económica 1997b. Organizacões da Sociedade Civil. Praia: second version of unpublished proposal document.

15. Ministério da Coordenação Económica, (1997c). Organizacões Não Governamentais e Outras Organizações Comunitarias do Desenvolvimento. Praia: third version of unpublished proposal document. Ministério da Coordenação Económica, (1997d). Organizacões Não Governamentais e Outras Organizações Comunitarias do Desenvolvimento. Subsídios para a regulamentação da Constuição e funcionamento das ONGs e outras OCD. Praia: fourth version of unpublished proposal document.

I am speaking in terms of an objective reading of the document. The intention could be something else. I am not challenging you, I am simply responding to what is written in the document.

How is the lawyer's reaction to be interpreted? I would argue that his frustration over accusations of control were due to his inability to communicate what he considered to be legitimate concerns for *accountability*. The word "accountability" does not translate easily into Portuguese which makes the dividing line between control and accountability harder to recognize. Although I would translate the word "accountability" by "responsabilização" or "prestar contas" the only word I ever heard throughout all of the discussions was "control". Consider the words from one of the participants of the meeting quoted below.[16] Is he expressing the desire to control or an underlying concern for the accountability of NGOs?

> If we are going to decentralize from the lowest level NGOs have to be organized within the ambit of the process of decentralization. Projects need to be co-ordinated from top to bottom and from bottom to top, hence the need for the agreement framework. I consequently don't see why you are against the presidents of the local councils presiding the municipal committees (of these frameworks), particularly if the national committee is presided by the Ministry of Economic Co-ordination.....It is the councils who have experience. NGOs should be given freedom of action but in a first phase, it is a matter of control, the councils should be more involved. This is my own personal opinion.

One of the directors of NGO A reacted immediately to this trigger:

> No-body is going to boss about the NGOs. When we submit a project there are presentation norms and control mechanisms in the project.

The limitations of the kind of project "control mechanisms" referred to by NGO A and the problems these limitations raise regarding who NGOs are ultimately accountable to, have been discussed in the literature on Northern NGOs (see Hulme and Edwards 1997; Marcussen 1996). Given that this is a contentious issue in the North, where NGOs are already firmly established within a democratic system, it should come as no surprise that the government of a young democracy, emerging from a long history of state control,

---

16. I was unable to identify which institution this participant represented.

should also be concerned with the accountability of NGOs. My reading of the events suggests that the necessary vocabulary for expressing this concern had not yet been formulated within the "universe of discourse" (Bourdieu 1977:168). There may be historical reasons for this (beyond the scope this chapter) related to the restrictions imposed by the colonial and post colonial authorities upon the delegation of power in Cape Verde.

It is evident that the government's intentions cannot be read from the work of the lawyer and his colleagues alone. Why, for example, did the government not assign more (competent?) lawyers to the task of producing a new law? Had this omission been deliberate? A lawyer whom I spoke to from the Ministry of Economic Co-ordination told me that she could not understand why she or some of her colleagues had not been included in the process. Whilst I cannot offer any answers to these questions, I would argue that the questions testify to the multiple levels and agendas of the state (Gupta 1995), which provide further evidence of the analytical limitations of creating a fixed "stakeholder" category. The way in which the stakes change according to context were exemplified by NGO A which allied itself with the NGOs in the consultation meetings regarding government "control" but was also in cohorts with the government in its attempt to undermine the "plataforma".

The dynamics behind the proposals for the creation of an agreement framework and a national fund demonstrate the way in which stakes were modified, negotiated and contested according to the immediate context of the actors' practical interests.

The Agreement Framework

The rationale for the creation of an "Agreement Framework" was to set up a permanent mechanism for negotiations concerning the basis for a working partnership between the government and CSOs. The third version of the proposal envisaged the setting up of both national and municipal committees, composed of representatives of central and local government, donors, NGOs and CSOs (1997f: 4).[17]

NGO criticism of the "Agreement Framework" was voiced both in the forum and in the consultation meetings. Many associations and NGOs dis-

---

17. Ministério da Coordenação Económica, (1997f). Quadro de Concertação Governo/ONGs. Praia: second version of unpublished proposal document.

agreed in principle with this proposal, on the grounds that the committees would make relations with the government more rigid and bureaucratic. Nevertheless, there were still intense discussions regarding who would sit on these proposed committees because the "undiscussed" issue at stake was to test the popularity of the "plataforma". The forum had become an arena of competition between different representatives of civil society.

The government had allocated two posts for NGO representatives and two posts for CSO representatives. The "plataforma" argued that it should appoint both of the NGO representatives. However, the two NGOs which had refused to join the "plataforma", including NGO A, argued that this would lead to their exclusion. Finally participants agreed to vote and the "plataforma" won the right to appoint both posts with a large majority.

The NGO directors who had lost the vote were furious and consequently tried to challenge the results by turning the debate back to the contested issue of definitions. Having failed to undermine the legitimacy of the representative role of the "plataforma" they were no longer interested in blurring the distinctions between the different kinds of organizations but rather in accentuating the differences. The NGO directors consequently protested on the grounds that as NGOs they could not be represented by the CSOs.

The moderator of the forum responded to their complaint by stating that the forum had already resolved the issue of definitions. It had already been established in a vote that NGOs constituted a subgroup of the CSOs. At this point the president of the council of Praia, who had made the appeal for the creation of a new federation of CSOs, also attempted to question the legitimacy of the vote. He pointed out that since there was no legal difference between NGOs and CSOs the forum should respect the fact that NGOs did not exist in juridical terms.

The president of the council of Praia had invoked the law in order to create the impression that he was aligning himself with the "up there state" that existed above local conflicts. As Bourdieu (1998:59) points out, the law serves to legitimize official representations of the state as "the site of universality and of service to the general interest." Yet the president's argument contradicted the claims of the NGO directors that NGOs could not be represented by CSOs. This contradiction was nonetheless compatible with the practical interest that they shared: to undermine the legitimacy of the "plataforma".

One of the voluntary workers of NGO A who was employed in the local council of Praia also found herself in a contradictory position in the vote for the representatives of local government in the "Agreement framework". In order to appear consistent in her opposition to the "plataforma" she was one of the very few people who voted against the motion that the Association of the Local Councils appoint the local council representatives even though she worked closely with the president. Despite all of these efforts, however, the opponents of the "plataforma" failed to overturn the results of the vote.

With regard to the voting procedures, it is interesting to note that everybody present was allowed to vote. This meant that government officials were able to vote upon what should have been an internal NGO affair and vice versa. Neither was the policy of one vote per organization adopted, since there were also various organizations that had more than one member present in the forum, all of which voted. Although this lack of rigor with regard to the voting procedures was commented upon later by some participants, it did not seem to be a major issue. After all, as already stated above, many NGOs were against the "Agreement Framework" in principle anyway. The voting had served an alternative purpose of testing the legitimacy and popularity of the "plataforma". The outcome was a show of strength which was celebrated as a major victory by the NGO members of the "plataforma" who were "in the know".

Most of the membership organizations, however, particularly those based in rural areas had not participated in many, if indeed any, of the consultation meetings. They were consequently only partially aware of the strategies that were being employed on both sides. When I later asked the President of one of the OASIS affiliated organizations if he had voted, he replied somewhat dismissively that there was no point. The President claimed that the "plataforma" was only concerned with administrative issues and that organizations in rural areas were simply left out. There had been no victory or defeat for this association. One section of "civil society" had remained marginalized from the whole process.[18]

Mechanisms for the Creation of a National Fund for the Support of Grassroots Initiatives

The proposal for setting up a fund identified the concepts of "decentralization" and "participation" as fundamental elements of the government's national program and announced its commitment to the "reinforcement of the

---

18. Lest we become too mired in "nostalgic" sympathy for rural authenticity I should add that on a return visit to Cape Verde in 2002 I discovered that this particular association president had immigrated to Portugal taking all of the association funds with him.

participation and autonomy of civil society", with specific reference to a program to support the development of NGOs (1997e: 3–4).[19]

This proposal generated prolonged discussions during the forum. Some of the CSOs saw no reason to reject government funding. The director of an association for entrepreneurs, for example, argued that the fund could be used as a form of collateral for associations to take out loans. Some of the NGOs, on the other hand, were very critical of the idea, seeming to prefer the current system of signing contracts with the government for specific projects. Their major criticism was related to safeguarding the autonomy of NGOs.

Notwithstanding these criticisms, none of the participants actually voted against the fund and an ad hoc committee was set up instead, to study the matter further. One explanation that was offered to me to account for this unexpected turn of events was that the NGOs had decided that voting against the fund would alienate some of the CSOs from the "plataforma". Another possibly complementary explanation was simply that when it came to the crunch, the NGOs could not resist the temptation of government funding.

The moderator of the forum whom I had interviewed beforehand had been prepared for the strategies and counterstrategies that I have described above. He compared them to rival military operations to seize a contested territory. He went on to explain that both government and NGOs were in competition with each other to dominate the process of the insertion of NGOs into the "development process". Due to the preference for NGOs by foreign donors, the government had realized that strengthening NGOs was a means of bringing in more resources for Cape Verde. However, the government did not wish to be marginalized from the process. The NGOs, on the other hand, aware of their institutional weaknesses, knew that although their survival depended upon entering into the "development process"; this could not be done in opposition to the state.

Conclusion

In this chapter I have tried to provide an insight into the nature of "local" political struggles to establish the legitimacy to represent "civil society". My analysis of the effects on NGO-government relations of transnational donor policies to reach the grassroots has produced a more complex scenario than

---

19. Ministério da Coordenação Económica 1997e. Fundo Nacional de Apoio As Iniciativas de Base. (Proposta de um Mecanismo para a sua Criação). Praia: third version of unpublished proposal document.

pitting "civil society" against the "state". The eagerness of all parties to reap the benefits of donor policies resulted in alliances between NGOs and the government in competition with other NGOs. That the member associations were oblivious to what was really going on raises the question as to whether their policies brought the donors any closer to hearing the voice of the grassroots. But what is "the grassroots"? The dynamics of the local political struggles described in this chapter also raise a number of questions regarding our use of analytical categories.

It is tempting to argue that the membership organizations represent the "authentic" grassroots in opposition to the "worldly" NGOs; however, these organizations are also part of the "transnationalized local" identified by Ferguson since they were created within the ambit of a USAID development program. Unlike the NGOs, the membership organizations had had limited contact with the workings of the development apparatus and were consequently less skilled in bending the rules of the game to meet their own needs. Is this what it takes to be seen as "authentic"? I would argue that it is misleading to conclude that people who are "mired in doxa" are the only "authentic grassroots" because this smacks of romantic paternalism: if you lose your "innocence" you become "disqualified". This approach not only denies the grassroots access to knowledge and power but also fails to recognize the mobility between development categories. Some "development outsiders" gradually become "development insiders". Relevant here is Ferguson's discussion (2004) of the ways in which the grassroots is able to link its local struggles to global causes. And yet for every example that he gives how many more examples are there of dispossession and alienation at the grassroots level? Ferguson himself argues that his paradigm of transnational topographies of power does not replace but co-exists with traditional conceptions of the "grassroots".

So how then are we to theorize the grassroots? Critiques of romantic conceptions of "community" may be helpful here. It has become commonplace to state that the "community" is neither homogeneous nor harmonious; why not talk of a *heterogeneous grassroots*? It too is shot through with unequal power relations and conflicts of interest. If we conceive of the grassroots in this manner then we are less likely to overlook the "worldly and well connected" or those who are "mired in doxa". The latter are clearly in a majority and, in the case of Cape Verde, are not only represented by the member organizations. What about other ad hoc informal institutions in Cape Verde, and in Africa in general, which have remained beyond the reach of the development apparatus? Most of the people represented by these institutions will never become sufficiently "worldly" and "well-connected" to master the rules of the game. It could also be argued that it is in the interests of the "development insiders" for them to remain "authentic" outsiders. Their "authenticity" is a well sought after commodity in the development industry; however, this is not to argue that as analysts we should take their "authenticity" at face value.

Theorizing the grassroots requires making a distinction between "grassroots" as a category of analysis and "grassroots" as a normative discourse that appeals to notions of the "authentic" and the "local"; nonetheless, the latter should not be taken lightly. Normative discourses of the "authentic grassroots" are very important for securing the legitimacy of the work of African NGOs vis-à-vis donors and the state. As Kelsall and Igoe point out, in the introduction to this volume, NGO researchers cannot escape the slippery challenge of elucidating the ways in which normative discourses gloss over the complexities of "local realities" while simultaneously revealing the ways in which they may ultimately come to shape those realities. Our analysis of universal categories such as "civil society", "grassroots" and the "state" requires us to adopt the stance of the ancient deity Janus whose two faces enabled him to look both forwards and backwards at the same time.

Works Cited

Abrams, P. 1988. Notes on the difficulty of studying the state. *Journal of Historical Sociology* 1 (1): 58–89.

Bigman, L. 1993. *History and Hunger in West Africa: Food production and entitlement in Guinea-Bissau and Cape Verde*, London: Greenwood Press.

Bourdieu, P. 1977. *Outline of a Theory of Practice*. Cambridge: Cambridge University Press.

_____. 1998. *Practical Reason: On the theory of action*. Cambridge: Polity Press.

Cardoso, H. 1993. *O Partido Unico em Cabo Verde: Um assalto à Esperança*. Praia: Imprensa Nacional de Cabo Verde.

Carreira, A. 1982 [1977]. *The People of the Cape Verde Islands: Exploitation and emigration*. London: Hurst and Company Limited.

Chabal, P. 1983. *Amilcar Cabral: Revolutionary leadership and people's war*. Cambridge: Cambridge University Press.

Chambers, R. 1994. Participatory Rural Appraisal (PRA): challenges, potential and paradigm. *World Development*, 22 (10): 1437–54.

Commins, S. 1997. World Vision International and donors: too close for comfort? In *NGOs, States and Donors: Too close for comfort?*, edited by D. Hulme and M. Edwards. London: Macmillan.

Crewe, E., and E. Harrison, 1998. *Whose Development? An ethnography of Aid.* London: Zed Books.

Crush, J. (ed.), 1995. *Power of Development.* London: Routledge.

Davidson, B. (1969). *The Liberation of Guiné: Aspects of an African revolution.* Middlesex: Penguin Books.

Dow, S. 1995. *Non-Governmental Organizations in Cape Verde: An analysis and suggestions for their greater involvement in the development of Cape Verde.* Praia: unpublished UNDP report.

Escobar, A. 1984. Discourse and power in development: Michel Foucault and the relevance of his work to the Third World. *Alternatives* X (Winter 1984–85): 377–400.

_____. 1991. Anthropology and the development encounter: the making and marketing of development anthropology. *American Ethnologist* 18 (4): 658–82.

_____. 1995. *Encountering Development: The making and unmaking of the Third World,* Princeton, NJ: Princeton University Press.

Farrington, J. and A. Bebbington. 1993. *Reluctant Partners? Non-governmental organizations, the state and sustainable agricultural development.* London: Routledge.

Ferguson, J. 2004. Transnational topographies of power: beyond 'the state' and 'civil society' in the study of African politics. In *A Companion to the Anthropology of Politics,* edited by J. Vincent and D. Nugent. Oxford: Blackwell.

Foy, C. 1988. *Cape Verde: Politics, economics and society.* London: Pinter Publishers.

Furtado, C. 1993. *A Transformação das Estruturas Agrárias numa Sociedade em Mudança—Santiago, Cabo Verde.* Praia: Instituto Cabo Verdeano do Livro e do Disco.

_____. 1995. Efeitos da prática política no tecido social Caboverdiano. In *De Mindelo para Cabo Verde: Convergência para a Solidariedade,* edited by C. Araújo. Mindelo: Forum Convergência.

Gardner, K., and D. Lewis 1996. *Anthropology, Development and the Post-Modern Challenge.* London: Pluto Press.

Grillo, R. 1997. Discourses of development: the view from anthropology. In *Discourses of Development: Anthropological perspectives,* edited by R. Grillo and R. Stirrat. Oxford: Berg.

Grillo, R. and R. Stirrat (eds.) *Discourses of Development: Anthropological perspectives.* Oxford: Berg.

Gupta, A. 1995. Blurred boundaries: the discourse of corruption, the culture of politics, and the imagined state. *American Ethnologist* 22 (2): 375–402.

Hobart, M. (ed.) 1993. *An Anthropological Critique of Development*. London: Routledge.

Hulme, D. and M. Edwards (eds.) 1997. *NGOs, States and Donors: Too close for comfort?* London: Macmillan.

Langworthy, M., and T. Finan 1997. *Waiting for Rain: Agricultural and ecological imbalance in Cape Verde*. Boulder: Lynne Rienner Publishers.

Lobban, R. 1995. *Cape Verde: Crioulo colony to independent nation*. Boulder: Westview Press.

Mitchell, T. 1991. The limits of the state: beyond statist approaches and their critics. *American Political Science Review* 85 (1): 77–96.

Moran, E. 1982. The evolution of Cape Verde's agriculture. *African Economic History* 11: 63–86.

OECD. 1995. *Development Co-operation: Efforts and policies of the members of the development assistance committee*. Paris: OECD

Pigg, S. 1992. Inventing social categories through place: social representations and development in Nepal. *Comparative Studies in Society and History* 34 (3): 491–513.

Powell, M and D. Seddon 1997. NGOs and the development industry. *Review of African Political Economy* 71: 3–10.

Rahnema, M. (1990). Participatory Action Research: the last temptation of saint development. In *Alternatives: Social Transformation and Humane Governance* 15 (2): 207–8.

Sachs, W. (ed.) 1992. *The Development Dictionary: A guide to knowledge as power*. London: Zed Books Ltd.

Smillie, I. 1995. *The Alms Bazaar: Altruism under fire—non-profit organizations and international development*. London: IT Publications.

Stewart, S. 1997. Happy ever after in the marketplace: non-governmental organisations and uncivil society. *Review of African Political Economy* 71: 11–34.

CHAPTER 10

Western Beliefs and Local Myths: A Case Study on the Interface between Farmers, NGOs and the State in Guinea-Bissau Rural Development Interventions

Marina Padrão Temudo

Researcher, Instituto de Investigação Científica Tropical (IICT), Lisbon

marina_temudo@hotmail.com

NGOs and Community-Based Conservation in Guinea-Bissau: Rhetoric and Reality

"The honey they put in my ears does not arrive at my mouth"

—Statement by a local farmer about development interventions.

Cubucaré, March 1st, 1995

When I first arrived in Guinea-Bissau in November 1993 to conduct field-work for my PhD dissertation my head was full of "romantic" ideas about

NGOs,[1] farmer associations, and the potential of participatory methods to progressively change the "traditional" trend for "failure" that had so far characterized development in Africa. As time went on and my knowledge of the local lingua franca (Crioulo) increased, along with the trust farmers put in me, I was struck by a completely different reality. Only then I discovered that for almost one year my perception had been not only ideologically driven by my western beliefs, but also distorted by the multi-layered scenarios constructed by different actors for visitors, whether these visitors were donors, project evaluators or researchers.

The myth of the moral and operational superiority of NGOs to African states was the first to go. Most of the NGOs I observed resembled Meillassoux's (quoted in Geffray 1991:117) "social bodies": organizations produced by a particular social class, whose only aim is their own reproduction by expanding and increasing turnover, guaranteeing the jobs, and increasing the privileges of those employed. This situation was exacerbated by donor agendas and the strings attached to the donor funding on which these organizations depended for their institutional survival. It also had profound implications for the relationship of these organizations to their constituents in rural communities, as well as for the nature of the civil society that they claimed to represent.

The details of this situation stand in stark contrast to the neo-Tocquevillian ideal of African NGOs as a bulwark against corrupt and inefficient African states. In fact, as I shall demonstrate below, they raise fundamental questions about the putative boundary between "the state" and "civil society." Farmers in my research area of Cubucaré rarely distinguished between state-sponsored development interventions and those sponsored by NGOs. As far as they could make out, there was a continuum of external interventions—"projects"—and their agents were roughly the same persons. Furthermore, from their perception, "the state" and "civil society" (NGOs) shared similar organizational cultures, while trying to introduce technological and/or organizational innovations that were barely distinguishable from one another.

The words with which I opened this section expressed the farmers' perception of the contradiction between the rhetoric of the development agents who visited their community and the almost zero benefits that they, the targeted beneficiaries, actually received. Indeed development rhetoric, especially when it concerns NGOs and participatory intervention, has a very broad appeal. For

---

1. In this paper the concept of NGOs is only used to refer to service organizations.

local people it holds out the elusive promise that they will finally have a say over the processes that affect their daily lives. For western donors it offers opportunities to realize their ideals of liberal democracy and community empowerment. Because of the wonderful promises of NGO rhetoric, the realization that it is out of step with actual NGO interventions is understandably difficult to accept. While this painful realization usually becomes quickly apparent to local people, it is doubly difficult for western donors because of the time and expense involved in conducting detailed community-level evaluations.

Farmers' metaphors and statements like the one with which I opened this chapter drove me to understand development interventions as "arenas of struggle" (Crehan and von Oppen 1988) or "arenas of negotiation for strategic groups" (Bierschenk 1988) and to apply ethnographic methods to study the conflicts between the different stakeholders. This study and the identification of the strategic groups (see Olivier de Sardan and Bierschenk 1994), both with an actor-oriented approach (Long & Long 1992), seemed to me the best way to decode what was really happening at the "impact point" (Olivier de Sardan 1995:9). Living for a long time in the "development arena,"[2] I could daily observe and register several indicators of the organizational culture and of the results of the projects: external agents' and farmers' perceptions and attitudes toward each other, the management style of the organizations, the analysis of project proposals and reports confronted with on-going routine activities and with project results, and the conflicts between actors arising from the intervention process.

As I shall argue in this chapter, bringing clarity to this discrepancy is essential in providing constructive support to African NGOs and creating interventions that yield concrete benefits to local people through participatory processes. In order to understand the nature of African NGOs and the interventions that they sponsor, however, it is first necessary to address their relationships to two institutions: 1) the western development agencies and organizations that provide the funding that allow them to run; and 2) the agencies within their own governments that ostensibly monitor and regulate their activities. Furthermore, these relationships must be understood in the context of colonial history, postcolonial political conflicts, and IMF-sponsored structural adjustment programs.

---

2. Field research was conducted in the Cubucaré peninsula (Tombali province) and lasted from 1993 until 1996 (total of 22 months) and was complemented by several shorter follow-up visits in 1999, 2000, 2001, 2002 and 2003 (total of 9 months).

In what follows, I shall firstly give a brief outline of the socio-economic and political background to the current NGO rural development boom in Guinea-Bissau. I shall then discuss the strategies followed by urban NGO leaders working in rural communities. Thirdly, I shall describe the ambivalent attitudes of farmers to development projects by analyzing their strategies of resistance and the initial acceptance and later redefinition of external offers in a case study of a project intended to create a Natural Park, called "Safeguard of the last sub-humid forests of Guinea-Bissau." I conclude with an analysis of the implications of my study for NGO interventions throughout Sub-Saharan Africa.

The State, NGOs, and the Donors in Guinea-Bissau

Guinea-Bissau is a small West African country bordered by Senegal, the Republic of Guinea (sometimes known as Guinea-Conakry), and the Atlantic Ocean. A former Portuguese colony, Guinea-Bissau attained national sovereignty in 1974 after more than ten years of liberation war led by the African Party for the Independence of Guinea and Cape Verde (henceforth PAIGC), founded in 1956 by Amílcar Cabral.

Following independence, PAIGC established a non-aligned one-party regime with a centralized economy. According to the official discourse of the newly independent government, agriculture would become the foundation for national development and industry its engine. As in many other newly independent African countries, however, the reality was quite different. In practice, agriculture was relegated to a function of supplier of food for the urban population, raw materials for industry and export commodities. Agricultural revenues were also taxed to finance growing state bureaucracies. The government maintained agricultural commodities at artificially low prices, assuming that farmers would not respond to price incentives, and forced producers into direct exchanges of crops for other essential goods supplied in a tremendously inefficient manner by state enterprizes. The supply of agricultural tools was also not assured. As with many other African countries, the aggregate effects of these measures were the stagnation of agriculture, the impoverishment of farmers, and the increase of informal trade (see Galli and Jones 1987 and Forrest 1992).

During this period, development interventions in rural communities were conducted primarily through state-sponsored integrated projects, which were heavily subsidized or funded outright by international aid. On the whole, such projects failed to meet the problems of rural producers, and investments in the agricultural sector never surpassed ten percent of the total spending (Galli and Jones 1987).

This generated a growing dependence upon international aid which in turn contributed to a huge external debt that by the end of 1988 reached $423 million and corresponded to 300 percent of GNP (Forrest 1992: 98–111). According to Forrest (*ibid:* 111) these conditions were exacerbated by the fact that the priorities of government leadership were "overly self-serving, as members of the state elite wish(ed) above all to secure the well being of their administrative offices. Thus, there [was] little reluctance to become increasingly dependent on foreign aid."

In the early 1980s the government adopted two economic and financial stabilization plans whose unsuccessful results lead to the adoption of an IMF-sponsored structural adjustment plan. The broad objective of this plan was to give priority to the agricultural sector, restrict deficit spending, reduce the state apparatus and urban real wages, devaluate local currency, and liberalize the market.

From the beginning of the 1990s, the structural adjustment measures and the adoption of a multi-party regime created the conditions for an NGO boom. Until then, foreign NGOs operating in Guinea-Bissau were compelled to work in close relation with the state (Rudebeck 1996: 36), who in 1984 created a governmental-non-governmental organization—the Solidami—to better control them.

The government approval of the NGOs Decree in 1992 finally allowed for the creation of independent NGOs. At the same time, SAP measures of restricting wage increases induced a "generalized lethargy" and a growing absenteeism among public servants, who oriented themselves to the development of parallel activities (Solidami 1994a: 38–39), including the creation of NGOs. Most of these organizations, therefore, were founded by civil servants seeking to diversify their financial portfolios.

Of course, this phenomenon was not specific to Guinea-Bissau. To quote Farrington *et al.* (1993: 45):

"these adjustment related policy measures have not spared the professional middle class (especially civil servants), who have seen their wages decline rapidly and in some cases their jobs disappear. Some of this economically displaced middle class appears to have moved into, or created NGOs in search of new higher paying jobs. This strategy has been aided by the increased availability of donor funding, which facilitated the creation of new NGOs. In some measure this has been an important element of the recent explosion of the NGO sector."

Western donors were critical of the exodus of redundant civil servants from state bureaucracies to the NGO sector, but also of petty corruption and a general lack of capacity within local NGOs (Solidami 1994b:85). However, Guinean NGO leaders refused to accept these critiques, arguing that their western partners neglected to address the myriad difficulties under which they had to operate every day. They counter-attacked by accusing western NGOs of disinvesting on their financial support and of having a paternalistic approach, which created an "inferiority complex" in rural beneficiaries (*ibid*: 75). These arguments frequently appeared to be part of a larger strategy to open space for their exclusive intervention, relegating their western partners to the role of intermediaries in the flux of aid funding.

The most powerful NGOs were created by the urban Creole elite (mainly educated in Europe or North America), who held, or had previously held, high positions in the state. As a result of their education and position, they enjoyed extensive connections to transnational development networks. Members of this emerging NGO elite quickly learned to master the crucial performance skills needed to have their project proposals approved as well as a clichéd language: "participation," "help for self-help," "poverty reduction," "natural resources protection," "gender balance" and so on. They also learned to be flexible in their approach, since each donor has its favorite themes, which can change from year to year. In short, Guinean NGO elites quickly learned the importance of being well-informed about what is offered in the "development market" at each specific moment. These skills were crucial for running an NGO in Guinea-Bissau, where (as in many other African countries) national donations, members fees and voluntary work, when existing, are insignificant. Consequently, Guinean NGOs are almost completely dependent on western donors for their survival.

In spite of donors' rhetoric that African NGOs represent a fundamental change from state-centered development, this dependency on external aid actually represents a fundamental continuity between these two periods in African development history. NGO-sponsored interventions, just as state-sponsored interventions of the past, are fundamentally influenced by the agendas and ideas of western donors. Since many of the leaders of Guinean NGOs were previously government officials, and since many continue to engage in the same sort of "rent seeking" behavior previously practiced exclusively within government agencies, it is often difficult to determine where the governments ends and the NGO sector begins.

In Cubucaré region, external interventions since 1977 have been mainly influenced by the activity of the Experimental Station of Caboxanque, a research centre of the Department of Agricultural Research (DEPA). From 1978 to 1991 the station's activities were included in the Integrated Rural Development Project of Caboxanque (PIC), financed by several bi- and multi-lateral aid agencies and some western NGOs.

In 1991, the local NGO Calbante[3] was founded by about forty members most of whom were still public servants. Its director was (and has been almost since its creation) the director of DEPA[4], whose international network connections made it possible to transfer some of the activities financed by western NGOs and some material resources of PIC to this new NGO. This competition for project resources, but also the fact that the Calbante director was, at that time, affiliated to the ruling party's opposition opened a conflict between the NGO and the state.

The project maintained the acronym (PIC) and some of the activities: agriculture, health, support to farmer associations, and training. Another project supporting farmer associations, which was financed by a Portuguese NGO was also transferred to Calbante. In farmers' words, "DEPA brought forth Calbante" in 1993, Calbante and two more local NGOs began the implementation of a project aiming at the creation of a park in the Cubucaré region. This project was called "Safeguard of the last sub-humid forests of Guinea-Bissau." The activities of these three projects overlapped and the new PIC was turned into a kind of umbrella with the other two projects duplicating the funding for some actions. For this reason, and also because the multiple micro-initiatives of the project had their own specific donor, it became exceedingly difficult to conduct an effective evaluation of any particular project.

This already difficult situation is exacerbated by the fact that, in order to get funding, NGOs must also have beneficiaries. In this respect, Guinea Bissau's NGO sector shares a great deal in common with the previous state-sponsored development interventions. Both state-sponsored and NGO-sponsored interventions are carried out in the name of "the people." In order to be perceived as legitimate by western donors, these interventions benefit marginal (usually rural) communities. Following the NGO revolution, it also became imperative for local people to be "participants" in NGO-sponsored interventions. Without local "participants" it became difficult for NGO leaders to find

---

3. In this paper the name of the NGO has been codified.

4. The DEPA, at that time, suffered a re-organization and changed the name to INPA. However, as a consequence of structural adjustment measures, its human and material resources had been reduced to a minimum with full consequences in its activities.

donor-support for their interventions. In the following section I address the relationship of Guinean NGOs to communities in Cubucaré, and how local people perceived and responded to their interventions.

Reaching Out to "the People": From State to NGO-Sponsored Interventions

Reaching "the people" has been a central imperative of rural intervention in Guinea Bissau. In late colonial times, the associational model was defended as an important development tool (Ferreira Mendes 1969:367; Spínola 1971:415; and JIU 1972:151). Since independence the aim of "structuring the rural world" through the creation of farmers associations, in clear denial of any traditional social organization, has been promoted both by the government, by donors, and more recently by NGOs.

Associations became the legitimate partners and the organizational levers for the implementation of development projects and the main receptacle through which development funding has been channeled to rural beneficiaries. In the first years of independence, rice de-husking machines, palm oil presses, trucks, bicycles, radios, cloths and other goods reached these associations through international donations. In the NGO era, funding of associations became linked to credit, mainly directed to purchase de-husking machines or palm oil presses, to create grain banks for the food shortage period, or to trade local productions and buy goods to sell at the association shop.

These associations have remained important in the years since structural adjustment, as western donors are anxious that the funding they provide should reach a legitimate institution at the village-level, representing "the people." As with NGOs themselves, farmers associations became institutional "nets" for capturing donor money. Even before the NGO revolution, the building of the village association, always located near the road, was an object of prestige and the maximum symbol of local engagement with externally-induced development. For the state some years ago, as well as for NGOs and for farmers themselves today, the association building was the main instrument of what Long and Ploeg (1989) called a "cargo-cult" strategy toward donors. Prior to any visit of potential donors' representatives, the association buildings and the local NGOs offices were painted and cleaned while some farmers were prepared by external agents to speak as representatives of local societies. A description of this strategy had been given to me by some of the farmers even before I had the chance to witness it myself.

A system of personal networks and dependencies was established between the project personnel and some of the farmers. The latter were chosen by their capacity to accept and reproduce the development "cargo-cult" rhetoric of the NGOs toward foreigners, be they evaluators, researchers or simple visitors: "we are poor but we work hard" (*anós i pobre, má nô pega teso*). The other farmers called them the project "bards" (*djidios*). In a rather horizontal society, these *courtiers du* développement, as Olivier de Sardan & Bierschenk (1993) would call them, were usually among the most charismatic and eloquent. They also appeared to be the ones most willing to mouth donor agendas in order to gain access to the material and symbolic resources that donors provided. In fact, they were the main direct beneficiaries of external intervention, which generated a belief among local people that there existed only one list of beneficiaries and target villages and that dojnors used this list in allocating funding.

Aside from this small group of beneficiaries, however, most local people took a critical view of urban-based NGOs and the interventions that they sponsored. Local NGO staff were essentially oriented toward private-for-profit activities, mainly trade using the project facilities, and absenteeism was quite high, which made farmers ask questions along the lines of "what kind of work are they doing now?" The salaries of high-level staff were paid in US dollars whilst the others were paid in a local currency that was suffering a continuous devaluation. This discrimination caused resentment and was used to legitimate the search for parallel activities and the appropriation of project facilities. These patterns of behavior originated from experiences within government offices where, especially after the adoption of structural adjustment measures, it was accepted to "steal" whenever possible and to develop parallel remunerative activities during work time. Local staff also shared a feeling of suffering a kind of punishment for living in the countryside, far away from the main towns. This was another reason given to justify absenteeism.

Those few NGO workers who were committed to actually making interventions successful were hindered by their position in the NGO structure. In spite of their participatory rhetoric, most of these organizations were hierarchical and centralized. Decisions were taken in urban offices without the feedback of rural staff, reaching the villages in a top-down fashion. In the rare cases when local staff wanted to give some feedback to their headquarters about the perceptions of the farmers and their forms of resistance to intervention actions, they were accused of taking sides with the beneficiaries and told they could lose their jobs (Temudo 1998, vol. II: 131). Ironically, NGO staff who advocated for "the people" were listed as trouble makers, while those who kept their mouths shut, but misappropriated NGOs resources, continued to prosper.

Local people also learned not to rock the boat if they expected to receive benefits from NGO interventions. The president of the main women's association in the Cubucaré region once told me with a pun: "you know, project is profit (*projeto i proveto*), because when the money [funding] arrives those who are closer to it take the full profit." I was immediately reminded of Olivier de Sardan's and Bierschenk's (1993:12) notion of a development project as a "system of resources and opportunities that everyone tries to appropriate in their own way." She went on to tell me that she had first said so in a project meeting some years earlier, and that since that meeting took place she had never been invited again, because "they" did not want farmers with critical attitudes. This informant, along with other farmers whom I interviewed, complained that external agents applied for funding in their name, but only a very small portion of the money ever reached them. Previous experiences, the "historical imprint" (Long and Ploeg, 1989: 230), obviously influenced the ways in which local people perceived and responded to new interventions, and to the idea of development in general.

Most of the better-off villages located near the main roads had development interventions, sometimes with more than one organization operating simultaneously. One after the other, there were constant meetings organized by NGO representatives with farmers inviting them to participate in a project they intended to create: "we want to bring a project into your village, what are your first priorities?" Yet, farmers complained that, for most of the times, after a consensus concerning the priorities had finally been attained by the villagers, "they" never came back and no project was ever implemented. Farmers confessed that they were completely fed up with meetings and therefore most of the times attendance was low. This was a problem for NGOs leaders, who depended on community participation to legitimize their initial activities. The ways to secure farmers' participation was sometimes rather extreme. Thus, on one occasion I witnessed the representatives of two NGOs waiting for people to come out of the mosque on a Friday in order to make sure they would attend their meeting.

However, after the project approval, "participatory" meetings with farmers were constructed with ritualized scenarios and an instrumental rhetoric in projects' reports to mobilize donor funds. As Richards (1995: 13–16) noted, we are now observing a "bureaucratization" of participatory methods, which become a kind of "flag of necessity." These meetings were always decided according to the agendas of NGO leaders living in the capital city who arrived at the end of the morning and wanted to go back the same day, and so the time needed for a full participation of farmers was rather limited. Discussions were never open-ended and farmers did not play any major role in determining their direction and resolution. I especially remember a meeting in 1996 that was expected to be conflict ridden, where the NGO leaders arrived at eleven o'clock and the discussions lasted till 4 pm without even an interruption for lunch. NGO leaders were sitting at a table in front of the farmers' representatives, sharing coffee and cookies among themselves, and circulating written notes whenever any farmer would pose any critique or troublesome question, in order to better react in unison. Farmers pointed this out to me, making clear their own perception of the strategies and "participatory" methods of the NGO staff.

Farmers associations created under the stimulus of external agents (initially the state and at that moment the NGOs) were, with one exception, unable to function effectively on their own. The moment that the flow of aid money ceased they ran into visible difficulties and soon stopped their activities. In addition to being oriented to external resources, these organizations have taken on an organizational type that is alien to the rural communities in which they operate. They do not draw from traditional leadership structures, and the trainings in managerial and administrative skills external agents provided to their leaders have been superficial and sporadic. Consequently, they are completely unprepared to implement an autonomous collective action.

Another difficulty for farmers associations is that external donors wanted them to be inter-ethnically united. For local people this was a bit of an irony, since NGOs constantly competed with each other to work with them. Nevertheless, only multi-ethnic farmers associations were supported by either the state or the NGOs. The only association that was an autonomous and sustainable self-help group had been organized around a traditional Tanda age group, although some elements from other ethnic groups were integrated into it so as to gain support from external funding agents.

What this arrangement achieves in effect is to create a predictable task environment for western donors working with Guinean NGOs. In other words, it makes it possible for donors to move money to discrete groups and projects, while ignoring the diversity and complexity of the communities that they are trying to aid. The trade-off, of course, is that donors work with small groups of people who frequently do not represent the interests of the communities in question. Unfortunately, the outcomes of the interventions they are sponsoring are frequently compromised in the process.

The effects of these problems can be clearly seen in the development and conservation interventions that I observed in Cubucaré. These interventions ignored the diversity of local people and the fact that they were not adequately represented by local farmer associations. Perhaps more problematically, however, it was undertaken without any study of traditional resource management or of the beliefs of local people concerning their relationship to the environment. Consequently it was nearly impossible for these organizations to design a project that would elicit the participation of local people and promote sustainable resource management practices. It was even more difficult for the implementing NGOs to predict how people would perceive and respond to the interventions that they did implement. This is the subject of the following section.

Ethnic Diversity, Views of Nature, and Conservation Intervention in Cubucaré

The Cubucaré Peninsula is home to a complex mix of ethnic groups, mainly Balanta, Fulbe, Nalu and Susu, with complementing and competing resource management practices (Temudo 1998, vol. I). Rice is the main crop and production systems follow an ethnic matrix. Leaving present dynamics aside, they can be described in a simplified manner: the Balanta are specialized in mangrove swamp rice, while Fulbe and Tanda are cultivators of rain fed rice (slash and burn system). Employing one of these production systems in varying proportions, the other ethnic groups can be placed between these two extremes.

Slash and burn, rain fed cultivation is rather work-intensive, and today producers prefer to invest in fruit production for the urban market. Consequently, self-sufficiency in rice is not attained by the majority of households. The undersupply of food is mitigated by a complex system of interethnic exchange mechanisms, which include an exchange of work and of other products (mainly peanuts and traditional soap) for rice and a system of loans based on strong social capital networks.

Traditionally, the Balanta have concentrated their activity on swamp rice production and have been the only cattle breeders. However, several factors have been moving them toward cashew nuts production, which depends on other habitats: namely the savannas and the forests.

Local patterns of territorial settlement also show this functional specialization; the Tanda and Fulbe villages lie on the uplands, near the forest. In the opposite side the Balanta villages are located in the savannas (*lalas*) surrounding the mangrove bushes and the rice fields. Nalu elders claim that they gave the Balanta that habitat to settle and erect their villages because people must live near their working place. The ethnic groups that rely on both cropping systems have their villages somewhere in between the uplands and the mangrove.

In the Cubucaré region, ethnic groups, no matter how strongly influenced by Islam, share the same cosmological paradigm, which conceives of the territory as inhabited by supernatural entities, similar in many ways to humans. These spirits are black or white (the latter are said to be the most powerful), good or bad, female or male, and have other human-like qualities such as the possibility of making friends with human beings. They can also be seduced and even corrupted. They especially like blood sacrifices and they possess gold. The spirits' world is organized in the manner of a country, with a president and several chiefs of territorial divisions, an army and some guards placed at strategic points of the borders between different spirits' provinces.

Through contracts with the spirits, who are conceived of as the true owners of the land, the heads of the founding lineages of the ethnic groups that first settled in Cubucaré, the Nalu, obtained the right to manage all the natural resources and to be called the "owners of the land." This contract of transference of power must be periodically renewed by means of certain rituals conducted by the heads of the founding lineages at the spirits' shrines. Traditionally, for anyone to have access to land (either to settle or to work), to access forest products, or to have rights to hunting and fishing, a request had to be submitted to the heads of the founding lineages, who then would have had to perform certain rituals to demand the spirits' agreement.

Each spirit's province is divided into three distinct areas: a sacred wood, a buffer zone surrounding it, and the land attributed to each village for habitat and farming. Access to sacred woods is strictly exclusive to the members of the founding lineage and no resource can be collected there. In the buffer zone, the access to resources was restricted by an environmental management system. Nalu custom establishes that each sacred forest must have someone nominated by the owner of the land to keep vigilance in order to control resource use (Temudo, 1998, vol. I: 421–38).

Since colonial times, the forests of Cantanhês, which encompass the two Nalu chiefdoms of Cubucaré region, were considered the most beautiful and some of the richest in biodiversity of "Portuguese Guinea"; accordingly, they were protected from timber extraction for the export market. During the liberation war, the density of the trees allowed farmers and the guerrilla fighters to escape Portuguese aerial attacks. At the same time the main commandants had entered into contracts with the spirit owners of the land, under the support of Nalu elders, in order to win the war and to be personally protected against death in combat. The invincibility of some of them, like Nino Vieira (the former President of the Republic), was attributed to these contracts with the spirits.

People's beliefs about the environment also reveal their perceptions of development interventions and how they influence their world. There is a generalized belief that every rich or famous person, every scientist and every powerful country has a spirit (or a group of spirits) working for them, and that white people (because of their resemblance) have the capacity to seduce the spirits into abandoning their land and going to live in the West, where even they can be offered better living conditions. This "human weakness" of spirits is the main argument used to explain the destruction of some of the sacred forests of Guinea-Bissau after Independence.

According to tradition, whoever settles in the region has the right to a piece of land big enough for household self-sufficiency and well-being. So the low population density of Cubucaré has also been an important factor in the maintenance of relatively large buffer zones in the forests.

The local system of natural resource management has been maintained over the years through a complex and inter-locked group of myths and taboos. Over the years there have been some major threats to its maintenance: the Islamization of the Nalu, the liberation war (the ritualized protection of the buffer zones could not be done in order to allow farmers and fighters to live and run across them), the nationalization of land and of all natural resources after Independence, and more recently the fear of the occupation of huge parcels of land by the urban elite. But it was the above mentioned conservation project that perhaps most heavily affected the heart of this traditional management system.

The strategy declared in the project proposal considered "repressive measures" (administrative and legislative) to be compatible with the "full participation of the population in every stage of the project" (CALBANTE et al., 1992:28). A full range of activities was proposed: credit schemes for the rehabilitation of swamp rice polders, as well as for increasing the production of fruit orchards and of valley-swamp rice. These projects were undertaken in order to reduce rain fed rice cultivation, because of its dependence on slash and burn. Other schemes supported the creation of farmers' associations, as well as promoting traditional fishing, eco-tourism, health services, and apiculture. However, the project invested most of its budget in the construction of a local office and a house for the project coordinator (a rather young local technician) and on his salary, in the purchase of two four-wheel drive vehicles, in studies of forest biodiversity, the delimitation of the boundaries of the

natural reserves conducted by foreign researchers, and in actions of information and sensitization toward urban public opinion and donors in order to
promote the image of the NGOs.

In the conflict surrounding this project it was possible to identify different
sources and different stakeholders (Temudo 1998, vol. II: 113–31):

> Firstly, the Nalu ethnic group, possessing a well-established resource
> management system, did not feel the need of a project to tell them
> what to do. Traditional land owners considered that NGOs and the di-
> rection of the main farmers' association (AFC) bypassed them both in
> the decision-making for the project approval and in the nomination
> of the forests guards, chosen among people of all ethnic groups. The
> nomination of guards of all ethnic groups could look rather demo-
> cratic but in fact it was going to provide power to outsiders who did
> not have the same cosmological relation to the forests and whose ob-
> jective was to maximize resource use. Nalu elders had also the suspi-
> cion that the true, if undeclared, aim of the external agents (NGOs
> leaders were by and large urban Creoles) was to steal their spirits. This
> feeling was increased by the fact that external agents and scientists
> working for the project entered the sacred forests without any permis-
> sion and without being accompanied by any representative of the lin-
> eage of the owner of the land.

Secondly, the producers of rainfed rice considered that the project did not
give them any training or material conditions to stop shifting cultivation, and
that mango and valley swamp rice productions were not the solution, especially because the price of rice increased a lot, because there was no guarantee of an external market for mangoes, and because valley swamp rice had several production constraints. Considering that the project forbade the hunt of
the most important crop pests (wild pigs and monkeys), they wanted to be
given metallic fences to protect their fields.

Thirdly, the guards of the forests wanted to be paid a salary and be given
uniforms and credentials so as to have their authority recognized (mostly toward the state forest guards who were totally corrupt and would happily let
people cut protected trees and hunt protected animals in exchange for money
or favors).

Fourthly, most of the local population wanted the project coordinator to be
replaced due to his lack of engagement in the work, the huge share his salary
and other amenities had in the project budget, and the arrogant attitude showed
toward the farmers. They complained about the reduced number of beneficiar-

ies of the project activities. They protested about the totally unfavorable credit conditions. They also protested against the prohibition to hunt the most important crop pests—monkeys and wild pigs—that grew uncontrolled because of the disappearance of their predators during liberation war.

Fifthly, the main beneficiaries of project actions—mainly attendance to meetings in the city or visits to exchange experiences in other regions or countries (paid with per diems) or even the privilege of buying or being given resources diverted from the project by NGO staff—had an ambiguous position that changed according to occasions. These usually were the project "bards" toward foreigners when the NGOs needed them.

Sixthly, the NGO local staff and headquarters leadership considered farmers to be a group of hypocritical opportunists, not grateful for the project's common benefits (Temudo, 1998, vol. II: 131).

Last but not least, the state suddenly appeared as a seventh stakeholder, and tried to instrumentalize farmers for its own benefit, i.e., to control the aid money for natural resource management through its National Commission for the Environment (CNA). This was possible because in 1994 a huge conflict arose between the direction of CALBANTE and the direction of the AFC—the farmers' association chosen to be the earmarked partner of the NGOs in all their interventions in Cubucaré. This conflict introduced a party-political dimension to the intervention arena (Temudo, 1998, vol. II: 95–110) as the majority of the "beneficiaries" were affiliated to the ruling party and the NGO staff belonged to the opposition.

All these unsolved conflicts led to a farmers' revolt in 1996 that slashed and burned land parcels to produce rainfed rice along the main roads (instead of the accorded 100 m inside), destroying the scenery the NGOs would like to maintain for donor visits. The "external" evaluation that occurred in January 1996, some months before I left the field (I only returned in 1999), was conducted by two Senegalese experts and another one from Guinea-Bissau. The latter was living in Holland and working in an international organization, but was also a member of one of the NGOs that was implementing the project. As could be expected, of the fifteen days accorded to the mission, only two of them were spent in the project region, and most of the time in meetings at the local office and in "rural development tourism."

The project ended in 1997, apparently because of problems between the three NGOs, which were evident to everyone who attended the project appraisal meetings. Conflicts with beneficiaries were never detected (or valued?) by the mid-term external evaluation. Self-evaluations, although "participatory" in rhetoric and including representatives of the beneficiaries (named by the NGOs), completely bypassed the criticisms expressed by the general population. The increased desacralization of nature and de-legitimization of customary authorities were the main factors creating space for an "open-access" to natural resources. The suspicion that the NGO personnel and the project researchers stole some of the spirit owners of the land opened fissures in the already fragile system of myths and taboos that maintained the traditional management of natural resources. Land conflicts grew in number and intensity, leading to a scramble for land and resource management practices that were unsustainable and harmed the environment. However, the impacts of these interventions were overshadowed by national political conflicts, which tipped the balance of ethnic power in Cubucaré. All of these processes had profound implications for local resource management practices.

Yet Another Project to Save the Last Sub-humid Forests of Guinea-Bissau in the Aftermath of Civil War

In June 1988, a military uprising erupted in the capital, and soon after a civil war spread to several parts of the countryside. The conflict started between President Nino Vieira and the Superior Chief of the Armed Forces (the brigadier Ansumane Mané), accused of having sold weapons to the Senegalese rebels of Casamance (see INEP, 2000).[5] The almost total support that Ansumane Mané received from the army after being removed from his post was rooted in a generalized social discontent among the troops, especially the ex-combatants of the liberation war, with President Vieira's politics. However, it was the invasion of the country by troops from Senegal and from Guinea-Conakry, called in to support President Nino Vieira, that represented a turning point in the opinions of rural people, civil society organizations, opposition parties, and even a faction of the PAIGC. The war ended with Vieira's defeat and his exile to Portugal.

Post-civil war elections in 1999 gave the power to a party organized along ethnic lines and as a consequence inter-ethnic cleavages and tensions gained an increased importance. After independence, the distrust of the Balanta, the

---

5. INEP stands for Instituto Nacional de Estudos e Desquisas Educacionois Aniso Teixeira.

most important ethnic group both in liberation and civil wars, toward the PAIGC elite, caused by the removal or even execution of their main liberation war commandants under the accusation of coup attempts, helped to set the stage for further ethnic tensions and conflicts.

With the election of the Party of Social Renovation (PRS) the Balanta reached the main positions in the state apparatus, which generated, at a regional level, the breakdown of the equilibrium of the inter-ethnic power relations with huge consequences in the management of natural resources. Land occupations by the Balanta ran unchecked, as customary mechanisms of conflict resolution by the owners of the land had been deactivated. A further bone of contention between the Balanta and the Nalu came from the destruction of the African fan palm forests for palm-wine tapping, which led to the death of the trees (Temudo and Schiefer 2003). The generalized inter-ethnic conflict was also rooted in the Balanta's refusal to control their cattle, which continuously destroyed other people's crops leading to food insecurity in some villages.

Conflicts between the Balanta and the other ethnic groups reached a climax after the assassination of General Ansumane Mané, accused of attempting a coup, and the imprisonment of all his supporters (mainly Muslims from the other ethnic groups and affiliated to the PAIGC). The Balanta secured a total control of all the state apparatus and at a local level they even refused to accept the authority of the Nalu chiefs.

While Nalu youths and women wanted to return to the practice of ritualized protection of the forests (mainly to secure the respect for their local hegemonic position as owners of the land), the elders were more favorable to strategies of negotiation, fearing that it could generate a local civil strife. Their main hope was that some external organization could help them to protect the forests and that the following elections (within four years) could give rise to a party-political power reversal.

In 2002, the International Union for the Conservation of Nature and Natural Resources (IUCN) approached the Nalu owners of the land asking for authorization to create a new project for forest conservation and eco-tourism promotion. The initiative was fairly well received by the Nalu, since it was seen as their only chance to preserve their resources against the destruction by the Balanta. So, once again, new forest guards from all the ethnic groups were elected in the villages near each forest. However, once again, only the Nalu elders were truly engaged in the protection of natural resources and the other ethnic groups much more oriented toward "side-effects" and the expected benefits of a future eco-tourism.

IUCN proposed that the owners of the land carry out what they thought was the "traditional" ritual protection of the forests.[6] However, the elders refused this idea, arguing that it would be dangerous to do so, since transgressors would die. In fact, the Islamization, the market economy, and development interventions have all contributed to an increasing individualization of social relations and to a change in values and beliefs. The search for an individual and immediate well-being has led to a growing challenge to previous beliefs and ritual activities. Elders knew that youths of today challenge the consequences of transgression of ritual prohibitions and therefore their authority. They determined that a system of fines would be put to work instead. Until March 2003, however, no transgressors had paid any fines. However the simple fact of there being an external organization supporting land owners in the protection of natural resources in a context of total disrespect for local rules was rather beneficial for the inter-ethnic balance of power, reducing the number of conflict situations.

Another interesting point in the analysis of the farmers' strategy toward external intervention lies in the importance of what Ferguson (1994) called the "side effects." In fact, the farmers movement against NGO development interventions that was visible in 1996 (Temudo 1998, vol. I: 463 and vol. II: 113–120) induced a disinvestment of this type of organization in the Cubucaré region. For that reason and also as a consequence of the civil war, the main road became rather degraded, making difficult the circulation of trucks that could secure transport for people and the draining of cash crops to urban markets. In farmers' perception, the presence of NGO staff in the region is a guarantee that that road is will be repaired regularly. This constitutes one of the most valued "side effects" of even undesired interventions.

Farmers also believed that if they prevented or even criticized NGO interventions, that the organizations in question would destroy their prestige and spread images of them as a troublesome people, unworthy of any development interventions. Farmers feared, therefore, that obstructing a bad development intervention would destroy the possibility of good development interventions being brought to their community. As a general rule, therefore, they accepted all interventions. Their main "weapon" of resistance (see Scott 1985), however, was to question the impact of the interventions and to throw back the responsibility of their successful implementation to external agents (especially when

---

6. At that time, IUCN experts had had access to two PhD dissertations on traditional natural resources management in the region (Temudo, 1998 and Frazão-Moreira, 1999).

they were not able to repay credit loans). On one occasion, upon asking a group of farmers why they were not refusing external interventions or organizations that they considered as contrary to their own objectives and priorities, one of them replied to me with another question: "If you have a dry well and another one with some water, which one will you choose?"

Farmers are not only or not always manipulated by external agents. Sometimes they are also able to use NGOs to attain their own agendas. This particular case study also showed how "side effects," as Ferguson (1994) had aptly proved, can be instrumental in the understanding and in the reproduction of "failed interventions."

Conclusion: Whose Myth Counts?

Development funding is not only tied to certain western beliefs, but also to methodologies of intervention and to certain types of organization. It is imperative, therefore, that intervention (governmental or not) as an object of study should be analyzed on two levels:

The first level concerns the discourse that constructs its own reality and whose final end is to continuously promote planned intervention (Long and Ploeg 1989:230). This analysis needs to decode from a historical perspective how the ideologies and political strategies of western donors shape interventions and recipient institutions. The need to construct a "virtual reality," where a given problem requires external intervention and where a linear relationship between problems, means and results is established, is of utmost importance for NGOs, recipient governments and even donors agencies to get political support and access to funding (Ferguson 1994 and Quarles van Ufford 1995). The functioning of the development machine depends upon maintaining a certain ignorance of the multiple realities at the starting point of intervention and of the problems arising from it. In this sense, I agree with Hobart (1995:10) that "the postulated growth of knowledge concomitantly entails the possibility of increasing ignorance."

The second level concerns what Olivier de Sardan (1993:11) called the "développement sur le terrain." This can only be understood by considering social change as a complex system of interaction, where actors' "life-worlds", perceptions, strategies of action clash with each other and by analyzing each situation as unique. Further meta-analysis may allow the construction of a typology of organizational settings prone to failure or success of development interventions under given rural societies, and also the creation of an early warning system to detect latent social conflicts and intervene in destabilized societies facing a process of anomie (see Atteslander, 1995). It is absolutely necessary not only for research, but also for development actions and evaluations to start with a clear idea of the historical trajectory shaping the development of NGOs in each country and of all the organizations intervening in a given region and the interface established between them. This "organizational landscape" (Temudo and Arvéola 2003) is the "ground" where development takes place. A researcher or an evaluator should then look beyond each specific intervention, contextualize it and try to understand the strategies of action of the different stakeholders that have influenced the course of any specific project. In order to understand what Balandier (1971) called the inside dynamics (*la dynamique du dedans*) it is crucial to study both the historical processes of transformation of local societies and their many forms of resistance to undesired interventions, as has insistently been argued by other authors.

Understanding the relationship between the discursive apparatus of development and "*développement sur le terrain* is one of the central challenges facing ethnographers working in developing countries today. This challenge requires rigorous scrutiny and analysis of the gap between plans attempted and results achieved, as well as what actually happens at the interface between NGOs and local communities. Such scrutiny and analysis can in turn be achieved through formal questionnaires, open-ended interviews, participant observation, and the cultural immersion that anthropological approaches and ethnographic methods make possible. These approaches and methods will help ethnographers to "demythologize" planned intervention "for the development of a critical analysis of policy and intervention practices" (Long & Ploeg 1989).

One of the most common of the "development myths" lies in the potential of southern civil society in promoting democratization and economic development (Howell 2002). In countries where NGOs have emerged after structural adjustment measures from the former "ruling group" (see Ferguson 1994: 268), the development industry allows this group to maintain its power by maintaining its status and by the creation of a clientelistic network that also includes NGO staff and some farmers. As in former state development interventions, the "efficiency of inefficiency" (Dutkiewicz and Shenton, quoted in Ferguson, 1994: 268) lies on the need to reproduce development interventions, and by that means the flow of money on which the elites in "civil society" depend[7]. Thus, "failure" becomes a vital piece of their social reproduction.

The problem lies in the "tiredness" of rural societies toward undesired development interventions. For that reason, interventions feed on the internal political and social disruptions of rural societies. In Guinea-Bissau the "upper crust" of this "ruling group" has party connections, which allowed its members to get high governmental positions after the civil war (1998–99). This in turn enlarged their power and financing strategies. The main Guinean NGOs are at this moment fully engaged in the opposition parties' electoral campaign. The most illustrative example of that can be seen in the pre-electoral statement of one NGO leader: "If my party wins the elections, I shall be a minister and I promise to construct a good road to Cubucaré." In that sense, it seems that even the non-governmental characteristic of NGOs can turn out to be a myth. The question is why this myth is maintained by the development industry rhetoric and practice. My argument is that the use of NGOs as "public contractors" by western donors makes it easier to impose western models of development than dealing directly with the state and that it helps to maintain a middle class necessary to attain social stability and to secure consumers for western imported goods.

Actual interventions, even the "participatory" ones, lie in "modernization theory," in the belief that traditional institutions are incapable of change and need to be substituted through social engineering. It is believed that the myriad of farmers associations recently promoted constitute a pillar for the empowerment of rural societies. Farmers' participation itself is perhaps the most generalized myth in development cooperation (see for instance FAO 1997 and Mosse 1996). Tied-aid funding is not only introducing western ideas of change and modernity, but also the western pace of change. However, the potential compatibility or indeed incompatibility between this western pace and directionality of change (the direction toward "development," "progress," "modernization," "globalization," etc) and African notions of time, especially as it is lived through in rural areas, remains largely unexplored. The myth of a universal development model dependent on the globalization of markets and on a western idea of democracy, instead of empowering farmers, is dispossessing them of their local self-reliance and autarchic systems, and increasing their external dependence. So their livelihoods are more and more controlled by the market and the political power of the "ruling group."

There are also plenty of 'taboos' in development interventions as to the weight of traditional authorities and institutions and that of the cosmological

---

7. A compelling argument, to which I subscribe, against the application of a clear-cut division between state and civil society in Africa is to be found in Chabal & Daloz (1999: 17–30).

sphere of African societies. In fact, the belief system of these societies is never considered in the intervention model a pillar of their resilience, as a risk-defense strategy (see Ploeg 1995: 216), or an instrument for reducing uncertainty of local agro-social systems (see Desjeux 1987: 102).

'Failure' in development interventions may be explained not only by political, ideological, economic, social, technical and institutional problems, but also sometimes by the confrontation between two opposite myth-worlds. Change must root itself in local institutions, in social and cultural logics, and in cosmological schemes. As one farmer so poetically put it to me, making a metaphorical use of one of the most transitional animals of the African landscape: 'Development must walk like a chameleon: looking behind, looking ahead; looking behind, looking ahead.'

Works Cited

Calbante *et al.* 1992. *Salvaguarda das últimas florestas primárias sub-húmidas da Guiné-Bissau. Documento de projecto (1992–1994)*. Bissau: unpublished report.

Atteslander, P. 1995. "Introduction to special Issue: Anomie: Social Destabilization and the Development of Early Warning Systems." *International Journal of Sociology and Social Policy*, 15 (8–10): 9–23.

Balandier, G. (1971) *Sens et puissance*. Paris : PUF.

Bierschenk, T. 1988. Development projects as an arena of negotiation for strategic groups: a case study from Benin. *Sociologia Ruralis*, 28 (2–3): 146–60.

Chabal, P. and Daloz J-P. 1999. *Africa Works: Disorder as political instrument.* Oxford: James Currey.

Crehan, K. and A. von Oppen. 1988. Understandings of projects: an arena of struggle. *Sociologia Ruralis*, 28 (2–3): 113–45.

Desjeux, D. 1987 *Stratégies paysannes en Afrique Noire: Le Congo*. Paris, Harmattan.

FAO (ed). 1997. *La Dynamique des Sociétés Rurales Face aux Projects Participatifs de Développement Rural. Réflections et Propositions d'action à Partir d'expériences d'Afrique de l' Ouest*. Rome, FAO.

Farrington, J. et al. 1993. *Reluctant partners? Non-governmental organizations, the state and sustainable agricultural development*. New York, Routledge.

Ferguson, J. 1994. *The Anti-politics Machine: Development, depolitization and bureaucratic power in Lesotho*. Minneapolis: University of Minnesota Press.

Ferreira Mendes, J. 1969. *Problemas e Perspectivas do Desenvolvimento Rural da Guiné*. Bissau: Centro de Estudos da Guiné Portuguesa.

Forrest, J. 1992. *Guinea-Bissau: Power, conflict and renewal in a West African nation*. Boulder: Westview Press.

Frazão-Moreira, A. 1999. *Apropriação Social da Natureza entre os Nalu da Guiné-Bissau: a etnobotânica num contexto de mudança*. Ph.D. Dissertation. Lisbon: ISCTE.

Galli, R. and J. Jones 1987. *Guinea-Bissau: Politics, economics and society*. London: Frances Pinter.

Geffray, C. 1991. *A Causa das Armas*. Lisbon: Afrontamento.

Howell, J. 2002. In Their Own Image: Donor assistance to civil society. In *Lusotopie: enjeux contemporains dan les espaces Lusophones*. Paris: Editions Karthala.

Hobart, M. (ed.) 1995. *An Anthropological Critique of Development: The growth of ignorance*. London: Routledge.

Hochet, A. 1979. *Études Socio-Economiques Conduits dans les Régions Administratives de Tombali et de Quinara Sud-Ouest: Etudes socio-économiques de base*. Bissau: Ministerio Coordenação da Económica e do Plano.

Instituto Nacional de Estudos e Desquisas (INEP) (ed.) (2000) *Soronda: revista de estudos guineenses*. Bissau, INEP.

Junta de Investigacoes do Ultramar (JIU) (ed.) 1972 *Prospectiva do Desenvolvimento Económico e Social da Guiné*. Lisbon: JIU.

Long, N. and J. van der Ploeg. 1989. Demythologising planned intervention: an actor perspective. *Sociologia Ruralis*, 29 (3–4): 226–49.

Long, N. and A Long (eds.) 1992. *Battlefields of Knowledge: The interlocking of theory and practice in social research and development*. London: Routledge.

Mosse, D. 1996. Local Institutions and Farming Systems Development: Thoughts from a project in tribal Western India. *Agren Network Paper* 64. London: ODI.

Olivier de Sardan, J. (1993) Le développement comme champ politique local. Marseille, *Bulletin de l' APAD*, 6: 11–18.

Olivier de Sardan, J. and T. Bierschenk, 1993. Les courtiers locaux du développement. *Bulletin de l' APAD* 5: 71–76.

———. 1994. ECRIS: enquête collective rapide d'identification des conflits et des groups stratégiques. *Bulletin de l' APAD* 7: 35–43.

Olivier de Sardan, J. 1995. *Anthropologie et Développement: Essai en socio-anthropologie du changement social*. Paris: Karthala.

Ploeg, J. van der (1995) Potatoes and knowledge. In *An Anthropological Critique of Development: The growth of ignorance*, edited by M. Hobart. London: Routledge.

Quarles van Ufford, P. 1995. Knowledge and Ignorance in the practices of development policy. In *An Anthropological Critique of Development: The growth of ignorance*, edited by M. Hobart. London, Routledge.

Richards, P. 1995. Participatory Rural Appraisal: a quick-and-dirty critique. *PLA Notes* 24: 13–16.

Rudebeck, L. 1996. *Buscar a Felicidade. Democratização na Guiné-Bissau*. Uppsala: Uppsala University.

Scott, J. 1985. *Weapons of the Weak: Everyday forms of peasant resistance*. New Haven:Yale University Press.

Solidami (ed). 1994a. *II Conférence des ONG: Document d'orientation*. Bissau: Solidami.

_____. 1994b. *II Conferencia das ONG. Desenvolvimento participativo e democracia*. Lisbon, CIDAC.

Spínola, A. 1971. *Linha de acção*. Lisbon: Agência-Geral do Ultramar.

Temudo, M. 1998. *Inovação e mudança em sociedades rurais africanas*. PhD Dissertation.Lisbon: ISA (4 vols).

Temudo, M. and A. Arvéola 2002. Questions about evaluation methodologies of rural development projects: case studies from Guinea-Bissau and Mozambique. Paper presented at The 2002 European Evaluation Society Conference, Seville, 10–12 October.

Temudo, M. and U. Schiefer. 2003. Disintegration and resilience of agrarian societies in Africa: the importance of social and genetic resources. A case study on the reception of urban war refugees in the South of Guinea-Bissau. *Current Sociology*, (3/4): 395–418.

Acknowledgments

The *Fundação para a Ciência e a Tecnologia* (Portugal) financed the research conducted since 1999, within the project "The disintegration of African agrarian societies and their potential for reconstruction."

I thank my editor Jim Igoe and my colleagues Dr Ramon Sarró, Dr Bernhard Weimer and Lorenzo Bordonaro for their comments and critical insights. Professor John Farrington and Professor João Cravinho had read an earlier draft and made very useful comments. While all these people helped me improve my arguments, I remain solely responsible for the shortcomings of the final product.

CHAPTER 11

CONCLUSION: NGOS, ETHNOGRAPHY AND POLITICAL ETHICS

Tim Kelsall, Erica Bornstein, Elizabeth Challinor, Sara Rich Dorman, Ben Rawlence, Marina Temudo, Stephen Jackson, Tim Docking, and Jim Igoe.

Editors' Introduction

Jim Igoe and Tim Kelsall

As this volume finally took shape, we, the editors, found ourselves in a discussion with some of the contributors on the implications of the various chapters for action, on the part of both academics and NGOs. Though there was agreement on some issues, it was clear that we were not speaking with one voice. Because of this, we thought it would be inappropriate to try and sell the readers a single editorial line. Instead we asked each of our contributors to write a couple of pages, reflecting on what they thought the implications of their own work for research and action in the field of NGO development might be. The result is a kind of conversation, reproduced here in the form of a conclusion.

Tim Kelsall

It is by way of conclusion that I would like to offer some remarks on the implications of ethnographic inquiry for those who work in the NGO industry. Ethnography is not of value to the NGO world for purely utilitarian reasons. It is useful, at the risk of sounding romantic, because it presents a living example of the ideals that gave birth to the NGO movement, but which now seem to be on the brink of extinction. Let me elaborate.

The interest in NGOs in the West began in part as a reaction to top-down, bureaucratic modes of developmental intervention and transformation. The attempt to transform society according to blueprint models was deemed to be a dead end that caused untold harm. NGOs, by contrast, were thought to be comprised of dedicated men and women who lived among the people for extended periods, who experienced their problems, and who worked together with them to try and improve their lives. The relationship was, ideally, a reciprocal one of learning and respect. Developmental improvements or solutions were not guaranteed; mistakes would be made, but the ethos of solidarity entailed by participating in the community was as important, perhaps, as any material aim.

In a curiously similar way, ethnographers, at least if they are good ones, do not live among the people they study with the intention of transforming them. They do not come armed with a blueprint or set of plans. Moreover, the material gifts they can bestow on their communities are typically modest. While most will have attended "research methods" classes in anthropology, these add up to much less than a tool kit to allow one to do ethnography. The latter, as honest ethnographers all know, is a profoundly unstructured process in which the key to future "academic" success is normally acquired through building personal relationships founded on trust. Acquiring such relationships is frequently a fraught and reversible process in which the ethnographer's physical not to mention emotional well-being are tested to a remarkable degree. Insight comes to the ethnographer sometimes sporadically, sometimes haphazardly, and is an unpredictable ingredient in the research process. Moreover, many ethnographers will return from the field feeling deeply ambivalent about their host communities and about their own role within them. Some may even refer themselves for post-traumatic therapy!

But by "subjecting yourself, your own body and your own personality, and your own social situation, to the set of contingencies that play upon a set of individuals, so that you can physically and ecologically penetrate their circle of response to their social situation," in the words of Goffman, cited in (Emerson, Fretz, and Shaw 1995: 2) one has committed oneself in a way more profound than have the armies of new NGO practitioners with their buzzwords, blueprints and air-conditioned vehicles.

And yet, for all the talk of participation, the practical, political detachment of the ethnographer is also a worrisome object of critique. Having experienced the travails of a community at first hand, how can the ethnographer walk away? James Ferguson's answer is that the ethnographer has to be prepared for the fact that he or she has little practical to contribute to the political struggles of Third World peoples: "The toiling miners and the abandoned old women know the tactics proper to their situations far better than any expert does. Indeed, the only general answer to the question, 'What should they do?' is: 'They are doing it!'" (Ferguson 1990: 281) His answer is that ethnographers have to focus their political energies on the domestic stage—combating misrepresentations of third world people, arguing against policies that will harm them.

But this, perhaps, is a little glib. For all Ferguson's deft deconstruction of the "poor," the "people," their "interests," any kind of political action on the part of the ethnographer, even on the domestic stage, entails a corresponding judgement, about the best way to act; and this judgement inevitably invokes a further set of judgements about who the "people" are, or, at the very least, who "my people" are, and this undoubtedly destroys the detachment of the ethnographer. That the people are a slippery, hard to pin down, diverse mass, that no knowledge rests on secure foundations, that there is no single plan that is going to solve all problems, does not mean that we can sidestep questions of political judgement, involvement and engagement. And once we admit that judgements have to be made, then a space for a re-insertion of political action in the third world is re-opened. It may be that judgement dictates that the ability to act is rarely exercised; but it cannot be ruled out of court.

To act, trying to do what is right, while knowing that one might be wrong, is the very substance of ethical politics. The original NGO activists—both in Africa and in the West—need to have the courage of their convictions: to live among the people, to learn from them, and, when judged necessary, to struggle alongside them. A return to this philosophy will involve a radical rolling back of the remit of NGOs. Many in the industry, by heeding this call, would make themselves unemployable. It is less of a call to arms, than a call to throw away flipcharts and tear up logframes. To avert one's gaze from the ever more insidious poverty indicators, the latest fixation of governments and NGOs, and to see poverty once more through the eyes of those the west deems poor.

Erica Bornstein

The question of political engagement is thorny for both NGO workers and ethnographers. It is a question that has troubled me as well—both in the field and with the critical distance of writing ethnography. Anthropologists have long acknowledged that development, as a model for change, has its own baggage. However, despite persistent academic critique, development lumbers along in Africa. More importantly, perhaps, it is greatly desired. This is more than a hegemonic trance. The question at issue is not whether development is good or not, or whether development is done well or not. Instead, we must ask: what are the conditions of inequality that continue to make development desirable?

People want to get out of their poverty; in terms of both the material struggles of everyday life and the experiences of relative deprivation that are produced by knowledge about wealth in places where development acquires its capital. This is something we, as ethnographers and critics, should not forget from the comfort of our studies. True, as Kelsall has noted, ethnographers do not "live among the people they study with the intention of transforming them." However, NGO workers do just this. They aim to transform the economic conditions and behavior of their subjects; in this sense they are missionaries (Bornstein 2003). Unlike ethnographers, however, African NGO workers have webs of relationships that bind them to those they work with. Ethnographers leave. They may return for a visit or continue their research, or may nurture relationships, but in the end they leave, and this distinctly different social location is key to understanding the politics of differing intents.

In my research with NGOs in Zimbabwe, I saw how NGO workers experienced the economic perils that made development necessary in Zimbabwe alongside the constituencies they worked with. If NGO workers are privileged elites compared to the subsistence farmers they assist, they are only a few steps away from rural poverty themselves. For example, after I left Zimbabwe I received a letter from a former NGO worker who had lost his job. Faced with nothing but the prospect of returning to his rural home, he wrote to me (the foreigner, a possible donor) requesting a grinding mill for his village. He was desperate and could not turn to the NGO that had once employed him. As a development worker in Zimbabwe he had "walked with the people," queued for petrol, paid increasing prices for food, and faced the political complexity that made living in a "less-developed" nation an anxious affair. And then he became someone who needed help himself. While both ethnographers and development workers may feel ambivalence for "their communities," only ethnographers have the option of leaving the political context that makes development a sought-after endeavor.

Ethnographers are not NGO workers. The differentiating condition emerges as one attempts to write about development in Africa instead of doing it. I agree with Ferguson's directive that ethnographers must focus their political engagement on a stage where they will have impact: on policy, on representation, and on the politics and social inequities that make some nations developed and others in need of development. Ethnographers have a rare charge: of critically reflecting the common and taken-for-granted through a new frame. What NGO workers do with this reflection is up to them. Perhaps it is an ethnographic utopia to assume that politics will change through the articulation of critical ideas, a utopia that I share myself for lack of anything else. Ethnographers of NGOs in Africa fight poverty with their pens. This is tricky terrain, in which highly moralized categories—of what is right and what is wrong with development—are embedded in missionary and colonial histories, in coercive and charitable relationships that continue to play out in different ways in different places all over Africa. The consistent aspect of this inquiry is that the desire to "do good" is shared by ethnographers and NGO workers alike, even if they disagree on what good is.

In my chapter (this volume) I demonstrate how, in the politically volatile context of late 1990s Zimbabwe—both NGO workers and myself as an ethnographer, found that the only way to engage in political action and inquiry was to elide the category of politics. This, like the state in Ferguson's Anti-Politics Machine, was a form of political action. Thus I disagree with Kelsall's assertion, subtle as it is, that NGO workers are bad ethnographers because they aim to transform those they study, and that ethnographers are bad NGO workers because they have lost their call to political action. It is hasty to conflate the structural locations of ethnographers and NGO workers. Ethnographers have the option, and indeed the academic obligation, to leave a perilous political context. NGO workers do not—and the political stakes of this distinction are alarmingly clear to me.

This brings me to what I see to be a more serious divide: the chasm between those who write about Africa from afar and those who write about the same subjects from within. Often this gap is manifest as theoretical writing from Western scholars that is critical of development versus more applied writing from African scholars that suggests how to do development better. The two projects differ in intent, and part of this is structural. African scholars do not have access to as many theoretical sources. One political act toward altering this inequity would be to assist African academic institutions in obtaining more resources. The costs of political engagement also differ. African scholars are embedded in their political environment. Often, the dangers to themselves and to their families are extreme—sanctions are real and immediate for providing a counter to the hegemonic discourse of development. To this I am afraid I can offer neither a conclusion nor a way forward. Instead, I suggest an acceptance of things unfinished and of a subtle envisioning of the contradictions of political engagement.

Elizabeth Pilar Challinor

On a return trip to Cape Verde in May 2002 I was confronted with the anthropologist's eternal dilemma when an informant challenged me to "come up with the goods": what new ideas had I brought that could help to guarantee the economic viability of her association? I suddenly felt uncomfortably empty! I was no expert in this area and had no suggestions to make. In response to the look of surprise on my face she commented that after all these years of study abroad she thought that I would be able to come up with something new.

This incidence corroborates the point made by Kelsall above that ethnographers cannot sidestep questions of political judgement and engagement. This is particularly the case for ethnographers researching development: a form of directed social change in which value judgements are often explicitly formulated. In this context informants are used to discussing not only "what is going on" but also what is being done and/or what should be done to change "what is going on". Whilst in these circumstances it is not easy for the ethnographer to sit aloof on the sidelines, active engagement may be equally problematic, as revealed in the soul searching account by Hastrup and Elsass (Hastrup and Elsass 1990) of the pros and cons of becoming advocates for the Archuaco Indians in Colombia.

Kelsall's attempt to resolve the ethnographer's dilemma appears to rest on the notion of good intentions: to act, trying to do what is right, while knowing that one might be wrong. However, this is not only the substance of ethical politics; it is also the creed of many NGO practitioners who use it as a justification for trading the acquisition of local knowledge for timely intervention. NGO practitioners also use this creed to criticize academics (including anthropologists) for becoming too bogged down in irrelevant knowledge to be able to act effectively. I remember an NGO expatriate comment to me at the end of her postgraduate development studies at a British University that she felt she had become de-skilled. Whilst most NGO practitioners and ethnographers undoubtedly believe in their own good intentions they may have very different ideas regarding what constitutes relevant knowledge.

There were also moments in my fieldwork when I felt torn between applied engagement and critical detachment. The incidence described above was unsettling because it questioned the legitimacy of simply being a "nosy" anthropologist. The question left floating in the air was what was the point behind all my research? The answer to this may be relatively less problematic for classical anthropologists who make a conscious decision to steer clear of "development" (although this does not provide any immunity from postcolonial, reflexive critiques). Ethnographers who study development, however, do so with the knowledge that they are entering a field in which the question of "what should be done" is at the forefront of people's minds. To engage in this debate consequently becomes part and parcel of the fieldwork experience: putting participant observation into practice. And it is in this context where the ethnographer may carve out a middle ground between engagement and detachment: a space of critical engagement, free from donor "pressures" to produce simplified issues and solutions but which nonetheless offers support in a more informal, dialogical way. Although in the incident described above I had nothing to offer there were a few moments during my fieldwork in which I did make suggestions, some of which were taken into account by my informants. On these occasions I did not feel different to NGO practitioners. Fixed categories of "superficial", "interfering" NGO practitioners versus "honest", "respectful" ethnographers consequently still leave me uneasy. Whilst these two types of categories may exist there are also more nuanced, ambiguous positions in between.

Having failed to rise to the challenge of one of my informants I now find myself challenged by the editors of this volume to "come up with the goods"! What does my research reveal about how African NGOs may be strengthened in ways that would benefit African communities? I shall begin with a vignette.

The finances of the local associations created in Cape Verde within the ambit of a donor program were subject to audits. According to the logic of the program the surpluses that these associations generated—through contracting with the government for soil and water conservation work—were intended for income generation activities. However, there were frequent disagreements over what constituted a productive investment of these funds. The donor's classical interpretation of "economic return" did not recognize the associations' need for accumulating credit in the form of symbolic capital such as: employing more workers than they could strictly afford in order to build trust in the association and spending money on photographs of visiting officials who had made promises of financial assistance.

Supporting local initiatives requires a holistic, context specific approach rather than a standardized eligibility test. The conditionality of aid may stifle the potential for locally generated, creative alternatives by pushing the Western models that donors believe in: structured, safe, formal and rule bound. Why is it, for example, that there was no time scheduled in the Government-NGO Forum in Cape Verde for debating current development policies? I would argue that the funding stakes were too high for the NGOs to engage in such an "indulgence". The Forum was about learning and mastering the rules of the game, not about questioning them.

Those who make the rules of the game also have a weak spot: the craving for visibility. Most donors preferred to be based in the capital, Praia, where their work would be most visible. Lack of visibility was the reason behind the decision of a European bi-lateral donor to withdraw from the more remote island of São Nicolau. The challenge for African NGOs is to link aid visibility to issues of sustainability in such a way that donors develop their own need for embracing risk, informality, and flexibility.

Sara Rich Dorman

Gavin Williams argues that, as academics, we need "to understand the world, not to change it". This is not an idle or glib reworking of Marx. Williams emphasizes the importance of understanding development as an ideological project and proposes that:

> …radical intellectuals share with development agencies…and NGOs an orientation to realizing future plans. They start from the wrong end by postulating a desired state of affairs and then working back to the present.… *the one thing we can reasonably predict is that things will not turn out as we expect.*[1]

This raises the issue of what "engaged" academics are doing when living in the societies they study and contributing to their struggles. To draw too clear a line between "NGOs" and "academics" is surely arbitrary and unfair to both. In order to carry out our fieldwork, most of us participated within the very structures we then sought to describe and analyze. At ZimRights, the main subject of my contribution to this volume, I was an intern and a member of the organization. At another NGO I was an (unpaid) project officer for a year. At yet another NGO, one I have known for much longer, I continue to be treated as a member and am *expected* to attend meetings whenever I am in

---

1. Gavin Williams, "Political economies and the study of Africa: critical reflections" Paper presented to the African Studies Seminar, University of Edinburgh, November 2003, emphasis added.

Harare. So, to ask, as this volume does: "what is the relationship between NGOs and academia" is to artificially distinguish between those two roles. The very strength of ethnography as a methodological tool is in its blending of those two roles. The ethnographic approach enables us to ask the right questions, which I have argued in this volume and elsewhere, are rarely applied to NGOs, because of the tendency to romanticize and idealize them.

But for those of us studying political phenomena, the dangers of "engaged" research are particularly evident. My own research was stimulated by a desire to understand the social and political impact of structural adjustment policies.[2] Most research on this topic had assumed that NGOs would protest the implementation of neo-liberal economic policies. In order to understand why this did not happen, I worked with those few individuals and groups who were trying to challenge these policies and others.[3] Since then, many of the church and NGO initiatives that I documented and worked on, have fed into Zimbabwe's Constitutional Assembly, the Crisis Coalition, and the Movement for Democratic Change.[4] In doing so, I made my own small contribution to "change" in Zimbabwe while also trying to understand its deeper politics.

Working with those we respect and trust is "engaged" research of the best kind. But critical examination of struggles of all kinds—in NGOs or without—must not blind us to examining their limitations as well as their successes. Whether we position ourselves as political scientists, anthropologists, or NGO workers, valuable research comes from the study of "really existing" policies and processes: our duty is to act consistently in accordance with the demands of intellectual integrity—a path which in these times demands as much moral courage and personal commitment as the political alternative. [5]

But to conclude more positively, although I have chronicled what appears to be the collapse of ZimRights, and emphasized its weaknesses rather than its strengths, a recent research trip revealed a different picture. ZimRights is

---

2. Sara Rich, Non-Governmental Organizations and Civil Society in Africa: Zimbabwe's experience with structural adjustment, 1990-1995. Unpublished MPhil thesis, Oxford, 1996.

3. Sara Rich Dorman, "NGOs and State in Zimbabwe: implications for civil society theory" in Bjorn Beckman, Anders Sjogren and Eva Hannsen eds. Civil Society and Authoritarianism in the Third World (Stockholm: PODSU, 2001).

4. Sara Rich Dorman, Inclusion and Exclusion: NGOs and Politics in Zimbabwe (Unpublished Dphil thesis, University of Oxford, 2001).

5. Gavin Williams, "Political economies and the study of Africa: critical reflections." Paper presented to the African Studies Seminar, University of Edinburgh, November 2003, emphasis added, 27.

still in existence, despite several years without donor funding. Key members and staff remain committed to its regeneration. New projects are being developed, working with the urban homeless and poor.[6] ZimRights' continuing story—along with those of the other organizations detailed in this volume—reinforces my belief that neither undue pessimism nor romanticism should color our efforts to study NGOs. Rather we must use the methodological tools at our disposal to observe and to understand, but not to judge or to predict; in solidarity with those we study and with whom we work.

Ben Rawlence

Good social science does not avoid politics. Asking "why" the world is the way it is, is a political act. Answering that question in a convincing way also leaves many political questions hanging in the air. A good ethnography will have shown how social relations are articulated within a given community with subsequent effects. By implication it will have opened up the possibility for political action, since those who would remedy or change those effects can rely on mechanisms hitherto unobserved. But whatever the nature of the inquiry, the good social scientist asks questions for the sake of knowledge alone and distills the lessons for political action afterwards. NGOs generally start from a different place. "Something must be done" and then they set about doing it, often learning by doing rather than studied detachment.

NGOs and those that work with them, provided they can read English, should have much to learn from the ethnographies presented in this volume. A little reflection and comparative analysis can often save time and money and help spread best practice (both ethical and technical).

However, the moral and ethical dilemmas, surrounding the way in which northern countries engage with the Global South, are relevant to ethnographers and NGO workers alike. The spheres of their action—whether with the pen or the plow—may be different, but the pitfalls are similar, even if academics and activists stumble across them from different directions.

The terms of the inquiry or the intervention must be tightly drawn. What does "development" mean in any context? Is it the alleviation of poverty, the reduction of inequality, the improvement of living standards or the preservation of the environment? These are separate problems with different drivers and diverse solutions. Lazy definitions and inattention to the politics of the

---

6. Interview, Munyaradzi Bidi, 21 July 2003.

"development" process itself, including the presence of an ethnographer, can lead to inaccurate results, bad programs and even more suffering.

The actors and agents must be clearly defined. Some of the conclusions and statements in this volume are not sufficiently clear about who NGO workers are, while ethnographers are generally assumed to be foreigners. NGO workers come from within communities, from other countries and from elite groups within countries. The politics of relations between groups, and even between NGOs, must be properly understood before an intervention that changes those relations can be effective. Furthermore, is the goal espoused by the NGO shared by all members of the community? In some cases, the NGOs themselves are vehicles for political competition to which donors and ethnographers must be alert.

Ethnographers and NGO workers must clarify their own motives in any given context. Is it the pursuit of knowledge, or the desire to help that motivates an inquiry? What are the assumptions underlying the design of a program; have they been robustly tested? What is it about inequality/poverty/resource conflict in this place and at that this time that is worthy of inquiry and/or of intervention? In general the eschewing of altruism as a concept and suspicion of one's own motives will yield rewards.

Ethnographers and NGO workers must clarify their roles vis-a-vis other actors in any given arena. Who are the most legitimate actors in any particular context? What is the position of the elected government (assuming one exists) with regard to the actions proposed or the studies planned? If they are not cooperative, why not? Who is the best-placed person or institution to carry out the proposed research or development intervention, and how can you work with them? The ethics of research are just as important as those involved in practical interventions. The production of knowledge and its transmission to interested parties must also proceed in a way that helps rather than hinders the empowering of those "development" aims to assist. Translation and training are hugely important components of capacity building in countries with weak institutions.

The ethnographer and the activist must see themselves as they are seen. Often from the perspective of development's customers, its agents are all the same. The prejudices and preconceptions surrounding images of foreigners or the better-off have consequences for what is possible and for what is remembered in an intervention. Sometimes success can even entrench a feeling of helplessness since a community may believe itself unable to have achieved a particular goal alone. In many apparently remote places ethnography itself has a long history, an understanding of which will greatly facilitate an honest account.

In the final analysis, the urge to understand and the desire to help spring from very human instincts that should be celebrated and not demeaned. But where the capacity for assistance or inquiry represents a human liberty, we must be circumspect in ensuring that the exercise of one liberty does not impinge on the liberty of others. This is always a political question and essentially comes down to one of human communication and identity. In trying to understand what another person is and what they want, and in joining with them to achieve a shared goal there is no alternative but to be humble, to trust, to forgive and to do unto others as you would be done by.

Tim Docking

An analysis of civil society organizations in Mali reveals several important developments that have powerful implications for both Western and African policy makers. To begin with, Malian civil society has grown dependent on the West. Moreover, opportunistic local elites have in many cases assumed control of civic groups in Mali and across Africa and are more interested in capturing foreign funds than articulating the needs of their constituents to national decision makers. Yet despite such troubling trends, the international/local interface in Africa has produced some positive results and, as this volume illustrates, moved Mali (and other states) ahead on the road to socio-economic development.

Research on the international/local nexus shows that the direct flow of Western support to African NGOs can have a corrosive effect on the development of African civil society. The direct funding of local groups in the developing world by the West stemmed from a realization among international donors that traditional methods of aid giving have failed in Africa, and that aid allocated directly to the local level, circumventing transfers to the "corrupt" Africa state, will have a greater impact on political development and democratization.

Yet the unintended consequences of this policy have been profound. For as international aid to local groups grows, civil society has often become less reflective of, or accountable to, the society it purports to represent. In fact, today state/civil society relations in Africa are mostly characterized by vertical linkages, opportunism and a symbiosis between donors and local groups; a far cry from the Tocquevillian concept of civil society as a network of grassroots organizations that form a protective "bulwark" between citizens and the excesses of a predatory state.

Civil society organizations in Africa thus attempt to straddle the state and society at-large by grounding one foot firmly in each sphere. Nevertheless, evidence suggests that actors within Africa's civil society inevitably train their focus outwardly (with backs turned to local constituencies) as they search for international funds.

Nevertheless, in Mali the picture is mixed. A series of relatively enlightened and democratic leaders have led Mali since its revolution in 1992. During this period they have resisted the excesses that often characterize Africa's political class and maintained a commitment to democracy and the development of civic organizations. Indeed, several state institutions have been created to foster and support Mali's nascent civil society. And regardless of the high number of opportunists within the ranks of Mali's civil society, Mali houses a robust civil society sector including a number of groups that are based on conviction, and exist to serve local interests. Many of these groups have benefited from interactions with the West and in some cases, as the case study of SYCOV illustrates, these groups are making governments more accountable to their constituents.

These advances in state/society relations in Mali however are directly affected by the relationship that Western donors often share with their local partners. For the West continues to partner with Malians, and Africans in general, who can "speak their language", both literally and figuratively. Consequently, today the leadership of Africa's civil society sector is largely characterized by Western facing, rent seeking elites who are disconnected from the masses they purport to represent. In short, Africans have taken the old adage, "Think globally, act locally," and turned it on its head, so that today African representatives from civic organizations and NGOs, "Think locally and act globally."

This emerging dynamic could have serious repercussions on the African development agenda. In brief, civil society, conceived as the "missing link" by optimistic Western political theorists and development specialists during the 1990s may simply become another "weak link" in the process of African political development. And once donors perceive Africa's burgeoning civil society/NGO sector as self-serving and disconnected from the continent's struggling masses, the well-intentioned bridges built between international and local communities in the developing world over the past decade risk collapse.

Incumbent on the West at this time is a re-evaluation of its current political and economic agenda in Africa. For just as the West had to rethink its failed theory of modernization which was liberal, optimistic, and aimed at improving the lives of Third World peoples in the post-colonial world, it now needs to rethink its effort to help the people of the world's democratizing nations. Special attention must be given to assure that Western policies of conditionality and technocratic assistance are not interrupting the evolutionary processes that are underway in African civic culture. Perhaps more important, however, is a reassessment by Western governments of their Western and African NGO partners, with particular focus placed on organizational performance and accountability.

The West often "got it wrong" in Africa with its cold war-motivated, statist policies of 1960s–1980s. Yet, a blind redirection of development assistance to Africa's civil society presents new set of problems. This point mandates a more deliberative, gradual and nuanced policy by the West as it connects with Africa's civil society.

At the same time, all parties need to accept that efforts to strengthen and develop civil society in Africa will not be enough to correct the catastrophic course that the African sub-region is on. The profound challenges posed by the AIDS pandemic, armed conflict, collapsed states, crumbling education and medical services in Africa will not be redressed by the disaggregated community of local or international civil society organizations. African states—despite their often corrupt and inept structures—hold the potential centralizing capacity required to tackle these problems. While Africa's civil society must help in the fight against these scourges, theirs must be a supporting rather than a central role. In turn, the African state must both draw upon civil society to help meet its greater needs. Thus, the Hegelian vision of the state—one providing the administrative capacity, regulatory framework, rule of law, in addition to guidance to civil society and the public at large—ultimately will provide a more useful model than the oft-cited Tocquevillian vision. Western policy makers interested in breaking Africa's cycle of crises would do well to embrace such a model and increase their efforts to build state capacity on the continent.

Marina Padrão Temudo

Twenty years ago I was a volunteer at one of the best known Portuguese NGOs, created to support the liberation movements in the African colonies. One of the most important activities of that NGO was to "fight" for the freedom of East Timor (a former Portuguese colony) that had been occupied by Indonesia. Every afternoon a lot of volunteers arrived to the office to do whatever was needed: sticking stamps, reading and cutting important news from newspapers, organizing funding campaigns, and so on…Apart from fees we also made sporadic financial contributions for specific aims (and at that time it was rather difficult for some of us).

When I went to Africa in 1993 to conduct field research I still had in mind the previous ideas about NGOs and voluntary action. However, those were times of rather quick and profound transformations of the NGO scene, and while I was prepared to face failure of donor and state interventions, I still believed that NGOs were part of the solution and not the new component of an old problem.

The shock I had when facing the crude reality inspired me to study development interventions at the "impact point"; from the dual perspective of the organizations that implement them and of the beneficiary societies. What follows is a brief description of a potential solution to the perennial misunderstandings that seem to encumber development projects.

Early on I concluded that it was impossible to understand the impact of a development intervention without situating the current project in historical context, without analyzing the dynamics of the institutional framework and the various user groups, and without deploying both ethnographic and sociological methods to analyze the micro-perspectives of the actors involved and the macro-context of the development intervention.

During the research for my PhD dissertation I had a large time-span (three years of fieldwork) and ethnographic techniques had been my main tool. However, after that I felt a need to introduce more speed in the data collecting process, because research projects, like development projects, have financial and time restrictions. In cooperation with my colleague Alexandra Arvéola we developed a new methodology based on the characterization of the "organizational landscape" (the whole of the organizations intervening in a given territory and the relations established between them) and on in-depth ethnographic case studies of the target-societies' social organization, livelihood systems, priorities, needs, potential for self-organization and forms of resistance to undesired external interventions.

For the characterization of the "organizational landscape" of a pre-defined territory, we conducted semi-structured interviews with all development organizations (governmental, donor-agencies, NGOs, CBOs). Guidelines focused on: the characterization of each organization, the characterization of their interventions, and the characterization of the articulation with donor-funding politics and with the other implementing organizations (governmental and NGOs). Field visits to projects areas accompanying staff activities, together with taking a glance at their relationship with beneficiaries were a part of the research procedure, when accepted by the organizations. Analyses of the project proposals and reports were continuously confronted with field observations of results.

However, once again I felt that research results are normally useless for development actors, and therefore the next problem was how to transform the knowledge acquired into an efficient tool. Most of the literature on development evaluation stresses the need of creating networks and collaboration between all development actors, not only to generate a pool of information (there is a lack of base-line, monitoring and evaluation data) and a flow of ideas, but also to improve methods and approaches in order to encourage mutual learning and increase development interventions' impact. Competition, duplication of efforts (and errors) and the absence of a synergic action between development agencies (governmental and non-governmental) are also frequently noted.

The construction of a database continuously updated can introduce an eclectic, flexible and adaptive methodological procedure and a free sharing of information between all partners involved in development aid and research, making compatible the accountability and lesson-learning objectives of projects evaluation, and above all contributing to increase development efficiency, and to reduce the negative effects of intervention on the target-societies.

Keeping that in mind we constructed a simulation of a database[7] that works like a page on the World Wide Web, in which all the information concerning the target societies and development intervention in a given territory is introduced and analyzed. Information about the region's demography, climate, soils, economy, infrastructures, and so on is also included. All these data are the main constituents of what we call the "development landscape."

The main idea is to create organizational and "organizational landscape" memories, providing a tool for the evaluation of each organization and of the whole landscape performance. Through a grid of indicators and variables each authorized actor (evaluator, researcher, CBO member) may introduce her/his classification into a ranking matrix. At regular times, commissioned experts can also do a rating analysis of all the organizations and of the landscape as a whole. These indicators and variables of the evaluation system can constitute good descriptors for the construction of both a local and an international NGO taxonomy and performance classification. Targeted societies should also be evaluated with concern to social capital, well-being, production level, market integration, resilience, social disaggregation, potential for self-organization, participation in external interventions, and so on. In that way, a memory of their modes of endogenous and exogenous-induced change is also created and analyzed.

For the construction of the database intensive teamwork is needed to gather pre-existing data and to collect further information in order to characterize

---

7. The first simulation (Arvéola, A. & Temudo, M.P., 'SITID: Sistema de Informação Territorial para a Informação e o Desenvolvimento') with data from the province of Niassa, Mozambique, will be available in the web in 2004.

the organizational landscape and the beneficiary societies. For the updating and for introducing the classification process, the database must have a manager that represents all development actors (donors, recipient states, NGOs, donor-commissioned implementing agencies, grassroots organizations and institutions).

These databases have a distinct territorial coverage, and should be linked to others in the same country and in neighboring countries. They can then portray "development landscapes" at local, national, sub-regional and continental levels, revealing what are general trends and characteristics and what is the result of local political, socio-cultural, institutional and economic dynamics. In this way they can be seen as windows through which to observe wider phenomena of local powers, national governance, social, cultural and technical interfaces, social change, or globalization.

We do acknowledge that the approach as conceived is almost exclusively directed to improve the funding strategies of donors and the performance of implementing organizations. It almost bypasses the relations of power between external agents and the beneficiary societies, and the fact that these last actors (due to frequent illiteracy) would only have an indirect access to the databases and their process of rating the development organizations performance. However, if funding was based on a better knowledge of beneficiary societies' priorities, objectives, needs and modes of change, then it could be better oriented toward a program perspective, where contextual complexities could be addressed through a synergic action of complementary organizations—the ones with a well-documented high performance record.

Stephen Jackson

Spend ethnographic time with activists in the burgeoning local NGOs of the African continent and one thing rapidly becomes clear: the degree to which "civil society" has become the international aid's flavor of the month is amongst the factors threatening to kill it off. "Each man kills the thing he loves," wrote Wilde. "Some do it with a bitter look/Some with a flattering word…" I'm tempted to argue that Western donors are killing African NGOs by vacillating between both of these positions.

On the one hand, by over-praising the capacities of NGOs—to deliver equitable, sustainable and uncorrupted development coupled with root-and-branch democratization—they have set-up wholly unrealistic expectations. By over-funding the sector, they have directly incentivized the creation of fictive, "opportunistic" NGOs and fomented splits within long-standing and credible ones.

On the other, bitter looks often follow the sudden donor discovery of just such imperfections that they themselves have had a hand in engendering. Donors favor NGOs with a "community basis," but then show themselves alarmed when the basis of "community" turns out to be "ethnic." Or else they look harshly upon the proliferation of rival coordination networks and NGO platforms, without realizing (or perhaps without acknowledging) that incautious funding strategies have helped to encourage them.

What can ethnographers offer in response? One possibility is that our techniques of getting up close and personal with social movements or political/economic organizations can reveal a much richer picture of what makes these tick than can the narrowly technocratic evaluative tools of the development machine. Logframes that weigh inputs against outputs, evaluations that depend on measurement of service delivery and a cursory glance at documents of association—currently development's standard measures—take little cognizance of the socio-cultural life of organizations. How such organizations react to external pressures and stimuli, and how, internally, individuals within those organizations react to each other, to their sense of purpose and mission, and their own everyday needs for economic and psycho-social fulfillment: these are some of the questions our work can enlighten.

I am calling, then, for a return to the highly uncomfortable and morally complex relationship wherein ethnographers operate, in part, as brokers and interpreters between the power and resources of the development machine and objects of that machine: in this case, Africa's NGOs. I base this on an article of faith that in the aggregate, Africa's NGOs can make a long-term difference to the betterment of Africans' political, social, cultural and economic lives, if they are not killed off or totally distorted by aid's impacts in the short term.

Jim Igoe

Like Liz Challinor, I am suspicious of fixed categories of "superficial, interfering NGO practitioners versus honest, respectful ethnographers." Ethnographers and NGO practitioners operate in overlapping networks of institutions, ideas, and money. It makes sense, therefore, that the ways in which they operate should also overlap. As Ben Rawlence points out, it is also important also to distinguish between Western NGO practitioners (usually donors) and African NGO leaders (usually recipients). Of course there are also African ethnographers. Ironically, however, many African social scientists wind up working as consultants to Western NGOs, in part because academic posts at African universities pay so poorly.

As Bornstein aptly asserts, the structural position of these different actors has implications for their ability to act and their relationship to African communities. African NGO workers tend to have lifelong social ties to specific communities. Western ethnographers, on the other hand, enjoy the option of walking away. It is also important to note that access to the development apparatus is a crucial element of these relationships. For most Africans, the development apparatus is a Holy Grail. In aid dependent African countries access to development money offers one of the few opportunities for a remunerative livelihood. Furthermore, access to development money promises improved standards of living for people in one's community.

But access to the development apparatus comes at a cost. The development apparatus is an insatiable beast, which must be constantly fed. Development practitioners, both African and Western, spend a great deal of time and energy feeding the beast. There are buzzwords to master and funding proposals to write. There are meetings and workshops to attend. There are vehicles and offices to maintain. There are projects to implement in a stipulated (almost always too short) period of time. All of these activities, and numerous others, must fall within the ambit of the development discourse *de jour*, while also meeting the short-term agendas of specific funding agencies. Meanwhile, academics plumb the bowels of the development beast for material to feed their own "publish or perish" academia beast. To mix my metaphors, everyone is operating with an institutional monkey on their back. Needless to say, this complicates things a great deal.

As Kelsall points out, the relationship of NGO leaders to the development apparatus has transformed local social movements in ways that excluded local people. I have observed community-based social movements lose steam as community leaders became increasingly beholden to the institutional demands of the development apparatus (see Igoe 2003). In the process, they were literally removed from their constituent communities. Most local people were mystified by this transformation. What had become of the community leaders who had inspired them to action? What had become of the promise of their movement and the NGOs they had helped to establish? NGO leaders meanwhile agonized over their inability to bring about the changes they envisioned in the context of formally registered NGOs.

As a young ethnographer in the field at this time, it was impossible not to get caught up in the infectious optimism that permeated the early stages of Africa's NGO revolution. Finally Africans were going to define their own problems and determine their own solutions. NGO leaders were going to "stay on the ground" for as long as it took, I was willing and able to "stay on the ground" with them. I watched their efforts to mobilize rural Tanzanians to improve their own lives. I shared their frustrations and watched them make mistakes. I made some mistakes myself. I learned a great deal, much of which was considered valuable by the NGO leaders I worked with. As Bornstein reminds us, however, "ethnographers have the academic obligation" to leave the field, and I was no exception. In 1997 I left Africa, and I have not returned.

Five years later I sat in an empty apartment in suburban Washington, D.C. with Tundu Lissu, a Tanzanian human rights attorney and NGO leader. He was returning to Tanzania and the movers had already taken the furniture away. We sat on the floor and discussed the institutional and political obstacles to bringing about positive change in Africa. For the past four years he had commuted between Washington and Dar es Salaam. Although he preferred to be in Tanzania all the time, he needed to be in the United States to secure funding for his organization and to drum up international support for the Tanzanian land rights movement. I had been working to start an NGO to advocate for indigenous land rights, and to get funding for a research project that would complement the activities of this organization, both with limited success. Toward the end of our conversation Tundu summarized our dilemma. To the best of my recollection, this is what he said: "Our challenge is to be relevant, be funded, and be in the right place at the right time."

Admittedly, Tundu's challenges are much more immediate than my own. He has been arrested and he is constantly concerned about his family's safety. Furthermore, his organization has been defunded because of the controversial nature of its work. His words, however, are relevant to anyone who seeks to take nuanced and flexible action in the context of development. The pressure to move money and produce tangible results means that the development apparatus selects against nuanced practitioners who point out complicated problems. African practitioners who "walk with the people," for instance, are frequently labeled as trouble makers. This is because they insist on meaningful participation by their constituents, a process that is cumbersome and tends to gum up the smooth operation of the development apparatus. Because these individuals spend a great deal of time "on the ground," they may not devote enough time to end of project reports. These proclivities make them difficult to work with.

Unfortunately, the development industry tends to favor individuals who toe the party line. To quote Chambers (1996: 246): "prudent (NGO) staff provide misleadingly positive feedback. The greater the need or desire for funds, the greater the danger of deception." It has been my experience that donors are less than appreciative of individuals who seek to debunk these deceptions. In fact, the NGO sector relies on these kinds of deceptions for its smooth operation. Individuals, both Western and African, learn to master the intricacies of the deception on which this system depends. Some do so in a cynical bid to gain money and social capital. Others do so because they have learned the hard way that they have little to gain, and much to lose, by rocking the boat. Of course these positions are not mutually exclusive.

Because of the conditions briefly outlined here, it is easy to despair that the development apparatus exists to perpetuate its own existence. It is also tempting to conclude that NGOs rarely benefit anyone outside of their own institutional purview. The people, as one Cape Verdean NGO leader explained to Liz Challinor, do not exist. Those who are able to become development insiders benefit (some much more than others), while those who remain development outsiders do not. While I am willing to entertain the possibility that this is not always the case, this scenario is consistent with my observation of NGOs in Tanzania in the 1990s. Development outsiders could see that development insiders were benefiting from development resources. By what means they achieved this, however, remained a mystery. I was frequently approached by Tanzanians who wanted advice on how to become a development insider.

While this is an admittedly gloomy prognosis, there are alternative networks of (quasi) institutions, ideas, and (a lot less) money. These networks are made up of individuals who are critical of the idea of development, many of whom are rural Africans. Many of my informants in Tanzania were less than enamored by the idea of development if it meant outsiders could come take their land, and local opportunists could enrich themselves in their name. While these people would like to have electricity and rural clinics, their most immediate concern is with keeping the land on which their livelihoods depend. Some of these individuals have networked with sympathetic individuals within the NGO sector, with academics, both at the University of Dar es Salaam and abroad, and with people in other parts of the world who have found themselves in similar straits. The loose network of which these people are part overlaps with the development apparatus, since some of its members are development insiders, but it also includes development outsiders. Of course, this network and others like it are not highly visible. This is because it is informal, and in some contexts clandestine.

While it would be premature to become overly enthusiastic about this network and others like it, its very existence indicates that the development apparatus is not all-pervading. It is fraught with institutional and discursive interstices in which it may be possible to insert alternative forms of discourse and practice. These interstices are evidenced by the existence of the anti-globalization and global indigenous peoples' movement. Individuals within these movements have exploited interstices in the development apparatus by starting their own NGOs and capturing not insignificant levels of funding. Of course such strategies are fraught with danger, which unfortunately are beyond the scope of this short essay (but see Niezen 2003). However, I believe they are the best alternative to mainstream development and governance interventions.

This brings me finally to the role of ethnographers in all of this. While I concur with Ferguson that Africans understand their own political struggles far better than any outside expert ever could, it is also the case that a good ethnographer is uniquely qualified to engage Africans and learn about their struggles through participant observation. Why should this matter? Because a good ethnographer is also uniquely situated to identify the institutional and discursive interstices that exist in the global development apparatus, upon which many social movements in Africa and elsewhere unfortunately depend for their success. I believe, therefore, that ethnographers have an important role in working with community activists to identify institutional and discursive interstices that are relevant to their cause, and helping them to connect with networks of likeminded people who may be able to assist them.

I agree with Kelsall, therefore, that there is a role for ethnographers in working directly with Africans in their struggle. I also agree with Bornstein that ethnographers also have a role "of critically reflecting the common and taken-for-granted through a new frame." Finally, I agree with Challinor that ethnographers have a role in calling donors' attention to important local imperatives that fall beyond the ambit of what they consider a productive investment of their funds. However, I also believe that all of these strategies should be part of the larger project of helping to institutionalize counter-hegemonic discourses and practices in the interstices of the development apparatus. This is a project that will be fraught with risk and mistakes, but one I believe is entirely necessary. In contemplating this project I echo Erica Bornstein's call for "an acceptance of things unfinished and a subtle envisioning of the contradictions of political engagement."

Works Cited

Bornstein, E. 2003. *The Spirit of Development: Protestant NGOs, morality, and economics in Zimbabwe*. New York, London: Routledge.

Chambers, R. 1996. The primacy of the personal. In *Non-governmental Organizations, Performance and Accountability: Beyond the magic bullet*, edited by M. Edwards and D. Hulme. London: Earthscan.

Emerson, R. M., R. I. Fretz, and L. L. Shaw. 1995. *Writing Ethnographic Field-notes.* Chicago: University of Chicago Press.

Ferguson, J. 1990. *The Anti-Politics Machine: 'Development', depoliticization and bureaucratic power in Lesotho.* Cambridge: Cambridge University Press.

Hastrup, K., and P. Elsass. 1990. Anthropological advocacy: a contradiction in terms? *Current Anthropology* 31 (3): 301–11.

Igoe, J. 2003. Scaling up civil society: donor money, NGOs, and the pastoralist NGO movement in Tanzania. *Development and Change* 34(5): 863–85.

Niezen, R. 2003. *The Origins of Indigenism: human rights and the politics of identity.* Berkeley: University of California Press.

INDEX